Ch... ...society in the late twentieth century

Chicano Politics and Society in the Late Twentieth Century

CHICANO POLITICS AND SOCIETY

in the Late Twentieth Century

EDITED BY DAVID MONTEJANO

University of Texas Press, Austin

Requests for permission to reproduce material from this work
should be sent to Permissions, University of Texas Press,
P.O. Box 7819, Austin, TX 78713-7819.

⊗ The paper used in this publication meets the minimum
requirements of American National Standard for Information
Sciences—Permanence of Paper for Printed Library Materials,
ANSI Z39.48-1984.

Library of Congress Cataloging-in-Publication Data

Chicano politics and society in the late twentieth century / edited by
    David Montejano. — 1st ed.
        p.   cm.
    Includes bibliographical references and index.
    ISBN 0-292-75214-8 (alk. paper).—ISBN 0-292-75215-6 (pbk. :
    alk. paper)
        1. Mexican Americans—Politics and government.   2. Mexican
    Americans—History—20th century.   3. Mexican Americans—Social
    conditions.   I. Montejano, David, 1948–   .
    E184.M5C447   1999
    973'.046872—dc21   98-15617

Pa' Willie (1944–1988) y César (1927–1993),
dos luminares del movimiento

CONTENTS

PART THREE: GENERAL STUDIES

Preface and Acknowledgments

One of the most striking aspects of public mainstream commentaries at the end of the twentieth century is the alarmist, dramatic tone of much discussion about Mexicans in the United States. The commentators, many of them East Coast based, seem to forget that a significant Mexican American population (some fourteen million U.S. citizens) exists and that these people understand the discussion going on around them. A more cynical possibility is that the commentators know these facts but believe that Mexican Americans are irrelevant to the discussion. The following studies establish their relevancy and in the process add a much needed voice to the discussion about Mexicans in the United States.

Not surprisingly, this voice speaks from a different perspective. The ten authors in this volume are all engaged in one way or another in a critical assessment of what can loosely be called the "politics of inclusion" that resulted from the civil rights movement of the 1970s. In this sense, these studies represent a collective postmovement assessment; "What went wrong? What went right? Where are we now?" are the questions that underlie much of the following discussion. The collective result is a wide-ranging portrayal of the complex situation of Mexican Americans as the twenty-first century begins.

An editing project such as this one requires considerable perseverance and institutional support. Among the several individuals and institutions that deserve thanks for their moral and logistical assistance are José Rivera, Tobías Durán, Rosemarie Romero, and Frances Rico of the Southwest Hispanic Research Institute and the Center for Regional Studies at the University of New Mexico; Robert Scott of the Center for Advanced Study in the Behavioral Sciences at Stanford University; and Verónica García-Contreras, Patricia Martínez, Sarah Guzmán, and Maribel Rodríguez of the Center for Mexican American Studies at the University of Texas at Austin. The Center for Advanced Study in the Behavioral Sciences, the Andrew W. Mellon Foundation, and the University Research Institute of the University of Texas at Austin provided generous support for sabbatical leave. Carlos Vélez-Ibáñez, now at the University of California, Riverside, and Luis Fraga of Stanford University were gracious critics. Finally, to the contributors who endured countless rewrites and pointed questions, many embraces and thanks: *por fin cumplimos*.

On the Question
of Inclusion

D A V I D   M O N T E J A N O

As we approach the end of the twentieth century, the national media
has begun to issue the inevitable, introspective analyses of American politics and society. In light of a number of prominent racialized events — the Los Angeles riots of 1992, the anti-immigrant campaigns of
1994–1995, the O.J. Simpson trial of the same years, the Million Man March
of 1995, the anti–affirmative action initiatives of 1995–1997, to name just a
few — the dominant tone of these media analyses has been a somber and anxious one. It reflects the anxiety of a nation obsessed with race, as one noted
sociologist put it: "we think race, act race, march race, tabulate race, celebrate
race, fear race." The prophecy of W. E. B. Du Bois, made in 1903, that the
problem of the twentieth century would be that of the "color line," may hold
up well for another century. On the eve of the twenty-first century, the most
active fault lines in U.S. society remain race and ethnic divisions.[1]

Not surprisingly, many of these national commentaries, noting the rapid
increase in the U.S. Latino population, have elaborated a common theme
around the notion of the "browning of America." Two disturbing lines of reasoning have characterized much of the public discussion. On the one hand,
some journalists and politicians talk in alarming tones about the possibility of
an "ethnic disintegration" of American society. An April 1990 issue of *Time*
put the matter bluntly: "What will the U.S. be like when whites are no longer
the majority?"[2] Whose history, values, language, and identity will count? One
commentator in the conservative *National Interest* warned his audience that
the Latino "value system" has been "the principal obstacle to human progress
throughout Hispanic America." Latino barrios, by reinforcing these values,
thus pose a special danger: "Poor enclave communities not only make it

easier for homeland values and language to persist, but they also possess the potential, particularly during bad economic times, for resentment-driven violence, such as the rioting in the Mount Pleasant district of Washington, D.C. in the spring of 1991 or the devastating April–May 1992 Los Angeles riots. One-third of those apprehended in Los Angeles for looting were illegal Hispanic immigrants."[3]

Such anxiety about Latinos is evident among liberal commentators as well. In the 1990s, the moderate magazine *Atlantic Monthly* has treated its readers to several ominous special reports on the U.S.-Mexican border, concluding in 1992 that "no one knows the consequences of Mexican immigration: it is a movement of the largest scale, immensely complicated, around which various arguments can easily be constructed . . . [but] these newcomers may indeed be the ones we cannot accommodate." One 1996 article, penned by Stanford historian David Kennedy, starkly warns of "the reconquista," of the possibility "that in the next generation or so we will see a kind of Chicano Quebec take shape in the American Southwest."[4] In short, conservatives and liberals alike have created a melodramatic, public discourse about threats to America from a growing Latino presence.

The second line of reasoning in this national discussion displays a righteous anger about the political "activism" of the U.S.-Mexican population. Nationally syndicated columnist Georgie Ann Geyer, for example, took a swipe in December 1992 at the "Hispanic advocacy movement," organizations that have consistently pushed for increased immigration, bilingual education, Spanish-language ballots, and "other such issues," by gushing about a "really surprising" poll of Hispanic Americans. The survey showed that Latinos actively want to reduce immigration, that they believe people living in this country should speak English, and that "the diverse and patriotic real Hispanic American community wants to adhere to the broader interests of the common good and of responsible Americanism rather than to the interests of professional spokespersons." Geyer, who in the 1980s believed that the Southwest was on the verge of becoming another "Lebanon," was plainly relieved by this finding—that Latinos are not so different, after all.[5]

Such reasoning—that Latinos are "not so different"—has led several conservative analysts to argue that Hispanics are guilty of "opportunism"—of abusing racial entitlements and preferences intended exclusively for African Americans. Political scientist Peter Skerry, for example, has argued that Mexican Americans are essentially immigrants who define themselves as a minority group only because their self-interested political leadership has been "seduced" by affirmative action "remedies" such as the Voting Rights Act. According to Skerry, Hispanics simply have no claim to such policies and remedies: "Whatever the merits of affirmative action for black Americans, it makes little sense to extend its benefits to those whose claims on the nation's conscience are far less cogent—and who come here expecting no special help." Skerry concludes that if we do not withdraw benefits from Hispanics, "we acquiesce in the rewriting of the social compact this nation has had with immigrants since its founding."[6] Ironically, Skerry does a considerable amount of rewriting of history and politics to carry out his polemical argument. In Skerry's treatment, the United States has no history of nation building worth exploring. Rather, the nation is assumed to have had a fixed space in which non–English speakers have been by definition immigrants.

Regardless of which line of reasoning is pursued, whether warning of ethnic disintegration or opportunism, these worrisome commentaries generally attempt no serious historical grounding. Skerry and others are free to portray Mexican and Asian Americans as "new" or "undeserving minorities" locked in a battle with African Americans for limited government resources. Or, as a rather naive article in the *New York Times Magazine* put it, "the new minorities' affirmative-action claims for fairness can't help but come at the expense of blacks."[7] The provocative, divisive nature of this neoconservative argument is hardly concealed. With the rise of racial tensions, even liberals take up the argument.

In a troubling *Atlantic Monthly* assessment of the 1992 Los Angeles riot, for example, Jack Miles warns of an emerging struggle between Latinos and Blacks "for the bottom rung." Because white employers fear or disdain blacks and trust Latinos, Miles argues, there is widespread preferential hiring of Latinos for menial jobs—"the largest affirmative-action program in the nation, and one paid for, in effect, by blacks." But, reasons Miles, if the Mexican border were sealed off, a desperately needed safety valve for Mexico would be eliminated, and this "could foster the rise in that country of a terrorist movement like Peru's Shining Path."[8] The horns of Miles's dilemma now become clear: regardless of which minority wins the battle for the "bottom rung," violence will probably result. Not once in his pessimistic analysis does Miles question his base assumption that the "bottom rung" should be a preserve for African or Mexican Americans.

Without much exaggeration, one could say that such unabashed speculation in the national media and academia displays symptoms of manic depression. Bouts of hysteria may be followed by reassurances or resignation, only to have the cycle repeat itself, sometimes within the same commentary. The delusion of the analysts lies in their unspoken belief that the race question refers to "those people"—Mexicans, Blacks, Asians—while they, naturally, speak for the "national" interest. Speaking for the "nation" disguises the "whiteness"— the race consciousness— of their perspective: their words are presumed to be part not of a racialized discourse but of an objective, transcendent American discourse. And so they speak "for the common good," composing a "national" discourse that manifests a profound ignorance and fear of Latinos and Blacks. Jack Miles's "browns vs. blacks" analysis, for example, was based on his long familiarity with the Mexican family that worked as domestics in the Miles residence. Out of such whimsical, anecdotal material have come alarming arguments with severe political implications.

These much publicized reactions and perspectives on the "browning of America" form the stark backdrop for the following collection of case studies. Needless to say, the general perspective of these studies is thoroughly different from that of the national print media I have just reviewed. The focus of the following essays is not on disintegration but on inclusion, not on opportunism but on activism to secure respect and equality.

By "inclusion" I refer to a basic recognition of Mexican Americans as a legitimate U.S. citizenry. Inclusion refers, in the most specific sense, to the extension and exercise of first-class citizenship. At the most general, it may refer to a broadening of the political culture and meanings associated with "Americanness." Defined generally in this manner, each of the following studies explores some aspect of inclusion; this is the common thread that makes the volume a collective whole.

The ten original contributions in this volume all take their departure point with the "Chicano movement," an integral part of the U.S. civil rights movement of the sixties and seventies. The concern in most of the case studies is to understand the type of "institutionalization" or "accommodation" that has characterized Chicano politics since the mid seventies. They describe various efforts to secure political influence and the contradictory results apparently achieved. In a sense, these studies represent a collective assessment of "postmovement" politics in the Mexican American community. What was achieved? What was lost? Where are we headed?

In answering such questions, the following studies provide a suggestive review of events and tendencies from the mid seventies through the early nineties. Rodolfo Rosales looks at San Antonio politics and the young Mayor Henry Cisneros to understand the unexpected consequences of single-member districts, at the time regarded as an important civil rights victory. Teresa Córdova, in her study of Chicago politics, describes the rise and fall of a progressive Black-Latino coalition under the brief tenure of Mayor Harold Washington. Mary Pardo's description of the "Mothers of East Los Angeles," a church-based community organization, outlines the manner in which activism and citizenship is "gendered." The bittersweet results of the creation of a state agricultural labor-relations agency, a goal long sought by California farmworkers, are analyzed in Margarita Decierdo's article. Phillip Gonzales's account of affirmative action politics at the University of New Mexico suggests the limits of "ethnic advocacy" as one moves up the institutional ladder. Both Christine Sierra and Antonio González, through their respective studies of immigration reform and Central American policy, provide insights into the unprecedented way in which "Hispanic" concerns and pressures have begun to influence national policy making. Eric Xavier suggests the problematic making of an American dream in the artistic and political evolution of Luis Valdez's work from farmworker theater to Hollywood production. And Martín Sánchez Jankowski, using survey data from three major cities, documents similar ambitions and dilemmas in the attitudes of former nationalists. Finally, in order to demonstrate that "inclusion" is a contingent and reversible circumstance, I use the forecasts of demographers and economists to outline a possible exclusionary future for Anglo-Mexican relations.

Together these studies suggest the increasing breadth and complexity of Chicano politics and society in the late twentieth century. Geographically the volume points to the importance of "Hispanic" politics in the Southwest as well as in Chicago wards and in the congressional halls of Washington, D.C., with ramifications in Mexico and Central America. The volume discusses "nontraditional" politics stemming from gender identity, environmental issues, theater production, labor organizing, and university policy making, along with the more traditional politics revolving around state and city government, the Congressional Hispanic Caucus, and various advocacy organizations.

What gives these various studies a sense of unity, as noted before, is the question of inclusion. In spite of different approaches and interests, the following studies clearly demonstrate that whatever political inclusion has taken place, it has been a partial one, uneven and full of contradictions. They suggest as well that inclusion be seen not as a permanent circumstance but rather as a contingent and negotiable one.

How can one speak of "inclusion" in light of the current backlash against immigrants, civil rights, voting rights, affirmative action, bilingual education? This question of inclusion draws its meaning from a historical as well as a present-day context. In other words, in order to understand this orientation, some basic background in history is necessary; then the individual studies can be properly introduced.

A HISTORY OF NATION BUILDING

The notion of inclusion suggests that we have witnessed a qualitative transformation of race relations from some pattern or history of exclusion and control. In the case of the Chicano or Mexican American experience, any historical assessment must recognize its nineteenth-century origins in the Mexican War and the annexation of the northern half of Mexico. It must deal candidly with the sentiments and structures of exclusion that were triggered by conflict and war. The fear about "Mexicanization" or "Latinization" can be traced back to such roots, as exemplified by a warning given at the 1845 Texas Constitutional Convention about allowing Mexicans the right to vote: "Silently they will come moving in; they will come back in thousands . . . and what will be the consequence? Ten, twenty, thirty, forty, fifty thousand may come in here, and vanquish you at the ballot box though you are invincible in arms. This is no idle dream; no bugbear; it is the truth."[9] More than a century and a half later, such sentiment still strikes a responsive chord in the American imagination.

What is important to note is the sharp reorientation that a frank nineteenth-century history introduces. Most pundits and scholars who comment on the worrisome immigration situation assume that the nation has had preformed, fixed boundaries into which poured immigrants who eventually melted into an American stock. There is no examination of the nation-building experience itself, a national experience that involved Indian wars, plantation slavery, wars with Mexico and Spain, and expansion to California and eventually to Puerto Rico, Hawaii, and the Philippines. Such failures of historical memory are critical, for only in this way can one ignore the manner in which nation building and conquests of "people of color"—reds, blacks, browns, and yellows—have fused race consciousness ("whiteness") and national identity ("Americanness") and profoundly shaped national politics.[10]

Immigration, of course, was and is a basic element of the American experience, but twentieth-century immigrants stepped into a world shaped by a past. The massive waves of European and Mexican immigrants of this century assimilated the cultural lore and political lessons of the nineteenth century, even as they put in place a contemporary modern economy. Assimilation occurred, but along ethnic-racial lines. Thus, for most of the twentieth-century Southwest, "American" generally meant "white," an identity that melted various European groups (German, Irish, Polish, Italian, Jewish) into one, while "Mexican" likewise referred to race and not to citizenship.

In short, the Mexican in the twentieth-century United States was seen as "another" race problem and handled in much the same way as the African American was, through segregationist policies and institutions. Indeed, in spite of their very different experiences in the nineteenth century, the parallels between African American and Mexican American experiences in the 20th century are extensive: exclusion or segregation for much of the first half of the twentieth century, as regional and local Anglo elites extended Jim Crow policies designed explicitly for Blacks to cover Mexicans, and a twenty-five-year period of change, 1950–1975, as these racial policies came under attack from various social movements demanding (among other things) first-class citizenship.[11]

THE CHICANO MOVEMENT

The question of inclusion also suggests a different kind of politics, a "normal" or routinized institutional politics that stands in contrast to the "politics of protest" that took place roughly between 1965 and 1975.[12] In the sixties, frustrated with the remaining segregationist limits and inspired by the Black civil rights movement, a general mobilization of the Mexican American community took place. The specific catalysts were the farm worker strikes in California and Texas in 1965–1966, which set off diverse organizing energies that quickly reverberated throughout the Southwest and later through the Midwest. These strikes ignited a broad civil rights mobilization among all classes of the Mexican American community—businessmen, professionals, college and high school students, factory workers, even the street youth. Unlike the assimilationist character of the earlier protests of the 1950s, these protests began to articulate a unifying nationalist vision that in its more militant guises was separatist. The activists took the pejorative lower-class label of *Chicano* and *Chicana* and transformed it into a powerful political identity.

Generally speaking, the Chicano movement scored few direct successes—winning a few rural county and town governments in Texas, fueling a land-grant reclamation movement in New Mexico, securing labor rights for farmworkers in California, and opening up universities throughout the region to Chicano youth.[13] The Chicano movement, nonetheless, set the stage for considerable political reform, both nationally and locally, and made the moderate established organizations more acceptable. It left its imprint in the creation of new advocacy organizations—the Mexican American Legal Defense and Educational Fund (MALDEF), the Southwest Voter Registration and Education Project (SVREP), the National Council of La Raza (NCLR), for example—that would carry out and monitor the mandated dismantling of segregationist practices and institutions. Ironically, then, the Chicano movement reformed the "system"—not in the sweeping manner that movement rhetoric demanded—but sufficiently to move Chicanos off the streets and into the waiting rooms of the "house of power."

This pressure from below, of unprecedented intensity and geographic scope, laid the basis for a politics of inclusion. One can arguably peg 1975, the year the Voting Rights Act was extended to "language minorities," as a defining moment. In the same year the passage of the California Agricultural Labor Relations Act signaled the extension of labor rights to farmworkers, thus also bringing some closure to the events that had started the movement in 1965. By the mid 1970s, the militant nationalist energy throughout the Southwest had dissipated, having been channeled on the one hand into cultural projects, community organizing, and nonpartisan political activities, and on the other into traditional partisan activities and business ventures. Generally speaking, the "Chicano generation" witnessed an uneven transition from segregation and powerlessness to integration and electoral influence, from the "politics of recognition" to the "politics of institutionalized power," as Christine Sierra describes it.[14]

Such basic change in American society led William J. Wilson to characterize the post-1975 period as one of the "declining significance of race."[15] This was somewhat an overstatement, for race continues to carry considerable significance. Nonetheless, as Wilson noted, the political and social context in which the fact of race is debated and negotiated has changed dramatically. Race relations at the end of the twentieth century are markedly different from those at mid century or even in the seventies. Indeed, in the case of Mexican Americans, the uneasiness evident in the national commentaries suggests that the feared "browning" has already taken place.

MEXICAN AMERICANS IN THE LATE TWENTIETH CENTURY

Numbering some fourteen million in 1990, the Mexican American population will grow to comprise near majorities throughout the Southwest, especially in the key states of Texas and California, within the next generation. Everyday features of Southwestern life—food, music, and art are among the most obvious—underscore the Mexican influence. Indeed, *Time* magazine declared in a special July 1988 issue that "Hispanic culture" had broken "out of the barrio."[16]

On university campuses in the region, the controversy over multiculturalism, while far from over, suggests that "Anglo conformity," the long-reigning cultural paradigm for the United States, is under siege as we enter the twenty-first century. In fact, the universities generally lag behind the elementary schools, where the reality of multicultural student bodies has influenced the curriculum for some time.

In the world of commerce, the consumer market of the Mexican American population has an estimated value of one hundred billion dollars and has gained the attention of major market promoters. Conservative projections estimate that by the year 2000 Mexican Americans will own 320,000 business firms with annual business revenues of twenty billion dollars. And while there may be disagreement over trade agreements between the United States and Mexico, no one disputes that Mexican Americans will become an increasingly important intermediary in such binational commerce.[17]

Nowhere is this influence more evident than in the political arena. Currently Mexican Americans play key political roles in all Southwestern states and in several urban areas outside the region, in stark contrast with the pattern of exclusion for much of the twentieth century. The growth in Mexican American political participation in the Southwest has been dramatic: between 1976 and 1988 the number of registered voters doubled to more than three million, while the number of Latino elected officials likewise doubled to more than three thousand. In the past two decades, the watershed elections of Henry Cisneros as mayor of San Antonio, of Federico Peña as mayor of Denver, and of Gloria Molina as county supervisor of Los Angeles County, as well as the gubernatorial elections of Jerry Apodaca and Toney Anaya in New Mexico, signified not just an exponential increase in political representation but a qualitatively different level of representation for the Mexican American community.

At the state level, the makeup of the 1996–1997 Texas legislature easily demonstrated the significance of Mexican American influence: of the 150 House members, nearly one-fifth belonged to the Mexican American caucus; of the 31 senators, almost one-fourth were caucus members. In California, in spite of an anti-Latino climate (or perhaps because of it), Mexican Americans in 1996 gained thirteen seats in the eighty-member state assembly, making Cruz Bustamante the first Latino speaker of the lower house.[18]

At the national level, the mostly Democratic Congressional Hispanic Caucus, numbering in the 1990s about a dozen members, had become increasingly effective in using the mechanics of "power brokering" not only to block detrimental legislation but, more importantly, to secure beneficial legislation. Despite the staunch Democratic Party affiliation of most Mexican Americans, the national Republican party has tried to make inroads with appeals to "family values" and business development; the result has been a sporadic competition between the Republican and Democratic parties for the Mexican American vote. Former President George Bush's appointment of Lauro Cavazos as secretary of education and Manuel Lujan as secretary of the interior, a serious bid to enlist Mexican Americans to the Republican fold, signaled national recognition of the Mexican American presence. The Democratic Party response was seen in President Clinton's cabinet appointments of Henry Cisneros as secretary of housing and urban development and Federico Peña as secretary of transportation for his first term, and the appointments of Peña as secretary of energy and Congressman Bill Richardson of New Mexico as UN ambassador for his second. These appointments suggest that Latino representation at the highest national level may have become institutionalized in partisan politics.[19]

In short, the "browning of America" proclaimed in the end-of-the-century accounts of journalists and pundits ironically suggests some measure of political inclusion. The friendlier commentaries describe Mexican Americans as "patriotic" and "real Hispanic Americans" and "worthy" (or "expecting no special help")—attempting, apparently, to soften the realization of an increasing Mexican presence in U.S. society.

The following studies look at the same reality with a different lens. Hopefully, they may begin to moderate the tenor and language dominating the current national discussion. At the minimum, they should demonstrate that voices on the other side of the American racial-ethnic divide are carrying on a very different discussion.

ORGANIZATION OF THE VOLUME

The articles in this book are grouped into three sections: community studies, institutional studies, and general studies.

Community Studies

In this section are grouped three studies that deal with the politics of specific urban communities, namely, San Antonio, Chicago, and Los Angeles.

Rodolfo Rosales, in his study of San Antonio politics in the 1980s, observes a curious result of the shift from at-large to single-member districts. As expected, single-member districts resulted in more ethnic representation on the city council, but they also promoted individualistic or "personal agenda" politics in place of the previous practice of collective or "organizational agenda" politics (which had been necessary for successful at-large campaigns). Presenting Mayor Henry Cisneros and Councilman Bernardo Eureste as examples of personal-agenda politicians, Rosales describes how community political influence remains elusive. Because the Chicano community has not forged a broad-based organizational agenda, the political field has once again been left to organized business interests.

Teresa Córdova's contribution takes us beyond the Southwest to the complex ethnic politics of Chicago during the mid eighties, a time when the old Daley political machine appeared to be unraveling. Córdova describes the rise of a progressive Black-Latino coalition with Harold Washington's mayoral victory in 1983. This coalition was unable to consolidate its power, however, until the special aldermanic elections in 1986, when four pro-Washington candidates—two Blacks, one Mexican American, one Puerto Rican—were elected. Shortly after the sudden death of Washington the following year, the coalition broke apart over the question of a successor. In 1989, with support from some former coalition members (including future Congressman Luis Gutiérrez), Richard M. Daley, son of the former machine mayor, was elected mayor of Chicago. Thus did the Daley Machine become resurrected, though with a decidedly increased Black-Latino presence.

The third contribution to this collection is Mary Pardo's study of the largest protest to emerge from East Los Angeles in the eighties. A grassroots protest movement, led by the church-based Mothers of East Los Angeles (MELA), was catalyzed by a State of California decision to locate a new prison in East Los Angeles. Pardo focuses on the developing political consciousness of the generally middle-aged, low-income women of MELA. Through their involvement they transformed their identities, especially of "motherhood," into a basis for militant opposition to projects that adversely affect the quality of life in their community. Pardo's study is a provocative account of the politicization of hundreds of working-class Mexican American women.

Institutional Studies

This section includes four studies that focus on the politics and policies of government agencies.

At the state level, we have Margarita Decierdo's assessment of California's Agricultural Labor Relations Board (ALRB) from 1975 through 1990, which touches on the unexpected consequences of a perceived victory. At the time of its creation in 1975, the ALRB was seen as the culmination of a ten-year struggle by the United Farm Workers, led by César Chávez, to secure union recognition and wage contracts with intransigent growers. From the outset, however, the new state agency faced serious obstacles in implementing the legal mediating framework intended to resolve the labor conflict. Indeed, the conflict itself was "imported" into the agency, with staff dividing itself into pro-grower, pro-farmworker, and neutral factions. The election of Republican Governor Deukmejian and subsequent pro-grower control of the ALRB led to a general purging of "pro-farmworker" staff. Thus the ALRB in the eighties, Decierdo concludes, ends up, ironically, being used as a mechanism to control farmworker union activities.

Phillip Gonzales grounds his analysis of university politics in a contentious dispute over affirmative action policy at the University of New Mexico in the mid 1980s. The determination of two influential Hispanic regents (one of them an ex-governor of the state) to pursue affirmative action alienated the university president and a large fraction of the Anglo faculty, who essentially countered by labeling the regents as ethnic politicians concerned with patronage. The ensuing public outcry against the regents' "meddling" led to the passage of a constitutional admendment adding two new seats to the Board of Regents, a move to undermine the Hispanic majority. Gonzales argues that this case illustrates the limits to ethnic advocacy as one moves up the institutional ladder, where "universalistic" goals are expected.

At the national level, Christine Sierra reviews a ten-year period (1976–1986) of Chicano efforts to influence immigration reform to understand how the Congressional Hispanic Caucus and a Latino lobby in Washington engage in the politics of compromise, often at the expense of the Chicano community. The Caucus and the advocacy lobby proved successful in blocking the Simpson-Mazzoli bill until the coalition fell apart over the question of legislative strategy. Some members of Congress and advocacy organizations felt that they needed to shed their obstructionist role and engage in "realistic politics" if they were to save the amnesty program. Sierra notes that while Chicano politicians and activists have demonstrated their ability to influence national policy making, they are now subject to pressure to moderate their demands and be pragmatic.

In similar fashion, Antonio González outlines the Chicano advocacy organizations' unprecedented consensus in the late eighties in opposing U.S. Central American policy, especially regarding the support of the Nicaraguan "contras." This coordinated opposition, led in particular by Willie Velásquez and the Southwest Voter Registration Education Project (SVREP), pressured the Congressional Hispanic Caucus to work to reverse Reagan administration policy, with success finally coming in 1988. For González, this suggests not only a qualitative advance for Chicano politics but also a historic possibility of moderating the Monroe Doctrine that has justified U.S. hegemony in the Western Hemisphere.

General Studies

As noted earlier, an underlying theme that unifies these various studies is a concern with understanding what happened after the movement. Two contributions provide explicit overviews of the transition from movement politics to institutionalized politics, but each does it in a distinctive way.

Eric Xavier begins his intriguing study of El Teatro Campesino and its founder, Luis Valdez, in the mid sixties and takes us through the late eighties. Xavier explores the relationship between the politics and culture of the Chicano movement by reviewing the evolution of El Teatro Campesino, from farmworker theater performed on flatbed trucks to the "American plays" staged and filmed in Los Angeles. Xavier interprets the change in specific dramatic styles according to the changing fortunes of the Chicano movement. Xavier thus provides us a case study of how one Chicano cultural form has become "integrated" into American society, with theatrical and movie success as the evidence. It is a curious integration, however, for Valdez's contemporary efforts to write "American plays" for a broad audience have been seen in Hollywood primarily as an opening into the Hispanic market.

From another vantage point, Martín Sánchez Jankowski employs a unique data set—a longitudinal survey of youth in San Antonio, Albuquerque, and Los Angeles—to find out what happened to the nationalists he first interviewed in 1976. Reinterviewing them in 1986, Sánchez Jankowski discovers that the "cultural nationalists" of the mid seventies have abandoned their position, whereas the "political nationalists" remain as committed as before. In this candid analysis of youth who have gone different political ways, Sánchez Jankowski notes that lower-class nationalists of the seventies generally remain the most radical, whereas many middle-class nationalists have turned to Republican party politics. Sánchez Jankowksi concludes that nationalism can reassert itself if inequality between Chicanos and Anglos worsens.

The volume concludes with my speculative study of the possible futures for Chicano-Anglo relations in the twenty-first century. The "politics of inclusion," I argue, basically reflects a certain understanding or convergence of interests between the prominent class groups of the Chicano and Anglo communities; specifically, the Chicano middle class, which wants political entry and opportunities, and the Anglo business elite, which wants support for its pro-development plans, have accommodated one another. Against this setting, I explore the implications of two much discussed projections: that the United States has already begun an economic decline within the world system and that ethnic demographic growth (or "browning") portends potential class polarization along ethnic lines. In summary, I argue that the convergence of these two projections poses serious challenges to the pro-development accommodation that makes for political inclusion.

ON THE POLITICS OF INCLUSION

What general points about political inclusion can be teased out from these wide-ranging studies? Three basic points appear to stand out.

The first is that inclusion, although referring to involvement in institutionalized problem-solving politics, is accompanied if not maintained by a politics of protest. All the community and institutional studies in this volume mention such mobilization. Protest politics catalyzed or underscored the various campaigns for voting rights (Rosales & Córdova), quality of life (Pardo), labor rights (Deciderio), affirmative action (Gonzales), immigration policy (Sierra), Central American policy (González), and cultural expression (Xavier). Put another way, political inclusion signifies the assertion of community autonomy or influence in the policy-making process. The degree or extent of inclusion is the result of negotiation and, sometimes, of conflict.

A second general point, closely related to the first, deals with the distinct perspective—that "un-American agenda" most feared by conservative commentators—that Mexican Americans are introducing in American public policy. Inclusion signifies access and participation in policy- and decision-making agencies. Such participation necessarily entails the advocacy of a definite position on such questions as affirmative action, labor relations, bilingual education, immigration, foreign policy toward Latin America, multiculturalism, and so on. Most of the studies in this volume describe an unprecedented political situation that promised a "historic" introduction of a Chicano perspective. A critical ingredient was the development of an organizational infrastructure that could at times effectively express such a perspective.

This leads to a related third point about pragmatic politics: that this distinct ethnic perspective is moderated, compromised, or contained by participation in institutionalized politics. Indeed, the institutional limits that moderate or contain ethnic issues comprise the core of most of the studies; it is the most developed theme in the volume. These various studies demonstrate rather evident advances in access and representation within institutionalized politics, but these advances all prove to be fleeting or ambiguous. In San Antonio single-member districts end up encouraging individualistic or personal agendas rather than community-wide organizational ones. In Chicago the insurgent Washington mayoralty turns out to be a temporary lapse from Daley machine rule. In California, the much heralded Agricultural Labor Relations Board becomes transformed into a regulating agency of farmworker labor activity. In New Mexico the Hispanic regents of the flagship university are basically censured for their "ethnic politics." At the national level, the Simpson-Mazzolli immigration bill finally passes with the compromised support of the Congressional Hispanic Caucus, while the U.S. policy of supporting the Nicaraguan "contras," although finally overturned, reveals sharp differences within the Hispanic Caucus.

What these studies suggest, then, is that participation in institutionalized politics, while providing routinized access to decision making, at the same time sets limits on political behavior, promotes compromise at the possible expense of the "community," and may even undermine community organizational effectiveness. Such are the contradictions of inclusion.

A FINAL WORD

A word might be said about the organization of this volume. There was no conference or shared intellectual discussion to pull together ideas, smooth over differences, or reconcile disagreements; all papers were written independently of each other, not in concert with some overall design. The various studies employ very different approaches: demographic analysis, survey analysis, participant observation, interviews, life histories, and straightforward library research. Evident also are differences in ethnic identification preferred by the authors — Chicano, Mexican American, Mexican, Hispano, Latino; these were left as the author chose.

There is no claim, of course, that this volume offers a thorough consideration of contemporary Chicano politics and society. Beyond Pardo's insightful
discussion of the changing consciousness and identity of women activists, there
is no treatment of gender or gendered politics. There is no theory of the "state,"
although Decierdo's provocative argument—that the state does not stand
above the fray but reflects the class conflict occurring around it—points the
way for further analysis. There is no sustained comparison with African Americans, although Córdova's description of Chicago politics is suggestive. Nor are
all the compelling issues that point to the limits, unevenness, and uncertain-
ties of inclusion—poverty and crime, school finance and school dropout rates,
language policy and multiculturalism, foreign policy with a restive Mexico,
for example—discussed in this volume. Nonetheless, these studies take an
important first step. Taken together as a whole, they provide a panoramic view
of post-movement politics and suggest directions for more research.

NOTES

1. Todd Gitlin, "Racial Obsession Taking a Toll," *Austin American-Statesman*, December 12,
1995; special issue on "California Fault Lines," *Nation*, Sept. 18, 1995; Mike Davis, "In L.A.,
Burning All Illusions," *Nation*, June 1, 1992, pp. 743–746; W. E. B. Du Bois, "To the Nations of
the World," address to the Pan-African Conference, London, 1900.

2. "What Will the U.S. Be Like When Whites Are No Longer the Majority?" *Time*, April 9,
1990.

3. Lawrence E. Harrison, "America and Its Immigrants," *National Interest* (Summer, 1992),
p. 45.

4. William Langewiesche, "The Border," *Atlantic Monthly*, May 1992, p.65; David M. Kennedy, "Can We Still Afford to Be a Nation of Immigrants?" *Atlantic Monthly*, November 1996,
pp. 52–68.

5. Georgie Anne Geyer, "Poll Shows Gulf Between Hispanics, Their 'Spokesmen,'" *El Paso
Times*, Dec. 27, 1992; also "States Conduct Own Foreign Policy," *Houston Post*, Nov. 10, 1983.

6. Peter Skerry, "Borders and Quotas: Immigration and the Affirmative Action State," *Public
Interest* no. 96 (Summer 1989), pp. 86–102. For a full elaboration, see Skerry, *Mexican Americans:
The Ambivalent Minority* (New York: Free Press, 1993).

7. William H. Frey and Jonathan Tilove, "Immigrants In, Native Whites Out," *New York Times
Magazine*, August 20, 1995, pp. 44–45.

8. Jack Miles, "Blacks versus Browns: The Struggle for the Bottom Rung," *Atlantic Monthly*,
October 1992, pp. 52–55, 68.

9. Quoted in Paul S. Taylor, *An American-Mexican Frontier: Nueces County, Texas* (New York:
Russell & Russell, 1971), p. 232.

10. See David R. Roediger, *The Wages of Whiteness: Race and the Making of the American Work-
ing Class* (New York: Verso, 1991); Reginald Horsman, *Race and Manifest Destiny: The Origins of
American Racial Anglo-Saxonism* (Cambridge: Harvard University Press, 1981); Ronald T. Takaki,
Iron Cages: Race and Culture in Nineteenth-Century America (New York: Alfred A. Knopf, 1979);
Tomas Almaguer, *Racial Fault Lines: The Historical Origins of White Supremacy in California* (Berke-
ley: University of California Press, 1994).

11. See Manning Marable, *Race, Reform, and Rebellion: The Second Reconstruction in Black America, 1945–1990*, rev. 2nd ed. (Jackson: University Press of Mississippi, 1991).

12. Protest activity, of course, antedated the sixties. There had occurred an earlier veteran-inspired civil rights movement in the late 1940s and early 1950s. This was the height of the "Mexican American Generation," a political generation that emphasized its American identity and progress toward assimilation. See Mario T. García, *Mexican Americans: Leadership, Ideology, and Identity, 1930–1960* (New Haven: Yale University Press, 1989).

13. See David Montejano, *Anglos and Mexicans in the Making of Texas, 1836–1986* (Austin: University of Texas, 1987).

14. Such recent entry into institutionalized politics signifies an ongoing learning experience. When the Congressional Hispanic Caucus proved successful in pushing for passage of the Voting Rights Language Assistance Act in August 1992, over the objections of Republicans and "English-first" advocacy groups, the event was hailed as the first time that Hispanic leaders had played the Washington influence game "as insiders" to score major legislation. See "Breaking the Beltway Barrier: Can Lobbyists Win the War for Washington Clout?" *Hispanic Business*, April 1993, pp. 16–22.

15. William J. Wilson, *The Declining Significance of Race: Blacks and Changing American Institutions* (Chicago: University of Chicago Press, 1978).

16. Bureau of the Census, *The Hispanic Population in the United States: March 1991*, Current Population Reports, Series P-20, No. 455. Washington, D.C.: U.S. GPO, 1991; special issue of *Time*, "Magnifico! Hispanic Culture Breaks Out of the Barrio," July 11, 1988.

17. See "The Hispanic Market: A Tremendous $200-Billion Marketing Opportunity For All!," *Telemarketing*, November 1992; "30 Million by the year 2000: Annual Hispanic Market Issue," *Hispanic Business*, December 1991. For different views on NAFTA, see "Opening the Door to Mexico's Riches," *Hispanic Business*, January 1993, and Southwest Voter Research Institute, "The Impact of the North American Free Trade Agreement on Latino Workers in California and South Texas," *Latin American Project Paper* 2 (September 1992); "Talking Free Trade," *Texas Observer*, April 9, 1993, p.4.

18. See, for example, Southwest Voter Registration Education Project, *Latino Vote Reporter*, vols. 1–2 (1996–1997); "Polanco's Efforts Bear Fruit with Latino's Rise in Assembly," *Los Angeles Times*, December 26, 1996; "Latino Turnout a Breakthrough Election: Group's Heavy Balloting Could Signal a Historic Pivot Point for Political Relations in L.A.," *Los Angeles Times*, April 10, 1997.

19. See "Breaking the Beltway Barrier: Can Lobbyists Win the War for Washington Clout?" *Hispanic Business*, April 1993; "What Clinton Will Do for Hispanics," *Hispanic Magazine*, Jan./Feb. 1993; "Clinton Administration's Number of Hispanic Appointments Graded at C− and 'Unacceptable' by NHLA and NCLR Respectively," *National Hispanic Reporter*, May 1993; "Hispanics Organizing as Republican Entity," *Austin American-Statesman*, July 1, 1995.

PART ONE

Community Studies

One

PERSONALITY AND STYLE IN SAN ANTONIO POLITICS

Henry Cisneros and Bernardo Eureste, 1975–1985

R O D O L F O   R O S A L E S

In 1977 independent political representation for the Chicano community finally arrived as San Antonio changed from an at-large system of representation to single-member districts, making it possible for the various sectors to elect their choice of representation to city council. The impact of this change for the Chicano community is obvious.[1] In the area of employment, San Antonio boasts the first Chicano city manager in a major city, along with a sizable number of Chicanas and Chicanos in upper-level city administration positions. In the area of allocational services, such as streets, drainage, libraries, and other primary services, the impact of single-member districts is quite significant — the streets in the westside, southside, and eastside are finally paved, lighted, and equipped with drainage.

However, the broader backdrop for this analysis is an urban market economy in competition for limited resources and investments in a regional economy that is moving rapidly to a more competitive global economy. Given its limited resources, San Antonio still finds itself in the face of these larger market forces, as have many other cities, limited in terms of what it can and cannot do. The social ills that San Antonio, especially its Chicano community, has suffered throughout this century are still painfully and pervasively present. One could argue that San Antonio is essentially imprisoned by the structure of a political economy that forces it to turn most of its attention to economic development as opposed to the various social and economic issues that face the community.

In this larger context, then, did the change in the structure of political representation create political inclusion for the Chicano community, or did it create an illusion, simply setting the stage for individualistic politicians to serve as brokers for the business community? Stated in another manner, can politicians in this system be held accountable to the needs of the community? The other side of the question is: Can the community electorally advance an agenda that is geared to its social and economic needs in a political system that is geared to economic development? To address these questions, this essay focuses on how two of the most prominent Chicano politicians whose careers were created by these structural changes shaped and fashioned their political agendas in the relatively more open political environment created by single-member districts.

STRUCTURE AND AGENCY: THE QUESTION OF EMPOWERMENT

While it is obvious that humans are not simply robots determined by the structures and rules around them, how do we come to an understanding of the interaction between the structures which, after all, were created by human action (agency), and the determinacy that these structures in turn impart on human behavior?[2]

In this context, Paul Peterson, in *City Limits*, argues that while cities are equipped to provide allocational services, their only realistic and therefore legitimate function outside the routine allocation of services is economic development.[3] In essence, the overall interest of a city is economic development. Cities are not structured or set up to address, for all practical purposes, social issues, which he defines as redistributional services. Redistributional services are for the most part the function of the state and national government. From this functional perspective of the city, then, the most legitimate agenda in city politics ends up being that of growth and expansion, and the major actors end up being the business community and its various allies. As a consequence, efficiency, rather than equity or equality, is at the heart of city politics. Political conflicts brought about by the demands of the community thus are seen as problems in the management of local government. In other words, Peterson depoliticizes the entire process through his narrow and overstructural definition of the function of a city as the "director" of development.

Michael Peter Smith, on the other hand, argues that beyond the influence of market forces and political structures, sociopolitical forces are at work in determining the shape and welfare of any particular city.[4] His focus is on the conflicts over space and politics that have shaped the urban political environment. Smith provides an approach by which one can then look at how communities win and lose in the struggle over space, quality of life issues, and ultimately the kind of political agenda that a city shapes for its constituents. The particular policy direction of a city is the outcome of political conflicts and not solely the consequence of political and economic structures.

Another very important approach to city politics and the status of communities is Manual Castells's classic study, *The City and the Grassroots*.[5] Castells's study, which is a cross-time and cross-cultural analysis of how communities define and confront the issues facing them, concludes that communities in today's global economy end up cutting out their particular spaces within their urban experiences as they adjust to their environment. His is both a pessimistic as well as an optimistic conclusion. It is pessimistic because he finds that these various communities across culture and across time submit to an overwhelming global political economy by covering their heads and end up concerning themselves solely with their own backs. It is optimistic, on the other hand, because he brings out the agency side of humanity—people's struggle to overcome odds that are sometimes beyond their control.

All three of these approaches concerning the influence of the larger forces and structures on what cities and communities can do have played some part in bringing us to our particular study. To address this question of structure and agency in contemporary San Antonio, we use a comparative profile method to present an analysis of modern San Antonio as it finally opened up the political system that had been closed to the Chicano community for most of this century. In this analysis we do not pretend to come to any concrete generalizable conclusions about Chicanos, urban politics, and political power. While I do look at larger forces, my premise is that the understanding of how communities cope with political and institutional structures can only develop from the kind of particularistic case study that this essay represents.

PARAMETERS OF THE STUDY

This essay arises out of a larger study of how the Chicano community mobilized to bring about changes in a political system that had excluded them throughout this century.[6] Beginning in 1951, when it successfully changed the city charter in order to set up a council-manager form of government based on an at-large, nonpartisan electoral system, the business community masterminded a politics of growth and expansion that excluded most of the social and economic issues facing the Chicano community.[7] By the early 1970s, the dominance of the business leaders was successfully challenged electorally as well as legally by the Chicano community, ending with the change to single-member districts.

This is not to say that the dominance of the business community and its agenda was not challenged prior to the 1970s. During the 1950s and 1960s, politics was almost completely dominated by two organizational agendas representing two diverse politics. The business non-partisan slating group, the Good Government League (GGL), represented the politics of growth and expansion. The Bexar County Democratic Coalition, a coalition of liberal Chicanos, Anglos, Blacks, and labor, on the other hand, represented a politics that focused on the social and economic needs of the community. With only one exception, no politician could afford to be independent.[8]

The notion of "organizational agenda" politics was an important concept for understanding the political reality of mid-century San Antonio. I employed the notion of "organizational agenda" politics to depict a political process in which the GGL dominated at the exclusion of the various sectors of the San Antonio community. The political reality that this style of politics reflected was one in which the Chicano community had to mobilize its resources in alliance with various other excluded sectors in their struggle for political inclusion. The notion of "personal agenda" politics, on the other hand, was useful in depicting a political process that had finally opened up to the various sectors of San Antonio, including the Chicano community. This kind of politics reflected a political process in which organizational agendas no longer played the dominant role that they had played in the past politics of exclusion. Politicians were now left to their own resources and organizations to define the politics and issues that they would pursue.[9]

In the 1950s and 1960s the two organizational agendas mentioned above dominated politics in terms of not only who ran for office but also who defined the kinds of issues addressed. While personal agendas certainly existed in that time, even the most maverick or independent individual required the support of or dovetailed into one or the other of the larger organizational agendas. Thus, organizational politics even defined the kinds of political conflicts that ensued.

From the 1970s, when single-member districts arrived on the scene, to the present, the personal agendas of politicians took the forefront. Our argument is not that organizational agendas do not exist today or that personal agendas did not exist in the 1950s and 1960s. Rather, we argue that the more open political process after 1977 made the pursuance of individual interests a very real possibility, changing the mode of political activity. Further, the argument is not that there were no existing organizations that influenced individual politicians. Indeed, the business community still maintains a very powerful presence through its lobbying and electioneering. As well, community organizations, such Communities Organized for Public Services (COPS), have had a tremendous impact on the politicians representing the areas where this organization is based. However, a formal process in which politicians are wedded to a particular agenda does not exist. Politicians in this more open environment are free to negotiate with various interests.

The political profile approach that we utilize in this study was very useful in both presenting a more personal account of two well-known political figures in San Antonio as well as in teasing out in more detail the particular manner by which both ultimately were products of a process that adapted the new mode of politics to its broader agenda of growth and expansion. What we set out to do in this study, then, is bring into relief through a profile of these two actors the particular political reality of the Chicano community in a changing political system. These profiles allows us to analyze how personal agendas in all their diversity ultimately reflect a political reality that is tied to the logic of the ever looming market economy.

We begin with a brief discussion of the process that led to single-member districts. Next we provide a discussion of Henry Cisneros and his remarkably astute climb to political legitimacy for all of San Antonio. Then we compare this profile to Bernardo Eureste's seemingly more radical style so as to bring out how, ultimately, despite their different styles and different agendas, they both are products of the same process. We end with a brief discussion of how social and political forces and conflicts shape the particular patterns of city politics in the context of personal agenda politics.

A POLITICAL ENVIRONMENT IN FLUX

In 1973 the GGL lost a majority of the city council seats for the first time since they had gained control of the city council in 1955, with the "new Northside money" gaining a majority of the seats. After those elections, different groups in the business community tried to reorganize but to no avail. In November of 1974 San Antonio voters approved a city charter amendment to elect the mayor directly instead of allowing the city council to select the mayor from among its own members as it had done since 1953.[10]

The San Antonio city council elections of 1975 were the first in this century in which there was not a dominant group in a position to successfully capture a majority of the council seats. Those elections presented the first seemingly pluralistic political environment in San Antonio. The competing views and interests that had been set loose in the 1973 elections now represented a framework of personal-agenda politics as opposed to the organizational agenda politics that had dominated the San Antonio political scene since 1951.

More importantly, Chicano political activists, caught in the rising expectations of an open, pluralistic political environment, were intensely mobilizing forces against the still intact at-large system of electing city council members. For the Chicano activists the goal of single-member districts was the one structural method by which to insure parity in representation for all citizens in San Antonio. Even with the 1950s municipal reform ushering in San Antonio as a modern Sunbelt city, the Chicano community had yet to gain independent political access to government. The overwhelming majority of city council members elected in the at-large system came from the more affluent Anglo northside of San Antonio, with token representation coming from the other sectors of the city.[11]

There were at least two important factors that ultimately ensured the institutional change to the present single-member district system. The first of these was the demise of the municipal at-large elections, which began with a 1971 Texas court ruling that ordered the state to change the legislative representation system from a multimember (county at-large) system of representation to single-member districts.[12]

Another major factor was the 1972 city council decision to annex various far-northside affluent, Anglo-dominant precincts into the city. The annexation was a double-edged sword for the Chicano community. In the first place, it was part of the overall growth and expansion goals of the "new money" business community. The inclusion of these communities would add, in the eyes of the Chicano community, to the neglect of public services for the Chicano communities. In the second place, this new annexation would have a negative impact on Chicano voting power. The at-large system of representation effectively disenfranchised a large sector of voters in the city of San Antonio. Reinforcing this was the fact that in the 1971 elections, a barrio slate of four candidates, two Chicanas and two Chicanos, won overwhelmingly in the barrio precincts, only to ultimately lose in the at-large voting.[13] Finally, the 1972 annexation provided the means by which to bring the U.S. Justice Department into the picture, making the issue of representation a legal matter. In 1976 the Justice Department objected to the annexations on the grounds that the proportion of Anglos to Mexican Americans in the annexed territory (approximately 3 : 1 Anglo) diluted the majority status of the Mexican American population in the city. The Justice Department indicated that "unless the city altered its method of electing council members to provide more equitable representation of language and racial minorities, the nine precincts added in 1972 would have to be deannexed."[14]

The city council elections of 1975 represented a threshold of various sorts. The direct election of the mayor, while insignificant in terms of formal power, represented a tenacious hold by the GGL when mayoral candidate Lila Cockrell (a GGL council member since 1965) won the election handily. The election of Cockrell was a first for women in San Antonio mayoral politics. In addition, while most of the GGL candidates lost, Henry G. Cisneros was the only other GGL candidate elected as a council member. More significantly, the 1975 city council was forced to address the issue of single-member districts. The ensuing debate and final vote by city council to present a single-member district plan to the voters represented the threshold for a young politician who would rise to political prominence unmatched by any other young contemporary Chicano politician in the United States. Emerging out of this critical point in San Antonio's history was an articulate, smooth, Harvard- and MIT-educated young man who could represent the common man, especially the Chicano, in San Antonio as well as propose technically advanced ideas that were well received by a media and a public ready to see San Antonio take its place as a major U.S. city.

A Rising Star

The issue of single-member districts would finally be confronted by the San Antonio city council in the fall of 1976. In October of that year the city council was forced to decide whether to de-annex or to develop a plan of electing city council representation that would satisfy the section of the Voting Rights Act requiring a more equitable representation of language and racial minorities. The immediate reaction by some city council members was to take the Justice Department to court in order to bar its order. When this proposal was taken up by the city council, the vote was split down the middle, with the young first-term council member Henry Cisneros providing the deciding vote against going to court.

Cisneros eventually joined in the campaign for a "10-1" plan that would provide for ten single-member districts with the mayor running at large. The campaign was successful, and in 1977 the at-large system of electing city council officials was changed by the electorate to single-member district representation. This effort on the part of Cisneros showed an independence that brought him great popularity in the Chicano community.

Cisneros proved to be a meticulous and astute politician in choosing the steps to take in order to fulfill his personal political goals. As early as 1977, Cisneros was touted by the media as mayoral material. But he was careful to avoid running for mayor until Mayor Cockrell was out of the picture and he was able to secure the backing of some of the most prominent names in San Antonio business and political circles. As Rick Casey, a journalist for the *Express News*, put it: "Whether it's selling out or coalition building, it is nothing new to Cisneros. He owes his status to a large extent to two individuals and a political organization: To himself for seven years of single-minded work toward becoming mayor, to Mayor Cockrell for leading the city through a difficult transition and then resigning at the height of her power and to COPS for picking a fight that led to a public consensus of extraordinary intensity."[15] His "single-mindedness" and cautious, meticulous method were the key characteristics of a young man who had to satisfy two radically different sectors in San Antonio: those who wielded the political and economic capital he needed and those whose enthusiastic support would become a cornerstone of his meteoric rise to political prominence. Ironically, in spite of his cautious approach, these diametrically opposed sectors of the community would bring him to the brink of a disastrous conflict several times, endangering his relationship with those economic and political forces critical for his political future.

But Cisneros seemed to be gifted in the art of compromise. For example, from his first term in office, Cisneros consistently opposed development over the Edwards underground aquifer. The Edwards underground aquifer is an underground pure water source that provides water not only for the San Antonio metropolitan area but for eleven counties. Part of the limestone recharge zone which purifies the underground lake lies underneath northern San Antonio, where most of the development was taking place. Cisneros's support of a comprehensive master plan to regulate expansion set him directly in conflict with various powerful developers and their representatives on the city council.[16]

Further, development over the aquifer brought forces together that ordinarily would not have worked together. The Aquifer Protection Association (APA), a liberal environmentalist group, allied itself with COPS, an aggressive community action organization in the Chicano west and southwest sides of San Antonio, in protesting any development over the aquifer. In August of 1975, the city council unanimously adopted a resolution which closely controlled development over San Antonio's sole water source. But at the same time, the city council approved, by a 5 to 4 vote, a zoning variance for a shopping mall over the recharge zone. Cisneros took the side of the APA and COPS and led the opposition against the mall on the basis that it threatened the purity of San Antonio's water source.

By February of 1976, APA and COPS successfully brought a referendum on the city council's business zoning over the aquifer to the voters. With 57,000 votes cast, a referendum overturning the council's decision passed. But the city council, by a vote of 6 to 3, with one absent, voted against the ban on the zoning over the aquifer. Again Cisneros voted for the ban. APA and COPS eyed a possible "recall of councilmen" after the vote.[17]

This, of course, brought excellent publicity for then council member Henry Cisneros as a protector of the community's sole source of water. Considering Cisneros's mayoral ambitions and his own admitted propensity to avoid conflict, this highly risky episode instead brought him greater visibility and further enhanced his reputation as a new kind of Chicano politician who could stand on his own two feet. The young Cisneros was developing an image of himself as a populist — one who knew about and cared for the problems of the community.

Cisneros's astuteness in using the media and picking the right issues was again apparent in a conflict over a proposed 30-percent hike by the City Water Board. As the City Water Board's general manager Robert Van Dyke was explaining the changes in the City Water Board's master plan, Cisneros decided to bring back into discussion the proposed hike: "They [CWB] want this [supplement] approved and we want something changed on the rate hike." Van Dyke retorted that "it makes no difference to us if you adopt this or not." He stated that the presentation was merely a courtesy so that the city could update its overall master plan which it must maintain current to continue securing federal funds. He went on to explain that the supplements to the master plan were basically engineering studies that outlined what the utility must do to serve the fast-growing areas of the city's northwest and northeast.[18]

The significance of this last encounter was that Cisneros took a highly visible position against an institution that had consistently subsidized developers of subdivisions in the northwest and northeast white middle-class neighborhoods by providing water hookups at the expense of the rate payers at large. Cisneros had taken a populist position against an institution that was seen as serving the interest of particular groups without any accountability to the public it was supposed to serve.

Cisneros also raised critical questions as to the viability of governmental structures and institutions and their relationship to people.[19] On several occasions he made it a point to visit with the common person in his or her own environment. In June of 1975 he collected and emptied garbage cans for about four hours to learn first-hand the problems of the sanitation department. He also walked a beat with a policeman and aided ambulance attendants in giving first aid. Finally, in a visit with a family in a public housing unit, he dramatically stated, "These are really private enterprise people . . . they want to work and to better themselves. Their problems are ones that the city can no longer ignore."[20]

At the same time, Cisneros, who enjoyed the resources and visibility of the GGL establishment while not being confined directly to its agenda, was building an image that went beyond San Antonio politics. In 1981 San Antonio elected Henry G. Cisneros as the first Chicano mayor of a major city in the United States. In 1983 he was reelected with 93 percent of the vote. In the presidential elections of 1984 he was among the few considered as a vice-presidential candidate by Mondale, although publicly he emphasized that he still had too many goals to accomplish as mayor. In 1985 he was also considered as a potential gubernatorial candidate for the 1986 state elections, again responding that he was not available.[21]

Cisneros was able to craft a personal-agenda politics based on an image of a young leader with sleeves rolled up and coat over the shoulder—flashbacks of another young mayor (John Lindsay of New York City)—who was able to bring various distinct and sometimes conflicting interests together in a marriage that would ultimately bring the city into national prominence.[22] Here was a young leader who could place San Antonio on the map.

District Politics and the Molding of a Mayor

Henry Cisneros's first two terms (1975–1979) as a city council member were characterized by the astute maneuvering of a young politician with a personal agenda that promised to gain wide support in not only the Chicano community but the broader San Antonio community as well. While Cisneros was seen challenging certain policy matters tied to the priorities of the business class, he was careful at the same time to ally himself with those same groups in emphasizing growth.

Even in the issues that put him seemingly on a collision course with the economically more powerful business community, the context of these conflicts was always carefully articulated so as to separate them from any radical tinge. Thus, Cisneros stood for protection of water, not opposition to growth and expansion; for support of public housing but as an expression of faith in the free enterprise system. Cisneros molded a political agenda that cast him at once as a leader concerned with issues that affected the community and as a leader who was committed to building San Antonio as a great "center of profit" in the scramble for business investment throughout the Sunbelt.

The advent of single-member districts in 1977 and the resulting election of independent Chicano candidates, however, brought onto the scene new actors who presented to Cisneros his greatest challenge. These new actors not only expressed an indifference to the business community's objective of growth and expansion but were actually antagonistic to northside Anglo dominance of city politics.

An important consequence of this new political environment was the opportunity for any member of the city council to engage in debate over any item on the council agenda. Thus, this new kind of politics constituted more than merely a change in form. It reflected the lack of organizational direction and order provided by the GGL for two decades. With the entrance of independently elected council members came the possibility of routine conflict over public policy rarely seen before in city councils under the dominance of the GGL.

Indeed, some of Cisneros's friends were concerned that "the outspoken anger" exhibited by newly elected council members Rudy Ortiz (District 6) and Bernardo Eureste (District 5) would "stir ugly sentiments among the city's Anglos."[23] After the first single-member district elections in April of 1977, both were vocal in joining Cisneros in his challenges to what had been heretofore routine policy matters concerning rate hikes, expansion, bond issues, and even the relationship of institutions such as the city water board and the city public service board to the city council's governance. In fact, Cisneros's populist position seemed to erode alongside these two angry challengers.

In the summer of 1978, 300 Chicano garbage collectors were fired by the city manager, Tom Huebner, for illegally going out on strike. This occurred over the public objections of Ortiz and Eureste, with Cisneros supporting the city manager's action. Ironically, while the entrance of political actors not well rehearsed by the dominant political machine of the GGL seemed to undermine Cisneros's "star trajectory," it would also prove to be the molding that ultimately shaped Cisneros as the most acceptable Chicano politician for not only the Chicano community but also for the more affluent Anglo northside.

On the surface at least, San Antonio city politics had finally introduced a pluralistic politics that allowed an important sector of San Antonio formally to participate in the policy-making process in an independent manner. But then in 1979, Rudy Ortiz was narrowly defeated by Bob Thompson in District 6, an area almost evenly divided between Anglos and Chicanos and between middle-class and working- and lower-class communities. This election signaled the beginning of a process which was to be dominated by the contrasting styles of two significant Chicano leaders, Henry Cisneros and Bernardo Eureste. One represented the repressed interests of the Chicano barrios, and the other represented the equally repressed aspirations of the Chicano community for a Chicano as mayor, as leader of San Antonio. An intense conflict developed after this election, as Cisneros and Eureste not only fought over the approach to issues but over the kinds of issues that should be raised before the city council. For the next eight years, this distinct political relationship, especially after Cisneros was elected mayor, determined a political climate that allowed Cisneros to expand his electoral support to the most conservative and historically anti-Chicano sectors in San Antonio.

Eureste, a product of southside San Antonio and educated at the University of Michigan, was at the time of his election a professor at Our Lady of the Lake University. Eureste served four consecutive two-year terms (1977–1985) on the city council. His district represented the most densely populated, poorest district to be found in the south and west sides of San Antonio. This district also was overwhelmingly Chicano. Perhaps because of the combination of his barrio background, earlier Chicano activism, and social work education, Eureste brought to the city council a political activism never before seen in the formal setting of city council politics.

During his tenure not only did Eureste consistently and loudly pit his district's needs against those of the more affluent Anglo middle-class districts, but he also extended this debate into the arena of class by challenging his colleagues in policy matters that concerned growth and expansion, the historic priorities of the business class. Further, in his first term Eureste quickly gained the reputation as a hothead, but a hothead who could "reason at breakneck speed and back opponents into a corner during his frequent periods of verbal jousting" and was known "to storm out of a council meeting only to return and fire another salvo at his colleagues over something they have long since forgotten."[24]

It is evident that Eureste was aware of what he wanted to accomplish and what he had to do to reach his goals. With barely a month into his first term, the newspapers reported that Eureste had prompted a city staff briefing on the controls that could be exercised over city public service and the city water board: "He wants CPS under full city control, better drainage for his district, street improvement, parks, libraries, better housing and more social services for the entire city, but particularly in his district."[25] At his first council session, he flatly told CWB general manager Robert Van Dyke he didn't like the way the water board was run, adding that the council should make changes if the utility didn't follow directions.

Some of the major issues that sent shock waves through San Antonio in Eureste's first term, and in which he played loud and major roles, were the Edwards Aquifer moratorium (a council resolution that placed a moratorium on construction over the aquifer recharge zone), a bond drainage election (which pitted the business sector against the south and west side communities), Central District funding (grants to develop the central city), and the garbage collectors' strike mentioned above. By 1978 Eureste had clearly defined himself, with considerable help from the media, as the "Champion of the Underdog."[26]

In 1981 he found a hidden million dollars in the city budget. He then successfully channeled a large part of it to Chicano arts as opposed to the traditional middle-class arts, such as the symphony and the museum. In that same year, he organized weekly community street demonstrations protesting the police-shooting death of Mexican national Hector Santiescoy, who was shot several times while hiding, unarmed, under a house. In 1982 Eureste organized barrio activists around the issue of public housing, advocating the construction of public housing units in the well-to-do northside middle- and upper-middle-class communities. Needless to say, this action created a controversy that polarized the entire community along class lines.

Throughout his four terms as city council member, Eureste would gain the reputation as a zealot for lost causes, even at the expense of alienating or embarrassing his fellow colleagues. In one city council session he was escorted out of the council chambers by the police because of his inflexibility on a particular issue. Eureste, in fact, in his seemingly endless energy, took on almost every institution that interfaced with his constituency, including the media when their editorials seemed to him too harsh or unfair. Responding to an editorial in the *San Antonio Light,* Eureste dramatically retorted: "Do you think that you have made me weaker in this attack? I do not think so. I have only become more determined to speak out for what is right. The voices of oppression, as I have seen in this editorial and others that you have written, cannot silence the protests of those who have been victimized by this oppression. I would rather die fighting for these causes than to be silenced by the faceless pen of your editorials."[27]

Throughout most of this period, most political observers, including the media, generally explained Eureste's militant explosions over issues concerning his district as long overdue compensation for the neglect of these areas of San Antonio. While certainly many of the issues Eureste raised polarized the San Antonio electorate, because of the single member district structure of politics, the polarization had little or no impact on his reelection bids in his predominantly Mexican American district. In fact, polls showed Eureste to have broad support among many middle-class Chicanos and white liberals across the city in the issues he raised, despite an abrasive style that offended many of them.[28]

In the electoral arena, Eureste was seen as a politician to be dealt with as his support in his reelection bids climbed from 63 percent in 1977 to 68 percent in 1979 to an overwhelming 81 percent in 1981. His growing electoral support in each subsequent election brought him attention from many aspiring state office seekers "anxious to stake their claim to a portion of the rapidly expanding Mexican-American vote." Among Eureste's political trophies was a successful Democratic primary campaign for Senator Ted Kennedy in the Twenty-First Senatorial District "in spite of overwhelming Carter odds."[29]

Through Cisneros's first term as mayor, 1981–1983, Eureste continued to gain prominence among significant Chicano organizations such as the Mexican American Democrats, the League of United Latin American Citizens (LULAC), and GI Forum. Indeed, Eureste gained regional prominence as a Chicano leader and spokesman on the various issues confronting the Chicano community throughout South Texas.[30] However, the trajectories of these two prominent Chicano political careers pointed in different directions. Cisneros was seen by most political observers as heading for at least state prominence if not national prominence, while Eureste was seen in more ethnic terms—as "The Champion of the Underdog." Eureste's politics, in contrast to Cisneros's politics of bringing distinct and conflicting interests together, was a process of exposing the status quo. In his own words: "I do not believe in hurting anyone physically, but you have to get attention if you want things done. If you expose a situation, you flush out the opposition. If something is wrong, you cannot let it take care of itself. You have to bring it into the open."[31]

The bottom line is that Eureste was a force to be contended with, perhaps "the most complicated politician to come out of San Antonio city government in 50 years." He took it upon himself to use his position to address issues at such a rapid pace that not even his most avid and die-hard supporters had an opportunity to keep up with, much less have an input into, his strategy. From issue to issue the lines seemed to be redrawn in terms of supporters and opposition.[32]

Eureste, thus, made Cisneros even more legitimate as the serious kind of Chicano who could go beyond what white middle-class America considered the "private-regarding" nature of ethnic politics, a political leader who could provide the kind of leadership that would enhance the entire community and allow San Antonio to grow in national prominence as a shining "Sunbelt city." It can be argued that Eureste's militancy offered the mayor an alter ego.

THE UNDOING OF A MILITANT

Eureste's meteoric rise to political prominence in San Antonio politics was certainly not a smooth, well-planned process that one can easily analyze. In one of many interviews of Eureste by the local media, the writer portrayed Eureste's citywide image in the subtitle of the article as an enigma: "Is Councilman Eureste a Racist, a Hero, a Future Congressman — Or All Three of These?" A description that attests to, and perhaps best characterizes, this meteoric rise is the portrayal of Eureste in the local media as "Bandit or Savior?" By his third term in office, Eureste had created such a controversy by mixing ethnic issues with class issues that he had alienated a large sector of the northside Anglo population. More importantly, he had become a menace to developers and businesspeople in their efforts to continue in their otherwise uninterrupted pursuit of city policies that enhanced their profit-making growth and expansion.

Aside from the fact that District 5 was predominantly Chicano and lower and working class, a powerful and active Alinsky-type organization also dominated his district. COPS, organized throughout the Roman Catholic parishes of District 5, was in full support of Eureste's defiance of the business community's priorities of growth at the expense of the poor south and west sides of San Antonio. The group's power was such in San Antonio politics that the business community made no effort to run a candidate against Eureste for his first three terms. Indeed, many of Eureste's campaign contributions came from the business community.

However, toward the end of his third term, in February of 1983, an incident occurred in a local park that brought humiliation and personal tragedy into Eureste's life. Eureste was mugged in the early morning hours in Brackenridge Park while in a compromising situation with his young female aide. This alone would have been a serious indiscretion for a married politician. But when Eureste seemingly abandoned the young woman to the muggers as he searched for police, "both Hispanic macho and South Texas Anglo morality let loose a flood of outrage." It was easily the worst moment in an already controversial political career, and it was made worse by the fact that Eureste faced a primary election in only a few months.[33]

Eureste recovered from the incident by apologizing to his constituency and by charging that the police department had set up the mugging. Whether the charges had any truth or not was never proven. The point is that this made Eureste a victim and thus helped him maintain just enough support in his district to win in a runoff election.

Nonetheless, the park incident can be seen as the threshold of defeat for Eureste, who had seemed up to now indomitable in his district. His charges against the police department alienated Mayor Cisneros, who withdrew his endorsement for Eureste's bid: "This prince of destruction, this prince of negativism, is not going to be the downfall of our city as long as I can stand up to him," Cisneros said. The mayor's outburst appeared to herald a serious rift in a significant political alliance and a fight for control of the city council majority after the April 2 municipal elections.[34]

By the filing deadline of March 2, 1983, six opponents had filed against Eureste for the council seat in District 5. That race proved to be the hottest San Antonio had witnessed in at least twenty years. The main challenger was Jesse Valdez, an urban planner who had big money from the northside. Valdez succeeded in gaining a runoff election against Eureste. The runoff was intense, dirty, and the center of attention of the city, with Eureste staying in character by calling his opponent "a homosexual" controlled by northside developers.[35]

After the park incident and his reelection victory over Valdez in the 1983 elections, Eureste seemed safe enough from outside interference in his seemingly impregnable district. Cisneros and Eureste mended fences and vowed to work together. Eureste now had a tenuous truce with the mayor but continued to create a growing army of enemies. Eureste took on a political fight with the district attorney that would come back to haunt him in his last reelection bid. Eureste accused District Attorney Sam Milsap of being a Nazi for his efforts to crack down on DWI cases, charging that ethnic groups were facing the brunt of the arrests. This fight would continue through Eureste's last two years on the city council. In August of 1983 he escaped a libel suit by San Antonio police when a district judge ruled that Eureste's charges "that local police were killers" were privileged comments presented during a city council session.[36]

Then, in the summer of 1984, Eureste attacked the Guadalupe Cultural Arts Center, which he had originally helped establish. As reported in the local media, the new executive director of the Guadalupe Center did not see himself in a position to have to take any of Eureste's directives. Eureste had tried to intervene on behalf of a fledgling Chicano theater group when it complained that the Guadalupe had not allowed it access to the theater. Eureste was also upset that the brother of one of the southside politicos was on the Guadalupe staff; the council member suspected that foes from a southside power base were moving into his territory at the Guadalupe. The board scheduled several meetings to appease Eureste, but he wouldn't budge: "He announced that he was the only one who played politics in his district and that he would throw the Guadalupe out of the West Side if he had to." Shortly afterward, Eureste, the council's most left-wing member, charged publicly that the Guadalupe was "rife with communists. They had gone to Cuba. They had met with Castro and smoked his cigars. It was a disgrace to the people of District 5."[37]

While the Guadalupe group was not seen as influential in electoral politics, Eureste's estrangement from it symbolized an eroding base of support in his district. In this incident Eureste incurred the wrath of Willie Velásquez, the director of the influential Southwest Voter Registration and Education Project (SVREP). Apparently the feud between Eureste and Velásquez had begun in a conflict over whom the Chicano community should support in the U.S. presidential primaries. Eureste, who had started out supporting Walter Mondale, switched sides when the Mondale machinery overlooked him in planning its strategy in Bexar County. Thus, when Eureste came out supporting the Rev. Jesse Jackson, an apparent feud began with Velásquez.[38]

When Eureste attacked the Guadalupe group, whose board of directors included some of Velásquez's close associates, Velásquez became a member of the board to fight what he saw as campaign fund-raising pressures being applied by Eureste. Accusing Eureste of "strong-arm" tactics, Velásquez said that the city council member had launched his political attack on the Guadalupe Cultural Arts Center "because center employees refused to meet his political fund-raising goals."[39]

The irony was that Eureste had by this time managed to alienate many of those who had benefited from his style of politics and his barrio strategy. Still, most observers felt that Eureste had a tight grip on his district. His squabbles with the Guadalupe center, the southside politicos, Willie Velásquez, and the district attorney seemed to energize Eureste and increase his strength in District 5. But he was soon due for another test of this strength in the elections of 1985.

SEA WORLD AND THE FLOOD IN DISTRICT 5

In the first few months of 1985, San Antonio politics experienced some of its most wrenching and exasperating moments before the biggest economic investment in the area was concretized. In its wake, political careers were ended, land speculators were left hanging with devalued property, local residents lost a chance in a lifetime to sell their property at an extremely high profit, and a most unique political relationship was severed forever. Indeed, a political era ended.

The straw that seemed to break the camel's back in Eureste's fifth reelection bid came in the midst of an episode that capped his whole political career. Eureste's last grand public antiestablishment bid proved his undoing. Perhaps if this incident had occurred at any other time, it might have boosted his political credibility in his district and with his other supporters across the city to the highest level. Instead, it only opened unhealed critical wounds in his political profile; it became the thread that unraveled his imperial wardrobe.

In January of 1985, Sea World Enterprises, Inc., announced, to the surprise of most, its intention of establishing a marine-animal theme park in San Antonio. The mayor and his supporters considered this his greatest coup. The arrival of Sea World promised to place San Antonio on top of the nation's list of vacation "hot spots," attracting more investment opportunities to San Antonio. The business section of a local newspaper gave full-page coverage to the Sea World announcement, including a large picture of the mayor and William Jovanovich, chairman of Harcourt Brace Jovanovich, Inc., the parent company of Sea World, embracing joyously over the agreement.[40]

In the midst of this, Eureste charged that certain land speculators had gained inside information from the deal months earlier. Despite denials by officials, Richard Klitch, a real estate broker, revealed that the Sea World announcement, although not made public until January, had been common knowledge in the real estate community for months: "That area where Sea World is has been hotter than a rock for the past three months." The references to suspicious "insider" information kept coming up: "At the City Hall this week, there was euphoria about Sea World coming to town and bringing a giant influx of other investments. But already there is intrigue behind the glossy official smiles," according to one newspaper account.[41]

Throughout the next months, while the media trivialized what they called "political intrigue," problems kept cropping up. First there was the conflict with a local garbage company located near the Sea World site, then there was a question of the legality of the city's method of financing the deal, and finally, "from way out there in left field charged Councilman Bernardo Eureste, screaming to the top of his lungs about completely unsubstantiated charges of inside land deals and possible federal grand jury investigations." Eureste managed to capsize the euphoric rapture that Cisneros had brought to San Antonio by focusing all the headlines on his charges. As one byline put it: "The combination of having a dump for a neighbor and a crackpot councilman for an enemy was apparently more than Sea World executives could bear."[42]

Eureste's actions, apparently more than any other element in the complex deal, forced Sea World to back off of its original plans. More significantly, Eureste had embarrassed the mayor about the way the deal had been made. Even though Sea World had publicly promised that it would still move to San Antonio, the secrecy of the whole process became a paramount issue facing the mayor. The stage was set for a final showdown in the elections of 1985, with the media coverage focusing on Eureste as one who was about to chase away the biggest investment in San Antonio ever.

The city council elections of 1985 witnessed the emergence of an anti-Eureste "alliance" made up of several different sectors. The elections were anti-climactic: Eureste was crushed, receiving only 30 percent of the district vote. He was crushed by a barrage from the media; by an opposition candidate who had formerly been an ally of his and who had much grassroots support; by indictments brought by the district attorney, whom Eureste had antagonized throughout his last term; by most of the other enemies he had created by his actions on the various issues he had raised.[43] Finally, he was crushed by a mayor who publicly made it a point to let the voters of District 5 know that Eureste was no longer a viable representative. Cisneros, in the meantime, was reelected mayor with 72 percent of the at-large city vote.

THE AFTERMATH

After Eureste's demise, Cisneros was able successfully to defeat a northside voters' association challenge in a referendum to cap city spending. In the next four years the city under his leadership was also able to quietly attract other major investments in San Antonio's economy, such as a $15 million donation by Dallas billionaire Ross Perot for a biotechnology research park, announcement of plans to construct a semiconductor plant, a major golf tournament called the "crown jewel of golf," a planned visit by the Pope from Rome, the Alamo Grand Prix, a major sports dome (the Alamodome) in the downtown area, another theme park (Fiesta Texas) in the northside of San Antonio, and plans to hold an Olympic Sports Festival in 1991. Indeed, the council was touted by Cisneros as one that was hard working and farsighted in its views of the needs of San Antonio. The media went so far as to characterize the council as a "me too Henry" council; ironically, they lamented the absence of Eureste's ability to poignantly bring out issues in relief.[44]

This apparent consensus, however, eventually began to bulge at the seams, especially after Cisneros decided not to seek reelection in 1989. Walter Martínez was busy mobilizing his district—indeed, the Chicano community in general—over cultural issues such as the showing of the movie *The Alamo* (because of its denigrating and insensitive portrayal of the Mexican role in that beclouded historical event); a city referendum to add fluoride to the water supply, publicly supported by Cisneros, was defeated; and in 1990, the voters of San Antonio voted to limit city council members to two terms. Most critically, a referendum endorsed by outgoing Mayor Cisneros to construct a southside drinking water reservoir, the Applewhite Reservoir, was defeated. The reservoir was seen as a project that would allow continued growth on the northside recharge zone over San Antonio's sole water source.[45]

Although a business-backed candidate for mayor, Nelson Wolf, won the 1990 election against Applewhite opponent María Antonietta Berriozabal, the first Chicana mayoral candidate in San Antonio's history, his margin of victory was a mere 3 percent of the vote. A crisis in the growth and expansion plans of the business community was evident. In 1994, in a second referendum on the Applewhite Reservoir, a grassroots coalition led by community activists with only a $12,000 campaign budget defeated the business community's million-dollar campaign supported vigorously by Governor Ann Richards. The margin of victory was 10 percent. In spite of this victory, community activists were not able to come up with a viable mayoral candidate for the city elections of 1995, perhaps because their coalition was too fragile to go beyond the community struggle over water. Politics in San Antonio at this point remains unpredictable. The major point, though, is that consensus was celebrated too soon.[46]

THE LEGACY OF PERSONAL AGENDA POLITICS

What did single-member districts bring about for the Chicano community? To be sure, Chicano demands on political institutions played a major role in the broadening of representation in San Antonio. Electoral reform has created greater direct representation for the Chicano community. Most political observers agree that single-member districts made a Cisneros and an Eureste possible. It is clear, however, that Cisneros could have drafted a strategy to reach his goal of being mayor of San Antonio without single-member districts. Indeed, the election of Cisneros as mayor of San Antonio can be seen as a result of an individual's own personal agenda. In fact, many political observers argue that Cisneros will be the last Chicano mayor elected in San Antonio for quite a while.[47]

Aside from Eureste's politics' enhancing Cisneros's image as an acceptable and sensible Chicano politician for the Anglo northside, what was the nature of the change that single-member districts brought to San Antonio politics? There are several facets to this complex question. These facets are rooted in the historical experience of San Antonio, especially in the rise of Chicano middle-class politics after World War II.

After World War II the rising expectations of Chicanos produced a broad and sophisticated infrastructure of Chicano organizations that allowed the Chicano community greater political resources to address the problem of political exclusion. Out of this complex process the Chicano community articulated diverse strategies in their struggle to gain political inclusion. There were those who proposed assimilation, those who proposed confrontation, and those who proposed separation.[48] These movements historically were all part of an effort to achieve greater access and participation in the political arena. The one major institutional result was the implementation of single-member districts, which enhanced independent political representation for the various excluded communities of San Antonio.

As this study shows, the legacy of this struggle for inclusion can be seen in the kinds of politics coming out of single-member districts. While neither Cisneros nor Eureste was guided by an organizational agenda, their political popularity as well visibility can be seen to be tied to that legacy. Cisneros's broad popularity reflects the need to deal with the deep cultural nationalist feelings in the Chicano community, even if done from an assimilationist position. Certainly, Eureste's politics reflected a strong cultural nationalist position, but they also reflected the class concerns of the coalition politics of the 1950s and the 1960s.

The irony in this is that while the change to single-member districts was brought about directly by intense Chicano organizational activity, single-member districts now tend to undermine the basis by which the Chicano community built political organizational agendas in the first place. The political environment now tends to be fragmented not only along district lines but within those districts as well. Citywide organizational agendas are now a thing of the past.

Another important facet of this question is the economic context of San Antonio as a Sunbelt city. After World War II San Antonio entered the race for capital investment at the national level. San Antonio went through an intense municipal reform movement in setting the stage to attract the business fleeing from the frostbelt as well as the developing high-tech industries. From a broad economic perspective, if San Antonio did not prove to be a "center of profit," then it could fail to attract these most lucrative investments. A most important consequence, aside from the cheap-labor nature of these new investments, was that the business community's concerns with growth and expansion continued to be priorities for city council policy making, whether in view of personal agendas or in that of organizational ones.

In this context, the lack of organizational agendas in contemporary San Antonio politics seemed to give the definite advantage to the highly organized business sector. While the business community lost direct control of the decision-making process in city hall with the demise of the powerful pro-business Good Government League, its ability to lobby and also to finance political campaigns has maintained its access to the decision-making process. The formula for this access has been a simple majority on the city council, along with its dominant role in electing the mayor. Indeed, the business community was content with what it considered Eureste's rantings and ravings as long as he did not enter directly into its business prerogatives. Eureste's downfall, while not discounting his erratic behavior, has to be analyzed in the context of the city as a "center of profit." His questioning of the decision-making process in the Sea World controversy proved to be too threatening to business interests.

The needs of a growing city, then, historically have favored the needs of the business community. While not absolute, the structure of the game (or as Katznelson would say, the "rules of the game") is paramount in the determination of political outcomes.[49] Certainly, Cisneros's election can be seen as a turning point for Chicano politics in Texas and the Southwest. But that mayor, or any other mayor, depends on his or her viability as mayor on the growth and expansion of San Antonio—on maintaining San Antonio as a viable "center of profit." This above all has been the overriding factor in creating the individualistic politician, best represented by Henry Cisneros, who is ultimately accountable only to her or his own personal agenda—and, of course, to his or her ties to particular sectors of interest—and only indirectly to the community.

But perhaps the most critical point is that because of the lack of organizational agendas, the community's participation and ability to voice its concerns have been at best fragmented and at worst muted. On the other hand, instead of allowing the business community to continue with its plans of growth and expansion with little or no opposition, this inability to participate has created for the business community its greatest enemy—community activists who need not worry about incumbency nor campaign funds. The end result has been, as mentioned above, a crisis in governance, with neither the community able to muster the resources to gain control of the governmental institutions nor the business community able to govern in a legitimate and acceptable fashion.

CONCLUSION

I began this study with very important questions. First, can the Chicano community define its political interest collectively in the face of a powerful business community whose market logic of growth and expansion overshadows any concerns for social issues? Secondly, and more importantly, can it mobilize to safeguard that interest in a political environment that, today at least, is structured to benefit business rather than community interests? Finally, can there be a coalition of interests across ethnic and class lines with the aim of defining and defending the community interests of San Antonio (the quality-of-life issues, i.e., the use values) in the face of market forces that buttress the domination of the business community in its relentless drive to turn all urban elements (water, services, development—urbanization in general) into moments of exchange value—into private profit?

In answer to the third question, it is obvious, with the latest electoral defeats of the various business community initiatives at the hands of a mixed ethnic as well as gender coalition, that the community can organize around quality-of-life issues. The major question is whether this kind of coalition can move beyond the particular issues in building a political agenda aimed at governance and not simply at vetoing offensive initiatives seen as working against the community welfare.

The possibility of that perhaps lies in whether the Chicano community can identify its interests. An important indication that that possibility exists is found in the election returns of the second Applewhite referendum. In looking at the predominant Anglo northside city council districts (8, 9, and 10), one finds that the election returns were evenly divided over the referendum, with not more than a hundred votes one way or the other. But when one looks at the Chicano districts and the one Black city council district, one finds that the returns were overwhelmingly against the referendum, with one district as high as two thousand votes and three others with as high as a thousand votes against the referendum.[50] The significance of these outcomes is that the Applewhite project was seen as working directly against the community interests of the southside and westside districts in particular, and the communities in those districts defied the stereotypic image of apathy in their communities and pounded their votes home.

This becomes even more significant when one recalls that all of the Chicano public officials, city and state, as well as the one Black city council member, came out vigorously in favor of the referendum. Apparently, these communities wanted to hear about quality-of-life issues and not about growth and expansion. The indication is that the Chicano community does have an organizational infrastructure that can begin that definition of its interests even in the face of powerful business forces and their allies.

Whether the Chicano community can then begin to organize and defend its defined interests is of course the one question that can only be answered through the continuing historical process. As Manual Castells concluded in his study of urban social movements, while the broader and more universal aspects of capitalism and its development tend to be out of any particular community's control, particular communities do recognize their political parameters and do act on them. In other words, they do make a difference locally.[51] San Antonio's political elite had better pay attention to a simple principle called political inclusion.

NOTES

1. J. L. Polinard, Robert D. Wrinkle, Tomás Longoria, and Norman E. Binder, *Electoral Structure and Urban Policy: The Impact on Mexican American Communities* (Armonk, N.Y.: M. E. Sharpe, 1994).

2. The question of structure and agency addresses the role of humans in the making of history. In a very general way, if the environment brings about the circumstances in which humans then act out their politics, is it a one-way street? Obviously not, but how then does the analysis capture human agency, especially through political change? The focus in this study is on the changing political behavior of politicians as the environment was freed from the powerful organizational constraints of the GGL or BCDC. The major question that arises in the more independent contemporary environment of single-member districts is couched in terms of accountability: Whom are these political leaders accountable to, now that there is no visible agenda? In an interview with historian Rodolfo Acuña in San Antonio, April 16 and 19, 1986, Acuña argued that the single-member district plan in San Antonio had actually produced brokers for the business class. His argument is based on the premise that without organizational constraints, the individual politician then becomes vulnerable to the larger forces found in the urban market economy that envelops city politics. In other words, without organizational agendas and the discipline to maintain them, the more powerful urban economic elites have a more powerful influence on individual politicians. However, as this study will show, while Acuña may perhaps be correct, the political behavior of individual politicians is not necessarily as predictable as one would assume given Acuña's argument.

3. Paul E. Peterson, *City Limits* (Chicago: University of Chicago Press, 1981). Peterson seems to be echoing the ideological claims of the Municipal Reform Movement and its insistence that the city was not a place for democracy and its notions of equity or equality but rather the core of the city was based on the rights of property and its need to develop in an efficient manner.

4. Michael Peter Smith, *City, State & Market: The Political Economy of Urban Society* (Cambridge, Mass.: Blackwell, 1992).

5. Manual Castells, *The City and the Grassroots: A Cross-Cultural Theory of Urban Social Movements* (Berkeley: University of California Press, 1983).

6. Rodolfo Rosales, *The Illusion of Inclusion: The Political Mobilization of the Chicano Community in San Antonio, Texas: 1951–1991* (Austin: University of Texas Press, forthcoming).

7. Luther L. Sanders, "Nonpartisanism: Its Use as a Campaign Appeal in San Antonio, Texas,

1961–1971," M.A. thesis, St. Mary's University, May 12, 1974, pp. 49–55. Sanders goes into detail in tracing the coming to power of the municipal reform–minded business community and its ultimate successful domination of city politics through structural reform. This structural change profoundly affected the role of the Chicano community in urban politics in San Antonio.

8. Henry B. González was the only independent to gain a seat in city council in the 1950s. In 1953 and then again in 1955, he ran unopposed. In 1956 he became the first Chicano state senator from Bexar County, thus ending his city council career. In 1961 he was elected congressperson from the twentieth congressional district. Throughout the 1950s Mr. González was by virtue of his politics very close with the coalition leaders. After 1965 he broke with them, and the gap between the coalition leaders and later the Raza Unida leaders from Bexar County widened.

9. Ibid. Sanders points out that the GGL, by controlling the nominating process, was able to exclude those who would not adhere to its growth and expansion agenda at the exclusion of all other issues. Rodolfo Rosales, interview with Rudy Esquivel, December 18, 1985. Esquivel points out that the difference between coalition politics and single-member politics was one of accountability. He pointed out that under coalition politics, one didn't have to worry about raising funds or running a campaign, but the catch was that the coalition then could exert discipline on its particular candidates to remain consistent with its social agenda. However, in single-member district politics, one had to raise one's own funds and run one's own campaign; therefore, agendas became personal. He preferred the latter, even though he had to organize his own campaign financing and his campaign strategy. Organizational efforts did surface during this latter period but in the form of nonpartisan community organizations, such as Communities Organized for Public Service (COPS); the Mexican American Unity Council (MAUC), a community development nonprofit organization; and the Mexican American Legal Defense and Education Fund (MALDEF), a nonprofit legal advocate for the Chicano community; as well as the older GI Forum and LULAC. Precisely because of their nonpartisan nature they were disconnected from the most accessible political infrastructure available, the Democratic party precinct network, and thus were fragmented at best and muted at worst in the political arena.

10. "Direct Vote for Mayor Plan Wins," *San Antonio Express/News*, November 6, 1974. The first challenge to this at-large system, which took the form of a city amendment presented to the voters in the fall of 1974, failed. This failure, however, further strengthened the argument coming from the Chicano community that the 1972 annexations had diluted their voting power.

11. Charles Cotrell et al., "Conflict and Change in the Political Culture of San Antonio in the 1970s," in John Booth, Richard Harris, and Bill Johnson, eds., *The Politics of San Antonio: Community, Power, and Progress* (Lincoln: University of Nebraska Press, 1984), pp. 75–94. Indeed, Cotrell et al. argue that the political rules in place after World War II, such as the poll tax, the long residence requirement, and annual registration, maintained and perpetuated political exclusion even after the municipal reforms were implemented. The legacy of these rules, which were generally eliminated by the early 1970s, however, affected political participation years after their elimination.

12. Rodolfo Rosales, interview with Joe Bernal, San Antonio, January 28, 1985. State senator Joe Bernal, a liberal local coalition member, was a plaintiff in the court case that established single-member districts for state legislative positions. Ironically, this led to his political defeat in the 1972 state elections and his subsequent retirement from public office.

13. Rosie Castro and Gloria Barrera were fielded as candidates in the 1971 city council elections as part of the Committee for Barrio Betterment, which was connected to the Raza Unida movement in Texas. While not successful, their candidacy proved to be the threshold for Chicana candidates in contemporary San Antonio.

14. Cotrell et al., "Conflict and Change." The San Antonio annexations were subject to review by the Justice Department even though they had taken place prior to the extension of the Voting Rights Act to Texas in 1975. In an interview with Gloria Cabrera, one of the Chicana candidates in the 1971 elections, she pointed out that one of the main reasons that she ran for city council was to establish proof that the at-large electoral system did effectively disenfranchise the Chicano barrios. In fact, the Mexican American Legal Defense and Educational Fund (MALDEF) effectively used the data from this election to bring the Justice Department into the picture.

15. "The Seductive Henry C.," *San Antonio Express/News*, February 15, 1981. Indications of Cisneros's "single mindedness" go back to an unpublished paper he wrote at MIT in which he describes a new minority voting trend and the kinds of strategies that would be needed to successfully gain electoral power in San Antonio. Henry Cisneros, "A New Minority Voting Trend—Its Causes And Impact: San Antonio, Texas," unpublished paper presented at George Washington University as a graduate student, spring 1970. Indeed, a profile of Cisneros will show that his political orientation goes back to the Committee for Community Progress, an informal arm of the GGL in the westside barrios during the 1960s and early 1970s. Rubén Munguía, Cisneros's maternal uncle, even though he denies ever being part of the GGL, was as a candidate for public office supported by the GGL various times.

16. Sidney Plotkin, "Democratic Change in the Urban Political Economy: San Antonio's Edwards Aquifer Controversy," in Booth et al., *The Politics of San Antonio*, pp. 157–175.

17. "Groups Eye Recall of Councilmen," *San Antonio Express/News*, February 14, 1975; "Council Okays Aquifer Protection Plan," ibid., July 18, 1975.

18. "San Antonio Revises Budget," *San Antonio Light*, July 24, 1975; "Council Studies CPS Controls," *San Antonio Express*, August 22, 1975. In another incident Cisneros got into conflict with the Northside Chamber of Commerce president. When the chamber president complimented the council on its decision to build the mall over the aquifer, he noted that the council's decision permitted orderly growth and progress to continue in spite of attempts by certain pressure groups to use the Edwards Aquifer issue as a tool to redirect the city's growth. Cisneros responded by asking if Slaughter (chamber president) meant that any council member who voted against the mall was an opponent of growth in San Antonio. See "A Compliment Stirs Argument," *San Antonio Express/News*, November 7, 1975.

19. "Cisneros Fiscal Health Plan Is Valuable City Planning," *San Antonio Express/News*, June 7, 1976; "Fiscal Notes Necessary," *San Antonio Light*, February 20, 1977; "Cisneros Raps City Garage Criticisms," *San Antonio Express/News*, August 30, 1975; "Cisneros Angered By Firing," *San Antonio Light*, June 17, 1975; "Councilman Loses Bid," ibid., June 25, 1975; *San Antonio Express/News*, November 2, 1976.

20. "In The Bag," *San Antonio Express/News*, June 1, 1975; "Cisneros Walks to Gumshoe Beat," *San Antonio Light*, November 6, 1975; "Cisneros Learns Poor's Problems," *San Antonio Express*, March 26, 1978. In another incident, Cisneros publicly criticized the state Public Utilities Commission for its favorable review of proposed rate hikes presented by the telephone company. See "Let PUC Know Stand—Cisneros," *San Antonio Express/News*, September 12, 1976.

21. "Cisneros Won't Take Envoy Post," *San Antonio Light*, October 19, 1979. Even before he gained national prominence as mayor he was courted by President Carter in 1979 to take a national position; but his response was: "My first priority is building San Antonio right now."

22. Ironically, the water issue would be Cisneros's greatest nemesis toward the end of his tenure as mayor, as it created the greatest gap between his role in creating greater economic activity in San Antonio and his role in meeting the needs of not only the Chicano community but of the community as a whole. While Mayor Cisneros crafted an ingenious plan to establish an infra-

structure for growth and expansion, this infrastructure would ultimately clash with the perceived needs of the community. In other words, the inevitable conflict between exchange value needs of the entrenched developers and bankers on the one hand and the use value needs of the community on the other ultimately created a contradiction that not even the smooth and articulate Henry C. Cisneros could resolve. For an incisive theoretical discussion of the contradictions underlying urban social movements, see Castells, *The City and the Grassroots.*

23. *San Antonio Monthly,* October 1977.

24. "What Makes Bennie Run?" *San Antonio Light,* May 2, 1982. "Some—including himself—view him as the voice of the Hispanic in South Texas. Others see Bernardo Eureste as a bumbling, arrogant, uneducated ethnic bent on destroying the gringo."

25. "Eureste to Practice as He Preaches," ibid., May 15, 1977.

26. "Bernardo Eureste: He's a Champion of the 'Underdog,'" ibid., November 5, 1978; "Eureste Has Caused Controversy Since 1977," *San Antonio Express/News,* February 20, 1985.

27. "Bernardo Eureste Answers Editorial by Light," *San Antonio Light,* July 19, 1982.

28. "Bernardo Eureste: Bandit or Savior?" *San Antonio Express/News San Antonio Style,* September 13, 1981.

29. "Eureste Has Caused Controversy."

30. "Eureste's Traveling Activism Show Stirs Hornet's Nest," *San Antonio Light,* January 29, 1983; "Eureste Creates Backwash in Corpus Christi," *San Antonio Express/News,* January 30, 1983.

31. "Bernardo Eureste: Bandit or Savior?"

32. Indeed, while Chicano art advocates were outside City Hall serenading him for his heroic finding of a million dollars in the budget, local public employee labor organizers from the National Association of Government Employees were in his office chastising him for taking money from the "sweat of sanitation workers." At the same time, those same labor leaders were marching with him in demonstrations, helping him with his reelection campaigns, and working with him in barrio-oriented issues. Perhaps the "most complicated politician" is in reference to Maury Maverich, Sr., congressperson in the 1930s and mayor in 1939.

33. Anna Marie Peña and Tom Bell, "Staying Power," *San Antonio Monthly,* March 1984, pp. 58–64.

34. "Bennie Blasts Cisneros for Lack of Leadership," *San Antonio Light,* March 18, 1983; Deborah Weser, "Cisneros Lashes Back At Eureste," *San Antonio Light,* February 23, 1983; "Park Incident Plays Key Dist. 5 Role," *San Antonio Light,* March 23, 1983.

35. Pena and Bell, "Staying Power"; "Eureste Has Caused Controversy."

36. "Eureste: Don't Jail DWI Cases," *San Antonio Light,* January 20, 1983; "Eureste Claims Hispanics Singled Out in DWI Arrests," *San Antonio Express,* January 14, 1983; "Eureste Has Caused Controversy."

37. "What Makes Bennie Run?"

38. "Eureste Shifts Support to Jackson Campaign," *San Antonio Express/News,* January 7, 1984. Despite his many feuds, Eureste supported and successfully brought the Reverend Jesse Jackson to the Guadalupe Theater for a rousing political rally during the primary elections of 1984. Thus, Eureste continued to maintain a degree of political credibility despite his seemingly erratic behavior.

39. Bill Hendricks, "Eureste 'Hit List' Target Claimed," *San Antonio Express/News,* February 18, 1985.

40. David Hawkins, "City Deal with Sea World Follows Whirlwind Courtship," *San Antonio Light,* January 13, 1985; "Sea World Eyeing City," *San Antonio Light,* January 8, 1985; David Hawkins, "City Manager Lists the People Who Helped Sea World Project," *San Antonio Light,* Febru-

ary 1, 1985; Ralph Bivens and Dale Rankin, "Sea World Boosts Area Prices," *San Antonio Express/News*, January 11, 1985.

41. David Hawkins, "Sea World Puts Webb's Campaign on the Rise," *San Antonio Light*, January 13, 1985; David Hawkins, "Sea World Deal Names Sought," *San Antonio Light*, January 30, 1985; "Eureste Asks for Details about Sea World Talks," *San Antonio Express*, January 30, 1985; Dale Rankin, "Land Buy Tip Denied," *San Antonio Express/News*, February 20, 1985.

42. Jan Jarboe, "San Antonio Wastes Its 3 Wishes," *San Antonio Express/News*, February 24, 1985; David Hawkins, "Sea World Faces Second Controversy," *San Antonio Light*, January 23, 1985.

43. "Eureste Calls Millsap Racist; Vows to Continue Fighting," *San Antonio Light*, March 28, 1985; "Martínez in Fight for His Life: Hopes District 5 Voters Have Had Fill of Eureste's Flamboyance," *San Antonio Light*, February 24, 1985.

44. "Council Sings Praises of Eureste, Alderete," *San Antonio Express/News*, April 26, 1985; "2 Outgoing Members Praised by Council," *San Antonio Light*, April 26, 1985; Roger Beynon, "The Plan," *San Antonio Monthly*, February, 1983; Carol Cirulli, "Splashing Up San Antonio's Marketing Effort," *San Antonio Light*, March 8, 1987; Charles Boisseau, "Perot Donates $15 Million," *San Antonio Light*, March 11, 1987; Charles Boisseau, "Semiconductor Plant Under Way," *San Antonio Light*, March 5, 1987.

45. "Berriozabal, Wolf Face Runoff as Cockrell Upset: Applewhite Gets Stop Work Notice," *San Antonio Express/News*, May 5, 1991.

46. "Voters: 'No Means No,' City Leaders Slapped with Stunning Defeat on Applewhite," *San Antonio Express/News*, August 14, 1994; "City Leaders Agree It's Time to Lay Applewhite To Rest," *San Antonio Express*, August 15, 1994. The coalition was led mainly by women activists from both the Chicano and Anglo community, including Chicanas María Antonietta Berriozabal; Judith Sanders-Castro, legal counsel for the Mexican American Legal Defense and Education Fund (MALDEF); Rosa Rosales, the state director of the League of United Latin American Citizens (LULAC); and Angie García, the San Antonio LULAC district director as well as so-called water activists from the northside, Kay Turner and Carol and Kirk Patterson, with only two public officials vigorously taking their side—State Representatives Karen Conley, the only Black state representative in Bexar County, and Ciro Rodríguez, the Chicano representative from the southside. The entire present city council, including the Chicano councilpersons from the southside and westside districts, with the exception of one city councilperson from district seven, Bob Ross, as well as almost all of the other Chicano public officials from the southside and westside, supported the business community's efforts to continue the Applewhite.

47. Tom Baylis, "Leadership Change in San Antonio," and Tucker Gibson, "Mayoralty Politics in San Antonio, 1955–79" in Booth et al., *Politics of San Antonio*. Baylis argues that the future does not bode well for another Chicano mayor in San Antonio. His analysis is based on the assumption that Cisneros was an exception and that after his departure ethnic politics will dominate, eliminating the possibility of another Chicano mayor.

48. Since 1951, when municipal reform was accomplished in San Antonio, a significant sector of the Chicano middle class took the political position that it was far better to be on the inside where appointments to boards and commissions were decided and policy decisions were made. Thus, their approach to politics was to learn the system well and to participate in it as it was. They were not for political change. Almost immediately, a sector of that middle class developed in the early 1950s who rejected the assimilationist approach began organizing an independent political base. This movement ultimately formed the basis for the Bexar County Democratic Coalition (mentioned at the beginning of this chapter). Their approach was that assimilation would not be in their interest since assimilation meant being co-opted into the business community's agenda of growth and expansion at the expense of the community. Finally, in the Chicano

movement, one found a complex movement in which separation as a goal was always a part because of its rejection of the racist political environment, especially the Democratic Party. Here one also found a politics of confrontation.

49. Ira Katznelson, *City Trenches: Urban Politics and the Patterning of Class in the United States* (New York: Pantheon, 1981).

50. "Voters: 'No Means No,' City Leaders Slapped with Stunning Defeat on Applewhite," *San Antonio Express/News,* August 14, 1994.

51. Castells, *The City and the Grassroots.*

Two

Harold Washington and the Rise of Latino Electoral Politics in Chicago, 1982–1987

Teresa Córdova

In the 1980s in Chicago, Latino activists turned their attention to the electoral arena as a means of obtaining civil rights and gaining empowerment for their communities. Neighborhood services and opportunities were being denied through machine control of city hall. Believing that they had the numbers to do something about it, Latinos joined Blacks to "reform" the electoral process by breaking down a patronage system they characterized as "plantation" and "hacienda" politics. The mobilization that ensued was centered around the charismatic leadership of Harold Washington and involved the coalescence of Blacks, Latinos, and progressive whites. This paper chronicles and characterizes the rise of Latinos in electoral politics in Chicago during their struggle for "fair representation." The first step for Blacks and Latinos was to define their relationship to Chicago's infamous "Machine."

The rise of political power of Blacks and Latinos in Chicago in the 1980s required the shifting of power away from an entrenched political Machine. The Chicago "Machine" had been one of the strongest, most tightly organized examples of a local power elite, but internal power struggles, the death of Richard Daley, and an inability to agree upon a single successor left the Machine vulnerable to the emergence of political power outside the "regular" Democratic party.

Blacks had been a reliable component of the Machine. They moved, however, to break the chains of what many had labeled "plantation politics" and used their large numbers to defeat the forces they had previously been instrumental in electing. They chose one of their own to vie for mayor, and in 1983 they were successful in bringing Harold Washington to City Hall. "Progressive" Latinos and whites, who were opposed to Machine neglect of their communities, joined the efforts to elect the first Black mayor of Chicago. The primary and general elections epitomized the racial divisions within the city and highlighted the refusal of the Machine to be easily defeated.

While Washington's success shook the foundations of a patronage system, he was limited in his reform by a city council majority of Machine warlords. The forces of "the Vrdolyak 29" (named for politician Edward Vrdolyak) prevented the passing of Washington-backed ordinances, appointments, and Machine dismantling. Until Mayor Washington could win the support of at least twenty-five of the fifty aldermen (in which case he could cast the tie-breaking vote), Black-Latino progressive political power could not be fully realized in Chicago.

Finally, three years after a successful coalition brought Harold Washington to power, the same coalition of Blacks, Mexicans, Puerto Ricans, and progressive whites took four aldermanic seats from the Machine and handed them to Mayor Washington. In early 1986, special elections took place in seven aldermanic wards due to a successful legal challenge against Machine gerrymandering. The Washington forces were successful in two of the three predominantly Black wards, one of the two predominantly Mexican wards, and one of the two predominantly Puerto Rican wards. The results of the 1986 special election gave Washington the twenty-five aldermanic votes he needed to deny the "Vrdolyak 29" their edge.

The successful wresting of power through the 1986 elections was significant for four reasons. One, it contributed to the further deterioration of the political Machine. Two, it made possible the implementation of alternative policies toward a redistribution of resources. Three, it ushered in an era of unprecedented electoral participation by Latinos. Four, it signified the continued rise of a Black-Latino coalition and its progressive agenda.

A council majority enabled Washington to move quickly on committee chairships, ordinances, and financial programs. By early 1987 the preoccupation again turned toward elections. After fierce mayoral and aldermanic races, Washington was reinaugurated to a second term and to an even greater edge on the council.

Suddenly, the dream ended with the shocking news that Washington had suffered a heart attack in his City Hall office. He was pronounced dead within three very long hours. While the city mourned, the politicians maneuvered. The Machine moved in fast, the Washington bloc fell apart, and new forces emerged—all within days of Washington's death.

Chicago had lost a great leader. The significance of Harold Washington to electoral politics and to the dream of a "progressive" coalition cannot be exaggerated. Despite the loss, certain net gains remain. Harold Washington had challenged both a tightly organized political Machine and the people of a tightly segregated city. In Washington's words, it would no longer be "business as usual."

For Latinos, Harold Washington was the spark that ignited electoral participation that continues today. The purpose of this essay is to trace the development of Latino electoral participation during the era of Harold Washington, showing the importance of this historical moment for Latino electoral involvement in the city of Chicago.

CHICAGO'S POLITICAL MACHINE

To the political observer, Chicago's most interesting aspect is the endurance of a political Machine that began with Mayor Anton Cermak in 1931 and was in its heyday during the twenty years of the Richard J. Daley reign. Despite internal struggles and challenges by reformists, it is still in operation today, remaining the "last of the great big-city Machines."[1] Richard M. Daley became chair of the Cook County Democratic Party in 1953 and mayor two years later. Using his control of the two top positions and his skills as an astute politician, Daley consolidated his power. From 1955 to 1976, Daley was "the boss."

Historically, Machines have been built with the support of low-income, uneducated, immigrant groups who were in need of the services and protection that a patronage system could provide.[2] Daley's Machine was even wider in its appeal, reaching across ethnic lines and including downtown business interests. His organized and highly centralized Machine was comprised of a cadre of loyalists whose overriding concern was the organization itself. The Cook County Democratic Party was the organization, and the ward committee members were its most influential members.

Ward precinct captains provided access to City Hall. Through him (ward Captains were almost exclusively male) one had streets repaired, lights replaced, garbage cleaned, and stop signs added. One could get one's kid into school, bail a relative out of jail, or clear up a bureaucratic mess. It was all part of the benefits of political paternalism. It provided the security of "being taken care of." In return, one offered the precinct captain loyalty best exhibited through one's vote.

AFTER DALEY

After Daley's death on December 20, 1976, control of the Democratic Party was up for grabs. Daley had left no directive for a successor for either the mayor or chair of the party. According to Milton Rakove, the ward committee members did not want another Daley who "had kept them all under his control, had strengthened the city government and the bureaucracy at their expense, and had forced them to bow to his concept of the public interest and the good of the city. They wanted a milieu in which they would have more power, free from the centralized control Daley had exercised."[3]

As part of the overall strategy to limit the power of any single successor, Machine leaders sought two different individuals for mayor and party chair. Michael Bilandic was selected as Machine candidate for mayor, and George Dunne was selected as chair of the Democratic Party. Through these choices, several interests were maintained. Influential committee men were guaranteed power and patronage, city bureaucrats were allowed to continue as before, and banking and labor interests experienced no major shake-ups. Bilandic became acting mayor and then was elected in 1977. The Machine, it seemed, would survive intact.

Anti-Machine sentiments, however, were growing. White ethnics from the northwest side were becoming increasingly dissatisfied with southside control. Lakefront liberals were emerging as a block vote, and an increasingly discontented and growing Black population was thinking more about autonomy than compliance with Machine politicians.

In 1979 Blacks, Lakefront liberals, and Northwest white ethnics united behind Jane Byrne, a mayoral candidate the Machine had not considered a serious threat.[4] The electorate was especially aroused when Bilandic failed to provide the city services necessary to deal with one of the worst snow storms in Chicago's history. The 1979 winter was followed immediately by a primary in which Jane Byrne won the Democratic Party nomination for mayor of Chicago.

Byrne appealed to those interested in reform as well as those who felt the current "regulars" had deserted Daley's agenda. After assuming office, she attacked ward committee members and replaced city bureaucrats. While she later developed ties with some key politicians she had previously called a "cabal of evil men," she did far more damage in her replacement of nearly every department head. According to Rakove, what Byrne did was to disrupt and bring down the party–government–private interest group system that Daley had created in Chicago.[5]

This might have worked for Byrne if she had replaced one system with another comprehensive plan. Instead, her tactics served to alienate her from the banking, business, and labor communities and the remaining lower-level bureaucrats. Nonetheless, her agreeable relationship with some ward politicians might have carried her to a reelection bid, but the political arena of Chicago was about to be transformed.

BLACKS AND THE MACHINE

Blacks have often been pivotal in elections in which their vote made a difference in the factional, religious, ethnic politics of Chicago. As early as 1915,
Black voters were decisive in giving the edge to "Big Bill Thompson," the Republican mayor who created an earlier version of "the Machine." Based on patronage, Blacks were courted for their vote and in return received jobs—as
porters, cooks, janitors, and errand and messenger boys. A token Black elite
developed.[6]

After World War II, Blacks became even more pivotal as they grew in population due to immigration from the Deep South. Their relationship to the
Democratic Machine had been characterized as "plantation politics," where
white and Black politicians controlled and "delivered" their Black wards in exchange for a few patronage favors. Despite their indispensability, the concerns
of Black communities were subordinate to the needs of the Machine itself.[7]

The maintenance of a biracial coalition required the avoidance of controversial issues such as race and discrimination. "Thus, the white leaders of
the Democratic Machine, by establishing the terms and limits of the political
expression, denied autonomy to the city's Black community. Blacks became
separate and unequal partners in the Machine's coalition—subjects, not citizens, of their city."[8] Richard Daley believed that segregated housing projects,
a few patronage jobs, and token appointments were sufficient reward to his
Black "subjects." Better educated and economically comfortable "white ethnic" forces supported this relationship and viewed the Machine as "defenders
of their values and interests, as the last hope for continued white control."[9]

THE RISE OF BLACK INDEPENDENCE

In 1940, Blacks comprised 8.1 percent (277,000) of Chicago's population; in
1960, 22.8 percent (812,000); and in 1980, 39.5 percent (1,187,000). As demographics and priorities changed, the Blacks of Chicago sought political influence beyond the paternalism of the Machine. Low Black voter turnout indicated a Black electorate that was increasingly dissatisfied with Machine
control. Between 1967 and 1971 support for Machine candidates in Black
wards fell by 7 percentage points, and it had dropped another 13 percent by
1975.[10] In the early 1970s, Blacks ousted Ed Hanrahan as state's attorney because he was seen as being responsible for the killing of Fred Hampton, a Black
Panther. Black dissatisfaction and emerging independence were intensified by
continued Machine exploitation and neglect, and by the civil rights and Black
nationalist movements.

Black voters expressed their break from the Machine when they helped elect Jane Byrne. They were again key in the 1983 election when they displayed not only their dissatisfaction with Jane Byrne's policies toward them but also their desire and ability to put forward their own candidate.

Harold Washington was not an ordinary Chicago politician. His early political career was shaped by his father's successful politics, which were loyal to the Machine. However, as Washington rose through party ranks, he soon developed an inclination for independence. Machine priorities and strategies were not to his liking. Instead, in the Illinois General Assembly and later in Congress, he sought policies to protect and better Black neighborhoods and sponsored legislation to create equality.[11] Washington took a leadership role in amending federal voting rights legislation from requiring "proof of intent" of discrimination to "proof of effect." The change was significant in that it allowed Blacks and Latinos to gain fair representation in city redistricting.

LATINOS AND THE MACHINE

As is the case for nearly all aspects of Latino life in Chicago, there is little written information about Latino electoral participation. Available accounts depict a two-tiered leadership structure, with the lower tier comprised of leaders of grassroots community organizations and a higher tier of "reputational" leaders who operated as "brokers" between the community and the "lower rungs of the dominant system." The latter were Machine affiliates who derived their power through the Democratic Party. While a few individuals profited from the Machine-based positioning, mobility within that system was determined by party bosses rather than grassroots sentiment. Community organization leaders were essentially "excluded from effective brokerage positions."[12]

The Latino electorate voted Democratic throughout the Daley years, but as in the case of African American voters, they became increasingly independent. At the same time that there were "Amigos for Daley" operating in some parts of town, there were others making moves to separate from the patronage fold. One well-known account of precinct politics describes efforts by Mexicans to assert power at the ward level in two steel mill communities of South Chicago.[13]

The two neighborhoods had a history of territorial rivalries but were united in the late 1960s by union leaders to form the Tenth Ward Spanish Speaking Democratic Organization. When Ed Vrdolyak became the ward committee member, he stripped them of the few patronage jobs they had, but later Tenth Ward coalition politics led him to attempt to co-opt the leaders. As the most influential Chicano union activist noted,

Vrdolyak said he'd make me president of the Tenth Ward Democratic Organization if I would agree to disband the Spanish Speaking Democrats. We would have something like it, but it would have to be completely inside the regular organization. There was no way we could go for that deal. Here he fires our guys, a few lousy jobs, nothing like Ward superintendent or stationary engineer, you know, and he expects us to turn around and join his organization like that. We couldn't have looked our people in the eye. We had to tell him we weren't ready for that.[14]

The group had fought hard for its autonomy and was not willing to return to the fold of the "regulars." Instead, they continued to organize at the precinct level and to pose opposition to Vrdolyak and his forces by running their own candidates.

Most likely because of this opposition, the "regulars" juggled the results of a census count to ensure districts most favorable to themselves. For the 1970 redistricting, Vrdolyak and Machine regulars gerrymandered the two Mexican neighborhoods, splitting them into separate districts, leaving only Irondale in the Tenth Ward. In doing this, the regulars engineered the demise of the community organization and contained the effort of Mexicans in Chicago to build their own autonomous political efforts. Not until the 1980s would Mexican opposition to the Machine resurface in any significant way. In the meantime, Latino electoral power was limited by an inability to obtain ward majorities. Demographics and successful court challenges would soon change this.

THE RISE OF A LATINO INDEPENDENCE MOVEMENT

The success of some Latinos within the Machine did not translate into well-serviced Latino communities. Or so thought the young Mexican activists of the Near West Side and the Puerto Ricans on the north side who were beginning to define themselves separately from the Machine. Indeed, these young activists believed that the Machine relationship with their communities was one of neglect, and they believed that Latinos had the numbers to do something about it.

Political activism was not new to Latino communities. They had their labor organizers and community-based organizers. The Puerto Rican community had *independistas*, and Mexicans had protectors of immigrant rights. Many had been protesters of the 1960s and 1970s—fighting "outside the system." What was new was that these activists turned their attention to electoral politics. Now these Latinos from Centro de Acción Autónoma (CASA), Brown

Berets, and Puerto Rican independence organizations were working "within the system." Their fervor and commitment remained strong as they formed organizations, registered voters, and influenced candidates.

The activists engaged in the world of electoral campaigns and voter solicitation with the "realization that the Machine used the political realm to deny services to the community." Everything from garbage collection to education was denied through the Machine, and so the major task was to beat the "regulars" at the polls. "The electoral process was the avenue to change the system—if it could be changed." [15]

In the early 1980s, Mexican activists formed the Independent Political Organization (IPO) of the Near West Side. Prominent leaders within the group, especially Rudy Lozano, rallied the electoral cause, claiming that Latinos had the numbers to make a difference. Political statistician David Cantor backed him up, supplying figures and the concept of a Latino belt that ran through the First, Twenty-Second, and Twenty-Fifth Wards.

Voter apathy had to be tackled as did the belief that "the only way to get things was through the Machine." The activists made it their goal to enfranchise the community, to create a sense of empowerment, a sense that "this is our neighborhood and we have a right to say something about it." They believed that if they could convince people that their vote could make a difference, then they could open up the doors for reform politics. They intended to build an organization that could generate a voting bloc.

Once organized, it became easier to run candidates and endorse others. By doing this, they were opposing Machine heavies of the First, Twenty-Fifth, and Twenty-Second Wards such as Fred Roti, Vito Marzullo, and Frank Stemberk, respectively. They knew they would not win immediately, but their vision was long term. The Near West Side IPO "created" a candidate of its own to run in 1982 for state representative of the Twentieth District.

The members of the Near West Side IPO, such as Rudy Lozano, Jesús García, Lidia Bracamonte, Linda Coronado, Arturo Vásquez, Carlos Arango, Juan Velásquez, and many others, formed the basis for a solid organization. Through their efforts Soliz obtained 33 percent of the vote and demonstrated the political power that was being gathered by the Chicano and Chicana activists. [16] These same activists already had a history of forming alliances with Blacks in surrounding neighborhoods, including leaders like Danny Davis and Art Turner from the West Side.

On the north side of town, many Puerto Ricans had been familiar with patronage politics. Here, too, young activists sought another way of doing politics. Individuals such as "Cha Cha" Jiménez and Reverend Jorge Morales were among those who were forming their own movement at the same time that they were responding to Rudy Lozano's moves to use his citywide contacts to build alliances across Latino groups. Lozano was also instrumental in bringing the Latino independents together with the Black and white progressives who were working to elect Chicago's first Black mayor.

THE ELECTION OF HAROLD WASHINGTON

Black politicians in the post-Daley era were, with few exceptions, controlled by the Machine. Black voters, on the other hand, were voting less and itching more for autonomy and a candidate of their own.[17] Harold Washington attempted to be that candidate and ran in the 1977 Democratic primary for mayor. A divided and controlled Black leadership did not, for the most part, support Washington, with Black voter turnout of only 27.4 percent of those eligible to vote. Though Washington lost the election, he set the stage for a more significant challenge that was to follow.

The Black community "came alive" to actualize its civil rights at the ballot box. Mobilization for voter registration and participation swept the Black community and was primarily prompted by grassroots forces including churches and community organizations. The campaign was successful and resulted in a jump in participation to 73 percent of the Black voting-age population by the 1983 general election — the highest Black voter turnout in the history of Chicago.[18]

Washington reluctantly submitted to the efforts to draft him for the 1983 mayoral race. His contenders were mayor Jane Byrne, who had alienated the Black community through her lack of appointments of Blacks to key positions, and Richard Daley, the son of the late mayor. The three-way primary race and the ensuing general election against the Republican candidate, Bernard Epton, were the most expensive, the hottest, and the most unpredictable of Chicago's mayoral elections. They were also campaigns in which race and racism were contentious and significant factors.

The importance of the internal struggle of white Machine leaders and the split in the white vote between Byrne and Daley facilitated Washington's victory. Lakefront liberals also supported the anti-Machine efforts of Harold Washington. But it was primarily a mobilized Black community that was the force behind the historic election of a Black mayor in the city of Chicago. Latino support, nonetheless, played a key role in the Washington coalition.

LATINO SUPPORT FOR HAROLD WASHINGTON

In December of 1982 the IPO of the Near West Side endorsed Harold Washington for mayor. It also ran its own candidates in the Twenty-Second and

Twenty-Fifth wards for the 1983 aldermanic races. In the Twenty-Second Ward (Little Village), Rudy Lozano took on Frank Stemberk, and in the Twenty-Fifth (Pilsen), Juan Velásquez challenged Vito Marzullo. While neither challenger was successful, Rudy Lozano came within seventeen votes of forcing a runoff. Rather than challenge the legitimacy of a suspect outcome, the candidates decided instead to see their vision as long term.[19]

IPO endorsement for Harold Washington translated into campaigning for him in local wards. In a different part of town, Puerto Ricans also heavily canvased their wards (26th, 31st) to obtain support for Washington. These efforts in the north side became the basis of the organization from which Luis Gutiérrez ran for committeeperson in 1984 against Dan Rowstenkowski.

The "progressive" Latinos put their years of organizing and their newfound electoral skills to the task of turning out the votes for Harold Washington. According to Board of Elections figures, in the primary on February 22, 1983, the Near West Side IPO pulled in 24 percent of the Twenty-Fifth Ward votes and 20 percent of Twenty-Second Ward votes for Harold Washington. In the Twenty-Sixth and Thirty-First wards, 9 percent and 17 percent of the votes respectively were cast for Washington.[20]

The general election in April which pitted Washington against Republican Bernard Epton more poignantly suggests the importance of the Latino vote for Washington. Of the 48,230 vote difference between Washington and Epton, 27,915 of those were cast by Washington supporters of the four wards where Latinos have the highest populations. Put differently, the Midwest Voters Registration Project conducted an exit poll on election day and found 80 percent of Chicago's Latinos voting for Washington for an estimated total of 51,000 votes.[21]

The relationship formed in 1982–1983 between Washington and "progressive" Latinos grew stronger throughout Washington's time in City Hall. Washington brought some of these "progressive" Latinos into his administration as deputy commissioners of city departments, and he created the Mayor's Advisory Commission on Latino Affairs.[22] Meanwhile, further efforts were made to advance "progressive" Latinos into the electoral realm.

In the Twenty-Second Ward the IPO again challenged the Machine by putting Jesús García, deputy commissioner of water, against heavyweight Frank Stemberk for the position of ward committee member, the ward organization's chief authority. The successful 1984 bid placed García on the Committee of the Democratic Party and right in the midst of maneuvering within Machine hierarchy. The ability of the Latino activists to successfully place García points to the effectiveness of the organizers. It was a signal of the increasing importance that Latino progressives would play in advancing Washington's reform agenda.

WASHINGTON AND THE VRDOLYAK 29

Washington's pledge was to reform the patronage system and to open the political process. He desired a more efficient bureaucracy, neighborhood development, and a redistribution of resources. However, when Washington won as chief executive of City Hall, he did not win the support of the City Council. The chair of the Democratic Party and alderman of the Tenth Ward represented the interests of the Machine as it existed (even with its divisions). Edward Vrdolyak and the twenty-eight aldermen who supported him became known as the Vrdolyak 29—and the thorn in Washington's side. The ability to make commission appointments, to staff committee chairships, and to prioritize the budget were all limited by the inability of Washington to obtain a council majority on crucial issues. When accused of doing little to change the direction of the City, Washington pointed to the paralysis caused by the "council wars." It was precisely this situation that made the 1986 special aldermanic elections so critical from the point of view of both Harold Washington and Edward Vrdolyak. The successful legal battle for fair representation made these elections possible.

THE LEGAL BATTLE FOR "FAIR REPRESENTATION"

The issue leading to the 1986 elections was one of fair representation. In the 1981 redistricting that followed the census count, the city council approved the mappings produced by the Council Subcommittee on Redistricting and the commissioner of the Department of Planning. Generally speaking, the guidelines for apportionment accord with the ability of a given incumbent to retain reelection capacity. The maneuvering is called gerrymandering, and it is as old as apportionment itself.

In November 1981 a new map of aldermanic districts obtained city council approval. The plan was challenged in summer 1982, when lawyers representing Blacks and Latinos filed complaints of voting rights violations.[23] The plaintiffs alleged violations of Section 2 of the Voting Rights Act and its 1982 amendment, the Fourteenth and Fifteenth amendments, various federal civil rights statutes, and several Illinois constitutional and statutory provisions.

The case was heard in Federal District court in late 1982. After the District Court denied most of the claims, an appeal was filed in the Seventh Circuit Court of Appeals. That court accepted the plaintiffs' claim that violations of the Fourteenth Amendment had occurred and that intention to discriminate could be found. The higher court upheld claims of minority vote dilution through packing, fracturing, and boundary manipulation. Moreover, the higher court called for a majority in nineteen Black wards and for the creation of four Hispanic wards, with 65 percent deemed the effective guideline to ensure "fair representation." The Supreme Court refused to hear the defendants' appeal and returned the case to District Court for reconsideration on the basis of the Appeals Court's declarations. The final map that satisfied the guidelines of the Appeals Court closely resembled the proposed plaintiffs' map.

If gerrymandering disenfranchised South Chicago Chicanos in the 1960s, then what was different about the 1980s? The court case against Machine maneuvering of political wards was possible for a number of reasons. First, between 1960 and 1980, the population of Latinos in Chicago grew from 110,000 to 423,000, or from 3.1 percent of the population to 14.1 percent of the population.[24] A demographic base made for increased presence and participation. Further, the existence of alert and committed Latino professionals meant that there were individuals who had the skills to pursue complicated legal technicalities. Finally, the alliance with Black attorneys increased the effectiveness of the court challenge. The successful redistricting lawsuit contributed to an awakened interest in the ballot box as an expression of civil rights.

As a result of the successful court challenge, seven wards were reshaped and not only corrected minority voting dilution, but also altered the jurisdiction of long-standing Machine aldermen. In the revised Twenty-Fifth ward map, the Mexican community of Pilsen was politically strengthened because Machine Alderman Vito Marzullo was mapped out of his district. Similarly, in the Twenty-Second Ward, where the 57-percent Mexican majority jumped to 71.7 percent, Alderman Frank Stemberk chose not to run for reelection. In the Twenty-Sixth Ward, Alderman Michael Nardulli was moved into a ward where successful challenge of the incumbent would be unlikely. The fourth Latino ward, the Thirty-First, already had Chicago's only Latino Alderman, Miguel Santiago. The situation in the three Black wards posed similar challenges to Machine incumbents. The remapping did not guarantee a shift in city council balance of power, but the chances were good that at least four of the seven seats could be gained by a Washington supporter, thus making the balance 25-25, with Washington able to cast the tie-breaking vote. The Machine affiliates would not let this happen without a concerted fight. The electoral fervor, however, would mark a new era for Latinos in Chicago.

THE 1986 SPECIAL ELECTIONS

"Louie! Louie! Louie! Louie!" The walls and the halls of Humboldt Civic Center reverberated from the clapping, the stomping, and the screams for Louie. The big halls, the hallways, and the stairwells were filled with the supporters of Luis Gutiérrez, Puerto Rican candidate for alderman of the Twenty-Sixth

Ward. They were campaign soldiers who had walked the precincts, knocked on doors, answered telephones, raised money, and circulated posters. They were workers in factories, social service agencies, cultural centers, schools, grocery stores, and city offices. They were primarily Puerto Rican residents of neighborhoods known as West Town and Humboldt Park. They were excited, they were elated, and they were convinced that their candidate would win.

Who would be the next alderman of the Twenty-Sixth Ward? Would it be the Washington-backed fiery orator, or would it be the candidate supported by the regular Democratic Party? The fierce exchanges throughout the campaign between Luis Gutiérrez and Manuel (Manny) Torres point to the importance of this race from the point of view of the people of the 26th Ward. The involvement signaled a belief that the outcome of this electoral battle would make a difference for the future of the neighborhood. Roads with potholes, alleys with garbage, and blocks with vacant lots were only part of the problem. Unemployment, gang violence, high drop-out rates, and decaying commercial districts plagued the community. These were the problems people needed solved, and these were the problems each candidate swore to address.

Across town in the Twenty-Second Ward (Little Village), Jesús García, ward committeeperson, had the support of Harold Washington and of the IPO. "Chuy" was described by his campaign manager as a strong leader "who has the ability to work in an organization and the ability to have strong people around him." His grassroots organization was sound. García faced several opponents in the 1986 elections, including Machine-backed Guadalupe García, a loyal worker in Stembert's ward organization.[25]

In the Twenty-Fifth Ward (Pilsen), Washington people backed Juan Velásquez, deputy commissioner in the Department of Streets and Sanitation, against Juan Soliz. Soliz and Velásquez had been on the same political side a few years earlier, but Soliz made a break from the "Progressive" Latinos and aligned himself with Ed Vrdolyak. According to many, Soliz developed resentments against Washington when Washington did not bring him into the administration as deputy mayor. Others say that Soliz emerged from the 1984 legislative race with debts that Ed Vrdolyak helped him pay. According to Soliz, he began criticizing Washington because he felt his record of Latino appointments was weak. In response to questions about his alliance with the "Regulars" he replied, "Since regular democrats couldn't beat me, they supported me. I had to go with the people that supported me." The Machine forces did support Soliz in the heated battle against Juan Velásquez and two others.[26]

In the Thirty-First Ward (Humboldt Park), three Puerto Ricans ran for alderman. The incumbent was Miguel Santiago, whose position epitomized the Latino version of "plantation politics." According to Gary Rivlin, "the only difference between him [Santiago] and the plantation politicians who preceded him was his race." He was a faithful Machine soldier who was made by the Machine and in whose interests he served, even at the expense of the community. Santiago's predecessor in the Thirty-First Ward, Joseph Martínez, had been appointed by Jane Byrne and then "dumped" in 1983 when caught in crossfire between Byrne and Ward boss Edward Nedza.[27] Santiago was chosen to represent the regular democrats on the city council. In 1986, Santiago would rely on Machine backing to wage his reelection bid against contenders Benjamin Rosado, a Streets and Sanitation Department employee, and Migdalia Collazo, the Washington-backed candidate.

In all four wards, Latino interest in electoral politics was heightened. Nearly everyone had a position and a favorite candidate. A particularly close race was predicted in the Twenty-Sixth Ward, where the battle between Luis Gutiérrez and Manuel Torres was a battle between Washington and the Machine. With such high stakes, the emotions ran high; battle lines were drawn and residents of the ward were forced to take sides. Verbal arguments in restaurants, bus stops, and neighborhood streets were indicative of the heightened importance of electoral politics. To wear a campaign button or to canvass a precinct was to take the risk of verbal or physical assault. Candidates were slandered, threatened, and run down by cars, and youth gangs were employed to carry forward a Chicago tradition of voter harassment. The community was alive with enthusiasm and antagonism.

The Twenty-Sixth Ward race was also the race the media found most interesting, particularly as the drama unfolded. One must ask why the Machine cared so much about this ward. The *Chicago Sun Times* thought the question important and headlined an article "Why Gutiérrez Scares Eddie." In the words of Vernon Jarrett, "Politicians like Vrodlyak, ex-Mayor Jane Byrne and State's Attorney Richard M. Daley view people like Gutiérrez as a threat to their political domination. . . . The Machine crowd cannot tolerate a Hispanic, or any intelligent minority spokesman, who can inspire his people, yet is not for sale. They shudder at the thought of Gutiérrez standing in the City Council inspiring other Hispanics to register and vote."[28]

Election day arrived. The fervor and the intensity were pervasive throughout the Twenty-Sixth Ward, the other six wards, and the entire city. In the Twenty-Second Ward, Jesús García was elected with an overwhelming majority. For years, his work had reflected his commitment, and many viewed his election with enthusiasm and hope. In the Thirty-First Ward, the Machine's Miguel Santiago remained seated, but contender Migdalia Collazo rallied a sizable chunk of the vote, a signal, perhaps, that next time she could win. Juan Soliz was elected in the Twenty-Fifth Ward, winning so easily that a runoff was not necessary. So far, of the three Latino aldermanic races, two would be part of the Vrdolyak forces and one would join with Washington's side.

In the three Black wards, one would join the Washington bloc, and another would join the Vrdolyak forces. A third race required a runoff, but all predictions pointed to an easy victory for the Washington-backed candidate. And what of the Twenty-Sixth Ward in West Town?

On election night, as campaign workers anxiously crowded around television sets in campaign headquarters, the votes started coming in. Torres, Gutiérrez, Torres, Gutiérrez—it was close. By the end of the night, Gutiérrez had more votes and it appeared that he had won. Still, the Board of Elections did not declare him winner. The Machine had an ace in its pocket. Mysteriously, uncounted write-in votes appeared for the third candidate, Jim Blasinski. There were just enough write-in votes to deny Gutiérrez a sufficient majority for victory (50 percent + 1) and to, therefore, require a runoff. Where did these ballots come from? Would Gutiérrez be declared victor, or would he have to face a runoff election against Torres? Torres's lawyers filed a suit with the Cook County Circuit Court requesting that the write-in votes for a third candidate count. Their request was granted and the runoff election was scheduled for April 29, when the eyes of Chicago would turn toward the Twenty-Sixth Ward.

Workers for Gutiérrez, however, knew the Machine had been up to its "old tricks," doing what it could to "steal" the election. The new campaign slogan became "reelect Gutíerrez." People from the Independent Political Organizations and the campaign headquarters mobilized, and supporters from all over the city poured in to "reelect" Luis Gutiérrez. Machine forces from the nearby wards of Nardulli, Nedza, and Gabinski also entered the Twenty-Sixth Ward for the battle.

The hottest campaign issue came over accusations of "control" by one faction or the other. Torres called Gutiérrez a "City Hall puppet," while Gutiérrez focused on Torres's Machine connections. Gutiérrez's campaign literature described him as a "long time community leader" who worked on bringing housing to the community, getting streets and sidewalks repaired, and increasing minority hiring and "led the successful fight for the remap of this Ward." At the same time he described the Machine as giving "our communities 20 years of neglect" and hand-picking a candidate "so they can maintain *their* control of *our* community."

In the runoff election the Machine became the target of more than Luis Gutiérrez. The two major newspapers, the *Chicago Tribune* and the *Chicago Sun Times*, endorsed Gutiérrez. The *Tribune* said that the Twenty-Sixth Ward contest resembled "a gang rumble more than an election." Behind the personal feuding between Mr. Gutiérrez and County Commissioner Manuel Torres was "a struggle for power involving Chicago's leading political heavies. Their maneuvering left the election a mess." Most everyone would agree that the fight was intense and fierce. Many others would say it was "dirty." [29]

The stakes were high. The council balance still placed Vrdolyak with the edge. The runoff election included a race in the Fifteenth Ward between Washington supporter Marlene Carter and incumbent Frank Brady, whose redistricted ward now was 75 percent Black. A united Black vote would likely give Carter the seat. With the pro-Washington victories of Jesús García, and in two of the three Black wards, the count was 25-24 in favor of Vrdolyak. This left the Twenty-Sixth Ward outcome as the deciding point on who would gain control of the council. If Gutiérrez won the election, the count would be 25-25; it would be a new administration for Harold Washington.

No day was so exciting as election day itself. This time around, the organization for election day was tighter, smoother, and very serious. Poll watchers were trained to detect fraud—even the most subtle—inside the polling place. Runners used the information from the inside to get out their counts. This time state attorney officials were part of the surveillance team to keep an eye on the action. Emotions ran high while votes were challenged and judges were scrutinized.

Each candidate was confident of victory. At the end of the day, as individual precinct votes were tallied, the word spread among campaign workers that Louie was winning. The workers converged in Humboldt Park Civic Center, knowing, feeling that they had won. The months of dedication, strategizing, and plain hard work gave way to smiles, laughter, and *gritos*. "Ganamos! Ganamos!" Gutiérrez received 53.2 percent of the votes (7,429) compared with Torres's 46.9 percent (6,549). These special aldermanic elections were pivotal in Chicago political history, in the rise of political power of Latinos, and in the further coalition building among "progressive" whites, Blacks, and Latinos.

Latino Representation in City Hall

Latinos now had four representatives in City Hall. Given the tightness of the 25-25 power balance, a Latino "bloc" was conceivable. Variation among the four, however, was noticeable, suggesting that Latino unity was not automatic. Juan Soliz issued several public appeals calling for the aldermen to form the bloc as a way to obtain benefits for the community. "They'll have to come to us. . . . Everyone recognizes that we can be stronger as a bloc. . . . Except maybe García and Gutiérrez, because they are on a leash. They have to depend on the mayor for everything."[30]

Both Jesús García and Luis Gutiérrez rejected the Soliz appeals and instead identified Soliz as a Machine affiliate who "has joined forces that have sought to deny the Hispanic community representation." Each said they would work to form a "Latino agenda" but that they wouldn't form a "bloc for the sake of forming a bloc." "Our natural allies now in the council are the black community and those who agree on a progressive reform agenda."[31] Though the four aldermen might have been able to agree on the "Latino agenda"— on the common problems in the four wards—they would not agree on how to solve those problems or with whom to affiliate in order to do so.

While Miguel Santiago clearly remained as a relic of "hacienda politics," Juan Soliz was divorcing himself from Machine affiliation and claiming himself to be an "independent." García and Gutiérrez had arisen from grassroots organizing and were now two of Washington's twenty-five. They often appeared together on the same platform and were part of a "progressive" or "reform" agenda.

For the Washington administration "reform" meant the breakup of the patronage system. He sought changes in awarding of city contracts, neighborhood improvement (for example, streets, sewers, and sidewalks), the opening of the political process beyond the "regulars," an opening of jobs to include minorities, and record keeping of city hall activities. After Gutiérrez's victory in the April 29 runoff election, Washington moved swiftly to obtain confirmation for fifty-one positions on boards and commissions. For example, through his allies in the City Council, he ousted Machine leaders from heads of the Park District and the board of the Chicago Transit Authority. Both of these positions controlled large numbers of patronage jobs.

García and Gutiérrez moved quickly to direct money to their communities. Neighborhood improvement projects, sewer projects, establishment of block groups, curbs and gutters, street resurfacing, health centers, new refuse collection systems, and advisory committees were part of their strategies to develop Little Village and West Town. Meanwhile, Latino residents of these wards, and of Chicago, sensed that they were part of something big.

THE 1987 ELECTIONS

In the following primary election of February 22, 1987, Washington went head to head with former mayor Jane Byrne and won with 53.4 percent of the vote. In the general election on April 7, 1987, he faced Republican Don Haider and Edward Vrdolyak from the newly formed Solidarity Party. The general election placed Washington ahead with 53.3 percent (600,290) of the vote, compared with 4.2 percent (47,652) for Haider and 41.6 percent (468,493) for Vrdolyak.[32]

Both battles were fierce, and though race was a major factor, it did not equal the intensity of the 1983 elections. Washington received the near total support of the Black community. The white vote was not so united. The candidacy of several whites not only split the vote but also heightened the division among Machine warlords, many of whom voted non-Democratic rather than support the candidacy of a Black reform mayor.

The Latino vote was courted in the primary by Byrne and Washington. Byrne had already built a base of Latino support from the previous elections, and this time she tried especially hard to impress them with occasional use of Spanish phrases. Part of her campaign strategy was to challenge Harold Washington to a debate—in Spanish. She lost favor, however, after a slip in which she referred to Puerto Ricans as "illegal aliens." In response, Latinos were saying, "We are not aliens, we are human beings for Washington."

Latino support for Washington remained high for the 1987 primary and general elections. For example, in the four wards with the highest concentration of Latinos, Washington carried 24,617 and 27,305 votes in the primary and general elections, respectively. This is in contrast to 8,597 and 27,905 for the 1983 elections. Washington carried Luis Gutiérrez's ward (26th) and drew a little more than half the votes of Jesús García's ward (22nd). Machine strength in the Twenty-Fifth and Thirty-First wards delivered the majority votes to Byrne. According to *Chicago Tribune* estimates, citywide, 53.4 percent of the Latino vote went to Washington and 46.1 percent for Byrne in the primary. In the general election, 62.3 percent of the Latino votes supported Washington, versus 34.6 percent for Vrdolyak and 3.1 percent for Republican Don Haider.[33]

The outcomes of the aldermanic races were again crucial for the Washington administration. According to the *Chicago Sun Times*, the key races were being waged in the four Latino wards and six Lakefront wards.[34] The four Latino wards were the same ones where special elections were held the previous year. Washington supporters Jesús García and Luis Gutiérrez won reelection easily in the Twenty-Second and Twenty-Sixth wards, with each obtaining over 40 percentage points more than his closest opponent.[35] In the Thirty-First and Twenty-Fifth Wards, a runoff election was necessary. The Machine lost in both. Machine incumbent Miguel Santiago of the Thirty-First Ward lost to attorney Raymond Figueroa. In the Twenty-Fifth, incumbent Juan Soliz, running as an independent, managed to defeat both Machine and Washington organizers.

The outcome of the aldermanic races left Washington with control of the council. Washington was able, for example, to lead a 40-9 council steamroll over the floor leader and Machine warlord, Edward Burke, and replace him by Black alderman Timothy Evans. The *Chicago Sun Times* headlines read, "It's Harold's Council Now."

HAROLD'S DEATH
AND THE ENSUING POLITICAL BATTLES

Despite the optimism and apparent unity, the "Washington bloc" fell apart almost immediately upon the tragic news that Washington had suffered a fatal heart attack on Wednesday, November 25, 1987, the day before Thanksgiving. While the city mourned, politicians scrambled to see which alderman could muster the needed twenty-six votes to become acting mayor. Vrdolyak and Burke forces met; Jesse Jackson returned home from the Middle East to exert a mediating influence; Blacks behind Eugene Sawyer met secretly with white ethnics who realized that they did not have the votes to elect one of their own; while a growing sentiment emerged among the Black community that the one most likely to carry forward the legacy of Washington was finance chair Timothy Evans.

Evans became the candidate of "the people," and Sawyer became the man that had cut deals with the "enemy." The battle lines were clear the night of Washington's burial during a memorial service held at the University of Illinois at Chicago Pavilion. The crowd was told of the ongoing political activities and was further aroused by Vernon Jarrett, close friend of Harold Washington and columnist for the *Chicago Sun Times*. In an emotionally charged tirade inspired by Frederick Douglass, Jarrett described the Sawyer forces as Uncle Toms who had "ceased to be men and women" and had sold their people into slavery. His speech of wrath was followed by Jesse Jackson's call to arms — for people to do what they had to do to ensure that the Washington legacy be carried forward. The following day the Sawyer aldermen were bombarded with phone calls, threats, and picketing. That evening thousands of Washington supporters who now backed Evans turned out at City Hall in the hopes that they could stop the aldermen from voting. Finally, by 4:00 A.M., when most of the crowd had fizzled, Eugene Sawyer received the necessary votes to make him acting mayor of Chicago. Blacks were stunned that their unity had not survived Washington's death.

Latino aldermen, however, had announced before that they would vote as a bloc, and they did.[36] García, Gutiérrez, Figueroa, and even Soliz all cast their votes for Timothy Evans, the candidate they believed would carry on the reform of Washington. Such a united vote placed hopes in the Latino community that Latinos in city council might be finally united. The pledge was one thing; the ensuing reality was another.

By 1989, when a special mayoral election was held to decide Washington's successor, the Washington coalition had not regrouped, and divisions were deep in the Black, Latino, and Lakefront liberal communities. Acting Mayor

Sawyer faced several challengers, including Richard M. Daley, son of the Machine mayor; Danny Davis, longtime Black activist and politician; and Timothy Evans. For progressive Latinos, the most devastating blow was brought by Luis Gutiérrez's declaration of support for Richard Daley. The alderman of the Twenty-Sixth Ward had been put into place by a grassroots movement that believed his oratory. Progressive leaders of the ward organization were committed to an agenda that they believed Louie shared. Their devastation was deep, leading to disillusionment and disappointment.

Daley won the primary and general elections and regained his father's seat as mayor of Chicago. According to the Board of Elections figures and Midwest Voters Registration Project, Daley won the Democratic primary with the support of two-thirds of Latino voters (as compared to the 53 percent they gave Washington in 1987). In the Twenty-Sixth Ward, 72 percent (6,782) of the voters went with Daley.

THE LEGACY OF HAROLD WASHINGTON

At the funeral of Harold Washington, Jesús García received a standing ovation after offering a rap-style eulogy. The eulogy expressed the sentiment of many Latinos:

> You came to our community
> help build the spirit of unity
> The seeds that we then sowed
> became the fruit that victory bestowed
> You walked through our barrios,
> our neighborhoods, and touched our hearts.
>
> And now that you've gone, we
> the people vow to stay strong.
> The unity of our coalition is a
> tribute to the Washington tradition.
> Today, today in '87, we know
> that you're in heaven.
> Adiós amigo. Adiós.

Although some insiders caution about glorifying him, Harold Washington changed politics for Latinos in Chicago. Insiders were clear about the limitations of his administration and the extent to which he adequately addressed the needs of Latinos.[37] Nonetheless, he was an inspiration to encourage grassroots activists to continue their search for solutions to their communities' problems through electoral politics. Washington supported Latinos to gain political office and expand their representation in city hall.

Representation in city hall meant increased dollars into the neighborhood and improvements of everything from garbage collection to sidewalks. Block grants, community development projects, and contract awards were directed to communities that had previously faced disrepair and neglect. The placement of Latinos in city hall also meant the creation of a middle-level broker class and the upward mobility of highly paid city hall workers.

Latino activists were convinced of the necessity of coalitions, particularly among themselves and with African American communities. Washington became the conduit for those coalitions. He promoted the understanding that Blacks and Latinos had problems in common and needed to form alliances to solve them. The structural conditions that each of the groups faced became the basis for coalitions whereby a charismatic leader was important in bridging the various groups. The nearly immediate breakup of the coalition following his death suggests how important Washington was to its existence.

Latino women and men became part of a reform movement that challenged "business as usual" in Chicago. They contributed to the deterioration of the Machine stronghold in city politics. Several longtime Machine "heavies" were forced out of office due to reapportionment that created Latino ward majorities. Latinos defeated Machine aldermen at a time when the balance of numbers was critical for Washington to exercise real legislative leadership, greater control over the budget, and broader and fairer access to jobs once completely controlled by the machine. Legal battles over "fair representation" were a necessary component of opening the doors to electoral participation.

After Washington's death several questions emerged. To what extent was the Machine destroyed and replaced by progressive politics? Certainly, the democratic process was opened, but just how far? Now that politics were opened to Blacks and Latinos, would it be "business as usual"? How would Latinos fit into the political scene?[38] While fully answering these questions may be beyond the scope of this chapter, this chronicle of electoral emergence offers insights for viewing the political participation of Latinos.

BEYOND WASHINGTON

Jesús García and Luis Gutiérrez were two young political activists who found themselves swept into office by an electoral movement of Blacks and Latinos in Chicago. A view of each of their political careers illuminates the path of Latino electoral participation in the City of Chicago.

After Washington's death, Jesús García maintained the vision of the early days—the enfranchisement of the community. In his ward, each of the precincts organized block clubs, and out of these ranks emerged neighborhood leaders. The Twenty-Second IPO continued to host an annual conference as a means for residents in the ward to articulate their needs and opinions. García was readily available to those who wanted to speak with him. As Lidia Bracamonte, an original member of the Near West Side IPO, put it, "Chuy's organization runs all the time. It's the difference between the Machine and a political apparatus that empowers people."[39]

In contrast, many believed that Gutiérrez developed his campaign around the individual. According to close observers, "Louie built a circle of people around him who followed the man and not the plan." Chuy, on the other hand, "has got the plan. That is what makes him so good." Many were not surprised when Gutiérrez chose to align with the Daley forces, a move which demonstrably bolstered his political career.

At the same time, the political choices of both García and Gutiérrez suggest something about the complexities and contradictions of participation in the electoral arena. Namely, they were now in the world of deals—"I'll vote for your bill if you vote for mine." The game that says you "don't make no waves" and you "don't back no losers." It's an arena where you run on ideology and then face the reality of patronage politics, leaving the question of whether entrenched patronage politics can ever fully be reformed. Both politicians have survived and both have gone on to develop strong constituencies that keep them in political office.

The political career of Luis Gutiérrez was visibly boosted through his affiliation with the new Daley regime. He became in 1992 the first Latino from Chicago to be elected to Congress. The newly created political district again demonstrated the demographic changes in Chicago and the importance of participation in the struggle to ensure that districting results in adequate representation. Despite certain presumptive behaviors upon arriving in Washington, Gutiérrez has managed to juggle many interests in his district. He went on in 1994 to win, against Juan Soliz, a second term. Many point to Gutiérrez's anti-NAFTA stance as an indication that he has not completely abandoned progressive interests.

Since 1992 García has represented his constituency in the Illinois Senate. He too juggles an array of interests within the four wards of his district and continues to fight for legislation that favors the interests of workers. García joins Miguel del Valle as a leader in the Democratic Latino coalition that is a formal organism of the state Democratic Party. Del Valle rose within electoral politics as a member of the State Senate during the same electoral fervor that nourished García and Gutiérrez.

To Latinos in Chicago, these three leading politicians continue to keep alive the notion that the electoral arena is still a vehicle to empower their communities. They are joined in political office by four aldermen and four state representatives. Latinos continue to work in coalition with each other and with many African American politicians. The era in which Washington was elected was inspired by a grassroots movement that saw the electoral arena as a vehicle for empowerment. The legacies of that movement are visibly seen in the presence of Latino elected officials as players in the local, state, and national levels.

REFLECTIONS ON A CHRONICLE

Widespread racism has characterized the Latino experience in the United States, as typified by Latinos' exclusion from electoral politics. Gerrymandering has been the most prevalent measure to deny "fair representation," and court challenges have been the most effective way to remedy it.[40] The Chicago case confirms the prevalence of gerrymandering and its likely continuance without the role of vigilant attorneys who make it their business to intercede. In this case, the Mexican American Legal Defense Fund (MALDEF) was a primary actor in setting the stage for the Redistricting Elections of 1986, which in turn was a critical moment in bolstering the Washington coalition.

Challenges over redistricting are not new to Mexican Americans but have been a part of their political history in several regions since the 1960s.[41] The Voting Rights Acts of the 1960s certainly made these challenges viable. Denial of Latinos' political rights seems to be the norm, necessitating, each time, a court challenge and all the time and expenses that accompany it. Where access to these legal resources are nonexistent, denial of fair representation to Latinos prevails. Even in cases of successful challenges, several years of access are denied while the challenge is being waged. Either way, vigilance on the question of fair representation is a critical measure toward inclusion in the political process.

Demographic shifts of Latinos in Chicago reversed previous size, residential patterns, and electoral participation rates, thus impacting their effectiveness in the electoral arena.[42] Activists were aware of the increasing numbers and concentration of Latinos, which influenced their decision to mobilize within the electoral arena. Demographics alone, however, does not explain the rise of a Latino consciousness. The structural conditions that Latinos face create a Latino identity that potentially provides the basis for mobilization efforts to combat the structured inequality.[43]

The ethos of the era was indeed one of Latinismo, and many spoke of the dream of Latino unity. Chicago had been somewhat unique in that large concentrations of several Latino groups coexisted. As Latino populations in large urban areas become increasingly mixed, the Chicago case may yield some lessons. An articulation of a cultural and racial identity contributes to the likelihood that Latinos will mobilize in unity. An articulation of the structural factors impacting Latinos and their causes is also an essential component of a mobilizing effort, so that "unity" doesn't become a euphemism for class domination within the races.

"Radical" grassroots activists led the plunge into electoral politics during the era of Harold Washington. Services were denied or granted through City Hall—and City Hall was within reach. "Progressive" politics was the rhetoric of the day, though it was never entirely articulated what this meant, other than access to services by destroying a patronage system that had previously denied them. Other politicians who were part of the reform movement had ascended through machine politics, and many of them returned once Washington had died. At the same time, becoming a part of the patronage fold is compelling, as Gutiérrez exemplified when he chose the new Daley regime as his political sponsor—he delivered votes in return for political advancement.

Whether politics fundamentally changed in Chicago is still an unanswered question. Are "hacienda politics" alive and well? From the point of view of many, it remained "business as usual," though less centralized. Political observers had predicted that a less centralized machine would allow for Latinos to participate in party politics, including some level of decision making.[44] The party machine itself, though perhaps not as total in its control, would maintain its stronghold on the electoral arena. Nonetheless, gains are made through electoral participation, most especially in the increased access to goods and services. Participation in electoral politics, despite stated goals, may not fundamentally change the nature of the electoral arena. Participation may, nonetheless, provide some access to which Latinos are entitled in a representative form of government.[45]

The potential of our numbers is enormous. The stakes are high. How clearly we articulate our vision for a just society will impact the extent to which our Latino identity will help us mobilize to fundamentally alter structured inequality. Electoral mobilization during the era of Harold Washington was a spark in Chicago to ignite the belief that formal politics was at least one arena which held hope for effecting social change. The dream, for many, continues.

Notes

I wish to thank the many political actors who shared their information and insights. I also wish to thank Ray Romero and Dora Arechiga, former directors of the Chicago MALDEF, for information on the redistricting case and David Montejano for his editorial work. I especially wish to thank Alma Rivera for her research assistance.

1. Milton Rakove, *Don't Make No Waves—Don't Back No Losers: An Insider's Analysis of the Daley Machine* (Bloomington: Indiana University Press, 1975), p. 1.

2. There are numerous treatments of Machine politics. See, for example, Edward C. Banfield and James Q. Wilson, *City Politics* (Cambridge, Mass.: Harvard University Press, 1963); Harold F. Gosnell, *Machine Politics: Chicago Model* (Chicago: University of Chicago Press), 1977; Thomas M. Guterbock, *Machine Politics in Transition* (Chicago: University of Chicago Press, 1980).

3. Milton Rakove, "Jane Byrne and the New Chicago Politics," in Samuel K. Gove and Louis H. Masotti, eds., *After Daley: Chicago Politics in Transition* (Urbana: University of Illinois Press, 1982), p. 224.

4. Latinos did not join the Byrne forces in large numbers. In fact, of 18.3 percent of eligible Latino voters who voted, the majority supported Bilandic. Paul Kleppner, *Chicago Divided: The Making of a Black Mayor* (Dekalb, Ill.: Northern Illinois University Press, 1985), p. 116.

5. Rakove, "Jane Byrne and the New Chicago Politics," p. 232.

6. See Ira Katnelson, *Black Men, White Cities: Race, Politics, and Migration in the United States, 1900–1930, and Britain, 1948–68* (Chicago: University of Chicago Press, 1976), pp. 86–104.

7. Kleppner, *Chicago Divided* pp. 71, 73.

8. Ibid., p. 71.

9. Ibid., p. 84.

10. Ibid., 1985, pp.34, 74–75. Also see Royko, *Boss: J. Daley of Chicago* (New York: New American Library, 1971), pp. 101, 137–138.

11. See Jean M. Terrell, *We Want Harold. We Want Washington! The Chicago Mayoral Election of 1983* (Chicago: MJ Terrell, 1984), p. 6.

12. For an account of the post-Daley era, see Joanne Belenchia, "Latinos and Chicago Politics," in Gove and Masotti, eds., *After Daley*, pp. 118–145; and John Walton and Luis M. Salces, *The Political Organization of Chicago's Latino Communities* (Chicago: Center for Urban Affairs, Northwestern University, 1977), pp. 94, 123.

13. William Kornblum, *Blue Collar Community* (Chicago: University of Chicago Press, 1974).

14. Quoted in Ibid., p. 169.

15. Personal interview, February 16, 1988, with Ronnell Mustin, Black activist, former member of SNCC and CORE and campaign manager for Jesús García.

16. Latino Institute, *Al Filo / At The Cutting Edge: The Empowerment of Chicago's Latino Electorate* (Chicago: Latino Institute, September 1986), Appendix D, p. 34.

17. See Kleppner, *Chicago Divided*; and Michael Preston, "Black Politics in the Post-Daley Era," in Gove and Masotti, *After Daley*, pp. 88–117.

18. Kleppner, *Chicago Divided*, pp. 146–149.

19. Mustin interview. Personal interview with Jesús García on July 22, 1991. Rudy Lozano's political life was cut short, however, by an assassin's bullet during a time when he was organizing workers at the Del Rey Tortillería.

20. Calculated from figures obtained in David K. Fremon, *Chicago Politics Ward by Ward* (Bloomington: Indiana University Press, 1988).

21. Ibid.; Midwest Voter Registration Education Project, "Special Report: Chicago Mayoral Election, April 1985."

22. Many believed the gains were too few and too slow. See Nena Torres, "The Commission on Latino Affairs: A Case Study of Community Empowerment," in Pierre Clavel and Wim Wiewel, eds., *Harold Washington and the Neighborhoods: Progressive City Government in Chicago, 1983–1987* (New Brunswick, N.J.: Rutgers University Press, 1991), pp. 165–187.

23. The plaintiffs were a group of nine Black voters, six Latino voters, and members of a Black organization called the Political Action Conference of the City of Chicago. Representing the Latino plaintiffs were lawyers from the Mexican American Legal Defense and Education Fund

(MALDEF). Defendants in the case included Mayor Jane Byrne, the City Council, and the Board of Election Commissioners. The lawsuit was preceded by a successful challenge against gerrymandering of state legislative districts, making way for the election of a Latino State Representative.

24. Latino Institute, *Latino Perspectives for 1990: New Numbers New Leverage*. (Chicago: Latino Institute, 1987), p. 3.

25. Mustin interview; Robert Davis and Manuel Galván, "50 Candidates Line Up for 7 Aldermanic Posts," *Chicago Tribune*, January 19, 1986, sec. 3, p. 3.

26. Personal interview with Juan Soliz, December 1987; Jorge Casuso and Ben Joravsky, "Party of Juan," in *Reader, Chicago's Free Weekly Friday*, April 24, 1987, vol. 16, no. 30, p. 18. The other two candidates were Virginia Martínez, a local attorney and former MALDEF director, and Phil Coronado, described as a "political unknown." Davis and Galván.

27. Gary Rivlin, "How Did This Guy Get to Be an Alderman?" in *Reader*, Friday, May 16, 1986, vol. 15, no. 33, pp. 30, 34, 42.

28. Vernon Jarrett, "Why Gutiérrez Scares Eddie," *Chicago Tribune*, April 5, 1986, p. 35.

29. "For Carter, Gutiérrez," *Chicago Tribune*, April 25, 1986, sec. 1, p. 22. Local commentators such as Tom Fitzpatrick and Vernon Jarrett wrote a number of feature articles.

30. Katherine A. Schmidt, "Disagreement over Hispanic Voting Bloc," *Lawndale News*, May 4, 1986, p. 1.

31. Ibid.

32. Board of Elections, Final Cumulative Reports. Municipal Primary and Aldermanic Election, Chicago, Illinois, Cook County, Tuesday, February 24, 1987, p. 5; and Municipal General—Supplementary Aldermanic Election, Chicago, Illinois, Cook County, Tuesday, April 7, 1987, p. 5. Independent Tom Hynes dropped out just a few days before the general race.

33. Jean Latz Griffin and Manuel Galván, "Hispanics Sided with Mayor," *Chicago Tribune*, February 25, 1987, pp. 8, 9.

34. "10 Aldermanic Races Hold Key," *Chicago Sun Times*, February 15, 1987, p. 10.

35. Board of Elections, February 24, 1987.

36. Tom Gibbons, "Hispanics Vow to Unite for Reform," *Chicago Sun Times*, November 30, 1987, p. 7; and Jorge Casuso, "Hispanic Bloc Gives Credit to Washington," *Chicago Tribune*, November 30, 1987, sec. 1, p. 5.

37. María de los Angeles Torres, "Latino Politics: The Focus on Foreign Policy," *Nation*, July 16, 1988, pp. 59–61.

38. Rakove, in his classic analysis of the Machine, said that "the time will come when Latino politicians of demonstrated political acumen will be taken into the party leadership, granted power and prerogatives, and utilized to advance the interests of a Black-Latino, white-ethnic Machine, as well as their own aspirations and interests." Rakove did not anticipate Harold Washington but may have anticipated Luis Gutiérrez. Rakove, *Don't Make No Waves*, p. 284.

39. Personal interview with Lidia Bracamonte, August 15, 1990.

40. Richard Santillán, "The Latino Community in State and Congressional Redistricting: 1961–1985," in F. Chris García, ed., *Latinos and the Political System* (Notre Dame, Ind.: Notre Dame University Press, 1988), pp. 328–348.

41. Ibid.

42. Luis M. Salces and Peter W. Colby, "Mañana Will Be Better: Spanish-American Politics in Chicago," in García, ed., *Latinos and the Political System*, pp. 195–200.

43. Félix M. Padilla, *Latino Ethnic Consciousness* (Notre Dame, Ind.: University of Notre Dame Press, 1985).

44. Salces and Colby, "Mañana Will Be Better"; Rakove, *Don't Make No Waves*. See also note 38, above.

45. Increasing levels of participation by Latinos in the formal political system, even by grass-roots activists, do not necessarily signal the decrease of "confrontational" politics. We need only to observe the Environmental and Economic Justice Movement to note that there are still groups of activists who are engaged in another form of political activity. See, for example, Teresa Cór-dova, José T. Bravo, Jean Gauna, Richard Moore and Rubén Solis, "Building Networks to Tackle Global Restructuring: The Environmental and Economic Justice Movement," in John Betancur and Doug Gills, eds., *Urban Challenges for Blacks and Latinos in the 1990s* (Newbury Park, Calif.: Sage Press, forthcoming); Teresa Córdova, "Grassroots Mobilizations by Chicanas in the Environ-mental and Economic Justice Movement," *Journal of Chicana/Latina Studies* 1, no. 1: 31–55; Robert Bullard, ed., *Confronting Environmental Racism: Voices from the Grassroots* (Boston: South End Press, 1993).

Three

Gendered Citizenship

*Mexican American Women and Grassroots Activism
in East Los Angeles, 1986–1992*

Mary Pardo

> *Más de 600 residentes del Este de Los Angeles desfilaron anoche con
> cirios encendidos y pañuelos blancos . . . en nueva protesta contra la
> construcción de una cárcel estatal en el distrito de Boyle Heights. . . .
> en la marcha de anoche, 450 serían madres de familia supuestamente
> agobiadas por el peligro que representa para sus hijos . . .*[1]

Every Monday evening during the summer months of 1986 and
1987, from 500 to 3,000 people carrying bilingual placards pro-
claiming "No Prison in ELA" ["No Carcel en East L.A."] marched
on the Olympic Street bridge that links downtown Los Angeles with Eastside
Los Angeles. A broad-based community group, "The Coalition Against the
Prison," eventually defeated the first state prison proposed for construction in
a densely populated urban center. Symbolic of the legacy of "dumping" un-
wanted projects on Eastside Los Angeles, the community victory marked the
culmination of eight years of community mobilization and illustrated the power
of grassroots activism in working-class communities as well as the significance
of women's participation.

In conjunction with weekly demonstrations in Eastside Los Angeles, a
group of 200 women, heads covered with symbolic white scarves, traveled on
chartered buses to demonstrate on the steps of the California state capitol. The
surprised looks of the legislators who passed the women on the capitol steps
revealed the gendered dimensions of politics at the grassroots, the stereotypical images of women of Mexican origin, and the often narrow ways in which

politics is conceptualized.[2] The political demonstration by Mexican American women, members of a group called "Mothers of East Los Angeles," illustrated that people enter politics as "gendered," not as "generic" citizens.

Gendered politics, in fact, was evident from the very beginning of the protests, when an elected official, Assemblywoman Gloria Molina, first voiced opposition to the prison project. Molina, considered an aggressive, relatively independent community advocate and an outsider from most of the "old boys' network" of the Democratic Party, astutely turned to grassroots mobilization.[3] In the process, she strengthened her base of support as preexisting community networks, especially among women, became politicized.[4]

Although Mexican American women have been prominent actors at the grassroots level, their activism has seldom been documented. Dominant definitions of political participation have failed to address the ways in which gender and ethnicity shape political activism. Indeed, predictions by "experts" attribute the low formal political participation of Mexican Americans to a set of cultural "retardants," including primary family ties, fatalism, religious tradition, and mother country attachment.[5] The core activists in the "Mothers of East Los Angeles" [MELA] may appear to fit this description: all the women live in a low-income community, identify themselves as active Catholics, claim an ethnic identity, and range in age from forty to sixty years. Only a few have attained education beyond high school. However, these women fail to conform to the predicted political apathy. Instead, they have transformed social identity—ethnic identity, class identity, and gender identity—into a catalyst as well as a basis for activism. In mobilizing their existing social networks, they transformed themselves as well.[6]

Using the term "gendered citizenship" redirects focus on how gender, along with ethnicity and class, *conditions* political participation, especially at the grassroots level. Unlike electoral politics, grassroots activism occurs at a juncture between larger institutional politics and family networks, a place where people sustain and renew community life. Women within families often take on the work of creating the social networks that create community, becoming activated as they meet the social responsibilities "traditionally" assigned them.[7] In fact, the hotly debated "quality of life" issues—affordable housing, toxic dumping, and community safety—are typically "women's" concerns. In grassroots politics, gender responsibilities often converge with civic responsibility.

The siting of undesirable public projects is predicated on the assumption that poor working-class ethnic communities will be less likely to mobilize meaningful opposition.[8] According to a "personality profile" commissioned by the state of California, "older people, people with a high school education or less, are least likely to oppose" undesirable facilities such as waste incinerators. In California, three out of five African Americans and Latinos live near toxic waste sites, and three of the five largest hazardous waste landfills are in communities with at least 80 percent minority population.[9]

In 1985, Republican Governor George Deukmejian anticipated little community opposition to his decision to place the 1,450-inmate institution in Eastside Los Angeles. Violating convention, the state bid on an expensive parcel of industrially zoned land without compiling an environmental impact report or providing a public community hearing. Shortly after the public announcement of the proposed prison, Eastside merchants and professionals, including Frank Villalobos, an urban planner, and Steve Kasten, formed a group called the "Coalition Against the Prison." They made concerted appeals to the Department of Corrections.

The state's violation of procedures and disregard for public information meant the only way to stop the process was to disrupt it. Within a few months, a group emerged representing community interests with different resources: moral authority and legitimation from the Catholic Church, invaluable research skills and political contacts from a few middle-class professionals, financial support from neighborhood merchants, and thousands of committed parishioners led by the "Mothers of East Los Angeles."

While many other community members made tremendous contributions, I sought the women's point of view about political activism in order to make visible the often ignored "gendered" dimension of an illustrative case of grassroots politics in a working-class Latino community. In order to tell about the mobilization against the prison from the vantage point of the women, I asked three questions: How did women begin their involvement? What strategies did they use? What theories and perceptions of their activism did women hold? That is, how did they see the relationship between their activism and the "private sphere" of home and family? To answer these questions, I used ethnographic methods — participant observation and in-depth interviews with core activists — that emphasized practices, processes, and context rather than women's individual characteristics divorced from social networks. The research method included putting women at the center, following their social relations in contemporary conflicts and back into their preexisting community networks.[10]

For the purpose of the analysis that follows, social identity is a multidimensional process rather than a list of characteristics. Ethnic/racial, class, and gender identities are not distinct or discrete elements. One may emphasize or combine these identities differently depending on the situation. The varied expressions of social identity are creative and dynamic. Social identities are expressed in social situations and often used as strategies to accomplish political objectives: to promote group unity, legitimate "moral" authority, confront the opposition, or redefine the state's definition of the "common good."[11]

When women activists accounted for their community work as an extension of family relationships, as "wives," "mothers," "sisters," and "daughters," I called these expressions of gender identity. Gender identity of Mexican American women is not "generic," but specified by class, community, and ethnicity. In East Los Angeles, as in almost all major U.S. cities, ethnicity and class often converge with the stratification of place. Segregated neighborhoods not only reflect inequality; they also help to organize it. Women who live in low-income, ethnically segregated neighborhoods often find ethnic identity a meaningful base of organization.[12] In short, I understand social identity—ethnic, class, and gender identity—as a network of social relationships rather than a rigid and unchanging entity. The remainder of the essay is divided into three parts. First, I describe the prison controversy and the mass protests by Eastside residents. Next follows an overview of women's accounts of how they became activated in the conflict and the strategies and networks they used to express their opposition. I conclude by discussing the outcomes of their activism and how this case underscores the need for more inclusive accounts of political participation.

THE PROPOSED STATE PRISON: A SYMBOL OF SOCIAL INJUSTICE

The Eastside opposition against the proposed construction of the state prison represents a long, complex, and continuing battle which began in March of 1985 when the California State Department of Corrections (DOC) publicly announced the site, a ten-minute walk from Boyle Heights, for the first state prison in Los Angeles County.[13] Boyle Heights, the Eastside neighborhood where opposition to the prison originated, is a heterogeneous community of approximately 89,000—twice the density of the City of Los Angeles. According to the 1980 U.S. Census, residents are primarily low-income ($12,767 median family income), blue-collar workers, and renters, and more than half of the population is foreign born.[14] Within community boundaries are two large public housing projects often recognized as the territory of dozens of gangs and five major freeways whose construction uprooted more than 10,000 residents and now criss-cross over 12 percent of the community land space. At the same time, it is an "ethnic heartland" and home where stable Mexican American families have raised and educated their children, many of whom have completed college, moved to suburbs adjacent to Eastside Los Angeles, and return regularly for family celebrations.

A casual observer would be struck by the internal differentiation in the neighborhoods of Eastside Los Angeles; certain blocks which have particular reputations for being quiet, clean, and well kept may be adjacent to blocks considered untended, noisy, and dangerous. Most media coverage, blind to the stable community elements, highlight drive-by gang shootings, poverty, and disorganization. On two occasions I heard journalists—one from West Los Angeles and another from Great Britain's BBC—express concern for personal safety and hesitation at driving out to Boyle Heights for interviews with the members of MELA. After seeing the community, they expressed surprise that, in contrast to news accounts, "it was not as bad as they had expected." Women adamantly countered the media image of the Eastside as crime-ridden and dominated by gangs and deviants. To accept a degraded image of the Eastside would justify placement of one more negative project in its boundaries. Historian Rudy Acuña aptly calls the pattern of degrading a community image and dumping negative projects on it "the arrogance of power."[15]

Such arrogance was unmasked in the prison issue. The final decision to place the county's first state prison in East Los Angeles occurred after several middle-class communities—the Santa Clarita Valley and the cities of San Gabriel and Lancaster—opposed its placement within their boundaries. The DOC argued that the site was more suitable than the other sites for two reasons: the proximity of the site to the courts in downtown Los Angeles and the fact that the majority of state prisoners come from Los Angeles County. Assuming that the prisoners' families lived in the Eastside area, the DOC argued that they could easily continue communicating with family members.[16]

California State Assemblywoman Gloria Molina vehemently opposed the Eastside site, arguing that it was too close to the long-established, densely populated Boyle Heights neighborhood and within two miles of thirty-four schools. She also pointed out that 75 percent of the county's prison population already resided in the five prisons located in her district; thus, another prison would add to the overconcentration of penal facilities in the East Los Angeles area. Governor Deukmejian and the DOC representatives completely disregarded Molina's objections. Shortly after the governor and the DOC dismissed Assemblywoman Molina's objections, she explored the possibility of grassroots mobilization.[17] The chances of success were seen as slim for the politically powerless Fifty-Sixth Assembly District, a district populated by poor Mexican immigrants unlikely to raise opposition to state projects.

In September 1985 the Senate passed the bill with no senator voting against it and sent it to the Assembly for an apparent endorsement. Opposition to the prison faced incredible odds at winning support. News editorials began appearing on a regular basis, with the *Los Angeles Times* initially supporting the Eastside site. One radio editorial belittled the mobilization efforts, stating, "Gloria Molina likens herself to a drum major in a march against the East L.A. Prison. Few have fallen in line behind her." The *Los Angeles Herald Examiner* questioned the fairness of the selection, and *La Opinión*, a Spanish-language newspaper, and the local neighborhood papers opposed it. The United Neighborhood Organization (UNO), a parish-based, Alinsky-inspired community group, felt the issue was unwinnable and declined to join the coalition efforts. Later, as the community mobilization gathered momentum and broad support, the *Los Angeles Times* began changing its position, as did UNO.[18]

In spring 1986 after much pressure from the Fifty-Sixth Assembly District office and the community, the DOC agreed to hold the first well-announced public meeting. Over 700 people attended the meeting held at the proposed prison site, a former depot and maintenance center for Crown Coach buses. From this moment on, the community mobilized, and according to James Vigil, Jr., of Molina's staff, the "tables turned and the community began calling the political office regarding hearings and meetings."[19]

By summer 1986 the community, now well aware of the prison site proposal and organized under an umbrella group called the "Coalition Against the Prison," began weekly protest marches on Monday evenings. The coalition included merchants, local political representatives, community members, and the "Mothers of East Los Angeles" (MELA), which began with a loosely knit group of over 400 Mexican American women. MELA members comprised the majority of the representatives who traveled to speak at Senate hearings in Sacramento.

WOMEN AND COMMUNITY MOBILIZATION

The mobilization efforts began with informing *preexisting networks* of people in the community. Different segments of the community, including merchants, professionals, extended family members who no longer lived in Boyle Heights, and Catholic parishioners, contributed their resources.

The merchants and professionals in the community had been meeting regularly as a group for years, taking issue with neighborhood developments they deemed negative. In 1984 they stopped the building of a junkyard across the street from a Lincoln Heights school for the mentally retarded. In August 1985 the business council brought 200 people in to testify at hearings at which the Rapid Transit District was proposing to cut back on bus service to East Los Angeles. According to one central member of the group, landscape architect Frank Villalobos, the business group was already primed for the imminent conflict over the prison.

Working in conjunction with Assemblywoman Molina, the business group made several trips to Sacramento to lobby and testify against the prison. Finally, Molina, well known as a forceful advocate for Latinas and the community, asked Frank Villalobos why there were no women traveling to Sacramento to speak against the prison. As he put it, "I was getting some heat from her because no women were going up there." On the other hand, Villalobos noted: "The Senators . . . didn't even acknowledge that we existed. They kept calling it the 'downtown' site, and they argued that there was no opposition in the community. So, I told Father Moretta, what we have to do is demonstrate that there is a link between the Boyle Heights community and the prison."[20]

The next junction illustrates how perceptions of gender-specific behavior set in motion a sequence of events that brought women into the political limelight. Father Moretta, the Italian American pastor at Resurrection Parish, decided to ask all the women to meet after mass. He told them about the prison site and called for their support. Asked about his rationale for selecting the women, he replied: "I felt so strongly about the issue, and I knew in my heart what a terrible offense this was to the people. So, I was afraid that once we got into a demonstration situation we had to be very careful. I thought the women would be cooler and calmer than the men."[21] Father Moretta named the group "Mothers of East Los Angeles" and selected its president and spokeswoman. Thus bolstered by the authority of the Church and by "a mother's responsibility to protect her children," the women of Resurrection parish entered the battle. In a short time the battle would take them far beyond their church-bound origins.

Father Moretta asked twenty-one other priests in the area to announce the many hearings and demonstrations from the pulpit that helped to mobilize hundreds of people. Clearly, the Catholic Church served as a primary catalyst in disseminating information through parish bulletins. But not all women became involved through the church. Some took their first step into the eight-year struggle by responding to local information sources — neighbors, the local newspaper, and letters from Assemblywoman Gloria Molina's office.

Juana Gutiérrez, active in the neighborhood for many years, found out about the group from Assemblywoman Molina's field representative, Martha Molina-Aviles. Molina-Aviles (no relation to Gloria Molina) grew up in Boyle Heights and used her intimate knowledge of the community to forge strong links among the women in MELA and other members of the coalition and the assembly office. In turn, Juana began to link up her previously established community networks, including local political offices, the Neighborhood Watch, and the local parishioners. Her husband, Ricardo, and a group of five women collected 900 signatures on petitions that Gloria Molina took to Sacramento to illustrate community opposition to the prison.[22]

Another core activist, a senior citizen and mother of two sons in their thirties, read local newspaper articles about the demonstrations. She recalls her first reaction to the article and photograph of Mexican women with white scarves: "I saw a picture of the women with the scarves and I wondered, who are these ladies? I thought they were nuns! Then, I read that they wanted help in the demonstrations on the bridge. When I went, I told them that I want to help in any way I can because some of them don't know how to be heard and I want them to learn how to defend themselves and not get this prison."[23] The woman, who had been active in the PTA and parish and community clubs, stressed the need to assume responsibility for those less able to defend themselves and the community.

Information also traveled by word of mouth through extended family networks and in neighborhood shopping areas. One MELA activist, asked how she encouraged more people to participate, reminded me that she comes from a large family born and raised in Boyle Heights: "All my six sisters came to the marches with my mom and my brother. I have a sister who lives in Commerce, another one in Monterey Park, one in Hacienda Heights, and two sisters that live here in Eastside L.A. Then, my sisters started bringing their daughters to the marches."[24] Although some of her family members no longer lived in Boyle Heights, they commuted weekly to the Eastside from their suburban communities to attend church and visit their parents. They added the demonstrations to their agenda.

These preexisting networks formed the core of the first groups who participated in the marches. After that, they took the marches through the Estrada Courts Housing Project, chanting as they made their way through the small walkways separating the hundreds of housing units. One women tells of the many times people didn't fully understand what the protests were about, although they gained some people as they marched through the housing projects. The negative responses came from people not "really understanding" and thinking they were "just a bunch of *viejas* [old women or slang for women in general] making a bunch of racket in the street." She recalls one woman yelling back at the marchers, telling them to "shut up and get out of here." She tells about the incident with energy: "One day, that same woman brought her kids to enroll in school at Resurrection. She talked to me and said, 'I remember that day you yelling for us and I told you to shut up. Now that I see what you are going through and how things are getting really serious, I am sorry.'"[25] An important aspect of the incident was the fact that the woman who had turned her back on the rally had to confront a member of MELA in parish school activities. Much like a net drawing in other people, the parish networks served to widen the basis for participation.

Given the powerful symbolic ethnic reference Eastside Los Angeles holds for the larger Mexican American community, Chicano student groups began joining the marches. *La Gente,* a UCLA-sponsored student newspaper, ran an extensive article on the issue.[26] Several of the women in MELA had children or grandchildren attending UCLA. Mexican Americans also joined as individuals or as representatives of state and national Latino organizations such as the Mexican American Political Association (MAPA), the League of United Latin American Citizens (LULAC), and the Mexican American Education Commission. Thus, a combination of family and ethnic ties formed the social networks for political action.

Motherhood as an Oppositional Identity

The MELA activists had strong preexisting associations and a civic consciousness historically rooted in Boyle Heights. In general, the women in MELA were longtime residents of East Los Angeles; some were bilingual and had lived in the community for over thirty years. All had been active in parish-sponsored groups and activities; some had experience working in community-based groups arising from schools, neighborhood watch associations, and labor support groups. In short, women entered into the struggle both as good Catholics and as "good citizens" angered by yet another affront to the quality of life on the Eastside. Given the organizational name "Mothers of East L.A.," however, it is the significance of gender identity and of "motherhood" that rings out most clearly.

Each of the core activists had a history of working with groups arising out of the responsibilities usually assumed by "mothers"—the education of children and the safety of the surrounding community. From these groups they gained valuable experiences and networks that facilitated the formation of "Mothers of East Los Angeles." In the process, the women transformed the definition of "mother" to include militant political opposition to state-proposed projects they saw as adverse to the quality of life in the community. Explaining how she discovered the issue, Aurora Castillo said, "You know if one of your children's safety is jeopardized, the mother turns into a lioness. That's why Father John got the mothers. We have to have a well-organized, strong group of mothers to protect the community and oppose things that are detrimental to us. You know the governor is in the wrong and the mothers are in the right. After all, the mothers have to be right. Mothers are for the children's interest, not for self-interest; the governor is for his own political interest." [27]

Juana Gutiérrez explained her activism by linking family, community, and ethnic identity: "As a mother and a resident of East L.A., I shall continue fighting tirelessly, so we will be respected. And, I will do this with much affection for my community. And, I say "my community" because I am part of it. I love my *raza* [people] as part of my family; and if God allows, I will keep on fighting against all the governors that want to take advantage of us." [28] Like the other activists, she clearly used motherhood and family as metaphors for civic responsibility and action. By doing so, she expanded her responsibilities and legitimized militant opposition to projects she judged to be detrimental to the community.[29]

Women not only redefined understandings of "motherhood" to include social and political activism; they also manipulated the boundaries of "mother" to include women who are not biological mothers. At one meeting a young Latina expressed her solidarity with the group. Almost apologetically, she qualified herself as a "resident," not a "mother," of East Los Angeles. Erlinda Robles replied, "When you are fighting for a better life for children and 'doing' for them, isn't that what mothers do? So you don't have to have children to be a mother."[30]

The women's accounts of how they discovered the prison issue illustrate that gender identity and civic responsibilities may blend together, as do the parish and community boundaries. The notion of civic responsibility was strengthened by the connections. Many studies argue that working-class women activists seldom opt to separate themselves from men and their families. In this particular struggle for community quality of life, they were fighting for the family unit and thus were not competitive with men. Indeed, they transformed organizing experiences and social networks arising from gender-related responsibilities into political resources.

"SELF-SACRIFICING" MOTHERS

References to the "intersection" of race, class, and gender fail to capture the fluidity and dynamic nature of the women's interpretations and actions. Social identity may be interpreted and used in numerous fashions; it is not predetermined. Moreover, it may be transformed as a result of political activity. The women of MELA crafted their identities as mothers to confront the state-sponsored project; in the process, they became visible political actors. The experience transformed the women's image of "humble mothers" into one of well-respected community activists.

Father Moretta named the group "Mothers of East Los Angeles" and asked them to wear white *mantillas* for practical reasons. He believed the name and the visual image the women would present could help generate empathy and support for the cause. After viewing the film "The Official Story," about the courageous Argentine women who demonstrated for the return of their children—*desaparecidos* (the disappeared)—during Argentina's repressive right-wing military dictatorship, he took the name "Las Madres de la Plaza de Mayo" and changed it to "Mothers of East Los Angeles." Taking the example of the

Argentine women who wore *mantillas*, Father Moretta bought yards of white cotton cloth and had them cut into scarf-sized squares for the women to wear during demonstrations.

The hundreds of Mexican American women wearing white scarves at the demonstrations achieved the desired effect. As soon as the media saw the women, they asked who they were and what they were all about. The media's delight with the visual appeal of "ethnic" women wearing scarves seemed to be simultaneously a curiosity as well as a confirmation of the way they perceived the women of East Los Angeles. Some of the women commented that wearing the scarves made them look like "poor homebodies." Juana Gutiérrez laughingly said that "el padre Moretta dijo que éramos unas madres muy abnegadas" [Father Moretta said we were the self-sacrificing mothers].[31]

The women faithfully wore the scarves at the beginning of the mobilization efforts. As the anti-prison campaign wore on for years, the number of women wearing scarves around the head and tied under the chin declined significantly. In respect for Father Moretta's request, they had agreed to wear them. Gradually they began resisting them. Some would say it was "too hot" or they "forgot them." One of the women described her surprise at the "pieces of white rag" the pastor called a *mantilla*, a word that actually means lace scarf.[32]

At subsequent demonstrations, protestors wore scarves in a variety of ways. Some of the young men and women twisted them and wore them tied across their foreheads as headbands. Others wore them around their necks or tied around their upper arms. One woman agreed that the scarves did attract media attention. Another wore the scarf but interpreted the white scarf as a sign that they were "protesting, but protesting peacefully." For the women, the scarves held a meaning different from the one intended by Father Moretta. Perhaps symbols of struggle cannot be so easily transported across national and cultural boundaries.

Voices Raised in Protest

The political work of the MELA core activists generated personal changes in the activists themselves. The core activists became recognized as "grassroots community leaders," developing a public presence — the topic of many newspaper interviews and popular magazine articles requiring them to speak at rallies and before television cameras. The core activists typically tell stories illustrating personal change and a new sense of entitlement to speak for the community. Lucy Ramos related her initial apprehensions after Father Moretta asked her to be a spokesperson: "'Oh no, I don't know what I am going to say.' I was nervous. I am surprised I didn't have a nervous breakdown then. Every time we used to get in front of the TV cameras and even interviews like this, I used to sit there and I could feel myself shaking. But as time went on, I started getting used to it."[33] Ramos noticed that this was a common experience among the MELA activists: "They were afraid to speak up and say anything. Now, with this prison issue, a lot of them have come out and come forward and given their opinions. Everybody used to be real 'quietlike,'" she said. For some core activists, speaking out was not a novel experience. As one senior citizen put it, "I am not afraid to speak because I had my club meetings and senior citizen meetings."

Learning to raise one's voice also meant insisting that Spanish be recognized as a public language. In the context of public hearings intended to allow community input and participation, language turned into a focus of protest, an act of resistance, and a critique of the state's disregard for non-English-speaking citizens. At one public hearing held in the State Building auditorium and filled beyond capacity by Eastside community members, Assemblywoman Gloria Molina approached the podium to speak against the prison project. She began to read a written statement, paused, looked from side to side, and then asked for the interpreter. There was none. She proceeded to turn back to the hearing panel, and then faced the audience and asked, "Who needs a Spanish translation of the hearing's proceedings?" The audience fell silent for a moment; no one responded. Then someone called out, "Ask that question in Spanish!" She did. About three-fourths of the audience raised their hands. She read her entire statement in Spanish and then in English, in spite of the panel's dismay at the time required for a bilingual presentation.

Although community members continued to ask for translators at all public hearings, the city seldom provided them. Some residents gave testimony in English and Spanish, demonstrating bilingual ability and unsubtle criticism of the absence of translators.

Quiet and attentive at most hearings, the women sometimes used disruptive strategies. At one demonstration about 150 women appeared at an Eastside Recreation Center where the DOC was holding a job fair for people interested in working at the proposed state prison. Rectangular tables lined the walls of the large recreation room. Representatives from the DOC stood or sat behind the tables displaying information leaflets and job announcements neatly arranged in stacks. It was raining heavily that day as the women filed in, some wearing the white scarves.

Juana Gutiérrez had a small bullhorn and led the women in chants, "No Prison in ELA; No Prison in ELA!" A DOC representative, seemingly oblivious to the passionate protesters, stood up and began speaking to the crowd about job opportunities. Then some of the MELA members started calling out remarks in response to the Department of Corrections representative's attempt to quell the demonstration: "Pues, yo no quiero trabajar en prisión!

Mejor mándame hacer pan!" [Well, I don't want to work in prison! Better have me make bread!] Another woman called out, "Yo quiero hacer pan dulce o tortillas!" [I want to make sweet bread or tortillas!] The other women began to laugh. Juana picked up the bull horn and in Spanish told the crowd to pick up the pamphlets, take them out, and throw them away. They followed her directions.

Dolores Duarte walked up to a Latino Department of Corrections representative and began talking to him. "You know you are on the wrong side of town," she said. "You have nerve to sit here in a Hispanic area and let them do that to YOUR people. You say you want to give jobs to people who don't want the prison here—your OWN people. And you support these gringos. You go along with them after the way we have been treated. You want to dump everything on us!" The representative made a feeble attempt to say that he was from San Diego where the community had willingly accepted a large prison. As she walked away, two other women standing a few feet away listening to the exchange cheered her on: "Give it to him Dolores!" The job fair ended in chaos, the intention of the demonstration achieved.

The disruptive tactics shattered the hackneyed image of docile, passive, unassertive Mexican women. At one community meeting, for example, representatives of several oil companies attempted to gain support for placement of an above-ground oil pipeline through the center of East Los Angeles. The exchange between the women in the audience and the oil representative was heated, as women alternated asking questions about the chosen route for the pipeline: "Is it going through Cielito Lindo [Reagan's ranch]?" The oil representative answered, "No." Another woman stood up and asked, "Why not place it along the coastline?" Without thinking of the implications, the representative responded, "Oh, no! If it burst, it would endanger the marine life." The woman retorted, "You value the marine life more than human beings?" His face reddened with anger, and the hearing disintegrated into angry chanting.[34] The proposal was quickly defeated.

FAMILY RELATIONS AND WOMEN'S ACTIVISM

The MELA women have become a public resource for other organizations—parent education projects, such as the Mexican American Legal Defense and Educational Fund (MALDEF), environmental groups such as Greenpeace, and local political representatives.[35] While the women have moved into the public sphere and have become "public persons," they have done so without drastically changing household relations.

The media coverage of MELA do not show the family concerns with which women have had to contend. Meeting places and demonstration times had to be planned around meeting household and family responsibilities. The children's schedules set what time the women could leave in the morning and what time they would have to return in the afternoon. As one woman observed, "If we go downtown and have a march, we can have it any time when the children are in school. But, if it is 11:30–1:30, they can't go. If it is before 8:30, they can't go." Likewise MELA's demonstrations in Sacramento represented financial and personal sacrifices. Women took their children along "because we were fighting for them and we wanted them to see what we were fighting for. We made sure they got us a motel that had a pool for the kids." Several women figured that "jealous" husbands were amenable to the women's trips because they had come to the marches and were well informed about the seriousness of the issue.[36]

Unexpectedly, the women who were active kept pace with household duties the majority of the time. Juana Gutiérrez, one of the most active leaders in the group, said she had time for all her housework: "I clean my house, I babysit for my grandchildren and other kids, and take care of my block because I am Captain of the Neighborhood Watch Program [laughing] . . . a lot of *metiche* [colloquial for someone who knows everyone's business]."

When her husband, Ricardo, was asked if Juana's activism bothered him, he responded, "No. See, we started when our kids were very young. We have always been involved with their education. To us education is the main thing. It is going to allow them to live on their own and have no one manipulate them. So it does not bother me that she goes out there and demonstrates. In fact, she tells me when she is on TV or the radio and as soon as we come in we turn on the TV and tape it." Ricardo has a conception of how the whole unit works, and it does not violate what he sees as conventional:

> The mother in a Latino community is the head of the household, and the man is the supplier . . . but the woman runs the whole show. She is the one that takes care of the kids, she is the one that goes here and there whenever something happens to the kids when they are in school. The macho image is a little different when you put it into practice. Sure, she does not do anything against my will. We always talk about it and then she goes ahead and does it. She has always been vociferous, maybe that is why we have stayed together so long.

According to Ricardo, the women do what the men have wanted to do all along: "they are carrying the flag for the family."

At critical points, grassroots community activism requires attending many meetings, phone calling, and door-to-door communications—all very labor-intensive work. In order to keep harmony in the "domestic" sphere, the core activists creatively integrated family members into their community activities. I asked Erlinda Robles how her husband, Valentín, felt about her activism, and she replied openly:

> My husband doesn't like getting involved, but he takes me because he knows I like it. Sometimes we would have two or three meetings a week. And my husband would say, "Why are you doing so much? It is really getting out of hand." But he is very supportive. Once he gets there, he enjoys it and he starts in arguing too! See, it's just that he is not used to it. He couldn't believe things happened the way that they do. He was in the Navy twenty years, and they brainwashed him that none of the politicians could do wrong. So, he has come a long way. Now he comes home and parks the car out front and asks me "Well, where are we going tonight?"

Valentín Robles, when asked about his role in MELA, stated: "I'm part of the coalition . . . all I can do is back my wife up. I can't be a Mother of East L.A. since I'm a man. They should be in control. They have started this fight. I think it's great." [37]

VICTORY

The final defeat of the proposed prison resulted from sustained political battles at several levels: mass community protests in the streets, litigation in the courts, and lobbying within the legislature. Eight years of community solidarity and sacrifice stalled the construction of the prison until 1992. The California fiscal crisis provided additional pressure on Republican Governor Pete Wilson, who finally signed Senate Bill 97, thereby eliminating the Eastside prison project and redirecting funds to expand existing prisons in other parts of the state.

However, the crucial turning point had occurred during the summer of 1986, when mass protest and trips to hearings in the state capitol created the possibility of stopping Senate Bill 904 authorizing $31 million for the initial cost of the 1,450-inmate prison. It was expected to pass the Senate easily. On July 7, 1986, MELA traveled to Sacramento on chartered buses. Hundreds of women marched with signs saying, "Our children need schools, not prisons—MELA."

As the Senate debated the issue, about 200 MELA members wearing white bandannas converged on the capitol. The strong show of community opposition to the prison had a major impact on the legislators. Hoping to discourage community presence, the governor's administrative officials tried to delay the vote until the next week. However, Democratic Senator David Roberti convinced Republican Senator Robert Presley to bring it to a vote. Senator Presley said that the environmental impact report (EIR) would be completed after the purchase of the land. MELA held up signs chiding Democratic Assemblyman Richard Polanco, a newly elected Eastside representative, for casting the vote that released the bill from the assembly committee. Passage had been all but assumed. That day the Senate reversed itself and rejected the plan to build the prison in Eastside L.A. by a four-vote margin.[38]

In order to sway the Senate, Governor Deukmejian agreed to a limited EIR to be completed before the purchase of the land. The governor was surprised when the Senate rejected the bill that it had passed 35-0 one year earlier, in 1985. Sent to a Senate Assembly conference committee, the Senate voted down the bill a second time in as many weeks. Surprised by the second defeat, the Governor had underestimated the strong lobbying efforts by Latino organizations. Democrats cast all the "no" votes; Republicans cast all the "yes" votes. Several senators who had been expected to support the measure feared antagonizing the Mexican American community.[39]

The battle then moved into the courts. Again, the presence of women at all the court hearings embodied community opposition and concern. Later, legal strategies meant fewer demonstrations and, consequently, fewer opportunities to bring large numbers of people together as had occurred two years earlier. By 1989 the Coalition Against the Prison meetings numbered only about forty to fifty people, who came to hear updates on the legal appeal of the environmental impact report. Until it was denied by the California Supreme Court in July 1992, the appeal continued to stall the prison construction.

Meanwhile, four alternative sites were identified, but Governor Wilson expressed ambivalence about changing the state's plans.[40] The eight-year battle faced a final decision when the Latino Legislative Caucus, led by Senator Art Torres, began lobbying Governor Wilson to stop the $147 million project. Capitalizing on the state budget crisis, the caucus succeeded in convincing the governor to sign the bill. The hard-won victory helped create a new political image for the Eastside.[41]

NEW COMMUNITY VOICES

MELA originated out of the prison issue, but it gradually took on an identity of its own. The women also decided to oppose a proposed toxic waste incinerator, a chemical waste treatment plant, and an oil pipeline.[42] When deciding to address other issues, opinions varied. Some felt they should concentrate on the prison issue and not "spread themselves too thin." When a local political representative informed them about the toxic waste incinerator in nearby Vernon, they decided they would fight it.

Whereas the fight against the prison engaged only the Latino community, when the women took up the fight against the toxic waste incinerator, they began linking up with other ethnic communities. Greenpeace joined in at some of the meetings and provided testimony at the hearings. They also invited MELA to other Greenpeace-supported demonstrations organized in other working-class communities. In November 1988 MELA traveled to the town of Casmalia, 150 miles north of Los Angeles, to join in a demonstration for the closing of a toxic dump site. Grassroots groups from other small California cities with large minority populations—Kettleman, McFarland, Richmond, as well as Casmalia—joined the march led by MELA.[43] These mass mobilizations bolstered the signing into law of Assembly Bill 58 (Roybal-Allard), providing all Californians with the minimum protection of an environmental impact report before the construction of hazardous waste incinerators.

The more significant result of MELA, of course, involved the politicization of hundreds of working-class Mexican American women. Core activists mobilized their social networks, established from many years of living and volunteering in the community. This mobilization, as noted, relied largely on the "traditional" gender identity of motherhood, which became transformed in order to legitimize opposition to a state prison project. As MELA became more than a single-issue group and began working with the environmental groups around the state, the women acquired a sharper sense of class and ethnic identity. Aurora Castillo told of an incident in this regard: "And do you know we have been approached by other groups? You know that Pacific Palisades group asked for our backing? But what they did, they sent their powerful lobbyist that they pay thousands of dollars to get our support against the drilling in Pacific Palisades. So what we did was tell them to send their grassroots people, not their lobbyist. We're suspicious. We don't want to talk to a high-salaried lobbyist; we are humble people. We did our own lobbying."[44]

Outraged by the proposed prison, the women of MELA have become empowered to speak out publicly on behalf of their community. Women such as Juana Gutiérrez, a forceful speaker, have taken leading positions as spokespeople on Eastside community issues. Interestingly, Gutiérrez distinguishes her advocacy for social justice and civil rights from being "political." As she puts it, "I don't consider myself political. I'm just someone looking out for the community, for the youth . . . on the side of justice."[45]

In 1990, Mothers of East Los Angeles divided into two groups, roughly along parish lines. Both groups continued to advocate for community well-being and to inspire and affirm other women's community activism. Juana

Gutiérrez founded Madres de Este Los Angeles, Santa Isabel (MELA-SI), a nonprofit community-based organization. The group developed a community partnership with a private corporation and the Metropolitan Water District. By promoting a water conservation project, the group generated jobs and funds that are reinvested in the community through a variety of neighborhood programs, including lead abatement and immunization awareness, scholarships for youth, and graffiti removal. In 1996 Elsa López, who is Juana's daughter and a member of MELA-SI, attended a water conservation conference and met representatives from the South African Ministry of Water Affairs and Forestry. In South Africa as in Southern California, water is a scarce resource and water management is a national priority. The representatives invited her to Johannesburg, South Africa, to share her community organizing experiences. During her 19-day trip she shared her experiences with women and men wishing to develop a community-based water conservation project similar to the one developed by MELA-SI. Impressed by Elsa's emphasis on the importance of women's activism, the South African women named their group Mothers of Hermanus (a township in South Africa).[46]

What analytical lessons can be drawn from the experience of MELA? The existence and activities of the Mothers of East Los Angeles attest to the dynamic nature of gender, class, and ethnic identities. The story of MELA reveals, on the one hand, how individuals and groups can transform a seemingly "traditional" role such as "mother." On the other hand, it illustrates how such a role may also become a social agent, drawing members of the community into the "political" arena. How women see their circumstances, how they legitimize and redefine issues as they become involved, is essential to understanding community activism.[47] This must become part of our analysis of the "political."

All too often women of color "disappear" in conventional social science frameworks of political participation. The disappearance occurs because the details of women's leadership, commonly based in the face-to-face interaction that takes place in households and communities, seldom fit into existing conceptual frameworks. Leaving out women and a gendered analysis inclusive of ethnicity and race represents more than simply an oversight; "it is a conceptual practice of power."[48] The social science practice of dismissing local and particular activities because they fail to conform or fit into abstract grand theories perpetuates a patriarchal bias that erases gender, ethnicity/race, and class. In short, social science concepts can obscure more than they reveal about urban politics. At the turn of the twentieth century, threats to the quality of life in working-class Latina/o communities demand that activists and those who write about activism develop a keen appraisal of what inspires successful grassroots organizing and active citizenship, including the "gendered" connections between everyday life, citizenship, and political participation.[49]

NOTES

Portions of the data in this chapter also appear in "Mexican American Grassroots Community Activists: Mothers of East Los Angeles," *Frontiers* 11 (Spring 1990): 1–7.

1. Carlos A. González, "Protestan contra prisión en ELA," *La Opinión*, August 5, 1986, p. 1.

2. Roberto Rodríguez, "ELA Residents Halt Prison Bill," *Montebello Comet*, August 21, 1986, p. 1. For a review of how anthropology has depicted Mexican Americans as "fatalistic" but "cheerful" victims of their own backward "traditional" culture, see Shirley Achor, *Mexican Americans in a Dallas Barrio* (Tucson: University of Arizona Press, 1978). For recent alternative research on women of Mexican origin, see the work of Chicana scholars Pat Zavella, *Women's Work & Chicano Families* (Ithaca, N.Y.: Cornell University Press, 1987); Vicki Ruiz, *Cannery Women, Cannery Lives, Mexican Women, Unionization and the California Food Processing Industry 1930–1950* (Albuquerque: University of New Mexico Press, 1987); and Margarita Melville, ed., *Mexicans at Work in the United States* (Houston: University of Houston, 1988).

3. For the first profile of Latina officeholders in the United States and an analysis of the relationship between electoral and community politics, see Paule Cruz Takash, "Breaking Barriers to Representation: Chicana/Latina Elected Officials in California." *Urban Anthropology* 22, nos. 3–4 (1993): 325–360.

4. Gloria Molina served as the first Mexican American California Assemblywoman (56th District) from 1982 to 1987, the first Mexican American woman Los Angeles City Council member from 1987 to 1991, and since April of 1991 has served as the first Mexican American and the first woman Los Angeles County supervisor for the First L.A. County Supervisorial District, created as a result of the court-ordered L.A. County redistricting and special elections. Members of MELA staunchly supported her campaign efforts in each election. See Rudy Acuña, "Behind the Vote for a New Prison Is East L.A.," *Los Angeles Herald Examiner*, July 8, 1986. Also see Rudy Acuña, "The Coming Battle in the New Latino District," *Los Angeles Herald Examiner*, October 31, 1986.

5. John García and R. de la Garza, "Mobilizing the Mexican Immigrant: The Role of Mexican American Organizations," *Western Political Quarterly* 38, no. 4 (December 1985): 551–564.

6. William Flores, "Mujeres en huelga: Cultural Citizenship and Gender Empowerment in a Cannery Strike." *HJSR* (1996): 57–81.

7. Harry C. Boyte, *Common Wealth* (New York: Free Press, 1989); Robert Fisher and Joseph Kling, "Community Mobilization, Prospects for the Future," *Urban Affairs Quarterly* 25, no. 2 (December 1989): 200–211; Bettina Aptheker, *Tapestries of Life: Women's Work, Women's Consciousness, and the Meaning of Daily Experience* (Amherst: University of Massachusetts Press, 1989).

8. Cerrell Associates, Inc., "Political Difficulties Facing Waste to Energy Conversion Plant Siting," report prepared for California Waste Management Board, State of California, Los Angeles, 1984.

9. Jesús Sánchez, "The Environment: Whose Movement?" *California Tomorrow* 3, nos. 3 & 4 (Fall 1988): 13. Also see Rudy Acuña, *A Community Under Siege* (Los Angeles: Chicano Studies Research Center Publications, UCLA, 1984). The book and its title capture the sentiments and the history of a community that bears an unfair burden of city projects deemed undesirable by all residents.

10. This essay draws on data from more than twenty audiotaped life stories of women activists, focused interviews with other key informants, and coded field notes from 2½ years of participant observation from December 1987 to June 1990, and news media accounts.

11. Teresa de Lauretis, "Feminist Studies/Critical Studies: Issues, Terms and Contexts," in Lauretis, ed., *Feminist Studies/Critical Studies* (Bloomington: Indiana University Press, 1986), pp. 1–19.

12. See Don Parson, "The Development of Redevelopment: Public Housing and Urban Renewal in Los Angeles," *International Journal of Urban and Regional Research* 6, no. 4 (December 1982): 392–413; John Logan, "The Stratification of Place," *American Journal of Sociology* 84 (1978): 404–414. Also see Cheryl Gilkes, "Holding Back the Ocean with a Broom," *The Black Woman* (Beverly Hills: Sage Publications, 1980).

13. Richard Connell, "Downtown Prison Site Selected," *Los Angeles Times*, March 21, 1985. The prison was to house 1,450 inmates. Opponents argued that half of the state's prisons were housing more than the overcapacity estimate of 190 percent on which an environmental impact report was based. Later, this fact became the basis for a Superior Court decision to uphold a court order requiring a new EIR based on the "worst-case" level before prison construction could begin. See Michael Cárdenas, "Community Scores Big in Anti-Prison Battle," *Belvedere Citizen*, August 1, 1990, p. 1.

14. Based on 1980 U.S. Census Data. UCLA Ethnic Studies Center, *Ethnic Groups in Los Angeles: Quality of Life Indicators*, University of California, Los Angeles, 1987. The percentage of homeowner-occupied units may vary from 3 percent to 75 percent from block to block, according to Raul Escobedo in Boyle Heights Community Plan, Department of City Planning, Los Angeles, 1979.

15. See Rudy Acuña, "Another Prison? No Rewards for Latino Unity," *Los Angeles Herald Examiner*, September 11, 1986. Gerald Suttles notes that "community images" may complement or denigrate the places they represent. As in the Eastside case, the community image may then become contested given different political purposes. Gerald D. Suttles, *The Social Construction of Communities* (Chicago: University of Chicago Press, 1972).

16. Roxanne Arnold and M. Seiler, "State Prison, A Birthday Gift They'd Like to Pass," *Los Angeles Times*, February 17, 1984; and Rodney J. Blonien, "The Los Angeles Crown Coach Prison Site—A Superior Location," *Americas 2001*, March 1986, p. 2.

17. Gloria Molina, "Response to Department of Corrections from Assemblywoman Gloria Molina," *Americas 2001*, March 1986, p. 6.

18. "Dawdling on the Prison," editorial, *Los Angeles Times*, January 27, 1986; "The Great Prison Holdup," editorial, *Los Angeles Times*, April 18, 1986; "Prison Urgency," editorial, *Los Angeles Times*, August 22, 1986; "Corrections vs. Molina," editorial, KNX Radio, March 15, 1986; Carolina Serna, "Eastside Residents Oppose Prison," *La Gente* (UCLA Student Newspaper) 17, no. 1 (October 1986): 5. For Alinsky's views on community organizing, see Saul Alinksy, *Reveille for Radicals* (New York: Vintage Books, 1969).

19. James Vigil, Jr., field representative for Assemblywoman Gloria Molina (1984–1986), personal interview, Whittier, Calif., September 27, 1989.

20. Frank Villalobos, personal interview, Los Angeles, May 2, 1989.

21. Father John Moretta, Resurrection Parish, personal interview, Boyle Heights, Eastside Los Angeles, May 24, 1989.

22. Juana Gutiérrez, born and raised in the Mexican state of Zacatecas, has lived in Boyle Heights for over thirty years. She stated that she has always been outspoken. In 1978 her husband, Ricardo, served on the first steering committee of the United Neighborhoods Organization (UNO). Juana Gutiérrez, personal interview, Boyle Heights, Eastside Los Angeles, January 15, 1988.

23. Anonymous, member of MELA, personal interview, Los Angeles, August 14, 1988.

24. Anonymous, member of MELA, personal interview, Los Angeles, September 14, 1989.

25. Ibid.

26. Serna, "Eastside Residents Oppose Prison."

27. Aurora Castillo, personal interview, Boyle Heights, Eastside Los Angeles, January 15, 1988.

28. Juana Gutiérrez interview.

29. See Gail Minault, "Introduction: The Extended Family as Metaphor and the Expansion of Women's Realm," in Minault, ed., *The Extended Family: Women and Political Participation in India and Pakistan* (Delhi, India: Chanakya Publications, 1981), pp. 3–18.

30. Erlinda Robles, personal interview, Boyle Heights, Eastside Los Angeles, September 14, 1989.

31. Reymundo Reynoso and Josefina Vidal, "Las Madres del Este de Los Angeles se proponen seguir luchando por sus hijos y su barrio," *La Opinión*, August 28, 1986.

32. Anonymous, member of MELA, personal interview, Los Angeles, California, September 14, 1989.

33. Lucy Ramos, personal interview, Boyle Heights, Eastside Los Angeles. May 3, 1989.

34. As reconstructed by Juana Gutiérrez, Ricardo Gutiérrez, and Aurora Castillo.

35. Sharon McDonald and Robert McGarvey, "The Most Beautiful Women in L.A." *L.A. Style*, September 1988, p. 245. Dick Russell, "The Air We Breathe: Viva Las Madres!" *Parenting*, November 1989, pp. 127–128; Louise Sahagun, "Boyle Heights: Problems, Pride and Promise," *Los Angeles Times*, July 31, 1983.

36. Anonymous, member of MELA, personal interview, Los Angeles, September 14, 1989.

37. Cited in Gabriel Gutiérrez, *The Founding of the Mothers of East Los Angeles*, pamphlet (Los Angeles: Gabriel Gutiérrez, December 1989). The author, one of Juana Gutiérrez's sons, completed his Ph.D. in History at UC Santa Barbara and wrote an excellent pamphlet documenting the founding of MELA. Also see Gabriel Gutiérrez, "The Mothers of East L.A. Strike Back," in Robert D. Bullard, ed., *Unequal Protection* (San Francisco: Sierra Club Books, 1994).

38. Linda Breakstone, "Foes of L.A. Prison Manage to Thwart Bill's Passage Again," *Los Angeles Herald Examiner*, August 14, 1986; Leo Wolinsky, "Prison Plan Loses in Senate 3rd Time," *Los Angeles Times*, September 24, 1986; and Leo C. Wolinsky, "L.A. Prison Bill 'Locked Up' in New Clash," *Los Angeles Times*, July 16, 1987.

39. Leo C. Wolinsky, "Senate Rejects L.A. Prison Site in a Blow to Governor," *Los Angeles Times*, August 15, 1986; Richard Paddock, "Governor Risks Latinos' Support on Prison Issues," *Los Angeles Times*, September 14, 1986.

40. See Tracey Kaplan and M. Gladstone, "4 Alternative Sites Found for Controversial Prison," *Los Angeles Times*, April 26, 1991.

41. Greg Spring, "Opposition Builds to Prison," *Los Angeles Downtown News*, August 24, 1992; Mark Gladstone, "Latinos Press Wilson to Sign Bill to Kill L.A. Prison Plans," *Los Angeles Times*, September 2, 1992; Louis Sahagun, "Mothers of Conviction," *Los Angeles Times*, September 16, 1992.

42. Miguel G. Mendivil, field representative for Assemblywoman Lucille Roybal-Allard, 56th District, personal interview, Los Angeles, April 25, 1989. The toxic waste incinerator proposed for Vernon, a small city adjacent to East Los Angeles, would worsen the already debilitating air quality of the entire county and set a dangerous precedent for other communities throughout California. See Dick Russell, "Environmental Racism," *The Amicus Journal* 11, no. 2 (Spring 1989): 22–32.

43. Judy Christrup and R. Schaeffer, "Not in Anyone's Backyard," *Greenpeace* 15, no. 1 (January/February 1990): 14–19.

44. Castillo interview.

45. Cited in Gabriel Gutiérrez, *The Founding of Mothers*.

46. Elsa López, member of MELA-SI, personal interview, Los Angeles, January 28, 1997.

47. See Ida Susser, "Working Class Women, Social Protest and Changing Ideologies," in Ann Bookman and Sandra Morgen, eds., *Women and the Politics of Empowerment* (Philadelphia: Temple University Press, 1988); and Beverly Thiele, "Vanishing Acts in Social and Political Thought: Tricks of the Trade," in Carole Pateman and Elizabeth Gross, eds., *Feminist Challenges, Social and Political Theory* (Boston: Allen & Unwin, 1986), pp. 30–43.

48. Dorothy Smith, *The Conceptual Practice of Power* (Boston: Northeastern University Press, 1990).

49. For a comparative study of Mexican American women activists in Eastside Los Angeles and women in an adjacent suburb and further discussion of methodological and conceptual implications, see Mary Santoli Pardo, *Mexican American Women Activists: Identity and Resistance in Two Los Angeles Communities* (Philadelphia: Temple University Press, 1998).

PART TWO

Institutional Studies

Four

THE STRUGGLE WITHIN

The California Agricultural Labor Relations Board, 1975–1990

MARGARITA ARCE DECIERDO

In 1973 there was a strike at Giumarra Vineyards. In the course of this strike as many as 80,000 boxes of grapes were burned, five fields completely destroyed by fire, two labor camps burned down. Picketers were beaten and many seriously injured by company cars that swept through the fields without stopping. Molotov cocktails were discovered in several labor camps. And two United Farm Workers Union members were killed.

Two years later in the same fields, a California State official entered Giumarra Vineyards and approached the foreman in charge. She instructed him to call out the crews and stop production. She then told him to leave and wait at the edge of the road until she finished speaking to the workers. With much emotion in her voice, she read a state official notice: the State of California, for the first time in its history of agribusiness, had made a law to protect, encourage, and allow farmworkers the right to freely choose union representation. It was in this manner, in similar episodes repeated throughout the state, that the Agricultural Labor Relations Act came into effect.[1]

For many, the historic creation of California's first farm labor law represented a resolution to the violent conflict between growers, farmworkers, and labor unions. Yet, after years of intense and bitter unrest, during which tensions and confrontation had often resulted in violence and sometimes death, an end to this struggle would not occur overnight. The intervention of the "state" in California's race and class struggle did not represent the end of this conflict. On the contrary, it meant the "importation" of the grower-farmworker struggle into the very agency designed to mediate it. Ultimately, it also meant the regulation of a farmworker labor movement.

Much has been written about the role of the state in mediating or managing class relations in capitalist society. The literature is generally clustered around two basic positions, the "instrumentalist" and the "structuralist." Briefly, the instrumentalists maintain that the state serves the interests of the ruling class, and the structuralists argue that the state can act independently of the ruling class and maintain a degree of autonomy. As outlined by James O'Connor, Ralph Miliband, and Claus Offe, relative autonomy is viewed here as the state having the flexibility in surpassing the specific or immediate class interests of the elite and responding to various organized interests of other class groups.[2]

This case study of "state intervention," by fleshing out this generally abstract discussion, suggests that these two theoretical positions have been excessively drawn out. In tentative fashion, this study suggests that the state is not simply a committee of capitalists, nor will it "stand above" the class struggle in any removed or autonomous sense. While the state serves as an instrument that carries out different class interests, it is sufficiently resilient to accommodate conflicting interests. In fact, the complexity of the state indicates that different components, like the police, Immigration and Naturalization Service, and county officials may carry out contradictory policies. Under pressing economic and social conditions, the state will reflect the class struggle occurring around it. When viewing state intervention, therefore, one must understand the relative strengths and weaknesses of the oppositional forces within the political and economic arena. What role will the state play in order to accommodate the interests of the forces at hand? More critically, what will be the interplay of the oppositional forces and the strategic remedies available to each of them under specific economic, racial, and social conditions?

In this light, I will describe one form of state intervention — the historic implementation of California's first labor law, the Agricultural Labor Relations Act (ALRA). The discussion is divided into four parts. The first part will provide the background for understanding the strategic positions and strength of the three political actors, the United Farm Workers of America, the Teamsters Union, and the fruit and vegetable growers, in the drafting and passage of the ALRA.

The second section introduces the Agricultural Labor Relations Board (ALRB) and describes its first year of operations. Of special interest will be the board's attempt to place the bitter conflict of the three parties within the framework of the new farm labor law.

The third section looks at those who controlled the state agency, at times referred to as state managers or government officials. Here I describe the delicate interplay of state managers within the ALRB. For the purpose of this analysis, it will be important to identify the state managers as pro-worker, pro-grower, or neutral. In other words, to what degree did each state manager carry out a specific class interest in implementing the new law? The manner in which these political actors interpreted and implemented the law effectively imported the race and labor conflict into the internal operations of the ALRB itself. This internal conflict reached a climax with the formation of the ALRB Workers' Union of "pro-worker" state managers. The irony of this case, then, was that state intervention to pacify the struggle between growers and farmworkers imported the struggle "within" the ALRB. This agency, in effect, was an apparatus for confrontation and negotiation among state manager-officials.

The final section is a description of political changes that have affected the board and the UFW in the 1980s. Twenty years after the passage of the ALRA, the political topography of California has changed dramatically. The election of pro-grower Republican governors has virtually transformed the ALRB into an agency working to contain the farmworker labor movement.

PASSAGE OF THE AGRICULTURAL LABOR RELATIONS ACT, 1975

The chaotic and turbulent conditions in the fields—a conflict involving growers and two competing unions, the United Farm Workers Union and the Teamsters Union—provided the background for the ALRA. The creation of the ALRA itself was a complicated and delicate matter. In the mid-1960s the strategy of the United Farm Workers Union was to seek legislation under the National Labor Relations Act (NLRA). During that time, the NLRA seemed like the proper avenue to follow, for it provided for elections and union recognition. In 1968, however, the Union's position changed drastically. As a result of grape and lettuce boycotts, the UFW had won major contracts with grape and lettuce growers. UFW President César Chávez and movement followers were opposed to any legislation for fear that any form of state intervention would "take the wind out of its sails like it did to the Civil Rights Movement in the South." Under NLRA regulations, argued the UFW, the Union's right to boycott—the most powerful and effective tool against growers—would be eliminated. Consequently, the Union halted its bid to be represented by the NLRA.[3]

In 1970–1972 growers, affected by the impact of the UFW's boycott success, pressured the legislature to place the UFW under NLRA provisions and regulations. Several bills were introduced in the Senate which, although they provided for elections, did nothing else. There was no protection of farmworkers against grower discrimination and harassment, no system of unfair labor practice protection, no duty to bargain in good faith, and no right to boycott. The UFW was able to stop passage of these bills by holding mass demonstrations and marches in Sacramento. Chávez went on a fast on several occasions.

In 1973, after the grape and lettuce contracts had expired, growers decided not to renew their contracts with the UFW. Instead, they established and signed contracts with the Teamsters Union. Chávez charged that there was a conspiracy by the growers and Teamsters to keep the UFW out. In retaliation, the UFW called for more strategic boycotts and asked for the financial assistance of the AFL-CIO. The support was given; the AFL-CIO, however, wanted the UFW to actively seek legal arbitration.

In 1974 the political reality changed. Gerald Brown, a farmworker sympathizer and longtime friend of César Chávez, ran a successful gubernatorial race. During the course of his campaign, Brown had made a commitment to support the union's position for effective and democratic legislation. In December of 1974, Brown declared in his inaugural address that it was time to extend the rule of law to the agricultural sector.[4]

Three bills—AB 1, sponsored by the UFW; SB 308, by the Teamsters; and SB 813, by Brown—generally touched on the same major questions: secret ballot elections, strikes, existing contracts, labor court review, administration of the law, and voter eligibility. There were, as might be expected, distinct ideas on how these would be addressed. The UFW, for example, strongly supported the provisions for secret balloting in the choice of bargaining agents.[5] With a secret ballot provision, growers could no longer sign contracts with labor organizations unless there had been an election and workers had voted for an ALRB-certified labor organization.

The growers conceded to this provision only if the provision would allow a "no labor organization" choice in elections. The Teamsters, on the other hand, opposed such a provision unless they were assured that the contracts they had would remain in effect until a union representation election was held.[6] After much heated discussion, it was agreed that representational elections would be held if 50 percent of those working signed petitions asking for an election and if these petitions were filed when employment on the farm reached 50 percent of peak employment total.

On the matter of recognitional strikes and the related question of secondary (consumer) boycotts, however, the growers were totally opposed. Les Hubbard, spokesperson for the Western Growers Council, stated that "the growers will certainly fight this bill or any other which authorizes the use of the secondary boycott. We are dead set against that."[7] The UFW, on the other hand, had scored some major contracts with grape and lettuce growers as a result of the boycott and were determined to keep their right to boycott. UFW President Chávez and his supporters held several demonstrations at the capitol protesting any bill that would eliminate the boycott clause. Finally, a compromise was reached that would permit secondary boycotts by unions that were certified as bargaining agents.

Another point of contention was the question of access. Any effective farm labor law needed a provision which allowed union organizers to enter the fields in order to inform farmworkers about union representation. Growers, however, opposed such a provision. They felt that a rule permitting access to the fields would help unionization of workers, and growers should not be required to provide such help. They further argued that the basic issue of private property rights was involved and that if union organizers were allowed on the farms those rights would be violated. The Teamsters' position with regard to the access regulation called for limited access. They suggested that limited access should be given to organizers and that growers be allowed to designate certain areas of their property for union organizers to meet workers. The UFW argued that union organizers should be allowed on farms to talk with workers before and after work and during lunch and coffee breaks. If growers were allowed to designate areas for union representatives, argued UFW attorney Jerry Cohen, then they could easily manipulate such situations by keeping the location under close surveillance and discouraging workers from going to the designated meeting places. After several weeks of heated debate, the end result was a complicated formula which allowed access to organizers at "reasonable times" (see Table 4.1).[8]

And so went the negotiating process until, after several weeks, a final compromise was reached. On June 5, 1975, the Alatorre-Zenovich-Dunlap-Berman Agricultural Labor Relations Act was signed into law by Governor Brown. It was a historic event. The State of California had extended the coverage of the National Labor Relations Act to agricultural employees. The ALRA now recognized the right of agricultural workers to associate freely, to organize in unions and designate representatives of their own choosing, to negotiate the terms and conditions of their employment, and to be free from the interference and coercion of employers or their agents. This was theory, however; much still had to be learned from actual practice.

ALRB, 1975: THE FIRST YEAR

On August 25, 1975, California's first farm labor law went into effect. The preamble of the ALRA itself was explicit about the need for "peace" and "stability": "In enacting this legislation the people of the State of California seek to ensure peace in the agricultural fields by guaranteeing justice for all agricultural workers and stability in labor relations. This enactment is intended to bring certainty and a sense of fair play to a presently unstable and potentially volatile condition in the state."[9] In technical terms, the ALRA gave agricultural employees the right to elect a representative for the purpose of collective bargaining and directed the ALRB to supervise elections. The ALRA

Table 4.1. Major Farm Labor Legislation, 1975 [10]

This is how the farm-labor bills stood before the Brown compromise measure was amended extensively. AB1 was sponsored by Cesar Chavez, SB 308 by the Teamsters (a grower-backed bill was substantially merged into SB 308), and SB 813 by Brown.

	Alatorre (AB1)	Zenovich (SB 308)	Dunlap (SB 813)	Compromise
Selecting Representatives				
Secret ballot election	X	X	X	X
Recognitional strikes	X			
Secret ballot elections with a "no-union" option		X		X
Election Timing				
Within seven days after petition filed			X	X
Within five days after petition filed	X			
Within 48 hours, if possible, after petition filed, if majority of workers on strike		X	X	X
Permits expedited election when no recognitional picketing		X	X	X
To be determined by board		X		
Voter Eligibility				
Employees on payroll immediately before petition filing	X		X	X
All employees who left work due to work stoppage and are not working elsewhere	X			
Employees terminated due to unfair election practice	X			
All employees discharged after petition filing			X	X
Persons displaced by strike	X			X
To be determined by board		X		

(continued)

Table 4.1 (*continued*)

	Alatorre (AB1)	Zenovich (SB 308)	Dunlap (SB 813)	Compromise
Labor Practices				
Secondary boycott				
Full prohibition		X		
No restriction	X			
*No restriction on secondary boycott by certified union to secure collective-bargaining agreement with primary employer			X	
*Permits appeals to consumers to not patronize a neutral employer where no election held in the last 12 months or no union certified			X	X
*Permits boycott publicity asking consumers not to buy a specific product at neutral employer's place of business	X		X	X
*Prohibits forcing employees of a neutral employer to strike or cease work to pressure employer to stop doing business with primary employer				X
Recognitional Picketing				
Prohibited				X
No restrictions	X			
Allowed for up to 30 days before filing petition (used only when no union is certified or where no election has been held within the last 12 months)		X	X	X
Strikes				
Recognitional strikes allowed	X			
Strikes at harvest permitted	X	X	X	X

Source: *California Journal*, June 1975, p. 192.

required a bargaining representative to be elected by majority vote in a secret ballot election and, unlike the NLRA, did not permit voluntary recognition of a union by an employer. The ALRA further defined unfair labor practices which could be committed by an employer or by a labor union. The Act authorized the ALRB to conduct administrative hearings and issue remedies when unfair labor practices had been proven.

Before the actual operation of the ALRB, there were definite indications that the new farm labor law would not resolve the conflict between growers and farmworkers. Governor Brown himself was realistic about the prospects of the new law: "of course I expect conflicts. But hopefully, the law will provide a framework to resolve that conflict." Rose Bird, Brown's representative, likewise noted that this new situation "involves the human response to new situations set up to deal with private individuals locked in a bitter struggle in an arena where the stakes are high, emotions volatile and the outcome uncertain."[11]

During the first year of implementation, two main issues surfaced. One was the issue dealing with union access on employer property and the other was election manipulation. According to the unfair labor practices filed with the ALRB in 1975–1976, the UFW was at a serious disadvantage. In a representative case, for example, two farmworkers from Salinas described what had occurred when three Teamsters organizers came to the field where they were working:

> They arrived . . . and told our foreman to stop the machine so they could talk to us. He made us stop working and the Teamster organizer talked to us for about 50 minutes about the benefits that we get when we are under Teamster contract. Many times before, organizers from the United Farm Workers have come to the fields where we have been working and have tried to talk to us. They have not been permitted to enter the fields on many of these occasions even though we were on our lunch break and they have been arrested on more than one occasion.[12]

Underlying the evident favoritism shown the Teamsters was outright grower opposition to the ALRB's access rule. When UFW organizers tried to enter the Ballentine grape ranch near Parlier in Fresno county, two Ballentine supervisors blocked the way of the organizers. According to UFW testimony, the organizers were recorded as saying, "we have a right to enter the fields and speak with the workers." The supervisor responded, "we know all that, and we don't give a shit about the law, we don't give a shit about Governor Brown. All we know is that you are trespassing on private property, so get the hell out."[13]

Some growers were reported to have set up armed vigilantes. In one incident in Fresno county, UFW organizers attempting to speak to tomato workers were met with dozens of men and boys carrying shotguns, rifles, and pistols who threatened to "blow heads off" if they set foot on ranch property. The leader later told a Fresno reporter that "all we are doing is trying to keep trespassers out, you wouldn't want those people in your living room, and this tomato field is this man's living room."[14]

The growers wanted the ALRB to change its policy on the access regulation by prohibiting any union organizers from entering their property. They argued that their property was private property and that no one should enter without express permission from them. The conflict was finally adjudicated in favor of the ALRB by the California Superior Court, which ruled that all private property is held subject to the power of government to regulate its use for the benefit of the public welfare.[15]

Despite such court rulings, the question of access continued to be a major problem in the face of grower antagonism. In an interview with the *Los Angeles Times*, Chávez stated, "without access to workers in the fields, the law becomes a hoax."[16] A county sheriff in Tulare county, for example, repeatedly maintained that he would honor the property rights of farmers and enforce trespass statutes rather than the ALRB access rule. This particular action had also encouraged sheriffs in other grower-dominated counties to take a similar position. Meanwhile, the ALRB General Counsel maintained that the agency was powerless to do anything about law enforcement.[17]

In addition to the controversy over the access rule, frequent charges of grower manipulation of elections were filed with the ALRB in 1975–1976. Among the many complaints recorded, some charged that growers were padding their payrolls with anti-UFW workers just before an election. On one such occasion, an employer hired two extra crews (a change from previous practice) which consisted of about 20–35 older farmworkers. These workers were known to be ex-Teamster members and did not favor the UFW. In another case, an entire crew who had supported and voted for the UFW were "coincidentally" laid off, an action justified by claims that there was no more work.

To further complicate matters, growers used several tactics to undermine the operation of the ALRB. They used anti-union attorneys specializing in farm labor law to stall negotiation, clogged the board's administrative machinery with thousands of unfair labor practices, and sponsored court challenges to the board's power and authority. Growers complained that the ALRB was not acting in an "impartial" manner and that specific board employees were colluding with the UFW officials and organizers.

On the other hand, the UFW accused the board's general counsel of attempting to undermine the law with his favoritism towards growers. AFL-CIO Director of Organizing Alan Kistler charged that there was no question that the vast majority of the elections that had taken place could not pass the tests of the NLRB. A UFW attorney likewise concluded that "some people in Sacramento don't want the Act to work." He noted that anyone with any experience in union organizing knows that "the time to investigate unfair labor practice charges is the time they are filed, not two or three or four weeks later when people have left or moved on with the crops to other areas, other states or Mexico."[18] The UFW claimed that such delays in investigating unfair labor practices worked to the advantage of growers.

These types of acts, then, had a serious impact on elections. According to a report filed by a key official of the ALRB, the UFW would have won between 15 and 20 percent more votes in the elections held in 1975–1976 if there had been no abuses of the law. Nonetheless, the results of the elections held in 1975–1976 indicated that the farmworkers' choice was the UFW. Out of 34,000 votes cast, approximately 22,000 were for the UFW. The UFW had won a total of 154 elections. The Teamsters, on the other hand, had won 91 elections and represented 10,000 farmworkers.[19]

The growers, the Teamsters, and the UFW were all unhappy with the ALRB. The UFW was claiming lack of aggressive enforcement, board bias in favor of the growers, and that unfair labor practices were not being resolved promptly. Growers, on the other hand, wanted some serious amendments to the ALRA, especially on the question of access.

The ALRB, however, had a more serious problem to deal with. On April 2, 1976, the board ran out of money because it had conducted more elections than had been anticipated. If no other resources were allocated, the board would have to be shut down completely.[20] In order to refinance the ALRB, enabling legislation needed to be introduced to the Legislature. There were, however, serious divisions within the Legislature. Pro-grower legislators were blocking any funds for the ALRB unless several amendments to the law were made. The UFW reacted by threatening to boycott Sunmaid Raisin growers, Sunsweet, and eight other Central California grape and fruit growers.[21] The UFW claimed that these growers were mostly responsible for blocking the appropriation for the ALRB. To break the impasse, the majority Democratic caucus in the Assembly forced reluctant Democrats, who were themselves grower representatives, to support a $2.6 million funding bill (AB 2886). The bill was finally passed with a 54-24 majority vote.[22]

There were some modifications made to the ALRA, however. One was concerning the access regulation. The rules now indicated that organizers could enter employer property one hour before work, during lunch break, and anytime after work. Also, the number of organizers that had access was limited to two per crew. This was basically a concession to growers. Other changes in the law included a developed procedure to expedite election objections and unfair labor practice charges. The Joint Oversight Committee, composed of legislators representing labor and agriculture, was essentially created to oversee the internal operations of the ALRB.

ALRB, 1976: A SECOND LOOK

An inside look into the board's internal affairs during its second "go-around" sets the chaotic scenario and struggle to implement the act. The very conflict that the state was supposed to monitor and mediate became the very conflict that was waged within the second year of the ALRB. It was no longer assumed by any of the parties concerned that "impartial" and "neutral" staff and board members were in charge of interpreting and administering the ALRA. The five-member Executive Board appointed by Governor Brown itself reflected the contending sides: two members were known to have worker sympathies, two had grower interests, and the fifth was a "neutral" bureaucrat with extensive NLRB experience. This was the executive committee which oversaw the entire operation of the ALRB. The executive secretary, who was responsible for the "judicial review" of election objections and other charges, was known to have worker sympathies; and the general counsel, responsible for supervision of attorneys, field examiners, and support staff in the seven regional offices, was known to be pro-grower.

Not surprisingly, this design of compromise at the upper echelons of the ALRB was reflected in the composition of the general staff of attorneys, field examiners, and clerical workers. Although only few personnel had been explicitly hired to represent the interests of growers or the UFW, the majority who may have been neutral or unfamiliar with the conflict in the fields soon learned and discovered, in the course of implementing the act, that they too had to take sides. Some attempted to remain neutral. By 1976, the ALRB staff of 206 employees (50 attorneys, 50 field examiners, and 106 support staff) were divided into pro-grower, pro-worker, and pro-management camps. So transparent were these divisions that an estimate of the relative strength of these camps can be made: of the 206 staff members, approximately 109 were pro-worker, and the remainder were either pro-grower or pro-management. Since these three groups played an important part in carrying out the new state law, let us describe them in more detail.

The pro-management staff were generally bureaucrats who had been civil service employees for many years. They saw their role simply as "neutral" state officials and were concerned more with personnel matters, job stability, and going home after a long eight hours of work. For them, the external struggle between the competing forces could be ignored as long as it didn't interfere with their routine or job stability. Yet it was this seemingly neutral air which led to the clumsy and careless implementation of the law. Their function, for the most part, was determined by the other staff members. Thus, they could easily be manipulated by either pro-grower or pro-worker personnel. Nonetheless, even this type of "neutrality" accommodated many personal prejudices. One UFW lawyer described them this way: "There is a certain amount of racism, a lack of understanding and knowledge of agriculture and . . . emphasis is on the good faith of the employer . . . the UFW is [seen as] a radical, troublemaking organization while the employers . . . and the Teamsters are good and honest."[23]

In contrast to these "neutral" bureaucrats were the pro-worker and the pro-grower staff who understood the seriousness of the external struggle, and who had very definite ideas about how the farm labor law should be interpreted and administered. For the pro-worker staff, aggressive enforcement of the law was key. This meant several things. For one, it meant that pro-worker staff would have to be given some positions of power and authority. It also meant that their relationships with the pro-grower staff had to be handled with the greatest discretion. If the pro-worker staff showed any hostility toward the pro-grower personnel, this staff would become hostile toward farmworkers. And this hostility toward farmworkers sometimes resulted in delays of investigation and resolution of unfair labor practice cases. The other important factor for the pro-worker staff was the type of relationship they established with farmworkers themselves. In order for farmworkers to respect and believe that the law was established to serve their interest, consistent communication between staff and workers had to be maintained. The pro-worker election team, for example, on a daily basis spoke with workers, outlined workers' rights fully, and explained the entire election procedure. This was critical, especially in light of the fact that many farmworkers had never voted, were not familiar with unions, and were generally frightened by state procedures.

The pro-grower staff had a different interpretation and interest. Not surprisingly, this personnel usually treated and regarded farmworkers with suspicion and spent the least amount of time in the fields with them. They were known to patronize the workers; and when elections were conducted by this staff, the election procedure would not be explained fully. As a result, many farmworkers complained about surveillance and intimidation.

The differences between pro-worker and pro-grower staff also surfaced in the investigation teams which were responsible for determining whether a case had merit or not. The pro-worker team spent at the minimum twelve to fifteen hours investigating cases per week. The pro-grower/bureaucrat team, however, was known to spend less than six hours weekly investigating cases. This type of attitude from pro-grower (and bureaucrat) teams affected the outcomes of numerous cases, again in favor of growers.

In order to appreciate the critical differences between the pro-grower and pro-worker staff, we turn now to the election process to study how the contending sides interacted with one another.

THE GALLO ELECTION

On June 27, 1973, Ernest and Julio Gallo Wineries signed a four-year contract with the Teamsters in order to avoid renewing the contract it had with the UFW. In response, the UFW called a nationwide consumer boycott against the nation's largest wine producer. Gallo officials never publicly admitted the impact of the boycott, but polls conducted with regard to its effectiveness revealed that 11 million adults stopped drinking Gallo wines.[24] The relationships among the UFW, Teamsters, and Gallo, of course, remained bitter.

In 1975, with the changing political climate in the fields due in part to the new law, the UFW attempted to gain lost territory and campaigned for an election at Gallo farms. Gallo officials and foremen announced that they would do everything in their power to stop the UFW. The testimony of a security guard made these intentions clear: "We are instructed by the company to keep our eyes open for UFW organizers and to harass, photograph, and keep under close surveillance farmworkers who support the Union. The Teamsters will be allowed free and open access to the Gallo property at any time they want." According to an account given by a worker, "the company only lets UFW organizers talk to workers for one hour, but the Teamsters get to be on the property any time during the day." Clear favoritism was shown to Teamsters in access to fields.

Intimidation of workers by both Teamsters and ranch foremen was common. Gallo security guards took pictures of workers talking to UFW organizers. UFW organizer Fred Ross, Jr., testified later that in forty years of community and union organizing he had never witnessed such blatant harassment of workers by company representatives: "I went door to door in the company housing. At each door I knocked on, a guard would take a picture of me talking to the worker. Then we had out cameras taking pictures of them taking pictures of us."[25]

For Gallo workers, there was continual threat of being fired, deported, or caused bodily harm. A worker at Gallo later testified as follows: "A Teamster organizer and a company man approached us and stopped to talk about the elections. The Teamster organizer told me and the other workers that we could lose our jobs at Gallo if we voted for Chávez. He also asked me if I had been having any meetings with the Chávez people at my house. He told me that he had seen me at the meeting with César Chávez and he told me that he could . . . get me fired . . . he said that he had a list of all the Chávez supporters at Gallo and that there were 11 names on the list and mine was one of them." The winery kept the threat of firing hanging over the heads of any workers who didn't "vote right" or who just showed too much interest in the UFW.[26] Typical of Teamsters tactics, the night before the election, half a dozen Teamsters interrupted a UFW meeting and taunted the one hundred Gallo workers who had gone to hear César Chávez.

During the election campaign, there were more than fifty accusations of unfair labor practices filed by the UFW. They included death threats to pro-UFW workers, the use of armed vigilantes to prevent UFW organizers from leafleting workers, manipulating the workforce to affect the outcome of the election, and providing unequal access to competing unions. Despite the allegations that workers were in fact being intimidated and harassed, the position of the ALRB was one of total disregard. The announced position of the ALRB's general counsel was "we have a procedure for running elections and we will let the parties prove their allegations after elections have been held." This "non-decision," however, encouraged the continuation of grower intimidation and surveillance. Workers, seeing the inaction of the ALRA, were afraid to exercise their rights, and many didn't vote at all. "The General Counsel's failure to try to correct unfair labor practices at the time they occur," UFW vice-president Dolores Huerta said, "results in tainted elections with unfair labor practice charges that have to be investigated, heard by hearing officers and many times taken to court. . . . All of this could have been avoided had there been an effort to secure a fair climate of elections in the pre-election campaign."[27]

Irregularities in the election itself were highlighted when about thirty Gallo security guards cast their ballots by marching toward the voting booth in a goose-step fashion. They were wearing uniforms and badges similar to ones used by Border Patrol officials. The action had its intended results. Several workers waiting to cast their ballots moved away from the voting both and told a board agent that they didn't want to vote. Another worker observed that he and others were brought to the polls in company buses: "The regular bus driver was not there and I notice the new one was the foreman from my crew. After the workers got out, he yelled 'don't forget to vote for the Teamsters!'" The pro-grower board agent refused to allow three workers to vote because their names did not appear on the employee list, even though the UFW observer recognized them as workers in his crew. The pro-worker agent, however, assumed responsibility and told the pro-grower agent that they should be allowed to vote but have their votes challenged with a postelection investigation to determine the matter. As a fitting conclusion to the Gallo elections, after the voting fifty workers were loaded on Border Patrol buses and taken away to immigration detention centers.[28]

After the election, two pro-worker attorneys and two people from Brown's Community Relations office proceeded to investigate the mounting charges of unfair labor practices against Gallo. The investigation concluded that "retaliation against workers after elections and failure of the ALRB to promptly remedy acts reflects on the ability of the Board and General Counsel's office to protect workers who have sought to exercise their rights under the Act." It was recommended that prompt investigation and action should be taken on retaliation charges. The pro-grower general counsel was reported to have been outraged at the report.[29]

THE IMPORTED STRUGGLE

The pro-grower staff, especially those in positions of power, did not sit passively while the pro-worker personnel aggressively enforced the act. They knew that they could easily change the situation and swing the law back into the hands of the growers. The general counsel and his pro-grower supporters developed a pattern of harassment of pro-worker staff. Demotions, bad probationary reports, juggling case assignments, arbitrary transfers, and firings were methods used to discourage the enforcement of the law.

The general counsel demoted competent attorneys and field examiners who were known to be pro-worker staff members and replaced them with pro-grower personnel. For example, a pro-worker attorney in charge of the ALRB's Coachella office began an investigation of unfair labor practice charges filed by the UFW against two legislators (John Stull and Tom Suitt) who were members of the Oversight Joint Committee. These charges accused the legislators of interrogating farmworkers on behalf of several agricultural employers. Several days before the hearing, the general counsel called the attorney and ordered him to dismiss the charges because the legislators had immunity. Much to the surprise of the general counsel, the attorney responded by asking for more legal research on the matter. Subsequently, the attorney was relieved of his duties and replaced by a field examiner known to be a pro-grower supporter. The general counsel then instituted a policy which specifically said that only non-attorneys could head field offices. The attorney who had refused to dismiss the charges against the legislators received his final probationary report, personally prepared by the general counsel, and was demoted to staff counsel.

Job security was no longer a question of whether one was officially qualified to handle the difficult intricacies of labor law, conduct elections, or recommend the proper legal decisions of cases, but was contingent on the general counsel's strategy to relax the enforcement of the act. The general counsel had succeeded in replacing most of the pro-worker attorneys and field examiners with pro-grower staff.

In response, pro-worker personnel began to campaign for the formation of a union within the ALRB. A workers' union within the board would protect personnel against discriminatory actions taken by the general counsel. After securing enough signatures from board employees and following several months of negotiations with the Personnel Board in Sacramento, the Agricultural Labor Relations Board Workers' Union (ALRBWU) was finally recognized in early 1977. Ironically, the very rights outlined in the preamble of the ALRA were the same rights inscribed in the preamble of the ALRB Workers' Union. The birth of this union, however, did not stop the discrimination and harassment by the general counsel. As a matter of fact, conditions only worsened for the pro-worker staff, who were now ALRBWU members.

A test case occurred immediately. The vice-president of the ALRBWU was given his final probationary report. The report, prepared by the general counsel, stated that his performance was substandard and that consequently the agency had to fire him. The employee filed a grievance with the ALRB Workers' Union claiming that he had been fired due to his union activities. After several months of hearings, the personnel courts in Sacramento decided that there was enough evidence to prove that this employee had been fired for union activities. The employee was reinstated to his former position with one year's back pay. This case, however, did not stop the general counsel from harassing and threatening pro-worker staff.

After numerous complaints of management harassment produced no results, the pro-worker staff from the seven regional offices throughout the state gathered and conducted an informational picketing of the ALRB headquarters in Sacramento. On November 22, 1977, more than seventy-five employees of the board gathered in front of Capitol Mall and began to call for the immediate resignation of the general counsel. The employees felt that the general counsel was obstructing the enforcement of the act by threatening and firing employees who sought only to carry out the spirit of the law for farmworkers.[30]

The governor refused to call for the resignation of the general counsel, and those employees who had participated in the picketing were severely punished. One well-known pro-worker employee was removed as chief of operation and demoted. Another three attorneys were subsequently discharged. The general counsel made it unbearable for many pro-worker staff to continue working with the ALRB—there were many demotions and more transfers. As a result, as many as twenty-five pro-worker staff left the agency or were discharged. Most of the pro-worker staff were gone by 1978. It was in this manner, then, that the "struggle within" was contained and pacified.

THE ALRB IN THE 1980S

By 1980 the UFW had won the right to represent over twenty thousand farmworkers throughout the state of California. The height of UFW success came

Table 4.2. Farm Worker Elections, 1976–1986

Victories	76–78	%	78–80	%	80–82	%	82–84	%	84–86	%
No Union	29	23.0	23	24.2	15	18.1	29	43.9	28	53.8
United Farm Wrks	70	55.6	31	32.6	53	63.9	30	45.5	14	26.9
Intrnl Un Ag Wrk	23	18.3	30	31.6	5	6.0	3	4.5	1	1.9
Other Unions*	4	3.2	11	11.6	10	12.0	4	6.1	9	17.3
Total Elections	126		95		83		66		52	
Total Voters*	17,937		6,513		8,831		8,477		5,440	

*Excludes the 69 victories of 420 dairy workers, organized as the Christian Labor Association, in 1976–1978. These elections merely ratified previous arrangements, and no elections involving the CLA were held after 1978.
Source: Agricultural Labor Relations Board: Annual Report to the Legislature, 1976–1987.

in 1980–1982, when the union won fifty-three of eighty-three elections (or 63.9 percent) compared with fifteen for "no union" (12 percent) and five for the Teamsters (6 percent) (see Table 4.2). The Teamsters Union, as a result of these defeats, left the fields in 1982 to organize elsewhere. Nonetheless, in 1982–1984, there was a noticeable decline in UFW victories, as workers split their support between the UFW (in thirty elections) and for "no union" (in twenty-nine elections). By the mid-1980s it was clear that something had definitely gone sour for the UFW. Of fifty-two elections held between 1984 and 1986, farmworkers voted for "no union" in twenty-eight (or 53.8 percent). The UFW won in only fourteen contests (26.9 percent). In the span of four years, the union had lost its widespread support. Why were farmworkers voting for no-union representations?

There had been much speculation about the UFW's loss of support. Many farmworkers complained about the poor job the UFW was doing in representing their needs. Others pointed to internal political problems. The union's difficulties, however, extended beyond organizational questions. One explanation notes the shift in consumer interest and support, which weakened the favored UFW boycott strategy. This conservative political mood was evident during Governor George Deukmejian's tenure (1983–1990). A more precise explanation points to the transformation of the ALRB into a pro-grower state agency. Shortly after his term began in 1983, Deukmejian, who had received significant financial support from growers, slashed the board's budget by 27 percent.[31] In addition, he appointed a new general counsel, Harry Delizonna, to head the investigative arm of the ALRB.

According to César Chávez and the UFW, this new general counsel went after them like "a bunch of criminals." In fact, the counsel made it clear that the board was never meant to be a pro-labor board and that he would do everything in his power to rid it of pro-labor bias. From the union's perspective, the new general counsel was a disastrous appointment. To take an example, Abatti Produce, a family farm employing 2,500 workers, had been found guilty of union busting during contract negotiations in 1978 and also of illegally firing union activists over a period stretching back to 1969. Under the "make whole" provision, whereby farmworkers receive compensation when the employer is found guilty of bad-faith bargaining, Abatti had been fined $8 million. Through his power to make final decisions on cases, the general counsel reduced the judgment to $1.76 million. ALRB staff who handled the Abatti case rejected the general counsel's recommendation as too small. In response, the general counsel reduced the award even further, to $1.06 million. After the Abatti ruling (*ALRB v. Abatti*, 1984), the remaining key ALRB pro-worker staff, including a regional director, left the board. The pro-worker staff were winning only 10 to 20 percent of their cases, and the Abatti case was the final setback.[32]

Growers in the meantime began breaking labor contracts rather than pay farmworkers what was owed to them. Following judgments of unfair labor practices, for example, Sun Harvest, Bruce Church, California Coastal, Hubbard Company, and Martori Brothers quit farming altogether. One UFW attorney regarded these shutdowns as fraudulent: "We've got compelling proof that a lot of these companies, like Sun Harvest and Growers Exchange and Bruce Church, are just changing their names, firing union workers, lowering wages and continuing operations with labor contractors who hire workers from the shape-up at 4 am along the street in Calexico, and then truck them to the fields at rock-bottom wages. We sent these shutdown companies letters, and they refuse to reply, saying they're not the same, so we have to file new charges with the ALRB."[33]

The decisions of the pro-grower general counsel forced the UFW to rethink its organizing strategies. They had used the state's machinery to win the right to bargain collectively with growers, but this had obviously proved to be a disappointing strategy. César Chávez stated the hard facts to a reporter for the *San Francisco Examiner:* "We thought we could redress our grievances through the board, but that is not to be. That is definitely not to be. We have no choice but to change our tactics now."[34]

The shift in tactics generally meant a return to the boycott in order to force growers to service union contracts. In the mid-eighties the union persuaded McDonald's, Lucky Stores, and A & P to stop buying lettuce from Bruce Church. But generally the boycott strategy brought mixed results. More criti-

Table 4.3. Unfair Labor Practices Complaints, 1976–1986*

	76–78	78–80	80–82	82–84	84–86
Charges Filed	742	2,116	1,868	2,116	1,190
Complaints Issued	285	321	242	150	93
Hearings Opened	68	173	177	155	59
Brd Decisions Issued	59	119	97	132	63

Source: Agricultural Labor Relations Board: Annual Report to the Legislature, 1976–1987.
*Fiscal Years, Beginning July 1, Ending June 30.

cally, the UFW had ceased efforts to organize workers. Chávez believed that the boards had swung squarely in the growers' favor and that this made union representation elections meaningless.

The UFW and farmworkers stopped using the board to address unfair labor issues. This can be seen rather clearly in the decline in the number of charges filed and complaints issued (see Table 4.3). Between 1978 and 1984 the number of charges filed ranged around 2,000 per biennium; in 1984–1986 these had declined by almost half to 1,190. The complaints issued likewise declined, from 150 in 1982–1984 to 93 in 1984–1986. Not surprisingly, the number of hearings and board decisions also declined sharply in this time period.

As a result, in 1986 the UFW reversed its position and began to actively campaign to defund the ALRB. The UFW attempted to persuade the state legislature to eliminate the entire $8.7 million annual budget of the ALRB. As UFW attorney Chris Schneider stated, "It's clear that the law is no longer working. That means you're going to see a lot of marches, more boycotts and economic action at the workplace. It's the only thing a lot of these growers understand."[35]

Growers, on the other hand, have kept trying to keep the board alive by publicly stating that the farm law has been a good law and must remain operating at all costs. In fact, the general counsel noted that "it would indeed be a dark day in California agricultural labor relations if the ALRB were defunded merely to satisfy the reckless agenda of one spoiled and disgruntled labor leader [Chávez] whose singular theme seems to have become 'sour grapes.'"[36]

By the mid 1980s California growers had effectively turned the operations of the ALRB in their favor. Through elaborate changes in their harvesting and hiring arrangements, the growers "removed" themselves as employers of farm labor. Joe Sahagun, a former ALRB field organizer, described the problem: "The concept of grower as it used to be is disappearing. Instead they opt to either hire contract laborers or custom harvesters who provide equipment along with workers, or small farm-management companies that carry out all aspects of an operation on a consulting basis. Fewer and fewer growers actually employ farmworkers directly."[37] Such fragmented hiring patterns, sanctioned by a pro-grower board, undermined the organizing efforts of the UFW.

As a consequence of these constantly fluctuating arrangements, the workers and the unions could not determine against whom they should file grievances. Because the names of the employers or companies were often incorrect, cases would be held in abeyance until further proof was provided. Such delays acted against the workers. As UFW attorney Mary McCartney put it: "The board has recently issued decisions and orders on cases that were four to five years old. This is terrible for us because the workers are not receiving the pay nor the benefits due to them. Consequently, the workers get discouraged at the ALRB and at us. And then they leave to harvest crops in other areas."[38]

The discouragement was evident in the significant decline in the number of charges filed against employers and board decisions rendered. In fiscal year 1988–1990, 522 charges were filed and only 26 board decisions rendered. This contrasts sharply with the years 1982–1984, when 2,116 complaints were filed and 132 board decisions made, and also with the years 1984–1986, when 1,190 complaints were issued and 63 board decisions made. The decline in the filing of unfair labor practices corresponds, not surprisingly, to a significant decline in overall representational elections, from 66 in 1982–1984 and 52 in 1984–1986 to 42 in 1988–1990.[39] Again, these figures suggest that the organizational decline of the UFW can be traced in part to the manipulation of the ALRB by the growers.

CONCLUSION

The Agricultural Labor Relations Act represented an attempt by the state to mediate the farm labor conflict between growers and farmworkers. Under regulations and procedures outlined in the ALRA, growers and the union were forced to settle their differences after years of bitter conflict. In the preceding discussion, the various moments in the implementation of the new farm labor law were outlined as they unfolded in the context of a class struggle.

The first moment described the competing parties and their efforts to tailor a law that would fit their special interests. In effect, the UFW, the Teamsters Union, and California growers reached an agreement and a farm labor law was finally passed. The UFW agreed to suspend the secondary boycott that had been instrumental in the success of the first table grape boycott. And the growers and Teamsters agreed to a farm labor law that would allow farmworkers the right to have representational elections.

The second moment discussed the first year (1975) of the ALRA and traced the relations of the UFW, Teamsters, and growers within the framework of the act. The contending parties, not surprisingly, pointed to each other's manipulation of the law in order to meet their own interests. Growers, for example, refused to obey ALRA statutes with regard to access and instead had private property laws enforced by local and state police.

The third moment looked at the political actors within ALRB and described the importation of the grower-worker struggle into the agency designed to mediate their conflict. The "state managers" clashed over the interpretation and implementation of the ALRA. This internal conflict led to the ironic birth of the ALRB Workers' Union, as the pro-worker state managers attempted to defend themselves from pro-worker state officials. From the actual making of the bill and throughout the actual implementation of the act, then, the farm labor conflict directly influenced the character of the mediating state agency itself.

The fourth moment described the transformation of the ALRB into a pro-grower agency in the 1980s. With the election of Republican Governor Deukmejian, the board was reshaped to reflect grower interests. This, along with the removal of growers as direct employers of farmworkers, undermined the organizing efforts of the UFW.

What do these moments say about the nature of state agencies? Certainly the "flexible" nature of the ALRB raises a fundamental question concerning the impartiality or neutrality of state officials. Clearly, state managers and employees do not automatically carry out the wishes of a "ruling class," nor do they "stand above" the class struggle in any removed or autonomous sense. They consciously make political decisions, feel the intensity of conflict, and select a "proper" strategy in the implementation of state policy. These state actors are not impartial because, in an important sense, they organize and actually shape the class struggle.

In the 1990s this struggle has turned in clear favor of the growers. Bill Camp, a Brown appointee on the ALRB from 1976–1985, notes that the agency was deliberately dismantled by Governor Deukmejian to the point where it now actually works against farmworkers. Governor Pete Wilson has continued the assault. "People ask why the UFW isn't going to the ALRB. Why would anyone go there when [Pete Wilson's] only appointment has publicly bragged that he is the enemy of the ALRB?" In the meantime, Wilson's allies in the legislature regularly introduce legislation to abolish the ALRB or merge it with other state agencies.[40] As of 1994, the ALRB had closed all its regional offices with the exception of Sacramento, Salinas, Visalia, and El Centro, another indication that its political support has diminished.

As for the farmworking class, their conditions have deteriorated in the

1990s. In the Salinas Valley, where vegetable and fruit crops were estimated to be worth $1.2 billion in 1990, farmworkers were earning $4.25 an hour. According to one farmworker, growers told them, "If you don't want it, we've got 100 people waiting." Likewise farmworkers who were paid $1.10 per carton of lettuce in 1985, were in 1990 being paid 95 cents per carton of lettuce. Not only do these conditions reflect the decline of the UFW; they also point to the vulnerability of the new immigrant workers, mainly Mixtec and Zapotec Indians from southern Mexico. Speaking only their indigenous dialect, these farmworkers are open game for grower abuse, as evidenced by the discovery of two hundred workers living in dugout caves and filthy plastic lean-tos in Monterey County in 1991.[41]

These were the challenges facing the UFW when César Chávez died on April 21, 1993. It is difficult to know what impact Chávez's death will have on the UFW. In the short run, it seems to have revitalized the farmworkers' movement and public support. To commemorate the one-year anniversary of this death, the UFW organized a 330-mile pilgrimage from Delano to Sacramento. The march began on March 31, Chávez's birthday, and when it ended 23 days later, ten thousand farmworkers and supporters had marched through Sacramento. Filled with historical symbolism, it recreated the pilgrimage that Chávez, Dolores Huerta, and several hundred farmworkers had made in 1966 in launching the farmworkers' struggle for recognition and justice.[42]

NOTES

1. The facts contained in this study, the quotes, election results, and ALRA amendments were drawn from several sources: UFW witness testimony, ALRB attorney briefs, the ALRB Bill of Particulars, worker testimony, conversations with farmworkers, and my own experience while I was working with the ALRB as a field examiner. The sources came from the following regional offices: El Centro, Salinas, Fresno, Delano, San Diego, Calexico, Sacramento, Oxnard, and Lamont. It is worth mentioning here that the conflict between growers and farmworkers was not simply a class struggle. This conflict had racial and ethnic meaning as well. For a more detailed account of the violent confrontation between growers and the UFW, see Jacques E. Levy, *César Chávez: Autobiography of La Causa* (New York: W. W. Norton, 1975). See also Sam Kushner, *Long Road to Delano* (New York: International Publishers, 1976).

2. See, for example, Ralph Miliband, *The State in Capitalist Society* (New York: Basic Books, 1969); James O'Connor, *The Fiscal Crisis of the State* (New York: St. Martin's Press, 1973); and Claus Offe, *Societal Preconditions of Corporatism and Some Current Dilemmas of Democratic Theory* (South Bend, Ind.: Notre Dame University Press, 1984).

3. Chris Bowman, "Brown's Farm-Labor Coup," *California Journal*, June 1975, pp. 190–192.

4. The ALRA was part of Brown's general campaign promise to give organized labor a voice in state policy making. In fact, during the first year of Brown's term, John F. Henning, executive secretary-treasurer of the California AFL-CIO, noted that twenty-four AFL-CIO–sponsored

measures had become law and called the 1975 session the "best in the history of labor." *California AFL-CIO News*, October 3, 1975.

5. *The Sabotage and Subversion of the Agricultural Labor Relations Act*, a United Farmworkers of America White Paper published in 1976; hereafter, referred to as the UFW White Paper.

6. The Teamsters declared that if the bill was passed, twenty-five thousand farmworkers covered by Teamster contracts in four states would strike. UFW president César Chávez called the Teamster threat "an idle one." *Los Angeles Times*, May 13, 1975.

7. *Los Angeles Times*, April 12, 1975.

8. The executive director of the California Peace Officers Association declared in an interview that they backed the growers on the issue of access, saying that trespass laws would be enforced. *Los Angeles Times*, August 29, 1975; Chris Bowman, "Brown's Farm-Labor Coup," *California Journal*, June 1975, pp. 190–192.

9. Senate Bill No. 1, Chapter 1, "An Act to Add Part 3.5 (Commencing with Section 1140) to Division 2 of the Labor Code, Relating to Agricultural Labor," 1975.

10. Other key differences in the proposed legislation were as follows:

	Alatorre (AB1)	Zenovich (SB 308)	Dunlap (SB 813)	Compromise
gaining Unit				
ard selects between employer, craft or farm units		X		
ly employer unit permitted unless employees rk in noncontiguous areas	X			X
ard selects most appropriate unit, but employer t favored			X	
sting Contracts				
mits existing contracts to be challenged ough election	X		X	X
urt Review				
24-hour notice before court orders are sought ning pickets				X
ard may ask a superior court to enforce its orders		X	X	
ties hurt by a board order may obtain court review		X		
ties hurt by a board order may obtain a review court of appeals	X		X	X
urt prohibited from issuing injunctions in labor putes	X			
ministration				
e-member full-time board (two labor, two cultural, one public)		X		
e-member full-time board (no specified resentation)			X	X
ard required to create regional councils (no cific representation)	X			

rce: *California Journal*, June 1975, p. 192.

11. Chris Bowman, 191–192.

12. UFW White Paper, p. 20.

13. Ibid., p. 22.

14. Ibid., p. 24.

15. *ALRB v. Superior Court*, 16 California Reports 3d, 392, 128 Cal. Rptr. 183 (1976).

16. *Los Angeles Times*, September 4, 1975.

17. UFW White Paper.

18. Ibid.

19. Ibid., p. 14.

20. *First Annual Report of the Agricultural Labor Relations Board*, for the fiscal years ending June 30, 1976, and June 30, 1977.

21. *The Packer*, February 14, 1976.

22. In the midst of this apparent deadlock, the UFW introduced an initiative to be placed on the November ballot that would have taken the ALRA funding out of legislative hands and placed it in those of California voters. The initiative, however, was defeated in November 1976. *California Journal*, September 1973, June 1975, November 1975.

23. UFW White Paper.

24. Ibid.

25. Ibid.

26. Ibid.

27. Ibid.

28. Ibid.

29. Ibid.

30. The *Bill of Particulars* (1977) was a document prepared by ALRB employees. The Bill highlights numerous representative examples of the mismanaged administration of the ALRB's general counsel. The incidents and examples provided in this document reveal several themes: the inability of General Counsel Harry Delizonna to administer the ALRB, his retaliation against employees who disagreed with him, and his reward of "cronyism" over competence.

31. *California Journal*, December 1983.

32. Richard Steven Street, "It's Boycott Time in California," *The Nation*, March 23, 1985, pp. 330–333.

33. *Los Angeles Times*, April 30, 1986; Street, "It's Boycott Time," pp. 330–333.

34. Street, "It's Boycott Time," pp. 330–333.

35. Ibid.

36. *Los Angeles Times*, April 30, 1986.

37. Elizabeth Schilling, "The ALRB in the 1990's: Do Not Disturb . . . Agency Asleep," *California Journal* 23, no. 3 (March 1992): 152–153.

38. Mary McCartney, United Farmworkers Union attorney, personal interview, La Paz, Calif., August 1994.

39. Agricultural Labor Relations Board, Annual Reports to the Legislature, 1987–1992.

40. The latest political assault on the board came from Senator Leonard Hill, who introduced a legislative bill (SB 81) to abolish the ALRB and have the Public Employment Board assume its duties as the renamed California Employment Relations Board. This threat disappeared, however, when Senator Hill was sentenced to a four-year prison term for accepting bribes. *San Francisco Chronicle*, September 13, 1994.

41. "Cave Dwellers Found at Luxury's Doorstep," in *San Francisco Examiner*, September 10, 1991.

42. See José R. Padilla, "A Tribute to César and His Lessons," *Race, Poverty & the Environment* 4, no. 3 (Fall 1993); Susan Ferriss, "Bitter Harvest: The UFW After César Chávez," *San Francisco Chronicle Image,* July 18, 1993; and "10,000 at Rally for Farm Workers: Lively Celebration After 330-Mile March," *San Francisco Chronicle,* April 24, 1994.

Five

Protest and Affirmative Action in the 1980s

The Case of the University of New Mexico

Phillip B. Gonzales

After 1965, Chicano politics were characterized by a massive tendency among Mexican Americans to engage in collective protest. Various mainstream institutions came in for innumerable challenges under the banner of the movement. Among them, university campuses experienced perhaps the most sustained amount and among the most intense levels of confrontation, primarily on issues related to ethnic exclusion. It is well known that as an important part of the movement a mobilized student sector struck the university hardest, militantly demanding curricular changes, special faculty recruitment, and university responsiveness to social problems in the community.[1] What is given less emphasis, however, is that in the momentum of the movement, many of the Chicano professors, staff, and administrators also contributed to the pressures placed on university administrations.

For whatever reasons, the overall extent of protest activity associated with the Chicano movement receded dramatically after 1975. In some sociopolitical domains it disappeared altogether. But if the movement was to impact the political character of any institution by remaining somehow within it, it stands to reason that it would be the university, an institution whose political character is more flexible and accommodating of reformism, but also not as subject to standardized rules of authority and governance as other public entities, rendering its internal conflict more dynamic if not chaotic.[2]

This chapter presents an illustration of how the protest arm of the Chicano movement extended itself across time to impact the administrative apparatus of one institution of higher learning in particular. It recounts a conflict that consumed the University of New Mexico (UNM) throughout the academic year of 1985–1986. The story involves a process of ethnic protest occurring some ten years after the Chicano movement declined. As will be seen, the affair was unique in terms of its primary combatants. This very uniqueness serves in turn to heighten the idea that the era of protest truly affected the nature of ethnic politics at the university.

THE DISPUTANTS

In the politics of higher education, relations between a university's president and its board of regents are often delicate. Operating in distinct spheres of responsibility, regents are appointed to hold the institution itself "in trust" while presidents take charge of organizational management. A contradiction appears, however, in that regents are legally responsible for all that goes on in the university. If at odds, regents often act to police the president and directly influence the running of the university. This happens often enough that, along with other major conflicts, "Angry disputes in public between . . . trustees and president . . . seem the normal state of the institution."[3]

It was just such a dispute that occurred at UNM in 1985–1986. Amid a flame of charges and counter charges, the chair and vice-chair of the university's board of regents gave the president a low job evaluation. The president defended himself by accusing the regents of political interference in university business. The strain of the conflict, exacerbated by the special interest that the press took in the story, covered a broad front of friction. The considerable and often caustic opinion expressed by faculty and the public, especially in criticizing the regents, was aggravated by the sense of crisis surrounding the funding of higher education in New Mexico.

The whole affair would have represented a conventional sort of fight in a basic American institution but for the striking ethnic element that coursed through it. First was the fact that the two key players on the board of regents were Chicano ("Hispanic" according to the nomenclature of the incident itself) while the president was white. Moreover, among the varied issues, a big one involved affirmative action, particularly as the regents vehemently questioned the president's commitment to it. Finally, the regents' actions were part of a collective outburst. Key roles were played by members in a contingent of Chicano administrators, some faculty, staff, students, lay organizations, and, not least, a governor.

Truly remarkable was the confrontational ethnic stance that the Chicano regents took against the president. It has been pointed out that for minorities in high public office, it may be acceptable to broker one's ethnic claims aggressively in the "corridors of dominant power," but the professionalism and universalism in such corridors act as powerful inhibitors of untoward militant advocacy.[4] Nevertheless, at UNM the two key regents saw within their ken the need to openly confront the president over ethnic matters. The force of their actions in the affair caused the president to resign from his office only a year and a half after having assumed it.

However, the regents paid a heavy public-relations price for their stance. Mass opinion, especially by Anglos, went heavily against them, in part because the president himself appeared fully committed to affirmative action. It was commonly charged that the regents were cynically exercising their power. Later, New Mexico voters passed a constitutional amendment that added two new seats to the board of regents.

To fully comprehend UNM's regent-president dispute, it is necessary to consider essential aspects that define the American university as a political community, showing how it was that a characteristically Chicano-movement form of behavior was able to wend itself into the higher reaches of the university structure. In the process, the account will point out the legitimate affirmative action issue that the Hispanic regents defended to the president in spite of the public's inability to recognize it.[5]

A Perspective

What can be seen in the regents-president affair is how a protest dynamic was able to penetrate the normative walls of the professional university through the cracks which exist in the political structure of higher education. According to Brown and Goldin, collective behavior occurs on campus when a relatively large collectivity, say a sector of students, working in a conventional fashion on projects is suddenly faced with an external threat or interference to its overall "collective construction." Collective constructions in this sense are vulnerable to external impact especially from higher authority. A principal source of tension and conflict in the university is the tendency of high office to exert control over the system. In striving to concentrate power, officials construct their power base. In doing so, they often interfere with the ongoing work of lower-order collectivities by threatening to usurp resources. As Brown and Goldin write, an analysis of this type of conflict requires "a discussion of patterns of interference among competing collective constructions of the situation and the points of confrontation at which competition is made explicit."[6]

As it has been widely pointed out, academic power in the university concentrates in the bureaucratic administration. Central administration establishes a sphere of professionalism that is sharply bounded from other strata in the university.[7] Also important is that, despite the university's political, economic, and social ties to the rest of society, a cosmopolitan academic ideology proclaims the university an independent enclave devoted strictly to the scholarly pursuit of knowledge. Academic autonomy, which is "widely endorsed by professors and administrators who write about the university and its place in society during periods of crisis," often conflicts with lower-order perspectives and the prior constructions among departments and collectivities.[8]

A useful way of referring to the perspectives of players in collective dispute is in terms of their "frame of reference." Snow et al. theorize that individuals get recruited to collective activity through a process of "frame alignment," which is the linkage of individual and collective interpretive orientations. The frame of an individual's "interests, values, and beliefs" become "congruent and complementary" with the "activities, goals, and ideology" of the collective movement.[9] It is entirely possible, as seen below, for lower-order collective and higher-order power constructions to become aligned in their frames of reference and that such alignment can lead to unified collective action.

THE CONTEXT OF CONSTRUCTIONS

With these general points in mind, what can be seen to have converged at UNM as 1985 approached were three major "constructions" around affirmative action. The first of these was an older collective construction reflecting the work of Chicano faculty and administrators. The term "affirmative action" first arose in the Kennedy presidential administration and was codified and given its authority under the 1964 Civil Rights Act. Agencies having federal contracts were required to integrate underrepresented minorities and to devise affirmative action plans. But federal guidelines allowed universities to tailor their affirmative action plans according to the way that the various academic markets affect them. In the 1980s, the Reagan administration began undercutting the federal enforcement of affirmative action compliance. As a consequence, affirmative action, more than anything, began to provide the sociomoral grounds for reform efforts at local sites.[10] In the university, affirmative action was most commonly monitored by minority and women activists who formed collectivities on specific campuses and university systems.

Affirmative action at UNM had always been attended to most effectively by Chicano professionals. Los Profesores, a loosely formed faculty/staff group, arose out of the ferment of the Chicano movement in the early 1970s. From the start, Los Profesores began consulting with UNM presidents on academic and administrative hiring, student aid and recruitment, grievance cases, and related matters. This work led to the university's 1978 affirmative action plan, which, as the university president at the time declared, was dedicated to the

Table 5.1. Hispanics in Professional Ranks,
University of New Mexico, 1977–1987

	1977	1979	1981	1983	1985	1987
Executive/manager/admin., academic rank/tenure	6	16	10	4	4	10
Faculty, full time	60	69	79	84	84	94
New hires, prof. nonfaculty	19	87	84	86	123	135

Source: Equal Economic Opportunity–6 Reports, 1979, 1981, 1983, 1985, 1987; Affirmative Action Office, University of New Mexico.

"building of a university that will be an outstanding international example of multicultural development."[11]

In the 1980s, Los Profesores gave way as an organization to the fact that some of its members were being incorporated into the central administration. At this point, affirmative action issues were taken up by a contingent of administrators, headed by a Chicano dean with help from a few faculty. By 1985 this group was drawing from a segment of nonfaculty Chicano professionals that had seen a relatively sharp rise in new hires, from 86 in 1983 to 123 in 1985. Between 1981 and 1983, however, the number of Chicano central administration officials had decreased from ten to four (see Table 5.1). Such ratios were at once significant and politically problematic relative to affirmative action— significant enough to form a collective process; problematic within a state population that was 38 percent Hispanic and in which parity as a civil rights goal was well established.

It is clear that by 1985, Chicano affirmative action had carved out a place of its own in the realm of campus power, only to feel some slippage in the central administration. In late 1984, Chicano affirmative action was spearheaded by three Chicano deans and other administrators who diplomatically planned to see that affirmative action remained high on the incoming president's agenda.

Another independent interest in affirmative action issues happened to be taken in late 1984 by Toney Anaya, New Mexico's Hispanic governor. It should be noted that UNM had fallen heir to a tendency toward external political influence in the 1970s, when a conservative state legislature reacted to campus protest by ordering control over student political activity and faculty expression. The chair of the board of regents at that time later wrote that he took this mandate seriously, resulting in tensions with his own president.[12]

In 1984, Anaya, a steadfast liberal, tried his own hand at academic power. Anaya was a progressive Democrat who, at the expense of much popularity, took on the role of national Hispanic spokesman while still governor. Anaya's reform program in New Mexico stressed education. His Commission on Higher Education required New Mexico colleges to form Affirmative Action Councils and annual affirmative action goals. In addition, Anaya appointed John Páez to UNM's board of regents in 1983, giving the board its first ever Spanish-surnamed majority.[13]

The following year, two more seats on the board of regents fell vacant. Anaya made support for affirmative action a major qualification in considering his appointments to university boards of regents. For UNM, he had a confirmed supporter in former Democratic governor Jerry Apodaca.[14] Apodaca participated in Hispanic business organizations, wrote on civil rights, and played broker for corporate foundation funds awarded to Hispanic organizations. Anaya also appointed Robert Sánchez, a young nuclear pharmacist, Republican, and outgoing regent of another New Mexico college. Sánchez's receptiveness to affirmative action was evident early in 1985 when he strongly favored UNM's divestment of stock in companies doing business in South Africa.[15]

Apodaca and Sánchez took their seats on the board of regents on January 1, 1985. On that same day, Tom Farer began his duties as UNM's new president. As an incoming university president, Farer was in some key ways unique. Most university presidents in the United States attain their offices by having moved through the administrative ranks of department chair, dean, and vice-president; by having had distinctly "local" or "parochial" working relations with the institutions that hire them; and by having developed a "reactive," conservative approach in order to handle the myriad pressures that attend a university administrator. None of these aspects of usual presidential professionalism applied in the case of Farer. He had had no previous higher education administrative experience and had been a law professor at Rutgers when he got the job of UNM president. Rather than moving up through the system, his hiring at UNM, facilitated through a professional "head hunting" agency, meant that Farer leaped over the boundaries of interstatus layers that typically characterize the university hierarchy.[16]

Finally, rather than take a normal cautious approach to his new administrative duties, Farer immediately became an activist president. In a move that faculty liked, Farer immediately proclaimed his academic cosmopolitanism. Coming from Rutgers, where he had been a distinguished professor of international law, Farer defined UNM as a regional institution in need of academic upgrading. As he would eventually explain, he went to UNM "on a mission," "to face a challenge," and to act as "an 'agent of change' as president." Farer's mission was to begin elevating UNM's level of excellence. "There ought to be a sense," he tended to say, "that we can be one of the outstanding universities in the country." In the belief that UNM could be instantly "outstanding," he immediately instituted "strategic action," a set of policies developed in America's "best" universities in order to meet the changing demands of academic management. Included in Farer's plan were the recruitment of faculty "stars" from around the world, a strategic planning committee, a "cabinet" form of central administration, and an "imaginative" personal style.[17]

The Pattern of Interference

In this setting, a process of interference among institutional players began in the fall of 1984 before the Hispanic regents came on board and as part of the process which resulted in the hiring of Farer as president. At the time, a divided UNM board of regents had voted to retain an executive search firm in order to conduct a secret national hunt for a president. Anaya juxtaposed regionalism with affirmative action and charged that the regents' strategy eliminated his wish to have special consideration given to "New Mexicans," minorities, and women. Controversy surrounded the fact that several names were mentioned as being on Anaya's list of preferred candidates. The governor was accused of interfering in the prerogatives of the board of regents. One editorial said that the governor "should relegate to second place questions of ethnicity, geography, sex and political persuasion in making his selections."[18]

When the regents accepted the search firm's second recommendation to invite Farer for an interview, Anaya threatened to have unsigned letters of resignation drawn up for the two regents he was due to appoint to ensure that they would break off any subsequent contract with the presumptive president. The attorney general called this a violation of the regents' constitutional autonomy. The regents said they would thwart Anaya by awarding their president a two-year contract that would extend beyond Anaya's term in office. Immediately after Farer interviewed in New Mexico, Anaya and one Chicano regent, soon to be replaced, announced opposition to him, saying that a necessary qualification for the university presidency was experience in and knowledge of the home state, or at least "Western ways." On a three-two vote, the regents offered Farer a two-year contract. Farer accepted, on condition that his contract be reviewed six months before its termination date; this would give him time to search for another job should the new regents not look upon his administration in favor.[19]

Anaya swore "a hands-off policy" toward the university at the start of 1985.

On his previous contract threat, he reportedly said, "I made many mistakes in 1984 and probably one of the most grievous is even suggesting such a move." Apodaca assured him that he was not under the governor's control and told Farer, "We want to work with you from day one." Despite later speculation to the contrary, there is no real evidence that Apodaca and Sánchez were hired specifically to oust Farer.[20] Nevertheless, Farer was well on his way to defining the situation in New Mexico as one in which the political system violated the principle of academic autonomy. He sensed that the regents were likely to interfere administratively based on the fact that from the very beginning, Farer had felt hostility from Regent Sánchez, whom Farer alleged wanted a friend promoted within the administration.[21]

The first stage of tension also included a clash of public images. Farer's cultivated style generated much appeal. Articulate, dapper, sporting a fedora that to many observers epitomized Eastern Establishment, Farer appeared before many community audiences. The media, already unusually attentive to the university for its fiscal problems, exploited Farer's public persona. Apodaca was drawn in sharp contrast. Not only was he associated with Anaya, a highly unpopular governor, but there was also the old rumor of ties to organized crime. The charge had never stuck legally, but this did not stop a conservative state senator from exploiting it by holding up Apodaca's legislative confirmation to the board of regents, before finally saying he had no information which would prevent Apodaca from serving on UNM's board of regents.[22]

THREAT TO THE CHICANO MEANING OF AFFIRMATIVE ACTION

As publicized from the start, Farer's distinguished career included extensive work in the area of human rights — in a presidential appointment to the International Human Rights Commission, as first American to head the commission, and as human rights counsel in Africa and South America. During his presidency, some of Farer's early affirmative action – related decisions appeared consistent with this experience. In five months he appointed two Chicanos to vice-president positions, acceded to the League of United Latin American Citizens' proposal for a Hispanic research position, and reinstated a Chicano programmer that community groups charged was fired by the university radio station for racial reasons.[23]

Farer also consulted with campus Hispanics over affirmative action. Here, however, total cooperation was aborted by what Farer himself called his "cabinet." Farer started the cabinet because, as he said in one of the biting academic evaluations he frequently threw at UNM, the previous provost system was

"both bizarre and dysfunctional." He made up his cabinet by personally selecting individuals for vice-president and other high-level positions. In addition, Farer set about creating his own informal "kitchen cabinet" from among
his many appointees.[24] What proved significant is that Farer's policy of hand-
picking central administrators conflicted with UNM's affirmative action
guideline, long understood by local Chicano administrators, that full-fledged
searches be undertaken within six weeks to permanently fill openings at this
level. The rule was intended to provide fair and open consideration of minorities and women. From the Chicano perspective, Farer circumvented what
had been sought-after procedures. A more moderate response among some
gave the matter less importance in view of Farer's previous affirmative action
overtures. The more circumspect, however, saw it according to the words of
one informant: "Does affirmative action [as law] mean anything or not?"[25]

It appears that when apprised on the cabinet, Regent Apodaca initially
defended Farer's assurance of affirmative action appointments. However, that
a new definition of the situation arose in his mind is indicated in a March 1
story in the campus daily newspaper which briefly quoted Apodaca saying that
the regents' "first goal will be improving excellence of the people in top administrative positions." A week later, on the occasion of his appointing a vice-
president without a search, Farer stood committed to the cabinet system, defending it against current affirmative action policies because "not all major
universities follow such a procedure when promoting a person from within.
'We need to address the question of whether this [policy of full searches] is a
waste of money and time.'"[26]

Farer continued making fiat appointments in the administration in the
coming months, including an executive assistant, a coordinator of external
relations, a deputy vice-president for student affairs, a vice-president for continuing education, two associate vice-presidents for academic affairs, general
counsel of the university, and the vice-president for academic affairs. Two of
these appointments were Hispanic; none were of other minorities. Chicano
skeptics considered it a significant bias that key members of Farer's kitchen
cabinet were taken from the law school, representing the president's own
discipline.

Governor Anaya came back into the picture on May 2, which suggested
to Farer the connection between affirmative action and political meddling in
the university. That day, the Advisory Committee to the U.S. Commission on
Civil Rights conducted a forum entitled "Affirmative Action Issues at the University of New Mexico." The committee's special concern was new statistics
showing the lowering in recent years of minority and women's participation
on the faculty and administration. Farer testified in the morning, pledging himself to vigorous minority faculty recruitment. In the afternoon, a series of gov-

ernment and community speakers of Hispanic, Black, and Native American backgrounds criticized UNM for allegedly excluding New Mexico citizens.

Anaya's director of the Human Rights Commission made obvious allusions to Farer. "[I]t's kind of interesting . . . to me," he said, "that someone coming from a state like New Jersey where there are large numbers of blacks and Hispanics is amazed when coming to New Mexico. We're amazed, as natives of this state, how ignorant some people are who are hired for some supposedly sensitive high paying positions from other parts of the country and they do not take time or it does not become a requirement for them to understand a culture and the needs of the people of New Mexico."[27]

Farer responded in ten days by amplifying his viewpoint in a speech at commencement. His themes were the ultimate purpose of a university and how a president of one should define success. Farer acknowledged in his speech that these were questions he had had "few incentives" to ask himself six months previously, when, as he said, "I was still living the relatively carefree, rather hermetic life of an academic."

Farer would conclude that the sole purpose of the university was to encourage the "passion to press against the frontiers of knowledge." First, he felt it necessary to cite other notions of UNM in particular. "One view I have detected," Farer told his audience,

is that the university is a form of legitimate political prey, a large cluster of jobs available for allocation to people who have paid their political dues or have the right sorts of friends or preferably both. Probably such a perception is inevitable in any state where the university is one of the largest single employers and where the public sector has historically provided an important source of political patronage. Since this notion of the university collides harshly with other ideas about the university's role, ideas often held by the very same people who are affected by what we might call the 'cluster-of-jobs' syndrome, the latter perception rarely surfaces openly except, perhaps, in the form of claims about the distinctive virtues or superior rights of New Mexico citizens competing with outsiders who would like to become citizens. As long as I am President of UNM, it will remain open to men and women from every part of the country and the world who possess the skills and the character and the commitment one finds on the campuses of all great universities."[28]

Farer had his commencement address reproduced on June 5 in the state's largest newspaper, the *Albuquerque Journal*. In mid June, a letter to the editor hinted at Farer's power of suggestion, as it praised UNM for having a president who at last "spoke like a scholar" and cited the "cluster of jobs" reference. Anticipating the tone of public opinion that would soon arise against the regents, the letter ended by referring to nameless "political hacks" influencing the university.[29]

BREAKDOWN OF DIPLOMACY

Collective episodes are usually sparked by dramatic incidents. The conflict that arose in this case was precipitated at a meeting Apodaca and Sánchez convened on July 2. No recording of this meeting was made. A news report later said, "In a move many on campus call unprecedented, Apodaca and Regent Robert Sánchez in early July called a meeting of UNM deans and vice presidents to talk about increasing the number of minorities in academic positions. Descriptions of the closed door meeting range from a pep talk to high pressure politics."[30] Similar recollections by informants reflect views of the meeting from three frames of reference: the president and his kitchen cabinet; those who pressed for affirmative action, including Apodaca, Sánchez, and two Chicano administrators; and several deans from the campus at large.

The regular deans sat as witness to a confrontation between the other two groups. The news report said that "Apodaca expressed satisfaction with Farer's commitment to affirmative action. But he is less satisfied with appointments by lower level administrators and by individual department chairmen." This alluded to the fact that in the meeting, Apodaca singled out one member of the kitchen cabinet for reproach on the law school's affirmative action record. Another cabinet member apparently rose to his colleague's defense. Apodaca's forceful counter, that no one should feel satisfied about affirmative action progress, closed off the exchange. A third cabinet informant recalled that "this was the first blow across the brow of President Farer."

In September, Farer ordered reprints of his commencement address sent to offices throughout campus. Shortly thereafter a series of stories in the media began projecting the regents and the president in a state of battle. The first issue, a proposal to improve the football stadium, did not involve ethnopolitics or affirmative action, but did lead a political columnist to see a "quickening campus maelstrom." What should have, but did not, serve to dampen one conspiracy theory was the stand the columnist attributed to Governor Anaya, who opposed the stadium proposal, while Apodaca supported it.[31]

As the stadium controversy drew the public line between the regents and the president, a volatile issue arose in October. The regents voted in a confidential appeal to overturn the one-semester suspension of a law student who was found to have falsified an application form. In addition to Apodaca and Sánchez, the split vote was carried by Regent Colleen Maloof, who had originally voted against the hiring of Farer. Once the decision was leaked, anonymous members of Farer's cabinet treated it as a gauntlet, charging a serious infringement on their daily operations. The first news account of the meeting quoted "sources close to the regents" saying that "[s]everal high-level administrators came close to resigning over the affair."[32]

Apodaca raised the Chicano issue regarding Farer's cabinet. That so many of its members had been law school administrators, he argued, meant that their acting replacements had weakened the law student's right to full due process. The case had run the official course and would not be formally dealt with again. Endangering his right to confidentiality, the press was told that the student involved was Hispanic and that his family was known to Apodaca. The vote split the Hispanic regents. John Páez, who had originally voted to hire Farer and who had voted against the law student's appeal, defended the administration, reportedly asking if the university was "entering an age of degrees by patronage, or diplomas by patronage? Not what you know, but who you know?" Anticipating the provision which said that continuation of Farer's two-year contract had to be settled six months in advance of its official termination, Páez said Apodaca was holding the contract renewal "hostage."[33]

Serving as a court of last resort is a traditional responsibility of a college governing board. But as one expert says, "Concomitant with the responsibility to act in this appellate capacity is the judgement to know when not to act." In short, the student's case should have been resolved prior to the need for an appeal in private agreement between regents and president. But such normal working relations had by this point broken down. To Farer, the root problem was the regents' political meddling. To Apodaca, it was the role of the cabinet. Reflecting a clash at the level of social constructions, Apodaca said, "While I'm there, the university is going to be responsive to the students, not to the prima donnas who have administrative posts."[34]

The law student's case produced serious campus discussion on student appeal procedures. But the public condemned and disparaged the regents. In claiming that the university was being subjected to "patronage politics, favoritism and personalistic particularism," an emeritus professor referred to the "political culture of Santa Fe," a phrase Farer would later pick up to explain his problems in New Mexico. Another professor, already famous for his cynical blasts at those he disagreed with, set out in his column in the campus newspaper to develop a satire of Apodaca as an Italian fascist lording over his (university) realm. "Finally," he wrote, "the UNM Board of Regents has a leader who is not afraid to lead and to exercise fully the god-given powers of La Tavola Nostra." Similarly, a Roswell citizen wrote that the regents "reeked" of "something like Nazism or the Politburo." A political columnist toyed with the suspicion allegedly held by the governor's enemies that Anaya was "feathering a nest" so as to become president of the university himself. It was further rumored, the columnist said, that Apodaca himself wanted the presidency and that he would "cut [the Governor] out of the action" when the time came.[35]

The law student controversy began to subside when affirmative action arose as a prominent issue in November and December. The regents had kept the affirmative action pressure up by requiring a monthly report on faculty hiring from the campus affirmative action officer. Apodaca also reminded the faculty senate and Farer of the possible violation of affirmative action laws as searches for the permanent appointment of top administrative positions had not yet begun. Farer, meanwhile, requested that the campus Chicano leaders submit their affirmative action concerns in writing. Eight recommendations were submitted, and on December 2 Farer convened a meeting to discuss them. Fifty to sixty Hispanic faculty and staff attended. In a long and tense session, Farer would agree to a special fund to attract qualified minority faculty, although on the cabinet he persisted in favoring permanence for most of those already in office.[36]

What dominated the meeting, however, were the caustic exchanges. Farer took immediate control, ousting a television news reporter and camera operator and making clear his displeasure that the core Chicano leadership had already met with the regents on affirmative action (though this had been announced to him in memo two months before). Ethnic sensitivities were aroused when Farer charged that the Chicanos present were lacking in the *cortesía*, traditional courtesy, he was accustomed to when dealing with Latin Americans. Farer called Anaya a "demagogue" for stating that Hispanic representation on the faculty should approach the proportion of Hispanics in the state's population. The director of UNM's Chicano Studies program reacted angrily to this charge. Peaceful discussion on the academic objection to absolute ethnic parity was short-circuited. To the Chicanos, Farer appeared as a name-calling outsider; to Farer, the Chicanos appeared as a political mob. The friction overall alienated many Chicanos from the president, and he from some of them, regardless of his stated commitment to affirmative action. Some Chicanos were not particularly put off, while still others were caught in what one described as a "moral quandary" between the ethnic tensions arising and the fact that the president had actually supported some Chicano causes on campus.

Farer held the reins against the Chicano collectivity, but lost them to the regents at their monthly meeting in Santa Fe a week later. Anaya gave perfunctory welcoming remarks and departed. The press reported on a nonethnic argument that had arisen in the meeting but neglected to make clear that it had preceded the one on affirmative action. Apodaca reported that legislators had complained to him about Farer's "boondoggle" alumni trip to New York. Farer implied in defense that the regents were shirking their responsibility to raise funds. The snide and rather anarchic exchange on the level of official conflict opened up the ground for a duel over affirmative action.

UNM's affirmative action officer presented figures showing that the university's long-established goals for hiring minority faculty were falling short. Apodaca and Sánchez took some time pinning Farer, suggesting that he was not moving quickly or effectively enough in this area. The press would depict the regents "shaking heads angrily" and "visibly upset." An editorial cartoon caricatured regents on a statement concerning the need for a rise in absolute numbers of minorities. Editorials and letters called the attack on Farer unseemly and the accusations unjustified, especially as Farer had earlier announced his fund for minority faculty recruitment and other related actions. The press scored the regents as Machiavellians wielding an affirmative action "club" in order to dispose of Farer.[37] While Farer believed affirmative action served meritocracy by expanding the pool of talent from which departments could draw, he still held to the academic ideal that the "most qualified" should be hired regardless of ethnicity. The public view held that on this score the regents were cynical, although Apodaca and Sánchez's response can be seen as having reflected a kind of "freedom now" civil rights demand.[38]

Sánchez told Farer in regard to minority representation on the faculty, "We want to get to the bottom of this issue and we want to meet these [established UNM faculty] goals." Farer at one point referred to the problems that arise when only "conspicuously inferior" persons apply under affirmative action. Apodaca called the comment "very disturbing," interpreting Farer to mean, "'Do you want us to continue to hire white males or do you want us to hire inferior people and hire women and minorities?'" Decrying his reticence, the regents wished to see Farer "out in the trenches," talking to deans and department chairs, instilling the commitment to hire minorities that the regents noted one department had already demonstrated. While the press called this a "brow beating," it more accurately reflected a classic confrontation between "those who regard the university as a facilitator of social mobility and those who place a premium on the university as a safeguard of academic (that is cognitively rational) traditions."[39]

Apodaca closed off the exchange, emphasizing that should Farer not realize progress, he would indeed "meddle" to instill the proper commitment in department heads. After other routine business, brief discussion ensued on the central administration and the cabinet. The meeting concluded with Farer grudgingly agreeing to the regents' call for national and local searches for all cabinet-level positions.

This should have been seen as an important point of compromise. But public opinion continued mostly against the regents, concluding variously that they were attempting to enforce illegal affirmative action quotas; that the "politicization of the university under the guise of affirmative action" would hamper the state's economic development; and that as "political provincials," the

Hispanic regents had someone else in mind for president. Apodaca and several other Chicanos responded with essays on the principle of affirmative action, inexplicably making little mention of the cabinet issue. These were met by philosophical, partisan, or ideological counters and attacks. One of the few ethnic allusions among the anti-regent statements was that as "reactionaries" opposing "visionaries," Apodaca and Sánchez were incapable of laying to rest their "ancestral persecutions and paranoia of outsiders, in order to move ahead in brotherly love with their Anglo brothers for a new beginning." Among the regent defenders, one letter writer asserted that the attacks on Anaya, Apodaca, and Sánchez were meant to reflect on the integrity of Hispanic politics itself. The reaction, he said, stemming from the "underlying racism that upholds structures of inequality," intended to portray the regents and the governor as "the slimy Hispanic patron, the dissolute Mexican power-players."[40]

OFFICIAL CONFLICT

As Farer relented on the cabinet at the December regents meeting, the threat to the Chicano construction of affirmative action had been lifted and the specifically ethnic protest against Farer ended. However, official tensions between Farer and the regents lasted another five months. As they did, Chicanos at large tended to sense a continuing ethnic conflict. The public record indicates that during the spring semester tensions eased and then rose again to a high resolving pitch.

One Chicano dean implied that Anaya's concern with minority faculty was misplaced. Departing from the confrontation with the president, he hand-delivered a petition to the board of regents from his college that objected to blaming a new president for affirmative action problems that were long standing in the university. In the weeks afterward, Apodaca appeared conciliatory, telling the Rotary Club he was willing to see if Farer had the ability to be a good administrator and expressing hope that his presidential term would be a long one. One editorial called Apodaca's words "a welcome departure" from his previous attitude.[41]

But the press speculated that the regents were prematurely reviewing Farer's contract. Regent Sánchez and an athletic administrator were reported saying that it was Farer who had himself previously attempted to secure a second, considerably longer contract. This sort of exchange served to keep public opinion aroused and mostly critical of the regents. In this election year, it also led to a joint legislative resolution that proposed to give the voters a chance to amend the state constitution by adding two more seats to UNM's board of regents. The bill's sponsors said its intent was to "dilute" the power of "certain" board members and to make it more difficult for a governor to control the board. (Ironically, the 1983 state legislature had defeated a bill supported by Anaya which proposed to give the boards of regents at New Mexico colleges greater diversity by increasing their membership from five to nine.)

The regents' consensus in February favored offering Farer a second term. He said this seemed like an expression of confidence for which he was "delighted." Editorials expressed hope for campus stability. The regents announced that they would have to review applicant résumés and approve administrative appointments. Farer reportedly said this was a "compromise we can all work well with."[42]

But feelings on campus still smoldered. With the prospect of negligible pay raises for faculty, the professor with the weekly column gratuitously wrote that a faculty strike should be proposed except that Anaya "would come up with a thousand in-laws to take our place." A Chicano student's retort stressed Anaya's favorable higher education record and said that the professor columnist "would best serve the dual cause of misguided Anglocentrism and increased faculty salaries by deferring to his intellectual superiors and retiring to the damp, dark, mucky underside of the eastern seaboard rock from whence he and his sort periodically and predictably emerge [where] he can comfortably renew his search for 'truth' unimpeded by the realities of Hispanic regents and governors." In the legislature, the bill to increase membership on the Board of Regents passed and was on its way to the November ballot.[43]

At the March regents meeting, Apodaca pressed Farer on thirteen administrative positions for which searches were not as yet underway. Without permanence in key posts, Apodaca insisted, important matters such as student rights of appeal still hung in the balance. Farer raised no objection. Contention between the two major parties was largely absent in the news. Instead, reflecting two generally activist administrations, the president and the regents each sparked their separate controversies. Saying he meant only to place his work station on par with any American university president, Farer was criticized for "extravagantly" renovating his office at a time when university funding was at low ebb. Shortly after, the five Catholic regents ordered a student film committee not to show the controversial movie *Hail Mary*, only to rescind the ban after the Associated Students filed suit. Public reaction, including picketing by community Catholics at the movie's showing, lasted close to a month.[44]

FINALE

Dispute at the top broke out again in mid April when it was reported that at the time of the *Hail Mary* controversy Farer was secretly interviewing for positions at two eastern universities. Apodaca reverted to an angry tone, reportedly saying Farer "did not care" about the university and wondering if it was in the best interest of the university to renew the contract of someone "who is only interested in enhancing his own career." Farer defended the job hunt, saying it was in November that he had begun making inquiries elsewhere because, he explained, the "overall setting" in New Mexico as well as the threat from Apodaca that he would "run him off" the campus (which Apodaca denied having made) caused him to doubt that he could accomplish what he had intended when he took the job. As the day scheduled for the regents to review Farer's contract approached, several names were mentioned in the press as possible presidential replacements.[45]

In late April the regents decided in closed session to extend Farer's contract. At that very time, however, Farer taped a television interview in which he returned to the theme of his commencement address. After the evening news had announced his new contract offer, Farer appeared on television in cosmopolitan frame of mind, saying that the regents operated according to a "culture of political cronyism, rewarding themselves, family and friends" while thwarting the meritocracy of academia which he said rewarded "people for their contributions to the end of the system." Farer claimed he had been "publicly lacerated" on affirmative action. Claiming he was stopped because he would not turn "yes-man," and feeling his integrity impugned in regard to his job search, Farer said he could continue as president only on an open pledge of support from the regents.[46]

Fallout from the interview lasted several weeks. A Chicano administrator whom Farer had accused of using pressure tactics to get a promotion called Farer a liar. Signaling the rupture of Farer's base, a member of his cabinet corroborated the Chicano administrator's version. Anaya was reported prepared to step in to bring the university under control if need be. Editorials and letters ran mostly anti-regents. Campus petitions and radio polls were interpreted as favoring Farer. Gubernatorial candidates and a group of city professionals deplored the university conflict, the regents' role in particular.[47]

The faculty, an estimated seven hundred strong, rallied to consider two resolutions: that they actively work for passage of the constitutional amendment to expand the board of regents; and that they vote no confidence in the board for discrediting, interfering, and not effectively leading the university. In a great show of indignation, in which some of the attempts to negotiate the terms of the resolutions were shouted down, these resolutions and a third calling on all five regents to resign were overwhelmingly adopted. A circular drawn up by IMAGE (Incorporated Mexican American Government Employees) was distributed at the meeting, asserting that President Farer had "grievously damaged the Hispanic community by holding us up to public ridicule and scorn and . . . impairing our image and standing within the university and in the community at large." Alluding to the original affirmative action grievance, IMAGE charged that in forming his cabinet "Tom Farer has employed the buddy system himself in his actions and appointments at the University."[48]

That afternoon Apodaca appeared as a guest on the television program that had interviewed Farer a few days earlier. Apodaca avoided Farer's allegations, emphasizing the board's willingness to start a new period of cooperation with him. Asked to reflect on the ideal candidate for UNM president, Apodaca all but eliminated any cosmopolitan outsider as he listed, in order of preference, a state resident, someone from within UNM, and someone who knew the state well. Soon after, and without a public pledge of support from the regents, Farer announced he would not accept another contract under any circumstance. He and the board of regents proceeded into negotiations for an early "buy-out" of his contract. The board announced appointment of a dean as interim president effective July 1, 1986.[49]

The conflict in UNM's authority structure ended here. That fall, New Mexico voters approved the constitutional amendment creating two more positions on the board of regents. They also elected Republican Garry Carruthers governor. The term of one of the board members ended in December. With three new appointments in the offing, UNM's board of regents was set for its second major recomposition in as many years. Carruthers appointed three Anglo males, one who had been living in the state but six months.

CONCLUSION

This chapter has described and accounted for the Chicano dimension within UNM's 1985–1986 regents-president dispute. The conflict overall involved more than ethnic conditions and events, some not included here. In this sense, the Chicano protest tactics meshed with the problems that otherwise inhere in the relations between trustees and presidents.

UNM's Chicano regents were led to become ethnically hostile with the president insofar as they took up the specific cause for affirmative action that the local Chicano perspective had defended. The link to the Chicano movement was provided by a core of Hispanic administrators whose activism stemmed from the original Los Profesores organization. President Farer's aggressive, cosmopolitan administrative practice interfered with the local Chicano construction of affirmative action. His reluctance to see eye to eye with the regents on the issue of cabinet appointments was reinforced by his definition of a politicized situation at UNM. While Apodaca attempted to call attention to the cabinet issue, it was practically impossible for the public to see the social importance of the preestablished rules on affirmative action that the Chicano group had worked so long to effect.

Farer's definition of a politicized institution was not entirely inaccurate. But much of what Farer included as undue political influence reflected a universal tendency toward power concentration throughout the bureaucracies of state institutions. Much of the rest stemmed from the classic standard in U.S. society that, as a public institution, the university should be an "'instrument of the people,' [placing] its resources at the disposal of all members of the state who need its aid."[50] In fairness, Apodaca and Sánchez appeared unwilling or incapable of recognizing the optimism that Farer supplied to a demoralized and underpaid faculty.

Oddly enough, despite the appearance of complete institutional breakdown in the dispute, affirmative action was served by both sides but on different tracks. Farer did in fact promote minority recruitment, as the League of United Latin American Citizens tended to point out (see Table 5.1), while the regents' concern did serve to open up opportunity in the central administration in accordance with the spirit of UNM's original affirmative action plan. In this regard, affirmative action appeared vulnerable to approach and construction from various points of origin. In principle, the governor, the regents, Chicano leaders, and the president all agreed on the need for affirmative action. But the question of its locus of control arose dynamically in the dispute, whether it would emanate as part of a cosmopolitan liberal construction or from the framework of campus collectivities.

By now, the language of affirmative action is largely supplanted by that of "multiculturalism." The specific goals of multiculturalism have yet to be clearly spelled out. But it is not entirely clear that affirmative action per se, which has been under attack from both the left and the right, could arise as the center of such heated dispute at UNM as was seen in 1985.

Out of the throes of the Farer controversy, some Chicano administrators created Hispanics for UNM (HUNM), an organization designed for Hispanic faculty, staff, and administrators from throughout the university. HUNM functioned a few years in various activities, including scholarship drives and greater-community projects. But the organization waned with the retirement of a key leader. The political center of gravity for Chicanos on campus shifted somewhat to the ranks of faculty, particularly in the College of Arts and Sciences, while the Chicano Studies program embarked on a new expansion. In line with a national trend, there was a resurgence of Chicano consciousness to be noted among the ranks of Spanish-surnamed students.[51] These are all indications that the ethos of the Chicano movement persisted at UNM.

For a whole complex of reasons (not least of which was a contest among powerful personalities), the president and the regents became locked in a personal and institutional antagonism that was destined to play itself out. At the least and in a context in which institutional inclusion arose as a dominant goal of Hispanic ethnopolitics, the regents-president dispute at the University of New Mexico demonstrates the sociostructural and political stakes that can arise as Chicanos set out to participate, as Chicanos, in the circles of institutional power.

NOTES

1. Carlos Muñoz, *Youth, Identity, Power: The Chicano Movement* (London: Verso, 1989), chaps. 3 and 5.

2. See Harold L. Hodgkinson and L. Richard Meeth, eds., *Power and Authority: Transformation of Campus Governance* (San Francisco: Jossey-Bass, 1971).

3. Jacques Barzun, *The American University* (New York: Harper & Row, 1968), p. 147n.

4. Joseph Rothschild, *Ethnopolitics: A Conceptual Framework* (New York: Columbia University Press, 1981), p. 142.

5. Several participants in the dispute consented to anonymous interviews; hereafter cited as Interview.

6. Michael Brown and Amy Goldin, *Collective Behavior: A Review and Reinterpretation of the Literature* (Pacific Palisades, Calif.: Goodyear Publishing, 1973), pp. 178, 201, 214; see also pp. 129–130, 201–204, 289–290. While authority figures or public opinion may define short-term collective outbursts as socially unauthorized, deviant, or unscrupulous, it is more accurate to regard it as "unauthorized socio-political action."

7. Ibid., pp. 255–256, 259.

8. Ibid., pp. 269, 215; see also pp. 141, 145, 261, 270, 276.

9. David A. Snow, E. Burke Rochford, Jr., Steven K. Worden, and Robert D. Benford, "Frame Alignment Processes, Microbilization, and Movement Participation," p. 464 in *American Sociological Review*, 51 (August 1986): 464. Frame alignment in this sense occurs through "frame bridging" ("the linkage of two or more ideologically congruent but structurally unconnected frames regarding a particular issue or problem"); "frame amplification" ("the clarification and invigoration of an interpretive frame that bears on a particular issue, problem or set of events"); or "frame extension" (an SMO extending "the boundaries of its primary framework so as to encompass interests or points of view that are incidental to its primary objectives but of considerable salience to potential adherents"). Ibid., pp. 467, 468, 472.

10. Ray T. Fortunato and D. Geneva Waddell, *Personnel Administration in Higher Education: Handbook of Faculty and Staff Personnel Practices* (San Francisco: Jossey-Bass, 1981), pp. 91–93; see Ron Simmons, *Affirmative Action: Conflict and Change in Higher Education After Bakke* (Cambridge, Mass.: Schenkman, 1982.), especially chap. 4; Willie F. Page, "Recruiting Black Faculty: A Brief History of Efforts by White Institutions of Higher Education Prior to Bakke," in George L. Mims, ed., *The Minority Administrator in Higher Education* (Cambridge, Mass: Schenkman, 1981), p. 3; Félix Padilla, *Latino Ethnic Consciousness: The Case of Mexican Americans and Puerto Ricans in Chicago* (Notre Dame, Ind.: University of Notre Dame Press, 1985), p. 84; and ibid., "Latino Ethnicity in the City of Chicago," in Susan Olzak and Joane Nagel, eds., *Competitive Ethnic Relations* (Orlando: Academic Press, 1986), pp. 163–164.

11. See, e.g., "Points of Concern of Hispanic Faculty Presented to President William E. Davis by Representatives of Los Profesores," manuscript, n.a., n.d. [c. 1980]; Sabine R. Ulibarri to Dear Colleague, "Emergency Meeting of Los Profesores," May 6, 1980; William E. Davis to Chairman Sabine Ulibarri et al., "William E. Davis, President, to Representatives of Los Profesores," May 27, 1980; *Ethnic Minorities at the University of New Mexico: A Presidential Progress Report* (Albuquerque: University of New Mexico, May 1977), p. 16.

12. See Calvin Horn, *The University in Turmoil and Transition* (Albuquerque: Rocky Mountain Publishing, 1981), chaps. 10 and 17; for a general view, see Ralph K. Huitt, "Governance in the 1970s," in Hodgkinson and Meeth, eds., *Power and Authority*, p. 176.

13. Cara Abeyta, "Hispanic Force 184: Collective Symbolism or Political Reality?" Chicano Studies Occasional Paper Series, University of Texas El Paso, November 1984; *The Future is Excellence: Report of the New Mexico Governor's Commission on Higher Education* (Santa Fe: State of New Mexico, 1983), pp. 8–9.

14. Nationally, Latinos form less than 1 per cent of members on all university boards of regents and only 4 percent of all members on public four-year single campus boards. See *Composition of Governing Boards, 1985: A Survey of College and University Boards* (Washington, D.C.: Association of Governing Boards of Universities and Colleges, 1986), pp. 9, 30. The University of New Mexico is an institution that, except for 1931–1933, has seen Chicanos serve on its governing board ever since its founding in 1889. Since 1940, nearly one-third of regent appointees at UNM have been Chicano (see Records of the University Secretary, University of New Mexico). UNM stands as an exception to the national trend of underrepresentation.

15. On Apodaca see, e.g., the *New Mexico Sun*, March 6, 1985; *Diálogo: Annual Report Issue for 1986* 2, no. 4, p. 12; and *Albuquerque Journal*, February 3, 1986. On Sánchez, see, e.g., *Albuquerque Journal*, May 7, 8, 1985.

16. Michael D. Cohen and James G. March, *Leadership and Ambiguity: The American College President* (Boston: Harvard Business School Press, 1986), pp. 1–2, 17–28. Brown and Goldin, *Collective Behavior*, p. 269.

17. Liz McMillen, "Feud between President and Regents Debilitates University of New Mexico," *Chronicle of Higher Education*, June 4, 1986, p. 23. *Albuquerque Journal*, May 1, 1985; and George Keller, *Academic Strategy: The Management Revolution in American Higher Education* (Baltimore: Johns Hopkins University Press, 1983), pp. 611, 125, 143–144. For the parallels between Farer's program and strategic action, compare Keller (chap. 5) with Farer's description of his own program in *Albuquerque Journal*, January 3, 1985; *Daily Lobo*, May 30, 1985; "State of the University: A Report from the President," University of New Mexico, September 1985.

18. *Albuquerque Journal*, August 8, 29, 1984. Anaya's regionalism reflected the kind of expressions that were common in peripheral areas against the national, international, and ideologically universalist dimensions of higher education. See Christopher Jencks and David Riesman, *The Academic Revolution* (Garden City, N.Y.: Doubleday, 1968), chap. 4. For New Mexico's history of education, see Robert W. Larson, *New Mexico's Quest for Statehood, 1846–1912* (Albuquerque: University of New Mexico Press, 1968), pp. 279–280; Phillip B. Gonzales, "Spanish Heritage and Ethnic Protest: The Anti-Fraternity Bill of 1933," *New Mexico Historical Review* 61, no. 4 (October 1986): 282–283.

19. *Albuquerque Journal*, September 5, 7, 19, 1984.

20. *Albuquerque Tribune*, January 3, 1985; *Albuquerque Journal*, January 17, 1985. Farer would eventually say that he had Apodaca's cooperation at the beginning. Moreover, Anaya clearly steered away from UNM throughout its turmoil in 1985–1986. See *Daily Lobo*, April 24, 1986. Bill Hume, "UNM Tug-of-War Could Pull in Anaya," *Albuquerque Journal*, November 10, 1985.

21. *Albuquerque Tribune*, April 24, 1986.

22. *Albuquerque Journal*, March 3, 1985; *Albuquerque Tribune*, March 6, 1985. Throughout 1985–1986, some of the bigger media stories on UNM involved the fiscal tug-of-war between a liberal governor calling for increases in higher education funding and a conservative legislature curtailing the proposal, course cutbacks, a brain drain to other universities, and management of the athletic department's budget.

23. *Albuquerque Journal*, September 10, 16, 1984; also, e.g., March 6, 14; April 19; May 7, 8, 1985; and *Albuquerque Tribune*, May 8, 1985.

24. President to Board of Regents, University of New Mexico, Nov. 1, 1985. For a discussion of the "dysfunctional" consequences of the cabinet style of leadership in higher education, see L. Richard Meeth, "Administration and Leadership," in Hodgkinson and Meeth, eds., *Power and Authority*, pp. 42–43.

25. Chronology of Hiring Process for Academic Personnel, UNM Affirmative Action Manual; and interview.

26. See e.g., *Daily Lobo*, March 1, 1985; *Albuquerque Tribune*, April 4, 1985; *Albuquerque Journal*, March 6; April 5, May 7, May 15, 1985.

27. Partial recording of forum proceedings, courtesy Vicente Silva; interviews. See also "Affirmative Action Issues at the University of New Mexico — An Update, Briefing Memorandum to the Commissioners: A Community Forum, May 2, 1985; New Mexico Advisory Committee to the U.S. Commission on Civil Rights; and *Albuquerque Journal*, May 3, 1985.

28. "The Purposes of the University: An Address Presented by Tom J. Farer, President of the University of New Mexico, at the Ninety-Third Commencement of the University of New Mexico," May 12, 1985, n.p.

29. *Albuquerque Journal*, June 17, 1985.

30. Mary Engel, "University Hiring Practices Still Draw Criticism," *The Sunday Journal*, August 25, 1985.

31. *Albuquerque Tribune*, September 18, 29, 1985. *Daily Lobo*, November 20; December 16, 1985. *Albuquerque Journal*, November 1, 11, 1985.

32. *Albuquerque Journal*, October 20, 1985; November 3, 1985; *Daily Lobo*, October 23, November 4, 1985.

33. *Daily Lobo*, November 13, 1985; *Albuquerque Journal*, October 20, 1985.

34. *Daily Lobo*, October 23, 1985. On the responsibility of college boards, see Morton A. Rauh, *The Trusteeship of Colleges and Universities* (New York: McGraw-Hill, 1969), pp. 8–9.

35. *Daily Lobo*, November 26, 20, 1985; (Roswell) *Daily Record*, November 22, 1985; *Albuquerque Tribune*, November 29, 1985.

36. *Daily Lobo*, November 13; December 16, 1985. This account of the meeting is based on the author's participant observation. The meeting is mentioned in *Albuquerque Journal*, December 3, 1985, and *Daily Lobo*, December 5, 1985.

37. Factual statements about this meeting are based on its official recorded proceeding, Office of UNM Secretary. See also *Albuquerque Tribune*, December 11, 20, 1985; *Albuquerque Journal*, December 11, 12 (editorial), 13, 15, 20, 1985.

38. John C. Livingston, *Fair Game? Inequality and Affirmative Action* (San Francisco: W. H. Freeman, 1979), pp. 4–5, 233–234. On the dilemmas of affirmative action facing the traditional cultural values of academia, see William H. Exum, "Climbing the Crystal Stair: Values, Affirmative Action, and Minority Faculty," *Social Problems* 30, no. 4 (1983): 384.

39. Neil J. Smelser, "Epilogue: Social-Structural Dimensions of Higher Education," in Talcott Parsons and Gerald M. Platt, *The American University* (Cambridge: Harvard University Press,

1973), p. 399; see also the discussion of Jeffersonian intellectuals vs. Jacksonian social democrats in Frederick E. Balderston, *Managing Today's University* (San Francisco: Jossey-Bass, 1984), pp. 272–273.

40. *Albuquerque Journal*, December 4, 19, 22, 1985; *Albuquerque Tribune*, December 24, 26, 1985; *Daily Lobo*, December 9, 1985.

41. *Daily Lobo*, January 20, 1986; *Albuquerque Journal*, January 17, 19 (editorial), 1986.

42. *Albuquerque Tribune*, January 11, 25, February 5, 1986; *Daily Lobo*, January 28, February 11, 1986; *Albuquerque Journal*, January 19, February 5, 6, 12, 1986.

43. *Daily Lobo*, February 12, 26, 1986; *Albuquerque Journal*, February 7, 1986.

44. Official transcript, UNM Board of Regents Meeting, March 11, 1986. *Albuquerque Journal*, March 11, 1986; *Daily Lobo*, April 22, 24, 29, 1986.

45. *Albuquerque Journal*, April 23, 1986; *Daily Lobo*, April 22, 1986.

46. *Daily Lobo*, April 24, 1986; *Albuquerque Journal*, April 24, 1986; *Albuquerque Tribune*, April 24, 1986.

47. *Daily Lobo*, April 25, 29; May 1, 12, 1986; *Albuquerque Tribune*, April 25, May 9, 21, 1986; *Albuquerque Journal*, April 25, 30, May 7, 1986.

48. *Albuquerque Journal*, May 9, 1986; *Daily Lobo*, May 12, 1986; participant observation; IMAGE de Albuquerque to Mr. Jerry Apodaca, April 30, 1986.

49. *Albuquerque Journal*, May 9, 25, June 4, 5, 1986; *Albuquerque Tribune*, May 20, 24, 1986.

50. J. J. Findlay, quoted in Barzun, *The American University*, p. 1. That trustees in general, who usually come from the world of business, tend to lack adequate understanding of academia, is argued in John J. Corson, *The Governance of Colleges and Universities: Modernizing Structure and Processes* (New York: McGraw-Hill, 1975), pp. 263–273.

51. See the *Chronicle of Higher Education*, October 13, 1993.

Six

IN SEARCH
OF NATIONAL POWER

Chicanos Working the System on Immigration Reform, 1976–1986

CHRISTINE MARIE SIERRA

An important transformation has taken place in the politics of Mexican Americans at the national level. In short, Chicano politics have moved from "recognition politics" to the politics of "institutionalized power."[1] During the 1960s and early 1970s, a period marked by social protest and broad-scale political mobilization, Mexican Americans sought national recognition as a legitimate and significant group within the American polity. With that end more or less achieved by the 1980s, attention turned to another goal: the institutionalization of group power in national politics. Over the past two decades, then, a critical challenge for Chicano politics has been the creation of a long-term, well-rooted basis of group power to impact U.S. policies at the national level.

Mexican American efforts to institutionalize their presence in national politics continue to evolve. It is important to examine both the nature and the consequences of Chicano attempts to penetrate previously inaccessible centers of power and decision making. This study analyzes Chicano efforts specifically directed toward the U.S. Congress to influence national policy on immigration reform.

Chicano activism on the issue of immigration spanning the decade of 1976–1986 serves as the specific focus for analysis. An important evolution in the nature of Chicano politics took place over this period of time. Chicanos moved from grassroots mobilization on the issue to the development of a new "Hispanic lobby" in Washington, D.C. In the end, the study reveals a growing presence of Chicanos in national politics. At the same time, it points to important challenges that confront the group as it becomes incorporated into the policymaking process.

UNDER THE CARTER ADMINISTRATION, 1976–1980

Immigration as a policy issue has appeared at the top of the nation's political agenda intermittently throughout the twentieth century. In recent times, it was President Jimmy Carter who promoted immigration reform as a national concern of critical importance. On August 4, 1977, President Carter proposed to Congress "a set of actions to help markedly reduce the increasing flow of undocumented aliens in this country and to regulate the presence of the millions of undocumented aliens already here."[2]

Carter's proposals included the implementation of employer sanctions, stricter enforcement of the U.S.-Mexican border, and an adjustment of status or "amnesty" for long-term undocumented residents in the United States. He also called for a restructured temporary foreign worker (H-2) certification program for farm labor. He indicated continued "cooperation with source countries" in pursuing U.S.-sponsored programs for economic assistance and called for a "comprehensive review" of existing immigration laws and policies. Carter acknowledged that his proposals developed from both "a thorough Cabinet-level study" of immigration, previously commissioned by the Ford Administration, and Congressional proposals that had been advanced since the beginning of the decade.[3]

In October 1977, Carter's legislative package was formally introduced into Congress as the Alien Adjustment and Employment Act of 1977 (S. 2252/ H.R. 9531). The "Carter Plan," as the President's package came to be called, launched Congressional efforts to solve the problem of undocumented immigration — efforts that would span the next ten years. The Carter Plan also triggered a rebirth of Chicano activism, which had been in relative decline since the early 1970s.

"Abajo con la Migra"

Chicano opposition to the Carter Plan was immediate. The day after the president unveiled his immigration proposals, Congressman Edward Roybal (D-Calif.) cited his objections to the plan. Meeting in Washington, D.C., with representatives from various Chicano and other Latino organizations, Congressman Roybal critiqued specific aspects of the proposal as "offensive" to the Mexican-origin community in the United States and basically exploitative in nature toward undocumented aliens.[4] Although Roybal was serving as chair of the newly formed Congressional Hispanic Caucus, he cautioned attendees at the meeting that he was not speaking on behalf of the caucus. According to one of those in attendance, Roybal explained "that the Caucus it-self had differing views of the various proposals being circulated and each mem-ber had to take into consideration the constituencies they [*sic*] represented. The members of the Caucus with farming communities have tended to sup-port employer sanctions and a limited amnesty program."[5]

The National Council of La Raza (NCLR), one of the few national Mexi-can American organizations at the time with headquarters in Washington, D.C., quickly distributed copies of Carter's message to Congress to all of its af-filiate organizations and other selected groups. Attached was a statement from the council's national director, Raul Yzaguirre, indicating general council sup-port for the "overall thrust and intent" of what the president had proposed. Yzaguirre noted, however, that while the president's proposal "provides a framework from which to work, . . . [it] does not go far enough and does not adequately address the root cause of the flow of undocumented aliens to the United States." At the same time, Yzaguirre expressed concern over the ef-fects of employer sanctions on Hispanics and other minorities and the limited legalization program.[6]

Other groups, such as the United Farm Workers Union (UFW), were more decisive in their criticism of the Carter Plan. The UFW advocated for "total amnesty to undocumented aliens," higher immigration quotas for Mexico and the Western hemisphere, and firm opposition to employer sanctions.[7] As the saliency of the immigration issue increased, a consensus of opposition rose from most sectors of the Chicano community who chose to speak out on the issue. Over the next several years, Chicano opposition to the Carter Plan found ex-pression through a number of organized groups and community forums. Broadly speaking, at least five major sources of activism can be identified: (1) single-issue groups, (2) professional-provider groups, (3) membership organizations, (4) national advocacy groups, and (5) formal political representatives.[8]

First, single-issue groups exploded on the scene. Their main intent was to defend the rights of immigrants in the United States, with or without proper documents. The nature of their memberships varied. In some cases, immi-grants, documented and undocumented, comprised the membership of some of these groups. In Los Angeles, the organization *La Hermandad Mexicana Na-cional*, begun by longtime activists Bert Corona and Soledad "Chole" Ala-torre, had such a membership.[9] On the other hand, Chicanos from the uni-versities and community representatives formed the organizational core of many, such as the Bay Area Committee on Immigration and the Sacramento Committee for a New Immigration Policy in Northern California, to name only one area of intense activity.

Most prominent among these single-issue groups in terms of its ideologi-cal impact on the immigration issue during this period was CASA, *Centro de*

Acción Social Autónoma, headquartered in Los Angeles. CASA advocated working-class solidarity among Mexicans on both sides of the border. It denounced past and present U.S. immigration policies, including the Carter Plan, as repressive measures that violated the rights of both immigrant and domestic workers.[10] Overall, these groups that rallied in defense of immigrants' rights were, perhaps, among all sectors the most unequivocal in their condemnation of Carter's stand on immigration.

Second, professional-provider groups could be counted among the opponents to the Carter Plan. They included Chicano professionals who administered to the needs of immigrants, through legal aid offices, social service agencies, and community centers across the country. These Chicano professionals took public positions on the issue as, literally, experts in the field. That is, their "hands-on" experience working with immigrants largely served as the basis of their knowledge and expertise. As an example, staff from Centro Legal de la Raza in Oakland, California, tirelessly offered their assistance to numerous local groups who sought information and education on the issue. Centro Legal lawyers spoke at numerous community meetings and public forums explaining the Carter Plan and its consequences.

Third, membership organizations constituted a major sphere of Chicano activism. These organizations may also be referred to as voluntary organizations, given that individuals voluntarily join them and coalesce around similar interests. They address multiple issues of concern to their membership. Because of the significance and anticipated ramifications of the Carter Plan, many chose immigration as one of their top issues of concern. These groups were wide ranging. Among them were political organizations such as the Mexican American Political Association (MAPA), Chicano student groups on numerous college campuses, and labor unions with large percentages of Mexican workers.

The fourth category refers to a select group of organizations who sought to play a leading role in the immigration policy debates at the national level. They laid claim to nationally based constituencies and spoke on behalf of not only Chicanos but the "Hispanic" population at large. While they continued to address numerous policy issues, they invested a major part of their organizational resources to work on immigration. As they set up legislative offices in Washington, D.C., their work turned more and more to active lobbying "on the Hill."

Finally, a fifth important dimension to Chicano activism included a wide array of Chicano political representatives—that is, public officials and political party activists. Chicano caucuses within the Democratic Party structure at the state and national levels took issue with the Carter Plan. Public officials across the country also spoke to the issue. Their reactions, however, tended to vary perhaps more than any other sector's. As indicated above, some Hispanic members of Congress immediately spoke out against the Carter Plan, while others did not. In any event, during the Carter years this sector of political representatives took a back seat to the local-level mobilization generated by the immigrants' rights groups and Chicano community organizations across the country.

Chicano activism, based within and among these five sectors, attempted to "Stop the Carter Plan" by employing tactics familiar both to social movements and to the more conventional types of interest groups. For example, workshops, community meetings, marches and demonstrations, and other forms of organized protest transmitted intense Chicano opposition throughout many local communities. There was also grassroots lobbying of individual policymakers in Carter's administration and in Congress.

Carter's newly appointed commissioner of the Immigration and Naturalization Service (INS), Leonel Castillo, came under intense criticism for his defense of Carter's proposals. The Committee on Chicano Rights, an organization active in the San Diego area, published an informational pamphlet on the Carter Plan which condemned Castillo's role in the controversy. The pamphlet prominently displayed Castillo's picture opposite the pictures of seven Chicano/a leaders who had spoken out against the Carter Plan. The question the committee graphically posed was "Which Side Are You On?/¿En qué lado estás?"[11]

Numerous groups launched campaigns to get people to send letters and telegrams to Congress to urge defeat of the legislation. Senator Edward Kennedy (D-Mass.) was a prime target for grassroots pressure since he was perceived as a liberal ally yet was a cosponsor of Carter's bill in the Senate.

Chicanos also appeared before Congressional committees to offer testimony on S. 2252. Some of those appearing in Congressional hearings held in Washington during 1978 included: Vilma Martínez, president and general counsel of the Mexican American Legal Defense and Education Fund (MALDEF); Domingo González, Rural Affairs and Farm Labor Program representative of the American Friends Service Committee; Rubén Bonilla, state director of the Texas League of United Latin American Citizens (LULAC); and Delfino Varela, representing the Mexican American Political Association (MAPA).[12]

When Congress sponsored hearings on the bill outside of Washington, groups from the immediate local area came to testify. For example, in September 1978, hearings were held in Tucson and Nogales, Arizona. Farm labor groups, represented by Jesús Romo and Guadalupe Sánchez, and Chicano faculty and students from the University of Arizona offered criticism of the Carter proposals. Chicano support for the Carter Plan sometimes surfaced in such hearings. However, this remained largely a minority position among Chicanos who testified before Congress.[13]

Chicano activism centered in major urban areas in the Southwest during this time. Chicano inroads into policymaking circles in the nation's capital were few but developing. National Chicano—or Hispanic—organizations with offices in Washington monitored Congressional legislation. However, these groups, which included the NCLR, LULAC, and MALDEF, were still relatively new to the Washington scene and in the midst of building their legislative offices or policy divisions.

Mexican Americans in Congress numbered only four in the House of Representatives during the Carter years. They worked largely as individual representatives, not as a unit. The Congressional Hispanic Caucus, formally established in 1976, did not have an office or staff until 1978.[14]

There was only one formally organized Chicano lobby group in Washington at the time. Known as the National Congress of Hispanic American Citizens, or El Congreso, its staff testified in Congressional hearings a few times. However, the group was short-lived and defunct by the late 1970s.[15]

In general, then, Chicano opposition to the Carter Plan was expressed through a number of important but largely disparate efforts. Some groups attempted to forge some cohesion to their efforts by forming into coalitions. However, for the most part, Chicano political activity remained as diverse as the sectors from which it emanated.

In the fall of 1977, there was a major attempt to unite the various activist groups. Approximately 2,600 persons from thirty-two states and Mexico traveled to San Antonio, Texas, to attend the National Chicano/Latino Conference on Immigration and Public Policy. Prominent among the delegates were representatives from immigrants' rights groups, CASA, LULAC, La Raza Unida Party (LRUP), and the Socialist Workers Party (SWP). All in attendance indicated unified opposition to the Carter Plan. However, organizational rivalry undermined a major purpose of the conference—to forge a collective plan of action against the Carter Plan. The conference degenerated into factional in-fighting, sending many disappointed people back to their communities without a collectively endorsed strategy for action.[16] But the momentum of opposition continued nonetheless.

The extent to which Chicano opposition to the Carter Plan gutted the bill is difficult to determine. There can be little doubt that it was a significant contributing factor to blocking the proposal. Jimmy Carter was unable to forge the coalition of support in Congress necessary to enact his legislation. Consequently, he had to settle for the establishment of a special commission to study the problem and report policy recommendations to the president.

Government's sponsorship of immigration reform thus became embodied in the work of the Select Commission on Immigration and Refugees, established in 1978. Chicano opposition to the Carter plan subsequently subsided as the clear target of attack—a specific legislative initiative—dissolved and immigration reform was put on the back burner.

The Consequences of Movement Activism

The overriding significance of Chicano activism on immigration reform during the Carter Administration lies in the following considerations. First, government-sponsored initiatives mobilized a community of shared interests, igniting once again some semblance of social movement activism that had been in relative decline in the 1970s. Consequently, a renewed sense of group cohesion and political revitalization took place, at least among Chicano community leaders and activists, if not the general public.

Chicanos introduced new terms for debate on the immigration issue. Chicano solidarity in defense of immigrants' rights had never been so widespread or unequivocal, as displayed through demands for "unconditional amnesty" for undocumented workers. Moreover, the notion of shared interests regardless of citizenship and legal status found new levels of expression, if not clear acceptance, within the Mexican-origin community as a whole.[17] This revitalized movement activism clarified the major features of a new Chicano position on immigration reform before the nation. The ideological thrust of the new position set the parameters for debate as Chicano leaders grappled with the issue during the 1970s and 1980s. Its impact was also felt in national policymaking arenas.

Finally, Chicano activism signaled an increasing sophistication and level of organization, for the most part. One scholar commented on the nature of Chicano involvement in the immigration debate of the 1970s as compared with debates in previous eras. She perceived a broader and more highly organized Chicano position on immigration. In past restrictionist eras, Ann Craig commented, no "national response from Mexican-American interest groups" had been forthcoming. Similarly, Gilberto Cárdenas noted that Chicano demands to end the "Bracero Program" in the 1960s were primarily articulated through church-based groups, labor unions, and local community service organizations rather than through "autonomous Chicano organizations" as was now occurring.[18]

UNDER THE REAGAN ADMINISTRATION, 1981–1986

The creation of the Select Commission on Immigration and Refugees had ensured that immigration would appear as a national issue well beyond Jimmy Carter's years in the White House. As newly elected Ronald Reagan assumed the presidency, the Select Commission issued its final report on March 1, 1981.[19] Immigration reform then entered into a serious legislative battle.

Two members of Congress, one of whom had served on the Select Commission, spearheaded the legislative strategy designed to bring the immigration "crisis" under control. On March 17, 1982, Senator Alan K. Simpson (R-Wyo.) and Representative Romano Mazzoli (D-Ky.) introduced their proposal on immigration reform, commonly known as the Simpson-Mazzoli bill. For the next five years, Congress attempted to pass this piece of legislation. The Simpson-Mazzoli bill died in the 97th and 98th Congresses (1980–1982, 1982–1984). However, a reconstituted version, which Simpson cosponsored with Representative Peter Rodino (D-N.J.), emerged victorious in the waning hours of the 99th Congress (1984–1986). During these years, Chicano activism on immigration reform continued; however, it changed in important ways.

Chicano activism on immigration reform began to follow more traditional—or mainstream—political strategies and priorities. Emphasis was placed on building power bases in Washington, D.C., in order to influence policymakers more directly. Politics on Capitol Hill now determined the outcome of immigration reform, insofar as a specific legislative act would set new policies and directives. Consequently, Chicano activism on the issue necessarily had to shift more toward lobbying Congress through conventional interest group tactics and strategies. As the debate over immigration policy became firmly planted within Congress, Mexican Americans sought ways to increase their influence within the national legislative arena.

CHICANO POLITICS "ON THE HILL"

Two of the activist sectors in the Chicano community previously described played increasingly significant roles in the immigration debates of the 1980s: national advocacy organizations and political representatives. Indeed, specific groups from each of these sectors became key players in the bargaining and compromise that dominated the policymaking process from 1981 to 1986. From the first sector, the following groups played pivotal roles: LULAC, MALDEF, the NCLR, and the UFW (AFL-CIO).

All of these groups, with the exception of the UFW, had set up legislative offices in Washington, D.C. Their staff monitored Congressional action on the immigration issue on a daily basis. They also began to establish working relationships with members of Congress. Their offices issued position papers and policy analyses on virtually every major provision of the immigration reform legislation. As their work on immigration increased, so did their visibility and familiarity with key members of Congress. Simultaneously, there was a narrowing in the number of groups who articulated a Chicano position on immigration reform before Congress. For the most part, the groups cited above became the dominant spokespersons for "the Hispanic position" on immigration reform at the national level. Indeed, these groups constituted the organizational core of a new "Hispanic lobby" in Washington—at least on the immigration issue.[20]

Among political representatives, the Hispanic members of Congress were key. Congressional decision making is, fundamentally, an insiders' game. Thus the role of these Hispanic representatives was considered central to Chicano success in influencing Congressional action on immigration reform.

Merged together, these specific actors represented Chicanos (with a Hispanic label) in policy making at the national level. To be sure, Chicano activism continued "outside the beltway"—that is, beyond the nation's capital as well. However, because of the predominance of the "insiders" in the politics of immigration from 1981 to 1986, their actions took on increased significance. We now turn to an analysis of their roles.

Hispanics in Congress: "Boring from Within?"

As elected representatives, Hispanic members of Congress may perform numerous functions within the legislative body. Fundamentally, they are charged with two overriding tasks: (a) to legislate—to make and enact laws; and (b) to represent constituent interests in the policymaking process. Constituent representation for members of the U.S. House of Representatives specifically relates to the representation of one's district.

There is at least one additional dimension to representation, however, for Hispanic members of Congress. They also assume the role of *ethnic group representatives*. That is, both within and outside of Congress, they are viewed as national spokespersons for Hispanics on issues of public policy. The controversial issue of immigration challenged Hispanic legislators to reconcile conflicting positions on this issue, expressed in their home districts, with the needs and interests of the ethnic group at large.

Two periods of legislative behavior become important to distinguish. The first period, 1980–1984, spanning the 97th and 98th Congresses, can be characterized as a period in which Hispanic members of Congress engaged in "veto politics" on the issue of immigration reform. The second period, spanning the work of the 99th Congress, 1985–1986, can be described as the "politics of compromise."

The years 1980–1984 saw the further development of the Congressional Hispanic Caucus. The caucus expanded in size and visibility. At the outset of the 1980s, Latinos in Congress numbered five voting members and one nonvoting delegate. All were in the House of Representatives. Mexican American legislators, all of whom were elected in the 1960s, included Edward Roybal

(D-Calif.), Henry B. González (D-Tex.), E. Kika de la Garza (D-Tex.), and Manuel Luján (R-N.M.). They were joined by Puerto Rican Congressman Robert García (D-N.Y.), who was elected in 1978. The nonvoting delegate was Baltasar Corrada from Puerto Rico.[21]

Elections in 1982 saw four new Mexican Americans seated in the House of Representatives: Esteban Torres and Matthew Martínez from California, Bill Richardson from New Mexico, and Solomon Ortíz from Texas. All Democrats, they were elected from new districts created through reapportionment. In 1984 another Mexican American representative, Albert Bustamante, a Democrat from South Texas, joined the Hispanic delegation. Consequently, in just four years, Latino representation in Congress increased by five, doubling the number of Hispanic voting members in Congress. While they still constituted only a tiny fraction of the total number (435) in the House of Representatives, the new members brought more visibility to the group. They began meeting on a regular basis as a caucus and increased the legislative activities of their group. In coordinating their legislative activity around specific issues, the caucus sought "to develop a united congressional effort on behalf of Hispanic Americans."[22]

The 97th Congress, 1981–1982: The Play of Veto Politics

With the release of the Select Commission's final report, the Congressional Hispanic Caucus (CHC) began to address immigration as a priority issue. The chair of the CHC, Robert García, used his prerogative as chair of the House Subcommittee on Census and Population to convene hearings on Hispanic immigration and the Select Commission's final report. García set up the hearings to permit a "Hispanic point of view" to be aired. During Hispanic Heritage Week in September 1981, the caucus sponsored seminars on immigration, which included the participation of Senator Simpson, Representative Mazzoli, Rubén Bonilla (LULAC), and Vilma Martínez (MALDEF).[23]

Using the Select Commission's policy recommendations as the basis for legislation, Senator Simpson and Representative Mazzoli introduced their bill for major immigration reform on March 17, 1982, during the second session of the 97th Congress. For the rest of the year, the caucus monitored progress on the bill as it wound its way through the various committee hearings and markups. But Hispanic action on the bill was more likely to emanate from individual members than from the caucus as a unit. No doubt this was a reflection of the fact that not all members shared similar positions nor equal commitments to the issue.

For example, caucus members communicated to the chair of the House Judiciary Committee, Peter Rodino, their concern that the Simpson-Mazzoli bill "[ran] counter to this nation's commitment to civil rights and due process for all people residing in the United States." But this message was sent under four individual names, not as a caucus-endorsed position. Similarly, only Edward Roybal and Robert García wrote to Rodino urging him to strike the temporary foreign worker (H-2) provisions from the bill.[24] But the visible actions of only one or two Hispanic members of Congress would be sufficient to consolidate caucus opposition to the bill by the end of the congressional session.

The Senate passed its version of the bill on August 17, 1982, by the lopsided vote of 81-18. But on the House side, the bill was blocked. Opponents of Simpson-Mazzoli introduced almost three hundred amendments to gut the bill. Congressman Edward Roybal led the opposition with over a hundred amendments of his own, drafted in late working sessions by staff from his congressional office and one or two Latino organizations, most notably MALDEF.[25]

In the end, a number of factors held the Simpson-Mazzoli bill hostage in the final hours of the 97th Congress. The complexity and scope of the bill and its last-minute consideration—in a lame duck session—were significant factors. Division among traditionally aligned interests within Congress presented an additional obstacle to the bill's passage. In particular, division within the Democratic party on the bill's merits was key. Chicano opposition to Simpson-Mazzoli clearly had whittled away the expected Democratic consensus on the bill.

Given these conditions, Hispanic opposition, combined with support from the Congressional Black Caucus and liberal allies, proved to be a necessary and sufficient force to stop the proposal. Journalists and political observers in fact claimed an "unexpected political victory" for Latino lobbyists and members of Congress.[26] Yet many recognized that with changing circumstances the Hispanic victory could prove to be only a fleeting moment of success.

The 98th Congress, 1983–1984: Veto Politics Revisited
Chicanos continued their battle against the Simpson-Mazzoli bill when it was reintroduced in the 98th Congress. But they quickly learned that the strategy of veto politics had its limitations. They were compelled to search for alternative ways to deal with the issue.

In May 1983, the Senate once again quickly and decisively approved the Simpson-Mazzoli bill by a vote of 76-18. As in the past, Chicanos had to exert what influence they had in the House of Representatives. That year Chicanos took their demands of discontent to the House leadership. Simpson-Mazzoli was ready for floor consideration by the fall of 1983. However, due to partisan politics and, in part, Latino lobbying on the bill, Speaker of the House Thomas P. "Tip" O'Neill kept the measure locked away in the Rules Committee, delaying action indefinitely on the bill. O'Neill also challenged Hispanic legislators to devise their own proposal.

Hispanic veto politics appeared successful once again in stalling progress on the bill. Certainly, commentators from across the country thought so. In opinion columns, letters to the editor, and editorials in the nation's leading newspapers, Latino opponents of Simpson-Mazzoli were heavily criticized for obstructing badly needed immigration reform.[27]

Latinos both within and outside of Congress began searching for a new strategy of opposition. Taking Speaker O'Neill's challenge to heart, Representative Bill Richardson (D-N.M.) expressed the new concern: "It's important that we not be viewed as obstructionist. We have to come up with a serious alternative. If we don't have a serious alternative, [Simpson-Mazzoli] deserves to pass."[28]

Once again the ball passed to Congressman Edward Roybal to sponsor the alternative legislative strategy: the drafting of a bill to rival Simpson-Mazzoli. Staff from several Washington-based organizations, including MALDEF, LULAC, and the NCLR assisted Roybal in drafting H.R. 4909, the Immigration Reform Act of 1984. Roybal introduced his bill at the start of the second session of the 98th Congress.

According to a former legislative assistant to the Congressman, Roybal felt that his bill should represent a "wish list" of Chicano policy recommendations for immigration reform. To be sure, the Roybal bill addressed the major concerns Chicanos had with the Simpson-Mazzoli bill. H.R. 4909 eliminated employer sanctions and the temporary farm labor program. It created a strong labor law enforcement package and provided for a more generous legalization program.[29]

The bill was appealing to Chicanos and their allies. It eliminated the worst aspects of Simpson-Mazzoli, and the opposition now could posture itself in a positive light, as working *for* immigration reform. Under the direction of second-term chairman Robert García, the legislative staff of the CHC sponsored briefings on the Roybal bill "in conjunction with a coalition of organizations supporting immigration reform, but opposed to the passage of the Simpson-Mazzoli bill."[30]

Chicanos across the country united behind the Roybal bill, which offered both a symbolic and a substantive alternative to Simpson-Mazzoli. Those organizations that helped to draft the Roybal bill generated letters of support from their own executive directors and other organizations to Speaker Tip O'Neill, requesting movement on Roybal's measure. The National Council of Churches wrote O'Neill to urge that H.R. 4909 "be considered an integral component of the debate [on immigration] and permitted . . . a hearing." The American Jewish Committee (AJC) urged serious consideration of the bill, noting that it was "sensitive to the needs of the Jewish and other ethnic communities in the United States." The AJC reaffirmed its position that immigration reform legislation was necessary.[31]

The flurry of activity around the Roybal bill, however, did not prove successful. This time Latino efforts to derail Simpson-Mazzoli were cut short. The Roybal bill never even got a hearing. Several things proved problematic. First, Hispanic members of Congress were divided on some provisions of the Roybal bill. Manuel Luján, the sole Republican in the caucus, opposed the legalization program. Kika de la Garza supported the farm labor provision in the Simpson-Mazzoli bill. The Roybal bill eliminated this provision. As one Latino lobbyist explained, "The growers put up the money for his campaigns and elections. Hispanics vote him in — are his base of support in terms of votes. But grower money constitutes his resource."[32]

Moreover, there was a general reluctance among Hispanic members of Congress to exert leadership on the issue. A congressional staffer for one of the Hispanic members of Congress explained that immigration is seen as a politically dangerous and costly issue on which to advocate. Her words were echoed by one scholar who stated that immigration is considered by many as a "politically no-win issue." One Hispanic legislator who was serving his first term in Congress characterized his role as offering "behind-the-scenes" support for Roybal's bill; he "didn't want to take away the thunder from Roybal or García."[33]

Congressman Roybal had had a long history of advocacy on immigration legislation in Congress. He felt personally committed to the issue. Consequently, his leadership came as no surprise. Robert García assumed some leadership responsibility because he was chair of the Congressional Hispanic Caucus at the time. However, aside from Roybal and García, Hispanic members of Congress seemed to shy away from visible roles on immigration.

Divided opinion on the merits of the Roybal bill and individual calculations of political risks prevented the caucus from formally endorsing — as a group — the Roybal bill. Without strong and firm CHC backing, it is no wonder that "a ferment of support within Congress" for the Latino alternative to Simpson-Mazzoli never materialized."[34]

Roybal's legislative style also came into play. While he found cosponsors for his bill from the CHC and other members of Congress, he did not lay the appropriate groundwork for pushing his bill forward. Several lobbyists and congressional staff characterized Roybal as a loner when it came to handling legislation. They claimed that he did not "wire" enough support for his bill through the expected intimate give-and-take with others, including party leaders, in Congress. One lobbyist went so far as to say, "If you want something blocked, give it to Roybal; but if you want something passed, find someone else."[35]

The failure to move the Roybal bill through the House also pointed to critical features of the congressional decision-making process. The key to drafting legislation and getting it passed in Congress rests largely in committee assignments. No Hispanic member of Congress served on the House Judiciary Committee, from whose subcommittee immigration legislation originates. Further, it was highly unlikely that an immigration bill that came from outside the subcommittee would advance. The rules of decentralized decision making within Congress would not allow this to happen easily.

Finally, the ideological position advanced by the Roybal bill ran counter to the ideological position the Congress has usually taken with regard to immigration policy. The Simpson-Mazzoli bill promoted in essence a restrictive immigration policy with a back door opened for the continued importation of a temporary "foreign" farm labor force. The Roybal bill promoted a liberal immigration policy with no provision for temporary guestworkers. It also advanced the rights of all workers by calling for the vigilant enforcement of this country's labor laws. Only the most intense and broad-based support could have pushed the Roybal bill beyond the ideological predispositions within the U.S. Congress—if even that were possible.

With their affirmative strategy on the rocks, Latinos once again resorted to veto politics. Roybal offered provisions of his bill as amendments to Simpson-Mazzoli during floor debate. The Congressional Hispanic Caucus issued guidelines on how to vote on several key amendments. Hispanic members argued passionately on the floor of the House for the elimination of employer sanctions and retention of the legalization provision in the bill. But, in the words of one legislative assistant, these actions were "too little, too late."[36]

On June 20, 1984, after one week of heated debate, the House of Representatives passed its version of the Simpson-Mazzoli bill by a mere five votes, 216-211. The Congressional Hispanic Caucus unanimously opposed the bill's final passage, although members deviated in their votes on particular amendments to the bill. The fate of Simpson-Mazzoli then passed to a Senate-House conference committee that had to reconcile differences between the Senate and House versions of the bill.

In the meantime, Chicano opposition "outside the beltway" pushed its way to the forefront of the battle. Groups across the country protested the passage of the bill. Chicanos took advantage of partisan politics during the 1984 presidential election year to make their position known. The Democratic party and its candidates were lobbied heavily to take firm stands of opposition to Simpson-Mazzoli. Televised proceedings of the Democratic party's national convention broadcast Chicano opposition to Simpson-Mazzoli to a national audience. Walter Mondale, the Democratic nominee for the U.S. presidency, subsequently withdrew his support for Simpson-Mazzoli.

By the time the Senate and House conferees met in September of 1984 to move the bill forward, a multitude of problems prevented final approval. It would take yet one more round for this legislation to become law. For Chicanos, it would be in the next round that a new politics of compromise would replace the veto politics of the past.

The 99th Congress, 1985–1986: The Politics of Compromise

The years spanning the life of the 99th Congress saw the breakdown of consensus among Chicanos on immigration reform. At the start of the new year, Congressman Edward Roybal, in a surprise move to friends and foes alike, introduced another immigration bill. However, his Immigration Act of 1985 had a striking resemblance to the previous Simpson-Mazzoli bill. In fact, Roybal's new bill contained the very feature condemned most virulently by Latino groups — employer sanction provisions.[37]

The Congressman maintained that he introduced his bill as "bait." He wanted to draw out Senator Simpson's true position on immigration. Roybal explained that with Simpson thinking the opposition was weakening, the Senator would introduce "an even worse bill." With Simpson adopting a more extreme position, Roybal felt that the possibilities of blocking congressional efforts to pass another version of Simpson-Mazzoli would improve.[38]

Legislative aides to Roybal indicated that employer sanctions seemed sure to be included in any immigration legislation passed by Congress. They contended that some of the Latino organizations in Washington were also thinking that a compromise on employer sanctions would be necessary. So Roybal decided to "call the question" in his own way. Roybal's aides defended the bill by pointing to how it still departed from the previous Simpson-Mazzoli bill, even in its provisions for employer sanctions.[39]

Regardless of Roybal's well-meaning strategy, Latino opposition to his '85 bill was immediate. MALDEF led the criticism. One of its attorneys commented, "He [Roybal] included sanctions without consulting anyone and made concessions without getting anything in return." On the other hand, Senator Simpson, as expected, hailed Roybal's bill as evidence that a new mood prevailed among Hispanics on immigration reform. The Senator commented: "It took a lot of courage for Ed Roybal to put in a bill with employer sanctions in it. . . . It showed me that he, too, wants to do something (about immigration)."[40]

In the end, the Roybal bill simply died for lack of support from the Chicano community. This was the only comprehensive legislative initiative offered by any Hispanic member of Congress for the duration of the 99th Congress. Some sponsored particular amendments to the reconstituted bill, cosponsored this time by Simpson and Peter Rodino (D-N.J.). But once again Latinos were unable to initiate successfully an alternative legislative package to rival the one preordained by congressional leaders.

A breakdown of consensus on immigration reform became increasingly apparent as the Hispanic congressmen and national advocacy organizations reevaluated their previous positions. The junior members of the Hispanic Caucus indicated a new willingness to support the Simpson-Rodino bill. They spoke to three primary considerations: (1) the need to engage in "realistic politics," (2) constituency pressure to "do something" on immigration reform, and (3) their desire to shed their obstructionist label and improve their stature within Congress.

Congressman Bill Richardson (D-N.M.) underscored the need to compromise and "mainstream" Chicano demands in order "to break into the political infrastructure." He claimed that employer sanctions were now inevitable. Chicanos had to push for antidiscriminatory safeguards against employer sanctions and fight for the retention of the amnesty program in the legislation. He leveled criticism at those who ignored the reality of the political situation.[41]

Several others pointed to constituent pressure to enact some type of legislation, but their constituents supported the measure for different reasons. Calls for action revolved around two prevalent concerns: the need to prevent further undocumented immigration into the United States and the need for a legalization program. In the spirit of political expediency, to "do something" on immigration, numerous members of Congress, including some of the Hispanic members, voted for the Simpson-Rodino bill because it was "better than nothing."[42]

Additional justifications for vote switching on Simpson-Rodino pointed to the concern that the time was now or never to enact a legalization program. Members expressed concern that increasing anti-Hispanic, anti-immigrant sentiment across the country would result in more restrictive legislation in the future if something was not forthcoming now. Bill Richardson characterized the bill as "the last gasp for legalization to take place in a humane way." Esteban Torres (D-Calif.) commended some of his colleagues for their "courageous" but "difficult" vote on Simpson-Rodino. In his "Dear Colleague" letter, Torres stated: "Public attitudes about the illegal immigration situation are becoming increasingly harsh. I am convinced that continued failure by Congress to address this problem would have resulted in a far more punitive measure in the future. The immigration bill that you supported is probably the best legislation possible under current political conditions."[43]

Five of the eleven voting members of the Hispanic delegation in Congress voted for the Simpson-Rodino bill. Divisions within the Hispanic caucus no doubt contributed to the collapse of opposition against the bill from other sectors. Only one Black member of Congress had previously voted for the Simpson-Mazzoli bill; this time nearly half of the Congressional Black Caucus voted for Simpson-Rodino. Final passage was achieved through the lopsided vote of 230-166.

The organizational core of the Hispanic lobby in Washington also experienced a breakdown in consensus from 1985 to 1986. Since the late 1970s, LULAC, MALDEF, the NCLR, and the UFW had maintained unified opposition to restrictive immigration policy. Not without their differences and disagreements, these organizations nevertheless coordinated their efforts to defeat Simpson-Mazzoli in previous Congresses. However, in the 99th Congress their consensus on strategy dissolved. Like the Congressional Hispanic Caucus, Latino lobby groups and their closest allies began to engage in the politics of compromise.

Breaking from its unequivocal opposition to any kind of guestworker program, the UFW lent its support to the agricultural/farm labor provision in the bill, known as the Schumer compromise. The UFW's interests were represented by Howard Berman (D-Calif.), who played a major role in crafting the Schumer compromise. The union remained concerned about various provisions in the bill, but it involved itself in the politics of compromise in order to strengthen its position and to protect its interests should the immigration bill pass.

The National Council of La Raza attempted a "reasonable approach" to immigration reform. Its staff considered employer sanctions inevitable, so the group attempted to bargain on employer sanctions to win other concessions. The NCLR also promoted the Schumer compromise "behind the scenes." Its staff considered that this was a good way to engage in "damage control" and contain the ill effects of the immigration bill should it pass.

The reasons compelling Latino groups to engage in their various strategies of bargaining and compromise included the following:

(a) The immigration bill was before Congress for the third time. The old strategy of veto politics would not work again.
(b) Grassroots interest and opposition to the congressional initiative were not as intense as in previous periods; public opinion polls showed a divided Hispanic community on immigration reform.
(c) The lobby groups wanted to maintain their credibility with members of Congress and other policymakers; they sought ways to continue to be part of the process of decision making.
(d) Ideally they wanted to kill the bill. If the bill did indeed fail but surfaced

again in the next Congress, they wanted to be in a stronger position to lobby on it.

(e) The groups wanted to cut their losses should they be unable to kill the bill.[44]

In contrast to the other groups, MALDEF continued its unequivocal opposition to the Simpson-Rodino bill. Consequently, it gained the reputation in Washington as being "purist" or "absolutist" in its politics. Lobbyists on immigration reform maintained that MALDEF's "hard-line" position was important in reaffirming certain principles. They suggested that MALDEF represented the position of "the left" on immigration reform. At the same time, they contended that MALDEF was no longer taken seriously by members of Congress. They said that the organization had damaged its own credibility by refusing to engage in the politics of compromise.

THE FINAL OUTCOME: A GENERAL ASSESSMENT

On November 6, 1986, President Ronald Reagan signed the Simpson-Rodino bill into law as the Immigration Reform and Control Act of 1986 (IRCA). Embedded in the new immigration policy were contributions made by Hispanic members of Congress and the Latino lobby groups. Perhaps most significant were Latino efforts to ensure that the final bill included a legalization program for undocumented immigrants. At the same time, major components of a restrictive immigration policy remained intact. Indeed, IRCA included an employer sanctions provision, a policy long opposed by Chicano activists as potentially discriminatory against racial and ethnic minority groups.[45]

In the end, divergent assessments of the costs and benefits of IRCA emanated from Chicano and Latino activist circles. At the same time, Mexican American and Latino public opinion on immigration reform revealed a good deal of ambivalence. Public opinion surveys showed Mexican Americans to be divided on various aspects of immigration reform. For the most part, Mexican Americans tended to support a legalization program for undocumented immigrants. On the question of employer sanctions, sentiments were less clear. In some polls, Hispanic support for employer sanctions ran as high as 63 percent in favor. In others, Hispanic opinion was evenly divided. Importantly, nativity appeared to be a key variable, with the foreign-born voicing much more opposition to employer sanctions than the native born.[46]

The full effects of a broad and complex piece of legislation such as IRCA will take years to unfold. What can be more clearly pinpointed, however, are the implications of the shifting politics pursued by Chicanos over this time period.

The politics of immigration from 1976 to 1986 point to an important evolution in Chicano politics. Chicanos penetrated policymaking arenas to a much greater extent than ever before. This is most clearly seen at the national level with the development of a Hispanic lobby on Capitol Hill. Hispanic members of Congress and national Hispanic organizations became significant players in congressional decision making on immigration reform. Overall, Chicano efforts to influence American public policy, from the local to national level, increased in their organization, political sophistication, and significance.

As Chicanos have found their way into the policymaking process, the nature of their political endeavors has also changed. In the case of immigration, Chicano activism on the issue initially evolved as a social protest movement against government policy initiatives. Over time, however, Chicano efforts to influence immigration policy increasingly reflected more conventional interest-group strategies and behavior, as Hispanic elected officials and national lobby organizations assumed predominant roles in the policymaking process. The transition from social movement to interest group politics reflects the successful penetration of previously inaccessible policymaking arenas.[47]

Scholars have noted similar patterns of development in the politics of other social groups, particularly Blacks and women. Since the 1960s, the struggles for Black political empowerment and women's rights have shifted from the politics of protest to increased participation in conventional forms of political behavior. In particular, these groups have vigorously pursued the incorporation of Black and female elected officials in the policymaking process and the development of strong lobby organizations at the national, state, and local levels. To be sure, scholars have argued that "protest is not enough" to empower previously disenfranchised groups and incorporate them into the political system. Electoral politics and interest-group lobbying are also necessary complements to protest strategies.[48]

As Chicanos seek to further their incorporation into the political system, they will face numerous challenges and political trade-offs in what is won or lost for the group's benefit. As seen in the politics of immigration reform, the process of incorporation pressures political elites—public officials, organizational leaders, and community activists—to moderate their demands on the political system. As Chicano leaders establish themselves within decision-making circles and learn the rules of the game, they are much more likely to pursue incremental policy goals—that is, narrow, short-term, policy gains—and to avoid formulating and advancing more comprehensive and far-reaching demands on the political system.

Political scientist Lenneal Henderson has described how the politics of incrementalism took hold in the Black community during the 1970s. According to Henderson, Black politicians spoke to the necessity of "incremental policy changes to insure black survival" in the 1970s. Black politicians "counsel[ed] the black community to be 'realistic' and 'pragmatic' in their policy demands and in their expectations of white and black politicians." Many Black leaders perceived a national backlash against programs and goals associated with the era of the Great Society. They consequently felt that Blacks had to concentrate on protecting the gains they had already won. Henderson thus argued that the politics of "idealistic protest" had yielded to a "cautious politics of backlash pragmatism." His concern was that backlash pragmatism would inhibit the further development of policy gains for Blacks under the Carter Administration.[49]

At least in the policy area of immigration, Chicano politics reveal a similar move from idealistic protest to the politics of backlash pragmatism. Hispanic leaders contended that a hostile political climate toward Latinos and immigrants compelled them to compromise in their issue positions in order to avoid more punitive measures against these groups. In the end, the pressure to compromise resulted in a breakdown of consensus among Hispanics, resulting in more modified positions than had previously been articulated.

The extent to which Chicano politics are expressed in the future within the framework of "backlash pragmatism" may prove problematic. Incremental and defensive policy positions alone will not, in the long run, adequately resolve many of the intractable issues confronting the Chicano/Latino community. The articulation of bold and comprehensive policies, oftentimes associated with social movement politics, could help to infuse Chicano politics — indeed American politics — with sorely needed challenges to "politics as usual" and galvanize fresh approaches to pressing public policy concerns. In the end, the institutionalization of group power requires not only "sitting at the table" with national policymakers; it also implies the ability to produce effective and longlasting benefits for those communities whose interests are being represented.

Notes

1. John A. García, "Chicano Political Development: Examining Participation in the 'Decade of the Hispanic,'" *La Red/The Net*, no. 72 (September 1983): 17.

2. President Jimmy Carter, the White House, Message to Congress, Press Release, Office of the White House Press Secretary, August 4, 1977, p. 1.

3. Ibid., pp. 1–7.

4. Cosme J. Barcelo, Jr., Staff, to Raul Yzaguirre, National Director, National Council of La Raza, Washington, D.C., Memorandum, August 5, 1977, pp. 2–4.

5. Ibid., p. 1.

6. Ibid., pp. 1, 2.

7. United Farm Workers of America, AFL-CIO, "Resolution 73," Resolution on Immigration Reform, Third Constitutional Convention, Fresno, California, August 26–28, 1977; Harry Bernstein, "UFW Denounces Carter Program on Illegal Aliens," *Los Angeles Times*, Sunday, August 28, 1977, part 1, pp. 3, 26.

8. This categorization results from the author's long-standing research agenda on Chicano mobilization on immigration reform.

9. For an insightful memoir from Bert Corona about his organizational experiences with *La Hermandad Mexicana*, see Mario T. García, *Memories of Chicano History: The Life and Narrative of Bert Corona* (Berkeley: University of California Press, 1994).

10. See David G. Gutiérrez, *Walls and Mirrors: Mexican Americans, Mexican Immigrants, and the Politics of Ethnicity* (Berkeley: University of California Press, 1995), chap. 6.

11. Committee on Chicano Rights, Inc., "Stop Carter's Immigration Plan!: A Chicano Perspective on the President's Immigration Proposals," pamphlet, c. 1977–1978.

12. U.S. Congress, House, Committee on the Judiciary, *S. 2252: Alien Adjustment and Employment Act of 1977, Parts 1 and 2*, Hearings before the Subcommittee on Immigration and the Committee on the Judiciary, 95th Congress, 2nd session, May 3, 4, 9–11, 16–18, September 1, 2, 1978.

13. Congressional Information Service, *Abstracts of Congressional Publications and Legislative Histories*, Washington, D.C., 1976–1979.

14. Interviews with legislative staff from the Congressional Hispanic Caucus, Washington, D.C., December 1985.

15. Congressional Information Service, *Abstracts of Congressional Publications*, 1975–1979.

16. Alan Bailey, "Hispanics Rap Amnesty Plan," *San Antonio Express*, October 31, 1977, pp. 1A, 10A; Danny García, "Near-Chaos Marks End of Chicano Meet," *San Antonio Light*, October 31, 1977, pp. 1, 12.

17. As noted in another section of this article, public opinion polls during this time showed Mexican Americans in general to be ambivalent on a number of issues concerning immigration.

18. Ann L. Craig, *Mexican Immigration: Changing Terms of the Debate in the United States and Mexico*, Working Papers in U.S.-Mexican Studies 4 (La Jolla, Calif.: Program in United States–Mexican Studies, University of California, San Diego, 1981), pp. 9–10; Gilberto Cárdenas, "An Assessment of Chicano Views and Reaction toward Undocumented Immigration," unpublished paper, Center for Immigration Policy Studies, Georgetown University, Washington, D.C., May 24, 1983.

19. U.S. Congress, House and Senate, Committees on the Judiciary, *U.S. Immigration Policy and the National Interest*, Final Report and Recommendations of the Select Commission on Immigration and Refugee Policy with Supplemental Views by Commissioners, March 1, 1981. 97th Congress, 1st session, Joint Committee Print, no. 8, August 1981.

20. See Christine Marie Sierra, "Latino Organizational Strategies on Immigration Reform: Success and Limits in Public Policymaking," in Roberto E. Villarreal and Norma G. Hernández, eds., *Latinos and Political Coalitions: Political Empowerment for the 1990s,* (New York: Greenwood Press, 1991), pp. 61–80.

21. Delegates in Congress are not allowed to vote on the House floor. However, they do vote in committees.

22. García, "Chicano Political Development," p. 9; Congressional Hispanic Caucus information sheet, 1985.

23. Congressional Hispanic Caucus, *Avance*, March 1981 and August–September 1981; U.S. Congress, House, Committee on Post Office and Civil Service, *Hispanic Immigration and Select*

Commission on Immigration's Final Report, Hearings before the Subcommittee on Census and Population, 97th Congress, 1st session, April 27, 28, 1981, Committee Print, Serial No. 97-16, p. 1.

24. Edward R. Roybal, Robert García, and Matthew Martínez, Members of Congress, to the Honorable Peter Rodino, Jr., Chairman, Committee on the Judiciary, U.S. House of Representatives, September 13, 1982; E. (Kika) de la Garza, Chairman, Committee on Agriculture, to the Honorable Peter W. Rodino, Jr., Chairman, Committee on the Judiciary, U.S. House of Representatives, September 14, 1982; and Edward R. Roybal and Robert García, Members of Congress, to the Honorable Peter Rodino, Jr., Chairman, Committee on the Judiciary, U.S. House of Representatives, September 14, 1982.

25. Interviews with congressional staff of Edward Roybal, U.S. House of Representatives, Washington, D.C., 1985–1986; also see Estevan T. Flores, "1982 Simpson-Mazzoli Immigration Reform and the Hispanic Community," *La Red/The Net*, no. 64 (February 1983): pp. 14–16.

26. Frank del Olmo, "Latinos Should Offer Own Immigration Ideas," *Los Angeles Times*, December 30, 1982, n.p.

27. See Leo R. Chávez, "Hispanics and Immigration Reform," *Nuestro*, October 1983, for an insightful critique of this national response and a clarification of the Latino position on immigration reform.

28. Karen Tumulty, "House Likely to Pass Immigration Reform Bill," *Los Angeles Times*, December 1, 1983, n.p., quoting Representative Bill Richardson.

29. Interview with Dan Maldonado, Washington, D.C., May 22, 1986; U.S. Congress, House, Congressman Edward Roybal introducing the Immigration Reform Act of 1984, H.R. 4909, 98th Congress, 2nd session, February 22, 1984, *Congressional Record*, pp. H781–H782; Hispanic Link News Service, "The Immigration Bills: How They Compare," *Hispanic Link Weekly Report 2*, no. 10 (March 5, 1984), Special Pull-Out Supplement, pp. 3–6.

30. Robert García, Chairman, Congressional Hispanic Caucus, to Representative Matthew Martínez, March 2, 1984.

31. William K. Du Val, Chairman, Immigration and Refugee Program Committee, and Dale S. de Haan, Director, Immigration and Refugee Program, Church World Service, National Council of the Churches of Christ in the United States of America, to the Honorable Thomas P. O'Neill, March 1, 1984; Howard I. Friedman, President, The American Jewish Committee, New York City, to the Honorable Thomas P. O'Neill, February 23, 1984.

32. Conversation with a Latino lobbyist, Washington, D.C., October 31, 1985; also Memorandum to Members of the Congressional Hispanic Caucus from Bob García, March 29, 1984.

33. Interview with Elaine Sierra, staff member, Congressional office of Representative Edward Roybal, Washington, D.C., November, 1985; Craig, *Changing Terms*, p. 13; interview with a Hispanic member of Congress, U.S. House of Representatives, Washington, D.C., July 16, 1986.

34. Interview with Dan Maldonado, Washington, D.C., May 22, 1986.

35. Conversation with a lobbyist, Washington, D.C., December 1985.

36. Conversation with the legislative assistant to a member of the Congressional Black Caucus, Washington, D.C., December 1985.

37. For a critique of several aspects of the Roybal immigration bill of 1985, see Leo R. Chávez, "Roybal Jumps Ship on Immigration Bill," *San Diego Union*, January 20, 1985, p. C-6.

38. Interview with Congressman Edward Roybal, Washington, D.C., July 22, 1986.

39. Interviews with Elaine Sierra, October 1985, and with Dan Maldonado, July, 1986, both in Washington, D.C.

40. Senator Alan Simpson quoted in Julia Malone, "Hispanic Groups Foresee Backlash, Ease Opposition to Immigration Bills," *Christian Science Monitor*, April 2, 1985, pp. 1, 60; Richard

Fajardo, attorney for the Mexican American Legal Defense and Educational Fund (MALDEF), quoted in Mercedes Olivera, "Hispanic Groups Oppose Immigration Reform Legislation," *Dallas, Texas News*, February 24, 1985.

41. Congressman Bill Richardson, speech before conference "Ignored Voices: Public Opinion Polls and the Latino Community," The University of Texas at Austin, October 18, 1985.

42. Interviews and conversations with Hispanic members of Congress and their staffs, Washington, D.C., 1985–1986; Nadine Cohodas, "Congress Clears Overhaul of Immigration Law," *Congressional Quarterly Weekly Report*, October 18, 1986, pp. 2595–2596. See also U.S. Congress, House, House Debate on H.R. 3810, 99th Congress, 2nd session, *Congressional Record*, October 9, 1986.

43. Esteban E. Torres, Member of Congress, U.S. House of Representatives, Washington, D.C., Dear Colleague letter, October 20, 1986; also Cohodas, "Congress Clears Overhaul," p. 2595, quoting Bill Richardson (D-N.M.).

44. Clarification and elaboration on most of these points were made by Dale Frederick Swartz, Director, the National Citizenship, Immigration and Refugee Forum, Washington, D.C., in an interview conducted on November 8, 1986.

45. Evidence suggests that Chicano concerns over the potentially discriminatory effects of employer sanctions were valid. See United States General Accounting Office, *Immigration Reform: Employer Sanctions and the Question of Discrimination*, Report to the Congress, March 1990.

46. For further elaboration of these and additional public opinion data, see Christine Marie Sierra, "Latinos and the 'New Immigration': Responses from the Mexican American Community," *Renato Rosaldo Lecture Series Monograph*, vol. 3, 1987: 33–61.

47. For a similar argument regarding the women's movement, see Anne N. Costain, "Representing Women: The Transition from Social Movement to Interest Group," in *Women, Power and Policy*, edited by Ellen Boneparth (New York: Pergamon Press, 1982), pp. 19–37.

48. Rufus P. Browning, Dale Rogers Marshall, and David H. Tabb, *Protest Is Not Enough: The Struggle of Blacks and Hispanics for Equality in Urban Politics* (Berkeley: University of California Press, 1984); and Ellen Boneparth, ed., *Women, Power and Policy* (New York: Pergamon Press, 1982).

49. Lenneal J. Henderson, "Black Politics and the Carter Administration," *Journal of Afro-American Issues* 5, no. 3 (Summer 1977): 244.

Seven

Chicano Politics and U.S. Policy in Central America, 1979–1990

Antonio González

Introduction

The formation of U.S. foreign policy is generally the province of cliques of East Coast think tanks, congressional committees, and the administration in power. The citizenry and its local leadership are usually ignorant if not oblivious to the details and implications of our nation's foreign policies. The Jewish lobby on U.S. policy toward Israel and the Middle East departs from that general truth. The advocacy of African American leaders regarding U.S. policies in southern Africa is also notable. Both efforts have injected a modicum of civic participation and oversight in the making of U.S. foreign policies.

In this essay, I argue that Chicanos are entering a period in which they will have increasing influence over U.S. foreign policy concerning Latin America. Demographic changes in the Southwest (Texas, New Mexico, California, Arizona, and Colorado) due primarily to in-migration from Mexico and Central America, coupled with the acquisition of political power by Chicano communities, have created the basis for unprecedented Chicano advocacy on U.S. policy in Latin America, especially the Caribbean basin countries (Mexico, Central America, and the Caribbean). I use Chicano advocacy on U.S. policy in Central America during the 1980s, and in Nicaragua in particular, as a case study.

U.S. intervention in Central America was arguably the nation's most contentious foreign policy matter of the 1980s. Visions of communist expansion in "our backyard," on the one hand, and becoming trapped in another Vietnam-type war without end, on the other, fueled a rigorous public debate. Over time, the massive migration of Central American refugees to the United States expressed the human dimensions of U.S. policy. Despite the political cost, the Reagan Administration's priority continued to be the destruction of the Nicaraguan revolution. In early 1988, Congress definitively halted U.S. arms supplies to the Contras, dealing a significant defeat to the Reagan Administration. Chicano politicians and community organizations played a key but unexplored part in defeating Reagan's interventionist policy.

The literature discussing the Chicano role in U.S. foreign policy is sparse. Conventional wisdom holds that Chicanos have no role in U.S. foreign policy. Some analysts believe that Chicano leaders have little expertise and that the Chicano community has no common self-interest. Rodolfo O. de la Garza argues that "the historical ties between Chicanos and the homeland have not produced a relationship strong enough to propel Mexican American political mobilization around issues related to U.S. policy toward Mexico." According to de la Garza, "given the heterogeneity of the Mexican-American population, even if it were interested in Latin America issues, it is unrealistic to expect that it could respond with one voice to political developments in Latin America, especially in view of the complexity of Latin American socio-political reality." [1]

Chicano political voices had, indeed, been quiescent and unfocused during the early years (1979–1984) of U.S. intervention in Central America. Prominent Chicano leaders in this period defended a range of positions: pro-Sandinist, anti-communist, anti-intervention, pro-containment, and so on. However, by 1984 Chicano public opinion coalesced into consistent opposition to U.S. intervention in Central America. This, coupled with the emergence of opposition to U.S. intervention among Chicano organizations, created a new consensus: active opposition to the U.S. policy of providing arms to the rebels (or Contras) fighting for the overthrow of the Nicaraguan government.

THE BROADENING OF THE CHICANO AGENDA

Historically, U.S. policy premises in the Americas have been twofold. Since the Monroe Doctrine, the U.S. has always considered Latin America and the Caribbean to be within its sphere of economic and military influence. Second, U.S. policymakers have, since the Mexican revolution, considered most revolutionary movements to be inspired by Marxism and thus threatening to U.S. interests.

Nearly two centuries after the proclamation of the Monroe Doctrine, these premises still define U.S. behavior. This is especially true in Central

America, where meaningful change in Central American political and social systems can be guaranteed only if U.S. domestic actors or movements prevent hostile U.S. action. Such activity implies altering the terms of the policy debate with a critique of U.S. premises. Such a political space is ideally suited for Chicano leaders.

The creation of such space for Chicano leaders and organizations did not occur in a vacuum. It was paralleled and organically connected to developments in the Chicano community. Since the mid-1970s Chicanos have experienced an unprecedented expansion of political power, reflected in a doubling of registered voters, an increase in the number and size of community organizations, and a doubling of elected officials.[2] The growth of Chicano political power has broadened the Chicano political agenda. Nationally, between 1980 and 1990, the Chicano membership in Congress increased from four to ten. In addition, Chicano state legislators and officers number over one hundred.

In view of these developments, the late William C. Velásquez argued that Chicanos were entering a new period of political power and were thus obliged to begin addressing national and foreign policy issues. Velásquez maintained that given historic, cultural, linguistic, and economic relationships, migration patterns, and a pattern of problematic U.S. policies, Latin America was a natural beginning point for Chicano political action on issues of U.S. foreign policy. Latino leaders, according to Velásquez, should develop "Hispanic alternatives, not just to the Nicaragua problem, but Hispanic alternatives to the development of U.S. policy."[3]

A second general factor concerned Latino in-migration. Twenty years of Mexican and Central and South American in-migration have altered the social fabric of the U.S. Latino community. The 1986 Immigration Reform and Control Act (IRCA) legalized nearly three million undocumented immigrants, 90 percent of whom were Latino.[4] Their integration into the barrios of the Southwest (where a great majority have settled) has replenished the strength of Latino culture and consciousness in numerous ways. Moreover, their presence has helped sensitize the Chicano community regarding the causes of migration to the United States.

Voter opinion surveys conducted by the Southwest Voter Research Institute (SVRI) from 1984 to 1988 indicate that Chicano voters were substantially more supportive of the rights of Mexican immigrants and Central American refugees than Anglo voters. While Chicano voters in Texas favored amnesty for undocumented immigrant workers (50.8 percent in favor, 30.8 percent opposed), Anglo voters in the same precincts opposed such a measure (51.0 percent opposed, 36.4 percent in favor). While Chicano voters in California were sharply divided on hiring prohibitions for undocumented workers

Table 7.1. Chicano Voter Opinion on Contra Aid (in Percentages)

	1984	1986	1988
Favor	14	24	18
Oppose	62	59	66
Unsure	24	17	17

Source: Southwest Voter Research Institute statewide exit polls of 1,785 Mexican American voters in Texas, Nov. 1984; 2,300 Mexican American voters in Texas and California, Nov. 1986; and 5,722 Latino voters in Texas, New Mexico, and California, Nov. 1988.

(45 percent in favor, 41 percent opposed), Anglo voters in the same precincts overwhelmingly supported the hiring prohibitions (64 percent in favor, 22 percent opposed).[5]

At the leadership level, Chicano elected officials and organizational leaders were increasingly compelled to address the root causes of problems in their communities. U.S. military intervention, direct or indirect, in Central America stimulated the flow of hundreds of thousands of refugees to the United States.[6] These refugees settled in the urban Southwest (as well as other places) and impacted a range of municipal services. Thus, Chicano leaders seeking to deliver improved educational or municipal services to their constituencies were compelled to deal with a human consequence (the newly arrived refugees) of U.S. foreign policy in Central America.

Concurrent with the demographic changes in the Southwest, Chicano public opinion shifted from indifference regarding U.S. policy in Central America to opposition. In 1984, a SVREP exit poll of 1,785 Texas Chicanos showed 62 percent opposition to giving more U.S. aid to the Contras (Nicaraguan counterrevolutionaries seeking to overthrow the Sandinista government) and 60.6 percent opposition to aiding the dictatorial Salvadoran government. In 1986 SVRI polled 2,300 Chicano voters in Texas and California who indicated 59 percent opposition to giving military aid to the Contras. And similarly, the 1988 SVRI exit poll of 5,722 Chicano voters in Texas, New Mexico, and California showed 66 percent opposition to funding the Contras (see Table 7.1).

Surveys of elected officials and community leaders during 1984–1986 showed similar opposition to aiding the Contras and providing military aid to the Salvadoran government.[7] By the mid 1980s opposition to Contra aid contained all the rallying points for Chicanos, bringing together public opinion, progressive activists, mainstream elected officials, and community organizations. Of course, some Chicanos had opposed U.S.–Central America policy from the start. They were typically students or members of the peace community. But their activism was usually outside the scope of Chicano politics.

Chicano Leaders and U.S. Policy in Central America: 1979–1985

Washington, D.C., does not wait for communities and their leaders to analyze and arrive at consensus. While the Carter Administration (1979–1980) probed the possibilities for intervention, the Reagan Administration (1980–1988) set a brisk pace for U.S. intervention. National Chicano opinion leaders had no choice but to respond, even if lacking a consensus among their peers or a grassroots base of informed constituents. A review of the actions and positions of the most prominent Chicano leaders of the early 1980s provides some insight.

San Antonio Mayor Henry Cisneros attained national prominence by joining President Reagan's National Bipartisan Commission on U.S. Policy in Central America in 1983. Cisneros was the first Chicano to gain such prominent entry into elite foreign policy circles. Indeed, the star-studded commission, headed by former Secretary of State Henry Kissinger, was President Reagan's best early attempt at neutralizing public and congressional opposition to his Central America policies. The "Kissinger Commission" surveyed the political situation in Central America and made a set of policy recommendations to the president. Cisneros, though supporting the report as a whole, dissented on the commission's proposals regarding Nicaragua and El Salvador. The commission endorsed U.S. military intervention in El Salvador and Nicaragua. Cisneros argued in his dissent: "The Sandinista Regime should be encouraged to intensify dialogue with the hierarchy of the Nicaraguan Catholic Church, the private sector, and the opposition parties; expand its offer of amnesty for anti-Sandinist rebels; introduce details of legislation to permit the free functioning of political parties and the promise of elections in 1985; eliminate censorship of the press; fulfill its recent promises to the opposition newspaper *La Prensa* to acquire newsprint; and reduce the numbers of Cuban advisers and Salvadoran rebel elements from Nicaragua."[8] He added that the United States should suspend "covert" aid to the anti-Sandinist rebels "so that the Sandinista government can demonstrate its capacity to move toward pluralism and to fulfill its promise to hold free and fair elections." Regarding El Salvador, Cisneros did not oppose U.S. military aid to the Duarte government but instead proposed efforts to "convince FDR/FMLN [Revolutionary Democratic Front/Farabundo Marti People's Liberation Front] moderates . . . to take part in discussions concerning participation in a security task force to arrange security provisions for all participants on election processes [in El Salvador]." Regarding the FMLN guerrillas and the Salvadoran military, Cisneros recommended that "the Salvadoran security forces and the guerrillas should agree to a complete cease fire," after which discussions on security arrangements and election matters would determine the extent to which "meaningful dialogue on coalition approaches and structural reforms can proceed."

Mayor Cisneros's dissenting comments can be interpreted in two ways. On one hand, his participation in the Kissinger Commission legitimized Chicano involvement in foreign policy at the national leadership level. On the other hand, Cisneros's substantive positions, though dissenting from the right wing majority, embraced the practice of U.S. military intervention, negated self-determination, and ignored the root causes of the region's revolutions: poverty and repression. Cisneros advanced positions that, de facto, supported the repressive Duarte government in El Salvador. He opposed, for practical reasons, sending "covert" military aid to the Contras seeking to overthrow the Sandinista government in Nicaragua, but only if free and fair elections were held.

This moderate or, more accurately, centrist tendency in Chicano leadership advocacy is underscored by congressional voting patterns throughout the 1980s. Chicano members of Congress, while reaching a rough consensus in 1987 to oppose military aid to the Contras (they also voted against military aid in 1983–1984), vacillated until December 1989 on opposing military aid to the Salvadoran government. Generally, Congressmen Henry B. González of Texas and Edward Roybal, Esteban Torres, and Matthew Martínez of California opposed U.S. intervention in Central America. Congressmen Manuel Luján of New Mexico and Solomon Ortiz of Texas consistently supported U.S. intervention. And Congressmen Kika de La Garza and Albert Bustamante of Texas vacillated: they alternated between voting for and against Contra aid until 1986 and then tended to oppose Contra aid (see Table 7.2).

In the early years of the Central America debate (1982–1985), Chicano leaders only tentatively addressed issues of U.S. policy in Central America. Their actions were as likely to be pro-intervention as not. Mayor Cisneros's moderate anti-intervention stance was contradicted by actions like that of Congressman Bill Richardson of New Mexico, who in 1985 as Chair of the Congressional Hispanic Caucus played a public role in reinitiating military aid to the Contras (which had been prohibited by the Boland Amendment in 1983–1984). At the time Richardson was reportedly incensed by Nicaraguan President Daniel Ortega's visit to Moscow.[9]

Another characteristic of Chicano political action in the "early years" was the noninvolvement of Chicano institutions and organizations in the Central America debate. With some exceptions, e.g., Chicano student MEChA groups or Seattle's El Centro de la Raza, Chicano community organizations played

Table 7.2. Hispanic Members of Congress Voting Record on Contra Aid

Name/State	1983	1984	1985					1986			1987		1988	
			A	B	C	D	E	A	B	C	A	B	A	B
Bustamante—Tex.			N	N		Y	Y	N	Y	Y	N	Y	N	N
De la Garza—Tex.	N	N	Y	N	Y	Y	N	N	N	N	N	Y	N	N
García—N.Y.	N	N	N	N	N	N	N	N	N	N	N	N	N	N
González—Tex.	N	N	N	N	N	N	N	N	N	N	N	N	N	N
Luján—N.M.	Y	Y	Y	Y	Y	Y	Y	Y	Y	Y	Y	Y	Y	
Martínez—Calif.	N	N	N	N	N	N	N	N	N	N	N	N	N	
Ortiz—Tex.	N	N	Y	Y	Y	Y	N	Y	Y	Y	Y	Y	Y	N
Richardson—N.M.	N	N	N	N	N	Y	N	N	N	N	N	N	N	N
Roybal—Calif.	N	N	N	N	N	N	N	N	N	N	N	N	N	N
Torres—Calif.	N	N	N	N	N	N	N	N	N	N	N	N	N	N
Totals (%)	88.8	88.8	69.4					73.3			70.0		89.5	

Key: N = voted against pro-Contra measure, Y = voted for pro-Contra measure
Source: *FCNL Washington Newsletter,* nos. 464, 472, 516; Coalition for a New Foreign and Military Policy 1985 and 1986 voting records; Sane/Freeze, 1987 Senate and House voting records.

little or no role in the Central America debate. For the most part, influential groups like the Mexican American Legal Defense and Education Fund (MALDEF), National Council of La Raza (NCLR), League of United Latin American Citizens (LULAC), and Southwest Voter Registration Education Project, though probably critical of U.S. policy, steered clear of active opposition. Aside from the debate on immigration policy, none of them had any experience in foreign policy matters. Some, like MALDEF and NCLR, had explicit prohibitions on getting involved with foreign policy. Local community groups opposed to U.S. Central America policy generally joined Anglo-dominated peace committees.[10]

Chicano Organizations and Central America: 1984–1988

The pattern began to change with the initiation of the Latin America Project of LULAC. In 1984 LULAC National President Mario Obledo launched the Latin America Project. Designed to involve LULAC leaders in the national debate on U.S. policy in Latin America, the LULAC effort represented an important change for Chicano politics in the 1980s. Not only was the nation's largest and oldest Latino membership organization getting its leadership informed and involved in a new policy area, it was doing so in opposition to U.S. government policy and independent of the peace community.

Over the next three years the LULAC Latin America Project conducted a LULAC leaders' delegation to Mexico, Cuba, and Nicaragua (1984). It also sponsored a series of debates in Washington, D.C., and at its national conventions on the key issues of U.S. immigration and refugee policy, Contra aid, the Contadora negotiating process, the English Only movement, and the role of Hispanics in U.S. policy in Latin America. A publication series accompanied the symposia.

Though LULAC often took positions on these issues, with the exception of language and immigration issues, they did not create ad hoc or ongoing lobbying efforts. Rather, the emphasis of the LULAC Latin America Project was education and policy participation. Obledo argued in "The Role of Hispanics in U.S. Foreign Policy in Latin America" that, "[f]ocusing upon Latin America, our government looks upon the region with disregard. Latin America was and remains a second class citizen in the world community just as the Hispanic American has been and remains a second class citizen within U.S. borders."[11]

Obledo believed that Hispanics could make a substantial and significant contribution to the improvement of relations between the United States and Latin America. He felt that the cultural and historical relationship of U.S. Hispanics with Latin Americans "creates an environment whereby nuances, dynamics, symbols, facial expressions, temperament, customs, languages, philosophies, and emotions can be best understood." This unique Hispanic perspective could provide "an invaluable service to America." Yet Obledo felt "tremendous frustrations" because of the U.S. government's interventionist response to "circumstances and events—in Chile, Cuba, Nicaragua, the Dominican Republic, and so on."[12]

Congressman Esteban Torres, in response, emphasized the need for Latino political participation. "I simply have to look at the Department of State to see that there are very few Hispanics there," he said. Torres felt that the way to increase the role of Hispanics in foreign policy was "to get out there and promote political activity, right from the barrio up . . . to do all the necessary political tasks that eventually lead to election to the Congress, where they then can really influence the making of foreign policy."[13]

The pioneering LULAC initiative on Hispanic involvement in U.S. policy in Central America stressed participation and education. By 1986, however, prominent Chicano leaders were actively taking critical stands regarding U.S. policy in Central America and its implications in the United States.

A watershed in Chicano leadership dissent came with Governor Toney

Anaya's declaration of New Mexico as a sanctuary for Central American refugees in March 1986. Though symbolic in nature, the sanctuary declaration signified courageous opposition to the Reagan administration's discriminatory treatment of Central American refugees. Since 1983 the administration had opposed providing temporary asylum (extended voluntary departure) for Central American refugees, especially Salvadorans who were fleeing from a repressive U.S.-supported regime. Anaya, then the highest-ranking Hispanic in the country, essentially defied the Reagan administration, using his office to skirt the president's block on congressional action to protect Central American refugees.

Anaya argued against the administration claim that over 97 percent of these refugees were only "economic migrants," and thus deportable. Anaya held that these people were refugees, literally and legally. This definition applied to any person who was unable or unwilling to avail himself or herself of the protection of the home country because of "a well-founded fear of persecution on account of race, religion, nationality, or membership in a particular social group." Anaya asked rhetorically: "Doesn't it seem to you that anyone who migrates from El Salvador, a nation which has seen 1% of its population assassinated within the past few years . . . would qualify for a 'well-founded fear of persecution,' much less anyone who has actually tried to implement any change in that society?"[14] By declaring New Mexico the nation's first sanctuary state, Anaya also emphasized the connection between U.S. policy in Central America and its domestic implications. Indeed, situated along the border between the United States and Latin America, Chicano leaders like Anaya were ideally suited to remind the nation of its heritage of protecting the human rights of refugees and immigrants.

Chicano Advocacy against U.S. Intervention

Chicano participation in U.S. policy in Central America developed further in the summer of 1987 when Willie Velásquez, president of the Southwest Voter Registration Education Project (SVREP), launched his own Latin America Project. Based on the LULAC effort (which concluded in 1987), the Southwest Voter Research Institute (SVRI) Latin America Project has since 1988 conducted several delegations of Latino leaders to Mexico and Central America, including an observers' mission to the Nicaraguan elections. The project has also included an intensive leadership seminar series and a polling and publication series. The effort continues through the 1990s.

Politically socialized during the Chicano movement, Velásquez felt that U.S. intervention in Central America was misguided. Increasingly vocal in opposing Contra aid, he even threatened to run against San Antonio Congressman Albert Bustamante because of his support for Contra aid. Velásquez felt another Vietnam, with the incumbent racist effect on Chicanos (and Central Americans), had to be avoided. But he also knew that neither Chicano leaders nor the community at large were well informed on the subject. When the SVRI project was launched in 1987, Velásquez intended it to facilitate the emergence of a broad group of Chicano leaders that could develop and advocate a consensus Chicano perspective on U.S. policies in Latin America, especially Central America.

In launching SVRI's Latin America Project, Velásquez expressed his vision of the eventual Chicano role in U.S. policy in Latin America. Mexican American leaders, according to Velásquez, had to become "seriously involved as advocates for appropriate and genuine developmental aid" for a "peaceful resolution of conflictive situations" and had to act "as liaisons of communication and negotiation" in military or economic conflicts.[15]

Initiatives like SVRI's reflected a clear trend toward actively opposing U.S.-Nicaragua policy in Chicano politics. By 1988, there was no significant urban center in the Southwest where Chicano leaders and activists had not become involved in lobbying or organizing to change U.S. policy in Nicaragua. By 1987 groups as diverse as Texas LULAC, California MAPA, Southwest Organizing Project in Albuquerque, Southwest Voter Registration Education Project, and Texas GI Forum were organizing pressure campaigns on southwestern Congress members who had previously voted for the Contras or were undecided. Other groups, like the Chicanos Against Military Intervention in Latin America (CAMILA), conducted mass mobilizations in Austin, Houston, San Antonio, and Hondo, Texas. Prominent opinion leaders like New Mexico Governor Toney Anaya, Congressman Esteban Torres of Los Angeles, and Congressman Henry B. González of San Antonio repeatedly spoke out publicly at press conferences and protest events against Contra aid.

In fact, when the Central American presidents reached a peace accord in August 1987, Velásquez and Al Luna, chair of the Mexican American Legislative Caucus (MALC) of the Texas House of Representatives, traveled to Central America to survey the prospects for peace and the impact of U.S. policy. Their findings led them to intensify Chicano opposition to Contra aid and support the Central American Peace Plan. Luna publicly criticized U.S. policy: "If we want peace, we must do our part. President Reagan cannot credibly make public speeches for peace in Central America while at the same time advocating a three-fold increase in funding to the Contras." Luna felt that Nicaragua's government had taken deliberate steps to comply with the Central American peace plan. He also defended Nicaraguan self-determination:

"Whether we like it or not, the Nicaraguan government has a right to exist. It is legitimate . . . the United States cannot determine what social and political system should exist in Nicaragua. That is the right of the Nicaraguan people. That is called the right of self-determination. Our country is supposed to support that sort of thing. Isn't it?" Luna appealed to President Reagan to reverse this Nicaragua policy. "End your tenure in the White House, Mr. President, by acting for peace. The Contras have caused enough damage. Stop funding them. It's the right thing to do," he exhorted.[16]

In January 1988 when Speaker of the U.S. House of Representatives Jim Wright attempted to block the Reagan administration proposal for military aid to the Contras in violation of the Central American accords, Velásquez organized a historic delegation of Chicano leaders to visit Nicaragua and Costa Rica. The nine-member mission included Velásquez, Anaya, Mario Obledo, State Representative Eddie Cavazos (who was also vice-chair of the Texas MALC), refugee advocate attorney Linda Yáñez, and university professor Avelardo Valdez. Their report, presented on the eve of the vote to the Congressional Hispanic Caucus and Speaker Wright, was bitterly critical of U.S. policy. Delegation Chair Anaya charged at a national press conference on February 3, 1988, on Capitol Hill, that the Reagan Administration supported, in practice, the destabilization of Central America. Anaya, presenting the group's findings, "concluded that the missing element in the search for peace in Central America is the will of our government to genuinely support the Peace Plan." He argued that "the policy of giving aid to the Contras, whether military or non-lethal, must be terminated immediately." Importantly, Anaya explained that the U.S. moral standing was damaged by aiding the Contras: "the American contribution to resolving the conflicts in Central America ought not to be support for the Contras, whose claim to fame seems to be the wanton destruction of 25,000 Nicaraguans and $3.5 billion in economic damage. That's not the democratic way and not the American way."[17]

Later that day, the Congressional Hispanic Caucus, led by Albert Bustamante of San Antonio, a former supporter of Contra aid, voted 8 to 2 to oppose sending further military aid to the Contras. Every one of their votes were needed, as opponents of Contra aid won by 218 to 211, thus ending a six-year policy of arming the Nicaraguan counterrevolutionaries.

After six years of contradictory involvement, Chicano leadership opposition to U.S. policy in Central America had crystallized around the Contra aid issue and the Central American Peace Plan. A working consensus had been reached that included progressives and moderates, elected officials and organizational leaders. Congressman Henry B. González, a senior statesman of Chicano politics, explained the logic of the new Chicano consensus: "It is morally bankrupt and politically blind to support military dictatorships . . . our leadership is meaningless unless it stands for our own principles of law, decency and liberty. . . . With bombs and bullets, we are buying only fear and hatred. In the long run, our choice is between being an army of occupation, or helping Central Americans achieve what we would want for ourselves: decent government and a decent chance in life."[18]

CHICANO LEADERS DEBATE THE CHARACTER OF REVOLUTION

Chicano leaders that had first questioned and then actively opposed U.S.-Nicaragua policy remained involved with U.S.-Central America relations. Some focused on U.S. policy in El Salvador; some on refugee and immigrant issues. Others continued to monitor U.S. policy in Nicaragua, which had increasingly relied on building civic opposition to the Sandinista government. In one instance, an SVRI fact-finding mission in Esteli, Nicaragua, stumbled upon a meeting of Nicaraguan opposition leaders being conducted by the U.S. ambassador. For this blatant violation of diplomatic protocol, the ambassador was promptly expelled. After the defeat of Contra aid, the U.S. Embassy became an even more important center of intrigue, receiving an endless stream of Nicaraguan anti-Sandinistas.[19]

The scores of Chicano leaders who had visited Central America could not help but begin to ponder broader issues. Chicanos had viewed Latin America through "Mexican" lenses. Yet Central America made Mexico look rich, stable, and developed; the region was as different from Mexico as Mexico from the United States. The poverty was depressing. Repression and fear in El Salvador was palpable. New Mexico Secretary of State Rebecca Vigil Girón, upon her return from a SVRI fact-finding mission to El Salvador and Nicaragua in August 1989, put it succinctly:

> I have rage. I have a feeling of concern about what we are doing in
> El Salvador in terms of our dollars . . . going to killing people, harass-
> ing people — people that just want to be left alone . . . I felt a real
> fear, I do not think I have felt so much fear in any place in my whole
> life. . . . I heard shots outside of our hotel, and it scared me to death
> because I did not know what would come after that. . . . But it is
> a really horrible life for these people and yes, you could see it on
> their faces.[20]

Returning delegations of Chicano leaders regularly concluded that U.S. intervention mirrored its own internal racism. The issues of Central America were not capitalism versus communism, but the basics of human development: justice and human rights, land and jobs, freedom and democracy.

Still, the questions remained. How could progress occur? Were Central American societies doomed to perpetual cycles of poverty and repression, to revolution and counterrevolution and U.S. intervention? Could revolutions succeed in not only overthrowing dictators, but also delivering socioeconomic benefits and popular democracy?

In a debriefing session following their mission to Nicaragua in February 1988, Velásquez, State Representative Cavazos, and Attorney Linda Yáñez debated the nature of the Sandinista revolution. Velásquez began: "The Sandinista revolution truly is a revolution. . . . It is a classic revolution . . . designed to do something about the working people that have, for at least 300 years . . . gotten a very raw deal with fate." Velásquez felt that although excesses of power were likely, the revolution was basically Latino and Western oriented. Charges that the Sandinistas were Moscow-Havana style communists did not faze Velásquez.

> Then I would ask a question, what kind of communists? They're Latin communists who believe that there ought to be a private sector, capitalism. They believe that religion ought to be strong. They're communists who believe that there ought to be a press that's open. . . .
> That there ought not to be abusers, an abuser class, there's nothing wrong with confiscating their land and distributing it to the working people. And that laws and programs ought to be for the majority of the people as opposed to the elite. And I'd label that communism, Latino style.[21]

Cavazos disagreed, arguing that the Sandinistas were pragmatically "taking advantage of what's there": "And what's there is communist aid, Russian aid, Cuban aid or whatever. . . . Where are they getting their arms? That's the only place they can get them, or they won't get them. Where are they getting their gasoline? Ortega . . . and the Sandinistas are having to run a government by whatever means they can get."

Cavazos believed that Nicaragua could just as easily swing into the U.S. camp "if the tide was turned and all of a sudden we started dealing with them, they would be as pro-American as the next guy, simply because it's to their advantage."[22]

Yáñez differed with both, arguing that we cannot expect "United States-style democracy in Nicaragua any time in the foreseeable future or Soviet-style communism either." She believed that Nicaragua was developing "a social-political system that cannot be labeled." Yáñez observed that Nicaragua has not risen to "the level of closed, structured society currently in place in Russia."[23]

THE ELECTION OF VIOLETA CHAMORRO: A U.S. VICTORY?

Even as the Sandinista army defeated the U.S.-supported Contras, the country's economy went into shock. The resources diverted for fighting the Contra war had been too much. The economy collapsed. In 1988 inflation was 36,000 percent and in 1989 nearly 2,000 percent. The Sandinista revolution gave new meaning to the term hyperinflation. No government in modern history had endured such conditions, even less so in Latin America. The refugee stream to the United States, previously overwhelmingly Salvadoran, by 1987 was increasingly Nicaraguan. Nicaraguan exports dropped by half, to $233 million per year as rich coffee, pasture, and cotton lands located in battle zones went untended. Government programs making medical aid and education available to peasants and the urban poor were targeted and destroyed by the Contras or cut back because of scarce resources. Hyperinflation made private-sector investment in even secure areas risky and unprofitable.[24]

Though Presidents Reagan and Bush could not overthrow the Sandinistas by force, their policies effectively crippled the economy and exhausted the population. Support for the Sandinistas eroded. The beleaguered Sandinistas began to harden, creating further problems.[25] By the beginning of Nicaragua's electoral process in September 1989, questions on the future and character of the revolution were appropriate. Would the Sandinistas allow free elections? The previous 1984 elections had been fair and clean, but less competitive. This time 23 parties were participating, many receiving U.S. and European funds (as were the Sandinistas). Clearly, "había una perdida de sangre para los Sandinistas"; the Sandinistas had lost considerable popularity.

An eight-member SVRI fact-finding delegation (August 1989), led by Rebecca Vigil Girón, found electoral conditions more than adequate.[26] With an electoral accord signed by all parties, the credibility of the elections was guaranteed. The Contras were on their last legs. Indeed, confident Sandinistas plunged into an election campaign against a fractured and poorly organized opposition. All claimed the election would be a referendum on the revolution.

In March 1990, in a virtually flawless election with 86 percent voter turnout, the pro-U.S. candidate, Violeta Chamorro, upset Sandinista President Daniel Ortega. No one had predicted the upset. Afterward, the Bush Administration blustered that the Nicaraguan people had followed the example of Eastern Europe, voting for democracy and against communism.

Postelection analysis was problematic. The referendum was over, but what did it mean? Did the voters support the Contras and U.S. intervention? Did peasants want to return their lands to the "patrones"? Were the Sandinistas seen as communist oppressors? Or did the voters see Violeta Chamorro's candidacy as a way to obtain economic support from the United States, demobilize the Contras, and end objectionable Sandinista policies like the military draft? The SVRI's fourteen-member election observers' delegation, though united in supporting the elections as fair and clean, were divided on what motivated the voters. Juan Andrade, executive director of the Midwest Voter Registration Project, believed that the intent of the Nicaraguan electorate was very clear: "The vote was pro-Chamorro, anti-Sandinista, and a rejection of policies that have had negative impact upon the people." Andrade added that "Nicaragua's second clean election in six years suggests that the roots of democracy have begun to take hold." The Sandinistas, he argued, would have to be content with influencing "public policy as a legislative opposition party."[27]

Dr. Avelardo Valdez of the University of Texas, San Antonio, strongly disagreed. "The United National Opposition's, or UNO, landslide victory was both a protest vote and a vote for change," he said. "The electorate understood the United States clearly favored Violeta Chamorro's UNO party and was convinced that a victory for the Sandinistas, even a democratic one, would have meant a continuing policy of U.S. intervention."[28]

Chamarro's UNO won a landslide victory for president, for National Assembly (51 of 92 seats), and for over 90 percent of the 131 municipalities. But UNO's margin in the National Assembly did not approach the 61 votes needed to change the revolutionary constitution. Thus, the broad outline of the Sandinista revolution, including land reform, independent judiciary, Atlantic Coast autonomy, and a broad range of human, civil, and labor rights, remained legally protected. Moreover, within a month after their victory, Chamorro's coalition had gone into a crisis, with 23 of the 51 UNO deputies combining with 39 Sandinista deputies to elect most of the new National Assembly officers. This was inevitable, for the same breadth of parties in the UNO coalition—from communist to ultra-conservative—that allowed them to posture as a viable alternative to the Sandinistas, made programmatic unity difficult if not impossible.

Whatever the long-term outcome in Nicaragua, two things are clear: social struggles will be intense as the old elite seeks to reassert itself; and the U.S. will continue to be a wild card, altering through its purse strings and covert activity the range of possibilities. Interestingly, the end of U.S. aid to the Contras in 1988 brought about their collapse and also caused the end of Sandinista rule when Nicaraguans voted them out of power in 1990. Subsequent elections in 1996 confirmed the end of Sandinista rule.

TOWARD A REDEFINITION OF PREMISES

By the end of the 1980s many Chicano leaders viewed the revolutionary movements in Central America as indigenous revolts directed against age-old dictatorships and unjust structures. These movements, irrespective of their external allies, reflected a deeply rooted desire for land rights, jobs with decent conditions and pay, human and civil rights, and true democracy. These aspirations were not so different from Chicano aspirations.

Indeed, William Velásquez felt that U.S. intervention in Central America raised anew the great formative principles of the Chicano movement: self determination, social justice, human rights, and democracy. He felt that Chicano leaders' attitudes toward the intervention and the revolutions reflected their true potential as leaders. The best and brightest of them would naturally oppose intervention.

The debate on these questions was not academic. Enormous upheavals were taking place, not just in Nicaragua but in other Central American societies as well. The United States invaded Panama in December 1989, overthrowing nationalist dictator Manuel Noriega and installing a puppet government. More than one thousand people died in the process. El Salvador exploded in November 1989 with the biggest rebel offensive in the civil war. Thousands more died.[29] Guerrilla struggles and government repression intensified in Guatemala. It seemed as though progress toward peace and intensified civil war and intervention were two sides of the same coin. As progress toward peace seemed attainable, all sides launched offensives to improve their positions at the bargaining table. Then, with the end of the civil wars in El Salvador (1992) and Guatemala (1996), brokered by the United States and the United Nations, Central America fell off the foreign policy radar scope. Chicano attention also turned to other elements of U.S.–Latin America policy.[30]

Sadly, however, the battle to change fundamental U.S. premises in Latin America and the Caribbean continues. The failure of the United States to recognize the true character of the Central American revolutions and the invocation of ill-suited Cold War and Monroe Doctrine policies have squandered much Latin American goodwill toward the United States. Latin American governments were pushed into an oppositional stance toward U.S. policy. Indeed, U.S. military intervention created Latin American unity around the principles of nonintervention, self-determination, and respect for international law. This was unprecedented. Historically, U.S. intervention in the Americas has often been accompanied by some Latin American partner. The 1980s saw countries as diverse as Cuba, Mexico, Colombia, and Peru coordinate diplomatic efforts to change U.S. policy in Central America. Even the Organization of American States, traditionally a rubber stamp for U.S. policy, opposed it. In the case of Cuba, interventionist policies such as the Helms-Burton Act continue in force.[31]

The experience of Chicano advocacy on U.S. policy in Central America in the 1980s provides valuable lessons for the future. First, without a rough consensus within both the community and its leadership, Chicano leaders were not effective actors. Consensus against U.S. intervention in Nicaragua was finally achieved (1984–1985) around the principle of self-determination. This, however, did not stop Chicano leaders from criticizing the Sandinistas' abuses of human and civil rights or the numerous U.S. government–sponsored abuses. Human and civil rights were treated as absolute moral principles. Second, Chicano advocacy, even with an internal consensus, needed allies to be successful. In the Nicaraguan case, the allies were a U.S.-based anti-intervention movement and international public opinion. Third, effective Chicano advocacy saw foreign and domestic policy as interconnected. Cuts in social programs in home and massive refugee in-migration were understood and explained as effects of U.S. foreign policy. Finally, Chicano advocacy not only opposed U.S. intervention, but sought policy alternatives. For example, the Central American Peace Plan was immediately embraced by key Chicano leaders and served as an effective tool for broadening advocacy to other leaders and organizations.

Over the next generation the rapidly growing political and economic clout of Chicanos will make them a significant variable in U.S. foreign policy. Perhaps the Chicano role in the twenty-first century will be to challenge the Monroe Doctrine as the operative premise of U.S. policy in Latin America and the Caribbean. Chicano advocacy can act as the conscience of the nation, explaining that only respect for self-determination, coupled with long-term, equitable growth in Latin American societies, can truly benefit U.S. interests.

NOTES

1. Rodolfo O. de la Garza, "U.S. Foreign Policy and the Mexican American Political Agenda," in Mohammed E. Ahari, ed., *Ethnic Groups and U.S. Foreign Policy* (New York: Greenwood Press, 1987), pp. 105–106, 110.

2. Community-based Chicano organizations have grown in size and number. They have also extended into geographic regions and social sectors that were historically unorganized. For example, Texas LULAC maintains over one hundred councils. The Industrial Areas Foundation includes mass-based parish organizations in a dozen southwestern urban centers. Southwest Voter Registration Education Project includes activist networks in 160 cities.

Latino Registered voters in the five southwestern states of Arizona, California, Colorado, New Mexico, and Texas doubled from 1,511,500 to 3,002,900 in the 1976–1988 period. Southwest Voter Research Institute, Southwest Voter Registration Education Project, U.S. Census Bureau, Voting and Registration Series, 1976–1988.

Chicano elected officials also experienced dramatic growth, more than doubling from 1,379 to 3,066 during the 1973–1988 period. NALEO National Roster of Hispanic Elected Officials (Aztlan Publications, 1988); National Roster of Spanish Surnamed Elected Officials, 1973.

3. *SVRI Latin America Project Report 1, Views of Latino Leaders: A Roundtable Discussion on U.S. Policy in Nicaragua and the Central America Peace Plan,* 1989, p. 10.

4. Frank D. Bean, Thomas J. Espenshade, Michael J. White, and Robert F. Dymowski, "Post-IRCA Changes in the Volume and Composition of Undocumented Migration to the United States: An Assessment Base on Apprehensions Data," in *Undocumented Migration to the United States: IRCA and the Experience of the 1980s* (Washington, D.C.: Urban Institute Press, 1990), p. 3.

5. Southwest Voter Registration Project exit poll of 1,785 Mexican American voters and 919 Anglo voters in Texas on election day 1984. Unpublished summary, author's records. SVRI exit poll of 958 voters in California on November 4, 1986.

6. This is a conservative estimate. Douglas Farah, "Salvadorans Lining up to Get Out," *Washington Post,* December 28, 1989. Farah estimates Salvadoran refugees in the United States alone number about one million.

7. *SVREP South Central RPC Report 1,* no. 3 (March 1986): 4; *SVREP California RPC Report 1,* no. 5 (October 1986): 6; *SVREP Coastal Bend RPC Report 1,* no. 2 (January 1986): 4.

8. *Report of the National Bipartisan Commission on Central America,* January 1984, pp. 128–129.

9. In 1985, shortly after a close congressional vote in which Congress denied further funds to the Contras, Nicaragua's President Ortega departed for a visit to Moscow. Ortega's trip was touted in the U.S. press as a slap in Congress's face. Shortly thereafter, President Reagan reintroduced an aid package to Congress. Congressman Richardson of New Mexico, then chair of the Congressional Hispanic Caucus, publicly denounced the trip to Moscow and announced he was switching his vote. Other opponents of Contra aid switched, and President Reagan's proposal passed.

10. Chicano activists tended to join groups like the National Network in Solidarity with the Nicaraguan People (NNSNP) or the Committee in Solidarity with the People of El Salvador (CISPES).

11. *The Role of Hispanics in U.S. Foreign Policy in Latin America,* LULAC Latin America Project pamphlet 2, no. 1 (January 1987), p. i.

12. Ibid.

13. Ibid., p. 9.

14. Proclamation Declaring New Mexico a Sanctuary State, March 28, 1986, p. 2.

15. Founding Document of SVRI's Latin America Project (unpublished, October 1987), p. 6.

16. "Central America Deserves Peace Accord by Al Luna," *San Antonio Light,* October 11, 1987.

17. *SVRI Latin America Project Report 1,* pp.. 13–14.

18. Congressional Update Newsletter from U.S. Rep. Henry B. González, 20th District, Texas, October 15, 1987, vol. 20, no. 3, p. 4.

19. U.S. Ambassador to Nicaragua Melton was expelled for violating diplomatic privileges in July 1988.

20. Unpublished transcript of debriefing session of SVRI fact-finding mission to Mexico, El Salvador, and Nicaragua, August 1989, p. 7–8.

21. *SVRI Latin America Project Report 1,* pp. 5–6.

22. Ibid., p. 6

23. Ibid.

24. *Envío* (published by Instituto Histórico Centroamericano, Managua, Nicaragua) 8, no. 100 (November 1989), p. 7; *Nicaragua's Elections. . . a Step Towards Democracy?,* published

jointly by Hemisphere Initiatives, Washington Office on Latin America, Center for International Policy and Unitarian Universalist Service Committee, Section on Nicaragua's Economy, February 1990.

25. Amnesty International 1990 Report, pp. 176–177.

26. Unpublished transcript of debriefing session of SVRI fact-finding mission to Mexico, El Salvador, and Nicaragua, August 1989, p. 16.

27. *SVRI Latin America Project Report 2, Draft, Roundtable Discussion: SVRI Delegation to Observe the February 25, 1990 Nicaraguan National Election*, pp. 4–5.

28. Avelardo Valdez, "Nicaragua Vote a Plea to End U.S. Oppression," *San Antonio Express-News*, March 10, 1990.

29. Chicano advocacy continued in the El Salvador case. SVRI launched a campaign to oppose U.S. military aid to the Salvadoran government from 1989 to 1992, conducted a major election observation mission during the Salvadoran elections in 1991, and provided technical and financial assistance to over two dozen Salvadoran and Nicaraguan nongovernmental organizations on grassroots electoral participation in the 1990s.

30. Chicano advocacy dramatically expanded during the debate on the North American Free Trade Agreement (NAFTA) with Mexico and Canada. SVRI led the way, forming the Latino Consensus on NAFTA together with over a hundred key leaders and organizations. Other principal players included Congressman Esteban Torres, MALDEF, and the National Council of La Raza (NCLR). Through the Latino Consensus on NAFTA, Latinos were able to gain key concessions from the Clinton Administration (1992–present), in exchange for the support of twelve key Democratic U.S. Representatives. These concessions included a $3 billion border cleanup fund, called the North American Development Bank (NADBank), and a $100 million worker adjustment and retraining fund, called the NAFTA Trade Adjustment and Assistance Act. In many ways, the debate over Chicano (and Latino) participation in U.S.–Latin America policy was ended by NAFTA. Nearly every major national Latino organization (and numerous local groups) now conducts some type of international activity.

31. The Contadora Pact countries included Mexico, Panama, Venezuela, and Colombia. These countries sought to facilitate negotiations between the conflicting Central American forces beginning in 1983. The Grupo de Apoyo, or Support Group, nations of Brazil, Argentina, Peru, and Uruguay sought to support Contadora's efforts. Cuba actively supported both initiatives. All countries opposed U.S. military intervention, especially support to the Contras.

PART THREE

General Studies

Eight

POLITICS AND
CHICANO CULTURE

Luis Valdez and El Teatro Campesino, 1964–1990

ROY ERIC XAVIER

El Teatro Campesino and Luis Valdez continue to be the subjects of scrutiny more than three decades after their initial appearance. Writers in and outside the academy weigh the merits of their contributions to Chicano politics and culture, the trajectory of their artistic development, and the myriad reasons for the absence of any definitive successors to their struggle.[1] But few writers attempt to explain the cultural and political contexts in which Valdez and his troupe did their work, or the pivotal role they played in the formation of Chicano politics, nor the lessons their experiences may teach us about inclusion into mainstream society.[2]

In this essay I will outline a perspective from which these questions might be analyzed. My focus will be on the culture and politics of the Chicano movement from 1964 to 1990. During those years, I argue, the relation between Chicano culture and politics was, at times, mutually supportive and reciprocal. That is, individuals in each arena shared values and perspectives which helped legitimize many forms of artistic and political expression. As the Chicano movement reached its zenith, the affinity between artists and politicians seemed to increase. Early artists attempted to use their skills to suggest political solutions, while some politicians tried to incorporate artistic concepts to instill a sense of purpose and hope in their followers. Both these tendencies were expressed in the work of a contemporary Chicano playwright, Luis Valdez, and his troupe, El Teatro Campesino.

The argument in this essay suggests that artistic expression enjoys moments of relative autonomy, and thus has the opportunity to develop particular interests and influence human behavior. When art is created in the vortex of a political movement, as was the case of El Teatro Campesino, its impact can be traced both in the range of artistic vision and in the degree to which artists attempt to establish political agendas. In other words, artists may respond to political events in a variety of ways. At times they may accommodate art to dominant forces; at other times they may seek independence or resist accommodation, or they may actively oppose the status quo. As I shall demonstrate, the relative autonomy of Luis Valdez and El Teatro Campesino during the sixties and seventies allowed him to create new cultural forms which influenced Chicano political life and were in turn influenced by political events.

There have been few systematic attempts to analyze Chicano politics and culture as interactive processes. A review of the literature suggests two general misconceptions, which present serious obstacles for the study of culture in contemporary society. First, there is the assumption that cultural expression and political activity are autonomous and separate spheres.[3] This perspective is characterized by a degree of conceptual rigidity. Culture is usually defined as folklore, literature, "artifacts," or intransigent national traditions; in short, as specific and autonomous objects which can be analyzed as distinct components of a larger totality called "culture." The definition of politics, on the other hand, is usually confined to certain formalized activities: the electoral process, labor organizing, reform movements, for example. Each definition is limited by a fragmented view of reality, excluding many "intangible" processes such as art, the influence of media, and advertising which may have profound effects on political life.

A second assumption is that cultural expression is largely determined by economic and political forces. This perspective seems to acknowledge the relation between culture and politics but tends to assume the subordination of cultural expression to political forces. This approach suggests a one-to-one correspondence between culture and certain historical events. In doing so, some scholars suggest that sociopolitical developments are mechanically matched or reflected by periodic "flowerings" of art and subculture practice. Seldom do we see evidence that art may be political, or that politics may be creative, or that both share similar traits.

Thus, both perspectives obscure an understanding of the complex relations between culture and politics within the Chicano movement, and in society in general, over the past two decades. An alternative approach must begin with more flexible concepts. Culture should be conceptualized not solely as specific objects or "traits," but, as Raymond Williams suggests, "a constitutive social process, creating specific and different 'ways of life.'"[4] The analysis of these ways of life, or subcultures, and the artistic forms that result, can deepen our understanding of cultural practice in recent Chicano history. The

definition of politics, in the same way, must be expanded to include those activities which contribute to the creation and re-creation of organized ways of
political life. This expanded definition may include formal political routines,
such as elections, and also mechanisms which reproduce traditional political
relations through ideology, that is, through dominantly defined values and
stereotypes.

This essay argues that El Teatro developed a reciprocal relation to Chicano
political activity, largely because the theater grew from and helped shape the
intellectual currents of the Chicano movement. At the same time, the plays of
Luis Valdez developed the capacity to "distance" audiences from the dominant
ideology, primarily through humor and satire. Valdez's plays in particular attempted to separate audiences from this ideology by exposing and dramatizing
the contradictions of field work, by emphasizing the deeper social implications
of labor, and by demonstrating the vulnerability of cultural stereotypes. In so
doing, the division between Valdez the artist and Valdez the political leader
was often difficult to define.

The degree to which Valdez could maintain his independence and ideals
corresponded to the ability of El Teatro to give audiences a conceptual understanding of the Chicano experience. The implications of Valdez's changing
interpretation of that experience are drawn throughout the essay and evalu-
ated in the conclusion. The evolution of Valdez's work through the 1980s provides not only an example of how politicized art might be studied, but also a
case study of how one Chicano cultural form has become "integrated" into
Anglo society.

FARMWORKERS' THEATER, 1965–1967

Almost every discussion of Chicano politics points to the important role played
by the United Farm Workers Union (UFW), and with good reason.[5] The
Delano Grape Strike and Boycott of 1965, together with the Civil Rights,
Free Speech, and antiwar movements, served as catalysts for many Mexican
American organizations in the sixties. The grape strike and boycott were to
culminate in the first successful effort to unionize U.S. agricultural workers
since the 1930s.

The Delano strike quickly became a powerful symbol for many Chicanos.
Among them was a young college student named Luis Valdez. Valdez first heard
reports of the strike while writing and performing with the San Francisco
Mime Troupe. He later went to Delano to investigate the situation for himself; it was an experience that proved unsettling. As Valdez recalled in an interview a few years later, "There was this organizer, César Chávez, and all
these campesinos, Mexicanos, and Filipinos, marching through the streets . . .

it really grabbed me. We marched down Ellington Street. I was born on Ellington Street. . . . Marching past streets I had grown up in. I even saw some of my relatives. Some of them were even out in the fields scabbing. I had to straighten out a lot of things."[6]

Valdez returned to San Francisco after the march, but was soon drawn by the popular struggle in the fields. When Chávez came to the city to speak at a rally a week later, the student approached him with the idea to start a farmworkers theater.[7] Chávez responded favorably: "I said, 'Yeah, let's try it.' So he [Valdez] organized the original El Teatro Campesino with four or five farm workers. They played for the first time at the regular Friday night union meeting in Delano. Then people began to look forward to the next performance on the picket line or whenever the occasion lent itself."[8]

The first rehearsals were held in the back room of the union's headquarters. Using hand-lettered signs and improvising as they went along, the actors drew from their experiences during the strike. On picket lines, often within sight of armed guards and sheriff deputies, El Teatro began to take daring jabs at the traditional exploitation of agricultural labor. When direct access to farmworker audiences was denied—a frequent occurrence as their popularity grew—the troupe performed on flatbed trucks driven up to the fences of the labor camps.

From these first performances emerged several stock characters: El Patrón (the boss), Don Coyote (the labor contractor), and El Esquirol (the scab). Soon masks and other props began to replace the crude signs. As more workers were recruited, the number of characters and plots increased. Eventually, El Teatro's fragmented improvisations began to develop into a unique artistic form, which Valdez and his actors called the *acto*.

Initially a collective creation, the *acto* was also the result of Valdez's experiments with a variety of theatrical styles. The first drew from the work of the Spanish poet and playwright Federico García Lorca. Valdez was attracted to Lorca's work because of the latter's physical comedic style. Lorca also was one of the few European artists to break with the tradition of the formal stage by bringing performances to audiences in the Spanish countryside. Another source of inspiration was the *commedia dell'arte* style of the San Francisco Mime Troupe. This style, described as "a 16th century Italian method of broad comedy using stock characters, improvisation, and intense physicality," was infinitely useful to the union, and became the vehicle for much of El Teatro's early work.[9] The blending of comedy and satirical improvisation also had its roots in the agitation-propaganda tradition of Brechtian theater. As some writers have noted, in the early years El Teatro already showed evidence of a style that was "part Brecht and part Cantinflas." But when emphasizing the "alienation effects" of the former, the *actos* went beyond mere comedy. They began to acquire a pedagogical flavor. Valdez explained: "Brecht's technique of learning plays became a very real aspect of *teatro*, especially when we tried to teach workers about the grape strike. People can go on strike very simply. That's the easy part. What's hard to understand is what striking involves as well as the tactics of a prolonged struggle."[10]

The lessons Valdez and his troupe attempted to convey are evident in an early *acto*, "Las dos caras del patroncito" (The Two Faces of the Boss). More a series of short skits, the play attempted to counteract the myth of El Patrón's material and cultural superiority over the worker. If there was a moral lesson, it was that the "mask" of economic dominance worn by the grower was subject to the conditions of class struggle, a reference to the strike and grape boycott. Only when the farmworker could see that the grower's power was vulnerable could his weaknesses be exposed and the mask symbolically removed.

The realization that grower-farmworker relations were vulnerable also implied that certain kinds of struggle had effects on cultural relations as well. Here lay the strongest emphasis of the *acto*, for to Valdez the mask of economic dominance had a less obvious profile: cultural superiority. While exploitative relations supported the economic interests of the grower, cultural superiority suggested not only his dominance but also an acceptance of subordinate status by field workers. In order to counteract economic exploitation, farmworkers had to recognize and overcome the ideological supports inherent in cultural domination. Thus, as the curtain closed on this early *acto*, it became evident that the thrust of resistance was both economic and cultural. Audiences were shown the reasons for opposing the social relations and culture maintained by an agrarian elite. Valdez emphasized this theme when he observed, "We try to make social points not in spite of the comedy but through it. This leads us into satire and slapstick, and sometimes very close to the underlying tragedy of it all . . . the fact that human beings have been wasted in farm labor for generations."[11]

MOVEMENT THEATER

Although he did not fully realize it at the time, Valdez's work placed El Teatro at the forefront of a growing political movement in the mid 1960s. Just as the UFW reached the height of its struggle in California, activists throughout the Southwest were organizing. In New Mexico, Reies López Tijerina founded the Alianza Federal de Mercedes, an organization to recover lost land and water rights. In Colorado, Rodolfo "Corky" González, a former Democratic precinct captain, was providing legal and health services to Chicano youth through the Crusade for Justice. In East Los Angeles, more than ten thousand high school students walked out of their classes and staged a sit-in at the Board of Education. Similar walkouts and protests in Texas led to the founding of El Partido de la Raza Unida, a populist-nationalist alternative to the Democratic and Republican Parties. These and other events in the Southwest suggested the beginnings of a political strategy that called for self-determination by Latinos on several fronts.[12]

This reawakening suggested to Luis Valdez and his troupe that the issues raised in the early *actos* may have been limited. Activism from other quarters — blue- and white-collar workers, women, students, urban youth, and academics — suggested that the scope of the plays had to be expanded and redirected.

Despite the broader concerns brought about by this activism, however, El Teatro's future (in 1966) was still very much tied to the UFW. The close association between the organizations was not without conflict, and because of different priorities, may have temporarily stalled the theater's ability to address new issues and to reach new audiences. Valdez described some of the difficulties the theater faced during this period: "After the first month, the boycott against Schenley Industries (a major grower in the San Joaquin Valley) started and my two best actors were sent away as boycott organizers. There was a lot of work to rehearse so there was a lull for a month. That was due, in part, to the fact that most of my actors were taken away, and we were involved in picketing and boycotting and chasing trucks."[13]

The problem was not only a matter of union activities taking precedence over rehearsals. According to a former member of the troupe, the union's moderate leadership was dismayed by the actors' leftist orientation. There were also signs that Chávez's union was hostile toward some militant factions in the Chicano movement.[14] To Valdez, whose sympathies straddled both socialism and a developing Chicano nationalism, these rumblings signaled a coming philosophical rift. This may have been sufficient cause to seek other sources of organizational support. Not surprisingly, the first opportunities to do so were encouraged by the union.

Shortly after El Teatro Campesino performed for the first time at Stanford University, in 1966, Chávez asked Valdez to tour other college campuses to promote the grape boycott. Within a year El Teatro had attracted the attention of both critics and audiences. Much of the theater's notoriety was due to the talent of the performers and, significantly, to a new group of plays written for the tour. Two *actos* in particular, "Huelguistas" and "Vietnam campesino," continued the advocacy of the UFW struggle. The latter was especially skillful in highlighting the common interests of the growers and the military establishment. In a third *acto*, "Soldado razo," Valdez experimented with character development in a drama focusing on the experiences of a young Chicano soldier. Through the course of the play, the audience witnessed "Johnny's" gradual realization of the Vietnam war's tragic consequences not only on his own family, but on the Vietnamese, whose social condition Valdez believed to be similar to that of Chicanos in the United States. One of the most important *actos* of the period was "No saco nada de la escuela" (I Don't Get Anything From School). The play's value lay in its ability to portray the alienation of youth and the problems of teacher-student relations. In the playwright's hands both issues conjured up images of paternalism and latent racism.

The momentum generated by these productions moved El Teatro to broaden its critique to include issues that concerned not only campesinos but all oppressed groups. Valdez's intention was to inspire social action through the illumination of contradictions, which the actors were to address through satire and humor. The *actos* also were to hint at certain solutions that the actors felt to be consistent with the audience's thinking.[15]

On the basis of this new strategy and their early triumphs, the troupe began to win wide critical acclaim. This led to opportunities for national exposure. In 1967 El Teatro Campesino was invited to perform at the prestigious Newport Folk Festival. At the request of Robert Kennedy, the theater also performed before a Senate subcommittee on migrant labor. El Teatro's national reputation was enhanced once more by a special Obie award for, as the inscription read, "creating a worker's theater to demonstrate the politics of survival."

Eventually, the promise of an identity other than a "Farmworkers Theater" and unresolved political questions with the UFW leadership led to a formal separation from the union in 1967. Later, Valdez revealed his thoughts on the split:

> The strike in Delano is a beautiful cause, but it won't leave you alone. A cause is a living, breathing thing. It's more important to leave a rehearsal and go to the picket line. So we found we had to back away from Delano . . . to be a theater. That was a very hard decision to make . . . very, very hard. Do you serve the movement as being just kind of half-assed, getting together whenever there's a chance, hitting and missing, or do you really hone your theater down into an effective weapon? Is it possible to make an effective weapon without being blood close to the movement?[16]

These would be difficult questions for any artist intimately involved in politics, but the social condition of Chicanos throughout the sixties and the seventies made Valdez's inquiries that much more urgent. In the years that followed, the playwright would find himself wrestling with the same thorny questions. Could the theater continue to interpret faithfully in aesthetic terms the "lived experience" of audiences without belonging to a movement organization? Could Valdez continue to develop his artistic talents without compromising his self-proclaimed political objectives? The playwright soon realized that the answers to these questions were not immediately clear.

Teatro of Ritual, 1968–1971

The period following Delano was perhaps the most turbulent for El Teatro, as well as for the Chicano Movement in general. By the end of the sixties, state and federal authorities had mobilized to meet the challenge from the Left. In New Mexico, for example, the Alianza's ability to halt land seizures by the federal government was blunted by a lengthy court battle resulting in Tijerina's conviction and incarceration in 1967. In August 1970, the Los Angeles Chicano Moratorium against U.S. involvement in Vietnam quickly escalated into a "police riot," leaving more than four hundred people injured, three dead, and several million dollars in property damage. In Denver, Crusade for Justice programs lost support when organizers were continually discredited by local law enforcement officials. At the national level, political infighting at the 1972 La Raza Unida convention in El Paso was climaxed by a split between Chicano "pragmatists" led by José Angel Gutiérrez, and Chicano "socialists" led by Corky González. The division left La Raza Unida without a leadership that could gain consensus.[17]

The Farmworkers Union was also vulnerable to repression. By 1971 the success of the Delano strike and the national grape boycott were overshadowed by sweetheart contracts between the Teamsters and lettuce growers. Competition between the rival Teamsters union and the UFW was so intense that the latter was forced to seek the intervention of the AFL-CIO and the Democratic Party. By the 1972 presidential election, the UFW had become the link between Chicanos and the Democratic Party liberals. The new alliance sharpened simmering differences between traditionally oriented rural activists and urban organizers who distrusted white liberal Democrats. These differences also seemed to be widened as much by militant rhetoric as they were by political strategy.[18]

By the early seventies, a pattern of political realignments within and outside the Chicano movement was beginning to evolve. The previously assumed consensus based on nationalism was now being scrutinized in light of new organizational alliances and strategies. These, in turn, were affected by long-simmering regional and personal rivalries.

While repression and internal strife limited the effectiveness of other organizations, the increasing loss of confidence among Chicanos in the goals of the movement had lasting effects on El Teatro. The theater's contribution was largely its ability to convey a conceptual understanding of the world, to suggest an "experience" through humor and satire that contradicted ideological stereotypes. In this way the intrinsic value of the *actos* lay in their resistance to dominant values and their ability to foster trust in the efficacy of the movement's goals. These goals were assumed by Valdez to be shared collectively by others in the Chicano community. Once the fragile alliances that held the movement together began to crumble, the faith in common goals also began to wane. With that loss of faith, El Teatro's interpretation of events came into question.

This process first became apparent in the attitude of the actors. Pressures within the movement quickly fueled conflicts among members of the troupe.[19] Their differences threatened to inhibit both the theater's artistic development and its future as an organization. As Valdez stated in an interview, "Anger against the imperialist, anger against an unjust system, was very quickly satisfied by anger between members of our group. They let out their hostility toward injustice on each other. It complicated our own work because it destroyed the very unity that we needed to continue, and it destroyed the very reason we were doing all of this work, our own brotherhood."[20]

To overcome these obstacles Valdez pushed for better organization and more discipline within El Teatro. This meant streamlining the troupe according to specific tasks. Valdez became artistic director, while other members were assigned duties according to their theatrical or technical skills.

Valdez also sought new ways to continue the development of the theater's art, an activity without which, he argued, the theater could not survive. He began to dabble with different forms of theater and other media. In 1971 his screenplay for "Yo soy Joaquín," (an adaptation of Corky González's poem, "I Am Joaquín") won El Teatro a national film award.

The playwright also expanded the activities of the theater to attract the growing number of Chicano artists in the late sixties. During this period a significant number of activists turned toward aesthetic activities once opportunities in the political arena began to narrow.[21] To take advantage of this trend, Valdez divided the theater into two companies. One performed at San Juan Bautista while also serving as a training component, and the other company toured the United States and, eventually, abroad.

Among the new artists was a core of young playwrights who adopted some of Valdez's *actos* for their first productions. Their interest in Chicano theater prompted Valdez to publish *El Teatro* in 1970, a journal devoted to the exchange of ideas and techniques. During the same year the playwright organized the first "Festival de los Teatros" to provide a forum to show new work and begin sharing ideas. Following the second festival in 1971, Valdez and a group of directors and teatro representatives founded "El Teatro Nacional de Aztlán" (TENAZ), the first Chicano theatrical organization. According to one of its founding members, TENAZ was to stimulate communication among Chicano and Latino theaters and create a body to assist in "developing acting and staging techniques and in creating more esthetically politically sophisticated material."[22]

The creation of TENAZ can be viewed as an attempt by Valdez to secure a base of support to replace El Teatro's former tie to the UFW. Thus, TENAZ was organized to promote and encourage Chicano theater independent of other political work. More important, however, Valdez may have viewed TENAZ as a means to usher in a revival of the movement, a revival based on a commonly assumed acceptance of nationalism. In this regard, the playwright wrote:

> If Aztlán is to become a reality, then we Chicanos must not be reluctant to act nationally. To think in national terms: politically, economically, and spiritually. We must destroy the deadly regionalism that keeps us apart. The concept of a national theater for La Raza is intimately related to our evolving nationalism in Aztlán. . . . Consider a Teatro Nacional de Aztlán that performs with the same skill and prestige as the Ballet Folklórico of Mexico. . . . It would draw its strength from all the small teatros in the barrios, in terms of people and their plays, songs, designs; it would give back funds, training, and augment strength of national unity.[23]

Significantly, TENAZ's role implied a different kind of political strategy. Just as Chicano politicians were articulating a nationalist perspective, Valdez seemed to be proposing a new cultural agenda, which included a reevaluation of the movement's aims and a strengthening of Chicano identity. According to Valdez,

> beyond the mass struggle of La Raza in the fields and the barrios of America, there is an internal struggle in the very corazón of the people. That struggle too calls for revolutionary change. Our belief in God, the Church, the social role of women . . . these must be subject to examination and redefinition on some kind of public forum. And that again means teatro. Not a teatro composed of actos and agit-prop but a teatro of ritual, of music, or beauty and spiritual sensitivity. A teatro of legends and myths, a teatro of religious strength.[24]

One of Valdez's first attempts to create a "teatro of ritual"—the play "Bernabé"—illustrated the underlying premise of the new strategy: an acknowledgment of the Chicano Left's ambivalent relation to a hostile world. As the protagonist, Bernabé personified the Chicano caught between two worlds, the material world in which he was powerless, and the spiritual world from which he drew strength.

In the "real" world, Bernabé is portrayed as an outcast, a village idiot dependent on his aging mother. Bernabé's insecurity is painfully reinforced by his experience with Connie, a local prostitute. Rejection by Connie forces

Bernabé back into his role as the powerless child, a reference perhaps to the ill-fated attempts of Chicano militants to recover from their recent setbacks. Bernabé's inability to maintain the relationship with Connie, moreover, suggested the political and economic impotence of Chicanos during the late sixties. Without work, without a woman, without the dignity of an adult, Bernabé has no real link to the material world.[25]

By contrast, in the spirit world Bernabé is all powerful. He is the Vato Loco, the epitome of Chicano strength and, above all, the legitimate heir to an ancient philosophical tradition. As a Chicano and a man, Bernabé is shown to be one with the symbols of power, La Luna (the Moon), La Tierra (the earth), and El Sol (the Sun).

Despite achieving this status, however, Bernabé is never able to reconcile the two worlds, for in real life he has no power. He is unable to transfer his new spiritual status to the real world, largely because Valdez viewed Chicano political power to be on the decline. Since strength is achieved in the spirit world, the play's meaning becomes clear: the militant strategy had missed an important element, an acknowledgment of Chicano culture. The failure to recognize cultural identity, as represented by spiritual symbolism, Valdez suggested, was a major reason for Chicanos' lack of power. As long as Chicanos neglected their ancient legacy, they would remain mired in petty political squabbles. Armed with this vision, El Teatro entered the seventies.

THEATER AT ODDS, 1972–1976

The 1970s provided a chaotic atmosphere for Valdez to continue his work. By the middle of the decade, Chicano organizations had continued to disintegrate and seemed even further from a common political direction. Many factors contributed to this turn of events. They included the decline of UFW membership as a result of union-busting efforts by the Teamsters and the federal government; the infiltration of Chicano organizations by local, state, and federal intelligence operatives; and the general disorganization of student groups. Perhaps the most significant setback for the movement was the increasing fragmentation and decline of La Raza Unida Party. These events resulted in pockets of localized political strength in South Texas, but ultimately left the movement without a national leadership or a coherent strategy.

This scenario strengthened Valdez's convictions about the movement's weaknesses and his resolve to develop his art. Although some critics have suggested that Valdez's exploration of ritual theater in the seventies amounted to a political retreat, the playwright was motivated by other factors. Taking into account his proximity to the movement, it seems reasonable to suggest that Valdez may have been attempting to develop a broader analysis of the Chicano experience. Valdez may also have been trying to fill a void created by the lack of political leadership. In other words, the playwright was attempting to present a "cultural solution" to a political problem. Regardless of how Valdez's solution may be judged, his approach was vibrant, albeit at times perplexing.

El Teatro's development up to 1972 was the culmination of experiments undertaken at the troupe's new headquarters in San Juan Bautista. This phase is illustrated by two works, "La carpa de los Rasquachis" and the poem "Pensamiento serpentino."[26] In "La carpa" Valdez began with an *acto* which told the story of an underdog, José Rasquachi, and his family's struggle to survive in the United States. The *acto* was later expanded and refined through the use of *corridos* (poetry and stories set to music), which illustrated José's exploitation, the circumstances leading to his death, and the subsequent quest for power by his sons. Another form, the *mito* or myth, was introduced at the conclusion to suggest that only a spiritual reawakening among Chicanos, rather than material gain, held promise in the future. Reflecting on the play, critic Arthur Sainer summarized Valdez's position as an attempt to regain political perspective through psychological drama and satire. Thus, in "La carpa," rather than the politics being an end in itself, a "spiritual struggle now informed the social struggle."[27]

This perspective is reflected in Valdez's poem "Pensamiento serpentino." In contrast to the theme of *Bernabé* (the separation of the Chicano's role in the material world from the world of the spirit), "Pensamiento serpentino" promised a joining of both realms. Incorporating the ancient Mayan symbol of the Great Serpent, Valdez sketched out a theory in which he envisioned the social and political struggles of Chicanos continually evolving to higher states of consciousness. As the serpent shed its skin to emerge rejuvenated, audiences were shown by analogy that certain conditions also change, that Chicanos ultimately have the ability to withstand repression and internal strife. This realization, however, would only come if Chicanos were willing to be guided by religious "truths" born of Mayan philosophy. As the playwright observed, "La nueva realidad nace de la realidad vieja"—a new reality is born of the old.[28]

The basis of this new reality was the Mayan concept "Lak 'Eck," which Valdez interpreted humanistically as, "If I love and respect you, I love and respect myself. Whatever I do to you, I do to myself." This principle was to be applied within the movement. Chicanos were to find love by developing a common respect for each other. Self-respect, in turn, would cultivate trust for peoples of all races. Once Chicanos understood this logic and that love emanated from a supreme spirit, "La Energía that created the Universe," they could overcome the present obstacles facing them. Thus, Valdez wrote,

> As Chicanos
> As Neo-Mayans
> We must re-identify
> with that center and proceed
> outward with love and strength
> Amor y fuerza (love and strength)
> and undying dedication to justice.

Further on in the poem, he linked the Mayan way of life to a grand stage in which the Great Spirit took on multiple roles as "El great playwright del universe," "el scene designer y costume maker," and,

> El make-up man del teatro
> infinitivo
> que nos pone el maquiaje (the one who gives us faces)
> brown, white, black, yellow

None of the faces, Valdez continued, could be considered ugly or beautiful, although we may not always be content with them. "The point is to participate in the play (of life), not to reject the parts we are given to play." The Great Spirit gave Chicanos their roles for specific purposes. Valdez stressed that no one else had the Chicano part. "If a Chicano rejects his part," that is, denies his cultural roots for the sake of material gain, "he's going to mess up."

In the end, the role of Chicanos in this world is what the Mayans called "the limit," that is, the material existence which is physically separate from the world of the spirit. Beyond lay a realm that is not bound by the body. The key was that once Chicanos learned the material limits of the real world, they would "encounter your infinite potential. Encuentras a dios en tu corazón" [you find God in your heart]. For ultimately, the Great Spirit resides in all individuals and charts the course in the world.

The importance of Valdez's contribution to aesthetic as well as political discussion should not be lost in the poem's metaphysical tone. He was, in effect, proposing a humanistic approach to politics which attempted to incorporate nationalist sentiments. By doing so Valdez, along with other intellectuals, was opening the door for a broader analysis of the Chicano experience. Valdez's enthusiasm was matched by the zeal of writers who touted the higher truths offered by indigenismo, or those who called for "responsible and authentic relationships" among Chicanos, or others who wrote with the implicit assumption that humanism transcends politics, and could thus form a symbolic link among all Chicanos.[29]

In these and other examples, the emphasis on humanism was tantamount to a call on a fragmented class to take a closer look at itself, to find those intangible qualities which Chicano leaders had not taken into account. To Valdez the essence of the problem was that a materialist strategy was responsible for the factional differences within the movement. The solution was to reduce these differences to the most fundamental level. In short, Valdez sought to expand political horizons by embracing a spiritual aesthetic grounded in an emerging nationalist ideology.

Perhaps because he was one of the most prominent advocates of the spiritual humanist approach, Valdez came under intense criticism. Ironically, the same festivals he helped organize fostered debates over his art. At the fourth TENAZ festival in 1973, for example, controversy raged over Valdez's support of religious theater, which many observers believed diluted the political role of Chicanos. At the fifth festival, conflicts between community-based teatros and professional groups may have been fueled by Valdez's brand of aesthetics. This led to accusations from a number of artists that Valdez had lost touch with the developments of the movement.[30] An observer who witnessed a performance by El Teatro during the fifth festival described it as "entertaining, but confusing." He added, "A lot of it was Aztec and Mayan ceremony. The costumes were far-out and the choreography, wild. But it didn't really give people a clear message. When we talked to people afterwards, they said they liked it, but they couldn't explain what they saw."[31]

A major drawback to Valdez's approach was that the dialogue the plays generated was confined to a relatively small group of intellectuals. Several artists during the seventies enthusiastically embraced the playwright's position; their own work reflected the influence Valdez had on Chicano theater and Chicano art in general. In terms of a larger audience, however, "La carpa" and "Pensamiento serpentino" were largely foreign to the experience of working-class Chicanos. In effect, Valdez was asking them to accept on faith certain social and metaphysical principles which were not only unfamiliar, but also historically and politically suspect. The call to "turn the other cheek" suggested that Valdez's approach rested on an avoidance of social problems, and came very close to accommodation. The result was that instead of precipitating an examination and redefinition of concrete issues, Valdez's religious jargon may have obscured social issues and contributed very little to the development of political consensus during this period. Valdez's response to his critics can be gleaned from a letter he wrote explaining his position: "We do not feel that this is in any way inconsistent with our Chicanismo. Ask La Raza. They will tell you. Our people believe in the Creador, hermanismo. The Great Spirit . . . they are all manifestations of the same Cosmic force. Man is a spiritual animal. Man in his heart contains the divine spark. What we intellectuals struggle to grasp with our minds, La Raza más humilde has always known through sheer faith alone."[32]

The playwright may have overestimated the acquiescence of his audience to religious values. To observers in TENAZ it was apparent that some members of the audience were not content with merely watching theater; many wanted to become actively involved. As more activists joined the organization and began to participate in the exchange of ideas, they began to question TENAZ's approach to art and its relevance to daily experience. As Nicolas Kanellos noted, a number of groups "looked upon (TENAZ's) efforts at professionalism suspiciously" and considered them to be "too removed from their everyday reality." In Kanellos's words, "The members of these groups have formed teatros not because they consider themselves actors, performers or artists, but because teatro is a means of serving their communities in the struggle for civil rights and human dignity."[33]

Controversy emerged over the use of Valdez's original *actos* by the community-based theaters. To their members, the *acto* was more conducive to collective involvement than the *mito*, because the *acto* involved a wider range of individuals whose daily experiences became material for the plays. Those experiences were often specific to the region in which the troupe performed, and helped to create a close bond between actors and audiences. At times that relation was so intimate that actors and members of the audience exchanged roles during a performance. Themes reflecting a concern for specific issues, such as labor organizing, welfare rights, or ending barrio warfare, were often presented by individuals who were striving toward these goals in real life. On these issues, Valdez was silent.

There were, however, other factors which may account for Valdez's resistance to community-oriented productions. The playwright's adjustment to political struggles within the movement may have been influenced by El Teatro's increasing popularity outside the Chicano community. Despite the pressures on Valdez from within the movement, El Teatro was encouraged by the response of non-Chicano audiences. This recognition may have indirectly bolstered the playwright against his critics, while opening the way for a further development of his art, which moved further away from its original social base. At the same time, El Teatro's popularity took on a new meaning. What previously had been considered unusual or avant garde was suddenly in demand. Theatrical promoters had come to recognize the mass appeal and commercial potential of El Teatro's performances.

PROFESSIONAL TEATRO, 1977–1980

Valdez's courtship of these new audiences tended to coincide with the emergence of an influential strata of Chicano professionals. By the latter half of the seventies this well-educated, predominantly male group, the first to benefit from affirmative action policies, made significant advances toward equal opportunity. Organizations like TENAZ expanded their membership and adopted more sophisticated techniques. Like other racial and ethnic groups, however, Chicano professionals paid a price for their mobility by becoming estranged from the majority of working-class Chicanos.[34]

Perhaps a similar observation could be made of the founder of El Teatro Campesino. As Kanellos has noted, "For Campesino, professionalism was a goal fostered and realized through the efforts of the university-trained playwright and director, Luis Valdez. It represented the only avenue to a full exploration of the esthetic and cultural possibilities of the Mexican-American theatrical form that Campesino had helped to invent."[35] Valdez's efforts can perhaps best be understood by examining the stage production of *Zoot Suit*.

Zoot Suit dealt with a long-submerged incident in Chicano history, the Sleepy Lagoon Murder Case. In 1942 José Díaz, age twenty-two, was found dead from a fractured skull near a Montebello swimming hole known as Sleepy Lagoon, in the Los Angeles area. Police officials, goaded by the *Los Angeles Times* and the Hearst press at the height of World War II, eventually arrested twenty-two members of the 38th Street gang for Díaz's murder. Labeled "Zoot Suit Gangsters" because of their fondness for wearing exaggerated business suits popularized by young blacks in Harlem, the youth were the defendants in one of the most racially charged trials in California history. After many legal maneuvers and much public pressure, the convictions were overturned two years later for lack of evidence.

On the basis of his research on the Sleepy Lagoon trial and the infamous "Zoot Suit Riots" in Los Angeles in 1943, Valdez fashioned a musical drama focusing on the defendants and the historical events surrounding the case. *Zoot Suit* proved so successful in its Los Angeles debut that in 1979 the play went to Broadway. This marked the first time a Chicano production was able to break into the mainstream of American theater.

Zoot Suit's success owed as much to the staff of the Mark Taper Forum, where the production was first presented, as it did to the perseverance of Valdez and his troupe. A close relationship between the Forum's staff and the playwright was in fact a prominent feature of the play's early development. In 1977 Gordon Davidson, artistic director for the Taper, began a series of experimental productions called the "New Theater for Now." A major effort was made to produce plays involving local minorities in the Los Angeles area, particularly Chicanos, who make up a sizable but untapped audience. Davidson hired Kenneth Brecher, an anthropologist, to help develop works for the new project. One of Brecher's first visits was to San Juan Bautista to encourage Valdez to produce a play. Valdez recalled the discussions: "We talked about several things with the Taper. Finally, I said to Ken, how about a play about the pachuco era? He was pretty excited. And it turned out Gordon Davidson had just heard something on the car radio about the period so it was on his mind too. We researched the Sleepy Lagoon Case and the riots at the UCLA Chicano Library, but what we came up with isn't a Chicano play like the ones we do at San Juan Bautista. It's an American play." [36]

Commissioned by Davidson, Valdez immersed himself in six thousand pages of Sleepy Lagoon trial transcripts and read through hundreds of letters, defense papers, and newspaper clippings to reconstruct the events. Meanwhile, he and Brecher interviewed the principals of the case. Despite these efforts, Valdez's first draft was apparently not what Davidson had in mind. An article in the *New York Times* disclosed: "Instead of the excitement and theatricality of Brecht and Cantinflas, [Davidson] beheld a fairly conventional work of Odets-like naturalism. Immediately he sensed the problem: Luis Valdez had become overwhelmed by the myriad facts of his long research. Gordon counseled the playwright to start all over again, to abandon strict naturalism for a more theatrical structure, to find a metaphor for his tale that evoked the throbbing rhythms of his people, to splash color and fire across his pages." [37]

Valdez apparently accepted Davidson's assessment. In an interview with Dan Sullivan of the *Los Angeles Times*, the playwright acknowledged the obstacles he faced and gave a glimpse of the new direction the play would take. "You can see the problem: how to integrate it all," he explained. "If I used a naturalistic approach, I couldn't make it through the story. So the backdrop is symbolic. Some of the characters are based on real people, some are composite characters, and some are symbolic characters." [38]

The playwright's use of symbols is evident from the opening scene when the play's narrator, El Pachuco, slices through a huge World War II newspaper headline with a six foot switchblade. "When that enormous switchblade knife comes out," a reviewer commented, "it's clear that exaggeration will be one emotional keynote for the evening—we're meant to understand that we're in for something a little larger than life." [39] Exaggeration began with El Pachuco's costume. Dressed in a knee-length coat, billowing pants pegged at the ankle, a gold chain stretching almost to the floor, topped off by a wide-brimmed feathered hat, El Pachuco personified the legendary hero-gangster of the barrio. And that was apparently how Valdez envisioned him—part legend based on the Aztec "lord of education and experience," and part social misfit and nonconformist. By bringing to life this cultural archetype, the playwright instilled in the character a "subliminal power" designed to span the full spectrum of the barrio hierarchy: from the street personality who had taken on a godlike quality among Chicano youth, to the socially "deviant" gang member as seen from the perspective of more traditional observers. At the same time, Valdez was aware that his characters had to be relevant to other audiences; while El

Pachuco was "to be admired and despised at the same time by some of the same people," he was also to be funny and frightening. "I wanted to capture that energy in the play," Valdez said, "and use that as a bridge, the human bridge into mainstream America."[40]

The intention of reaching the American mainstream was not overlooked by early reviewers of the play. Some critics noted that because of Valdez's intention to attract middle-class patrons, it was obvious that Chicanos were not the play's primary audience. "I am certain that its popularity," Harold Clurman wrote, "is not due to a large attendance of Chicanos. . . . The majority of the audience at the Taper was, and perhaps still is, to a considerable extent unfamiliar with the various sections (of Los Angeles) inhabited by its minorities. What does Hollywood, not to speak of Beverly Hills, Brentwood, Bel-Air and Santa Monica know of Watts, Boyle Heights and other 'submerged' parts of the town where the others dwell?"[41]

Critic Gerald Rabkin wrote that Valdez, in responding to Gordon Davidson's commission to write a play, "was well aware that an evening of Actos and Mitos would not satisfy middle-class theatrical expectations."[42] Davidson's role as a promoter may partially explain Valdez's intention to direct the play "beyond the barrio." In Valdez's words, "I wanted to write a play that was not just a Chicano play but an American play. I wanted to make a single human statement, to invoke a vision of America as a whole including the minorities — using joy and humor."[43]

The desire to make a "single human statement" on a grander scale may have motivated Valdez and Davidson to take *Zoot Suit* to Broadway. Valdez explained that "*Zoot Suit* staying in the barrio would be like that pachuco putting on the zoot suit and staying in the barrio. The play had to come to Broadway because this is the Palladium of the theater. *Zoot Suit* belongs here."[44]

While *Zoot Suit* may have belonged on Broadway, the reality of the situation suggested otherwise. After only four weeks the play closed because of poor ticket sales. Part of the problems were strained relations between Teatro personnel and the play's New York promoters, the Shubert organization. The two parties apparently entered into the agreement with different goals, the Shuberts not concealing the fact that they viewed *Zoot Suit* as a potential hit, while Valdez and his troupe considered their very presence in New York as a political coup. Predictably, the differences eventually came to a head over finances. The Shubert organization initially allocated only $7,000 out of a $700,000 advertising budget for promotion in New York's Latino media. At the same time, the Shuberts saw no contradiction in paying $15,000 weekly for advertisements in the *New York Times*. Following negative reviews in the *Times* and the *New Yorker*, an additional $125,000 in advertising was spent as a last hope. With the troupe and the Shuberts working at such cross-purposes, the curtain quickly fell on El Teatro's Broadway debut.[45] Thus, despite Valdez's and Davidson's best intentions, the theater returned to California after only five weeks.

El Teatro's experience in New York was only a temporary setback. *Zoot Suit* proved to be a box-office hit in Los Angeles, continuing for many months to rave reviews. In 1981 a film version, which was a significant departure from the play, also made the rounds of theaters from coast to coast. Its use of montage and acknowledgment of the audience, its depiction of alternative lifestyles, and the political questions the film raises brought much critical acclaim.

EL TEATRO IN THE 1980S AND 1990S

Filmmaking was the next phase in the artistic development of Luis Valdez. It also illustrates the progression of Valdez's political thought. We will recall that in the sixties Valdez's work had criticized notions of cultural deference. In the seventies we saw him questioning the goals of the theater within the context of the Chicano Movement. By the eighties Valdez's introspection evolved into an ambiguous liberalism based on individual initiative. Filmmaking was an important element in this new strategy, for it provided the means of reaching new audiences and of ensuring the survival of the theater.

Soon after the success of *Zoot Suit* the film, Valdez indicated the direction the theater would take. In an interview, the playwright said his new goal was "to bridge the seemingly unbridgable gaps in life and politics." He concluded: "That's actually one of [my] approaches to life in general. If you feel you're shortchanged, fill the gap yourself. Why mope? Why feel angry? You've got the power to do something." This initiative is similar to the early goal of using theater to direct social action. Rather than focusing on specific contradictions, however, Valdez's new strategy is "to take peoples' minds off their problems by entertaining them."[46] He stated, "This relates to what's happening throughout American theater. People are experimenting with drama, dance, singing. . . . Look what's happening with MTV. Music is being visualized and that's what's happening on stage. . . . That's challenging."[47]

Perhaps most challenging was to use this strategy to create a place for Chicano Theater in American culture. As Valdez noted, "We are trying to build things that last, not only theater, but movies and videotape, an institution that can be used by others so this doesn't disappear."[48] Creative longevity could be achieved, Valdez suggested, through the cultivation of audiences for different media projects. After filming *Zoot Suit,* for example, Valdez signed a contract for distribution of the movie to video stores, collaborated with well-known television producers in a syndicated "video rock opera," and was hired by Jane Fonda's production company to write and direct other films. Between 1985 and 1986 Valdez developed a screenplay from his musical *Corridos*, a series of vignettes based on Mexican ballads; then in 1987 he narrated, directed, and staged the production for a public broadcasting station in San Francisco.

That year Valdez's most ambitious project to date, *La Bamba*, a film based on the life of Chicano rocker Richie Valens (Ricardo Valenzuela), made its debut. Contracted to direct by Columbia Pictures, Valdez fashioned a musical biography of Valenzuela's life as a field worker and an East Los Angeles teenager—a music career highlighted by the adaptation of a traditional Mexican ballad to a top-forty song, and Valenzuela's death in a plane crash with Buddy Holly and the "Big Bopper."

Critical and public reaction to *La Bamba* was divided. After the film opened, a *Los Angeles Times* critic described it as "no more electrifying than the ordinary '50's bio-pic. The charisma that Richie Valens had and the kind of energy that must have been there to propel a young Mexican American from picking fields and orchards into the world of music is missing." Yet audiences were eager to see the film. In the first three days of distribution, *La Bamba* grossed $5.6 million and was well on its way to recouping the $6.5 million Columbia had spent to make it.[49]

Much of the film's success was among Latino audiences. At Valdez's urging, Columbia distributed several Spanish dubbed and subtitled prints to thirty key cities with large Latino populations. Movie theaters in those cities consistently grossed more revenue than those showing the English versions. Favorable Latino audience response, in fact, was a decisive factor in the statements of studio executives. In an ironic twist, Valdez's efforts to reach the mass market were perceived by the studios as an opening into the "Hispanic" market. According to Columbia Pictures President David Picker, "If we can establish [Hispanics] as an on-going market, it will be a great asset to us. . . . One reason we are doing 'La Bamba' at all is that we have a market, that has never been addressed with the care and attention it deserves. If 'La Bamba' succeeds, it will create new avenues for Latino actors, writers, and film makers."[50] A representative for Universal Films took a similar view: "I want 'La Bamba' to succeed. . . . A success for a single Hispanic film is a success for all of us. If that movie makes money, then there's something to show to executives when they make the next film. Of course, success depends on how effectively Columbia reaches the Hispanic market."[51]

There is no question that *La Bamba* was a solid financial success. The film was profitable in theatrical release. Pay cable and home video distribution began in early 1988. Additional revenues have come from broadcast network play, independent television syndication, foreign release, redistribution, and the royalties from the music rights owned by Los Lobos, a well-known Chicano band. Had Valens lived longer, there would have been a sequel (*La Bamba: Part II?*), which would have begun the cycle all over again.

This potential has greatly increased Valdez's marketability among movie executives. It was not surprising that he used his new clout to create a pro-duction company, the current trend in the industry, in order to seek a long-term contract from a major studio. As this happened, Valdez moved finally in a position to give Latino arts some permanence, and perhaps demonstrate that it is possible to create, in his words, "an institution that can be used by others so this doesn't disappear." [52]

CONCLUSION

The final task of this essay is to evaluate Valdez's changing interpretation of the Chicano experience. What conclusions can be drawn by our examination of the turning points in Valdez's art? What can we learn about the cultural pro-cess as it exerted pressures on the artist over the years? Two articles illustrate an attempt to address these questions.

Dieter Herms argues that Valdez's work should be viewed as part of "unified cultural process and reality," in which professional and nonprofessional Chi-cano artists contribute to a "subversive praxis of philosophy." In a similar view, George Lipsitz suggests that the effort of Chicano artists in general, and mu-sicians in particular, to enter the cultural mainstream "reflects their struggle to assemble a 'historical bloc' [of advanced intellectuals] capable of challeng-ing the ideological hegemony of Anglo cultural domination." [53]

These scholars have highlighted some important aspects of Valdez's work. Certainly, Valdez's writings have drawn from and sought to inspire social ac-tion. Valdez has also played a significant role in the vanguard of Chicano in-tellectual thought. What has not been discussed, however, is the degree to which Valdez or other activists were able to maintain these positions and ad-dress social issues at particular points in their careers. I would explain these varying degrees of success as symptomatic of Valdez's "contradictory develop-ment" as both a cultural and a political figure.

The paradox that seemed to escape Herms and Lipsitz is that while artists are engaged in aesthetic activities, they also struggle with political processes that are rife with contradictions. Thus, we saw Valdez contending with the moderate UFW leadership while attempting to address wider social issues as a playwright. Valdez's break with the union only increased pressures on his troupe to function as a national theater. When political tensions worsened within the Chicano movement, Valdez found himself reassessing his strategies and weathering strife within his own theater. The result was a new spiritual emphasis, which met with movement criticism and drove Valdez to seek a larger audience.

Thus, Valdez's involvement in both cultural and political contexts *required* him to negotiate with the Chicano movement and the dominant culture for the right to be recognized as an artist. That negotiation was protracted and consisted of a number of stages which I identified throughout this chapter. Moreover, the need to negotiate has been by no means unique to Valdez. An entire generation of artists and social activists experienced the same types of pressures. The "price" Valdez eventually paid was his isolation from Chicano politics and recognition by mainstream theater critics as the premier "Hispanic" artist of his generation.

The final issue to be addressed is Valdez's diminished political role in the 1990s, in contrast to El Teatro's activities in the 1960s and 1970s. As we saw from the preceding analysis, the path taken following Teatro's break from the UFW led not only to creative independence but also to the need to develop independent financial and artistic support. This meant that Valdez and the troupe were immediately required to acknowledge "real world" needs, such as food, shelter, and clothing, as well as to cultivate audiences to support their new creative efforts.

In contrast, under the umbrella of the union, Valdez and other actors could rely on some level of support, while serving farmworker audiences as they struggled against the growers. "Politics" in the early stages for Valdez tended to come with the territory. El Teatro was part of the union, and therefore part of the latter's political and social struggles. As a result, the artists enjoyed a close "living" relationship with farmworker audiences, continually reinforced by the requirements of the strikes and the grape boycott.

Once independent of the union, however, political activity no longer took center stage for El Teatro. The process of creative production in itself became "politics" for several members of the troupe. To Valdez, cultural production meant moving away from overt political activity toward a philosophy of "professionalism" in all forms of expression. This process included regimented divisions of labor within the theater and layoffs of actors who did not fit the mold. El Teatro's new direction also led to commercially commissioned plays rather than plays developing out of social causes. In the eighties and nineties El Teatro and Valdez are best known for forays into movies, television, and multimedia, which initially attracted interest from the industry but led ultimately to the demise of Campesino as a theater company.

Some writers suggest that Valdez developed his apolitical themes at the time he sought to make the theater company more commercial in 1976–1977. I believe the process began as early as 1966, when El Teatro figuratively and creatively moved away from Mexican American farmworkers, and later from the urban working class in 1970–1971. Since then, the history of the theater can be viewed in some respects as the story of El Teatro's, and especially Luis Valdez's, search for a new sociocultural and political base. The Chicano movement was the most likely and compatible suitor. But once movement organizations disintegrated in the mid 1970s, El Teatro was left to its own devices. Many artists inside and outside Chicano theater sought creative refuge in religious and intellectual symbolism. Valdez's search continued through nationalism, humanism, liberalism, and professionalism, by blending the collective work of the troupe and his own individual initiative to develop unique — and ultimately marketable — art forms.

Despite this history, it is unfair and counterproductive to be too critical of Luis Valdez and El Teatro Campesino. In many respects, Valdez's efforts can be viewed as metaphors for our own adjustments to the contradictions of a dominant culture. We have only to listen to the doublespeak of this culture to realize its impact on our lives. Thus, we strive to hone our "professional skills" and continue our education to be more "marketable," all for the sake of affording the kind of "lifestyle" in which we can enjoy the fruits of our "labors" and pass on those values to our children, whom we subtly enlist into the ranks of a new "Hispanic" middle class.

The art forms created by El Teatro Campesino suggest alternatives to such values. Their plays capture the exhilarating events and disappointments of the sixties, as well as the realities of the movement's demise in the seventies and the Reagan aftermath in the eighties. The production of some early Teatro pieces in the nineties by a new generation of artists signalled possibilities for the future. Through its art, El Teatro has given us the means to overcome cultural and political obstacles and has motivated us to get on with our lives. Change is inevitable, we realize, but on whose terms? In the work of El Teatro we recognize the ability to push the boundaries of personal and cultural development, whatever the costs. In the long run, institutions like El Teatro Campesino and the artists they produce prepare us for a promising, and at times uncertain, future. Without their guidance, that uncertainty would seem overwhelming, and the promise of new vistas all too distant.

NOTES

Author's Note: This essay had its origins during the early 1980s in Berkeley. Since then, many colleagues and family members helped me in varying degrees to produce the final passages. My thanks go to the 1983–1984 U.C. Berkeley ChPEC working group, and to Tomas Almaguer, Larry Almada, Félix Alvarez, Jon D. Cruz, Margarita Decierdo, Troy Duster, Russell Ellis, Francisco García, Juan C. García, Todd Gitlin, Tomas González, David Montejano, Katia Panas, Brian

Rich, and Julie L. Sickert. Finally, this project is dedicated to my children, Nick, Russell, and Veronica, who as a new generation provided much of the impetus to complete the final draft. Any flaws which remain are my own.

1. See the following: El Teatro Campesino, *El Teatro Campesino: The Evolution of America's First Chicano Theatre Company* (1965–1985) (San Juan Baptista, Calif.: El Teatro, 1985); Arthur C. Flores, *El Teatro Campesino de Luis Valdez* (1965–1980) (Madrid: Pliegos, 1990); Yolanda Broyles-González, *El Teatro Campesino: Theater in the Chicano Movement* (Austin: University of Texas Press, 1994); Manuel de Jesús Vega, *El Teatro Campesino: Chicano y La Vanguardia Teatral, 1965–1975* (Middlebury, Vt.: Middlebury College Press, 1983); and Víctor Zavala Catano, *Teatro Campesino* (Lima: Ediciones Escena Contemporánea, 1983).

2. A notable exception is the book by Yolanda Broyles-González, op. cit. Mixed with some harsh criticism of Valdez, González illuminates the "dynamics of Teatro's creative production process" against the backdrop of sociocultural and political developments. The author lays bare the tensions within the troupe, particularly the conflict between the collective work of female ensemble members and Valdez's impulse to point the theater toward the mainstream. I would explain these and other conflicts as evidence of the unstable union between culture and politics within the Chicano movement, focusing on Valdez as a representative of Chicana/o artists who sought to present alternative forms of expression.

3. See, for example, Juan Gómez-Quiñones, "On Culture," in *Revista Chicano-Riqueño* 5, no. 2 (Spring 1977): 29–47; Juan Bruce Novoa, "The Space of Chicano Literature," in *De Colores* 1, no. 4 (1975): 22–42; José Limón, "Agringado Joking in Texas Mexican Society: Folklore and Differential Identity," *New Scholar* 6 (1977): 33–50; Tomás Ybarra Frausto, "The Chicano Movement and the Emergence of a Chicano Poetic Consciousness," *New Scholar* 6 (1977): 81–109; Joseph Sommers, "From the Critical Premise to the Product: Critical Modes and Their Applications to the Chicano Literary Text," *New Scholar* 6 (1977): 51–80; and Luis Davila, "Otherness in Chicano Literature," in James W. Wilkie, Michael C. Meyer, and Edna Manzon de Wilkie, eds., *Contemporary Mexico* (Berkeley: University of California Press, 1973), pp. 556–563. Analytical questions concerning culture and politics, of course, are not limited to Chicano studies. See also Terry Eagleton's *Criticism and Ideology, A Study in Marxist Literary Theory* (London: New Left Books, 1976).

4. Raymond Williams, *Marxism and Literature* (Oxford: Oxford University Press, 1977), p. 19.

5. See Armando Rendón, *Chicano Manifesto* (New York: Collier Books, 1971); Armando Navarro, "The Evolution of Chicano Politics," *Aztlán* 5, nos. 1 & 2 (Spring & Fall 1974); Rodolfo Acuña, *Occupied America*, 2nd edition (New York: Harper & Row, 1981); Tomás Ybarra Frausto, "The Chicano Movement"; and Gustavo Segade, "Identity and Power: An Essay on the Politics of Culture and the Culture of Politics in Chicano Thought," *Aztlán* 9, no. 1 (Spring 1978): pp. 89–99.

6. "Platicando Con Luis Valdez," *Rayas* (newsletter of Chicano arts and letters) 4 (July–August 1978): 11.

7. Ibid.

8. Jacques Levy, *César Chávez: Autobiography of La Causa* (New York: W. W. Norton & Co., 1970), p. 196.

9. Paula Cizmar, "Luis Valdez," *Mother Jones*, June 1979, p. 52.

10. Ibid.

11. Beth Bagby, "El Teatro Campesino: Interview with Luis Valdez," *Tulane Drama Review* 11, no. 4 (Summer 1967): 70–80.

12. Clark Knowlton, "Guerrillas of Río Arriba: The New Mexico Land Wars," in F. Chris García, ed., *La Causa Política: A Chicano Politics Reader* (Notre Dame, Ind.: Notre Dame Press,

1974); Stan Steiner, *La Raza: The Mexican Americans* (New York: Harper & Row, 1969); Carlos Muñoz, "The Politics of Protest and Chicano Liberation: A Case Study of Repression and Co-optation," *Aztlán* 5, nos. 1 & 2 (Spring & Fall 1974): 119–141; John Staples Shockley, *Chicano Revolt in a Texas Town* (Notre Dame, Ind.: Notre Dame Press, 1974).

13. Bagby, "El Teatro Campesino."

14. From an interview with Félix Alvarez, a former member of El Teatro, Oakland, California, April 1978; Olga Rodríguez, ed., *The Politics of Chicano Liberation* (New York: Pathfinder Press, 1977), p. 36.

15. Alvarez interview.

16. Sylvia Drake, "El Teatro Campesino: Keeping the Revolution on Stage," *Performing Arts*, September 1970, pp. 59–60.

17. Knowlton, "Guerrillas of Río Arriba"; Armando Morales, "The 1970–71 East Los Angeles Chicano-Police Riots," in García, ed., *La Causa Política*; Richard García, "The Chicano Movement and the Mexican American Community, 1972–1978: An Interpretive Essay," *Socialist Review* no. 40–41 (July–October 1978). See also Carlos Muñoz, Jr., and Mario Barrera, "La Raza Unida Party and the Chicano Student Movement in California," *Social Science Journal* 19, no. 2 (April 1982): 101–119; Juan José Peña, "Reflecciones sobre El Movimiento," *De Colores* 2, no. 1 (1975): 59–63; see Acuña's *Occupied America*, p. 389.

18. Rodríguez, *Politics of Chicano Liberation*; José Limón, "The Folk Performance of *Chicano* and the Cultural Limits of Political Ideology" (unpublished manuscript, 1979). Limón implies that the use of the term *Chicano* among young organizers was instrumental in creating distrust among older Chicano voters.

19. González, *El Teatro Campesino*, provides a vivid account of these conflicts in a section on the stereotypical roles endured by women members throughout El Teatro's history. In later years, Valdez's efforts to produce images of "colonization" for Chicano and non-Chicano audiences tended to reproduce tensions within the company when women continued to be cast as whores, prostitutes, or ingenues. See González's chapter 3, "Toward a Re-Vision of Chicana/o Theater History: The Roles of Women in El Teatro Campesino," pp. 129–163.

20. Theodore Shank, "A Return to Mayan and Aztec Roots," *Drama Review* 18, no. 4 (December 1974): 56–78.

21. Ybarra-Frausto, "The Chicano Movement."

22. Nicolas Kanellos, "Folklore in Chicano Theater and Chicano Theater as Folklore," *Journal of Folklore Institute* 15, no. 1 (Jan.–April 1978): 74.

23. *Actos: El Teatro Campesino* (Fresno: Cucaracha Press, 1971), p. 3. Aztlán, in Chicano writings, is a mental and physical state. Literally, it refers to a utopia written about by Aztec and Mayan philosophers and projected to the Southwest by Chicano writers in the 1960s.

24. Ibid.

25. For a vivid example of Valdez's attitude toward militants during this period, see his *acto*, "The Militants," in ibid.

26. Luis Valdez, *Pensamiento Serpentino: A Chicano Approach to the Teatre of Reality* (San Juan Bautista, Calif.: Cucaracha Publications, 1973).

27. Arthur Sainer, *Village Voice*, April 26, 1973.

28. Valdez, *Pensamiento Serpentino*.

29. See, for example, Rendón's *Chicano Manifesto*, and to some extent Gómez-Quiñones's "On Culture"; Raymond A. Rocco, "The Role of Power and Authenticity in the Chicano Movement," *Aztlán* 5, nos. 1 and 2 (Spring and Fall 1974): 167–176. See the work of the Chicano "formalist" school, particularly the writings of Juan Bruce Novoa. Ybarra's article, op. cit., cites other examples.

30. *Unity*, June 15, 1977; Juan Bruce Novoa and C. May Gamboa, "El Quinto Festival de Teatros," *De Colores* 2, no. 2 (1975).

31. *Unity*, June 15, 1977.

32. Personal correspondence from Valdez to Jorge Acevedo, April 12, 1973, on file in the Chicano Studies Library, University of California, Berkeley.

33. Kanellos, "Folklore in Chicano Theater."

34. See Acuña's criticism in his *Occupied America*, p. 385.

35. Kanellos, "Folklore in Chicano Theater," p. 79.

36. *Los Angeles Times*, April 16, 1979, p. 69.

37. *New York Times Magazine*, February 11, 1979, p. 99.

38. *Los Angeles Times*, April 16, 1979, calendar.

39. *Encore*, May 7, 1979, p. 32.

40. *Los Angeles Times*, April 16, 1979.

41. Harold Clurman, *The Nation*, April 21, 1979, p. 444.

42. Gerald Rabkin, *Newstatesman*, June, 1979, p. 962.

43. Cizmar, "Luis Valdez."

44. *Encore*, May 7, 1979, p. 32.

45. The play was unsympathetically reviewed by New York critics. See Brendan Gill in the *New Yorker Magazine*, April 2, 1979, p. 94; and Richard Eder, in the *New York Times*, March 26, 1979; also see Cizmar, "Luis Valdez."

46. *Los Angeles Times*, June 3, 1984.

47. *Los Angeles Times*, October 3, 1984.

48. *Los Angeles Times*, June 3, 1984.

49. Shelia Benson, "*La Bamba*: Flooded with Irresistible Music Yet Void of Raw Energy," *Los Angeles Times*, July 24, 1987.

50. Spanish-language prints averaged $5,300 per day in 77 theaters, while English-language prints averaged $4,886 per day in 1,174 theaters. "Richie Valens Film Boosts Prospects of Dubbing, Subtitles," *Los Angeles Times*, July 24, 1987.

51. Ibid.

52. *Unity*, December 17, 1990, p. 7. At the end of 1990, reports Gina Hernández, Valdez was working with actor Ted Danson and Paramount Studios on a television series based on the play "I Don't Need to Show You No Stinking Badges." There were also plans to create an artists' "pueblo" in San Juan Bautista that would include an outdoor amphitheater, recording studios, workshops, and a working farm. The Easter 1991 grand opening involved the production of *The Passion Play: The Way of the Cross*.

53. Dieter Herms, "Ideology and El Teatro Campesino," in Renate Von Bardeleben, ed., *Missions of Conflict: Essays on U.S.-Mexican Relations and Chicano Culture* (Tübingen: G. Narr, 1986), p. 115; George Lipsitz, "Cruising around the Historical Bloc: Postmodernism and Popular Music in East Los Angeles," *Cultural Critique* no. 5 (Winter 1986–1987): 157–178.

Nine

WHERE HAVE ALL
THE NATIONALISTS GONE?

Change and Persistence in Radical Political Attitudes
among Chicanos, 1976–1986

MARTÍN SÁNCHEZ JANKOWSKI

INTRODUCTION

In the 1960s the African American population in the United States began a
social movement that both challenged and changed the existing social and
political order in the country.[1] Chicanos experienced a similar awakening,
called *el movimiento*, and it captivated both the old and the young within Chicano society.[2] Like the Blacks, Chicanos had experienced a long history of racial prejudice and discrimination; and in an effort to overcome this history, *el
movimiento* was a conscious campaign on the part of Chicanos to challenge
the existing social and political order.[3]

While Chicanos may have been generally united in their desire to challenge discriminatory practices and improve their socioeconomic condition,
they were anything but united on how politically to do it. Within Chicano
society there existed a myriad of political ideas, each with its spokespersons
and impassioned followers. The two most prominent political positions were:
(1) those who supported the U.S. political system, but wanted the government
to both take a more active role in guaranteeing the civil rights of Chicanos
and create more opportunities for economic mobility; and (2) those who called
themselves Chicano nationalists and displayed hostility to much, if not all, of
the existing socioeconomic and political order in the United States. However,
as the 1960s and '70s passed, less and less was heard from those who identified
themselves as Chicano nationalists, and by the late 1980s, there appeared to

be virtually no one who supported nationalist politics. Ironically, sociologists and political scientists have consistently identified nationalism as one of those political attitudes that is held most dear to individuals, and one which is difficult for most individuals to discard.[4] Thus, an important and perplexing question that concerns the Chicano social movement of the 1960s and '70s (*el movimiento*) has to do with how it is possible that a once strong Chicano nationalism appears, for all practical purposes, to have died; in other words, where have all the nationalists gone?

What factors led those individuals who supported nationalism to abandon it? Was it simply a time in which the protest politics that Chicanos had been engaged in had succeeded in forcing the system to include them as full participants within the political arena, and thus nationalism became irrelevant? This paper is an attempt to address some of the questions concerning what this time of enormous transition in Chicano politics meant for the individuals who experienced it. Was this a time when the radicalism associated with the time of inclusion gave way to the moderate politics of being incorporated?

In my endeavor to understand the decline of nationalism among Chicanos, I shall draw on the work of Daniel Latouche, whose study on this very question in Québec provides a theoretical guide for my analysis.[5] At the time of Latouche's research, the first referendum put forth by the separatist *Parti Québecois* asking the electorate of Québec whether they supported the government's effort to negotiate a new and more independent relationship with the rest of Canada had been voted down and there was little nationalist activism. In fact, independent of the support for separating from Canada, data from the general surveys of public opinion in Québec indicated that nationalist sentiment was also waning. Within this climate, Latouche undertook his study to explain what the determinants of the change in nationalist sentiment and activism were. He offered three possibilities to account for both the change and stability in nationalist attitudes in Québec. The first is what he refers to as the group-specific "air of the times" experiences, in which people are nationalists because that is the predominant attitude at the time. The second is what he refers to as "life-cycle" experiences, in which youth, who are more willing to adhere to new ideas, seize on to nationalism, but as they grow older they become more conservative and abandon it. The third is what he calls the "generation-specific" experiences in which those people who go through a particular intense event (such as World War II or the Great Depression of the 1930s) maintain the attitudes developed during that particular time throughout their lives.

Of course, more recently (1995), a new *Parti Québecois* government initiated a second referendum asking the general public for their support in directing the provincial government to begin talks with the national government concerning the creation of an autonomous Québec. This time, the referendum was barely defeated (49.44 percent yes vote to separate, against a 50.56 percent no vote to separate) which indicated that clearly there was cross-generational support for a separatist platform. More will be said in the conclusion about the cross-generational basis in the rise of pro-nationalist attitudes in Québec, and how that relates to nationalist attitudes among Chicanos. However, suffice it to say now that it would be difficult to understand the resurgence of nationalist attitudes in Québec without understanding the factors that influenced attitude change and persistence during a time when efforts were being made to accommodate French interests within the larger national Canadian context. Likewise, it would be difficult to fully understand the contemporary Mexican American political condition without understanding the dynamics of change and persistence in Chicano nationalism—the most dominant of the radical ideological positions of the time. Therefore, this paper is an effort to identify the factors that influenced Chicano political attitudes during a time of political inclusion, how stable these attitudes have been over time, and how they have influenced other attitudes and behaviors of Chicanos over time.[6]

In my effort to determine the origins of nationalism's decline among Chicanos since the 1960s, the first two theoretical positions ("air of the times" and "life-cycle") advanced by Latouche provide just such an explanation, whereas the third theoretical position in his paper ("generation-specific") tends to explain why people would have maintained their nationalist attitudes. Therefore, in the present inquiry into the status of Chicano nationalism, I shall partially test all three of these theoretical postulates. In this endeavor, the chapter's design is to look first at what changes occurred over time in nationalist attitudes, then move to an analysis of the factors that affected attitude change, and then finally to address how changes in attitudes toward nationalism have had an impact on party identification and political participation.

DATA AND METHODS

The data for this paper were collected as part of a longitudinal study commenced in 1976, with retesting done in 1982 and 1986. The 1976 sample consisted of 1,040 high school seniors living in San Antonio, Texas (335); Albuquerque, New Mexico (315); and Los Angeles, California (328). The 1982 and 1986 panels consisted of 300 of the original 1,040 respondents. The ages of the respondents were 17 or 18 in 1976 when the study first began and 27 or 28 in 1986. The sample was chosen using stratified and clustering techniques and provides an even distribution of respondents from middle- and lower-class backgrounds, as well as an even distribution of males and females. Further, the sample contained youth who were in the United States without proper immigration documents.

The data for the study comes from two sources. First, there was a formal questionnaire with both structured and semistructured questions. In each of the follow-up legs of the study, the same questions were repeated that were on the previous questionnaire, with some new questions being added that were appropriate for the new time period (1986). Second, all the respondents were given an in-depth interview with open-ended questions. These open-ended interviews (which were a part of the questionnaire for each panel) lasted about ninety minutes each and were important for generating more detailed information than what was possible with the structured questionnaire. They acted as a validity check for many of the structured questions as well.[7]

NATIONALISM FROM 1976 TO 1986

Table 9.1 shows the number of people who supported Chicano nationalism in the 1976, '82, and '86 panels. It is apparent that there has been a substantial decline across each city in those who identified with Chicano nationalism. Table 9.1 reveals that San Antonio had the largest decline in nationalist support, followed by Los Angeles and then Albuquerque. However, hidden in the data of the table is another change that occurred: there was a significant increase in commitment to nationalism on the part of those who had remained its supporters; in other words, those who maintained their support for nationalism had become even more committed.

There are two factors that have affected the decline in nationalism among Chicanos: (1) the type of nationalism that the respondents identified with in 1976, and (2) the type of city they lived in. Latouche, as well as many other researchers of ethnic nationalism, have assumed that there is a universally shared view of nationalism by the people they are studying.[8] However, this was not true in the case of the Chicanos in this study and suggests that it may not be true of other populations espousing support for nationalism as well. In a previous paper it was reported that in 1976 the Chicano respondents had two general conceptions toward nationalism: there were those who associated their nationalism primarily with Chicano cultural institutions (such as Mexican clothing, food, holidays, Catholicism, language, and customs) and thus were labeled as "cultural nationalists," and there were those who associated their nationalism with not only cultural attributes but with political concepts (such as national self-determination and national sovereignty) as well and were labeled "political nationalists" (see Table 9.2).[9] However, upon further analysis, it was found that it was necessary to go farther than was previously done and subdivide those who were identified as cultural and political nationalists into four distinct categories of nationalists. The data from the in-depth

Table 9.1. Summary Numbers of Support for Nationalism[a]

Chicano Nationalism/ Separatism	1976	1976[b]	1982	1986
San Antonio	50 (15%)	15 (15%)	14 (14%)	2 (2%)
Lower class	29	8	8	2
Middle class	21	7	6	0
Albuquerque	94 (30%)	34 (34%)	31 (31%)	22 (22%)
Lower class	78	27	24	12
Middle class	16	7	7	10
Los Angeles	141 (43%)	42 (42%)	40 (40%)	26 (26%)
Lower class	92	29	28	16
Middle class	49	13	12	10

Source: Mártin Sánchez Jankowski, *City Bound: Urban Life and Political Attitudes among Chicano Youth* (Albuquerque: University of New Mexico Press, 1986).

[a]The numbers in this table represent those who had positive attitudes toward nationalism and were derived from semantic differential raw scores. Those who were positive toward an ideology (i.e., those who scored the concept 1, 2, or 3) were included in the positive category, while those who scored the concept 5, 6, or 7 were included in the negative category. It should be noted that there is a space (labeled "4") for respondents to check if they do not care one way or the other, but no one checked this category. Neither did any of the respondents check the box provided for those who did not know what a particular concept was. Therefore, every respondent is accounted for in this table. For a description of the semantic differential method, see Charles Osgood, *The Measurement of Meaning* (Urbana: University of Illinois Press, 1957).

[b]This is the subsample of the 1976 sample that was selected as the panel to be retested in 1982 and 1986 (and any additional retesting in the future). This category is included in the table to indicate how this group scored in relation to the entire 1976 sample (i.e., to determine if they were representative) and in order to compare their scores over time.

interviews indicate that there were actually four different conceptions of nationalism among the respondents in 1976, two each under the more general cultural and political categories.

I begin first with the cultural nationalists. All of those who were labeled in 1986 as cultural nationalists did not view nationalism in the same way (see Table 9.3). The most prevalent view of nationalism from those generally describing their nationalism in cultural terms was that it was a means by which people could begin to express pride in who they were. For this group of people nationalism represented the act of asserting to the dominant Anglo American culture the position that Chicano culture was not inferior to theirs. This group

Table 9.2. Factor Scores for Chicano Cultural and Political Nationalism

	Factor 1	Factor 2
Mexican food	.65	.30
Catholic church	.59	.09
Compadrazgo (godparent system)	.66	.33
Curanderismo (traditional folk medicine)	.62	.19
Mexican music (*rancheras*, polkas, etc.)	.61	.25
Cinco de Mayo (Mexican Independence Day)	.68	.71
Spanish language	.72	.77
Mexican War/Texas independence	.19	.72
Chicano colonialization	.11	.65
National Liberal Movement	.07	.67

Source: Mártin Sánchez-Jankowski, "Change and Stability in Political Attitudes among Chicanos: A Panel Study, 1976–1986," paper presented at Western Political Science Association, San Francisco, 1988.

Note: Factor loadings were derived from the semantic differential scores and generated using the Varimax Orthogonal Rotated Method. Consult Charles Osgood, et al., *The Measurement of Meaning* (Urbana: University of Illinois Press, 1957) for description of the semantic differential technique; and consult Norman Nie, et al., *Statistical Package for the Social Sciences* (New York: McGraw-Hill, 1981) for a description of the Varimax Orthogonal Rotated Method of Factor Analysis.

of people saw their support of nationalism as a statement to the Anglo community (and also to themselves) that they would no longer entertain thoughts that their culture, or they themselves, as members of that culture, were inferior to Anglos. The comments of Raul, Susana, and Hector express this view.[10] Raul, a seventeen-year-old (in 1976) son of a janitor in San Antonio, responded:

> Anglo society has always put us [Chicanos] down. They think that Chicano culture is inferior to theirs and then they try to tell us that we as Chicanos are inferior to them because of our culture. It is a way to keep us down so they get to keep all the good jobs. I used to believe that shit! But now things are different, Chicano nationalism is telling the Anglo that we are as good as anybody and that our culture is as good as his and we will make something of ourselves. I know I feel much better about myself and I know a lot of other Chicanos feel better about who they are because of the *movimiento*.

Susana, an eighteen-year-old (in 1976) daughter of a house painter in Los Angeles, said:

Chicano nationalism has said to the Anglo *basta* [enough]! We are no longer going to think that Chicano culture is inferior to other people's. Because we come from families that speak Spanish we don't have to feel inferior to Anglos. Most of us Chicanos used to feel bad about who we were, we didn't think that we were as good as the Anglo. They [the Anglos] used to make you feel that way, but that's changed now, there is some pride in who we are and where we came from. . . . I know I feel better about myself, and people who feel better about themselves are more successful. I think I'll be more successful now that Chicano nationalism has given us Chicanos pride in who we are.

Hector, a seventeen-year-old son (in 1976) of an auto mechanic in Albuquerque, described his feelings this way:

Chicano nationalism says to the Anglo society that we don't believe they are superior to us anymore. That we as Chicanos have a culture that is as good as theirs and we don't have to feel like ours is inferior to theirs. . . . Chicanismo is also a help to feel better about who we are. We don't have to believe Anglos when they try to tell us we ain't as good as they are or when they try to tell us that we're only good enough for the low-paying jobs.

This particular form of nationalism was very similar, if not identical, to the nationalism expressed by the Black Consciousness movement within the African American population in the beginning phase of the broader Civil Rights movement.[11] For Chicanos, it was first a reaction to the long period of discrimination that they had experienced in American history, a discrimination which, similar to the experience of Black Americans, involved psychological scars from being portrayed as inferior to the white society.[12] Thus, this type of nationalism was used as a resource in order to strengthen a positive self-image for the pursuit of a better life. The use of nationalism for such purposes was predicated on the logic (with a good deal of empirical support) that people who have a positive self-image tend to do better than those who do not.[13] For that reason I have designated this type of nationalism "self-image oriented."

The second view of nationalism that was present among those Chicanos who were labeled "cultural nationalists" is one that saw nationalism as something that could be used as a resource to persuade/pressure people in authority to provide more benefits and opportunities to those who held such views.[14] This type of nationalism I have designated "self-interest" nationalism. The people who adhered to this idea of nationalism did so in order to gain concrete material advantages. The desired advantages most often cited were opportu-

Table 9.3. Respondents Identifying with Different Views of Nationalism by City, Class, and Year*

1976

	CULTURAL			POLITICAL		
Self-Identity	*Lower Class*			*Lower Class*		**Electoral**
Nationalism	SA	6		SA	1	**Empowerment/**
	ALB	7		ALB	7	**Civil Rights**
	LA	5		LA	7	**Nationalism**
	Middle Class			*Middle Class*		
	SA	0		SA	5	
	ALB	0		ALB	1	
	LA	1		LA	1	
	Total	19		Total	22	
Self-Interest	*Lower Class*			*Lower Class*		**Separatist**
Nationalism	SA	0		SA	1	**Nationalism**
	ALB	0		ALB	13	
	LA	0		LA	17	
	Middle Class			*Middle Class*		
	SA	2		SA	0	
	ALB	6		ALB	0	
	LA	9		LA	2	
	Total	17		Total	33	

*Each subject was asked what he or she meant in saying he or she was a nationalist. From their answers to this question, subjects were assigned to a particular nationalist category. After that was completed, three independent judges were asked to assign the same individuals to the various nationalist categories. The agreement rate among the four judges (including the author) was .976.

nities for high-paying, high-status jobs; and increased opportunities for acceptance into the elite higher-educational institutions. The comments of Alicia and David are indicative of the people adhering to this type of nationalism. Alicia, a seventeen-year-old (in 1976) daughter of a lawyer in Albuquerque, said:

> Yes, I think nationalism is very important. . . . I think of myself as a Chicano nationalist because I think that it can get Chicanos better jobs. You see, the Anglo authorities feel pressured to do something to hold down the complaints that they have been racist, so being nationalist can be used to get opportunities you wouldn't get other-

Table 9.3. (*continued*)

1986

CULTURAL			POLITICAL		
Self-Identity	*Lower Class*		*Lower Class*		**Electoral**
Nationalism	SA	0	SA	2	**Empowerment/**
	ALB	0	ALB	2	**Civil Rights**
	LA	1	LA	3	**Nationalism**
	Middle Class		*Middle Class*		
	SA	0	SA	0	
	ALB	0	ALB	6	
	LA	0	LA	2	
	Total	**1**	**Total**	**15**	
Self-Interest	*Lower Class*		*Lower Class*		**Separatist**
Nationalism	SA	0	SA	0	**Nationalism**
	ALB	0	ALB	10	
	LA	0	LA	13	
	Middle Class		*Middle Class*		
	SA	0	SA	0	
	ALB	1	ALB	3	
	LA	2	LA	6	
	Total	**3**	**Total**	**32**	

wise . . . I believe in Chicano cultural things, but not a lot of the other nationalist stuff; but I do support it because I think it's useful. Yeah, I know this sounds like I am kind of opportunistic, but hey that's what you have to be.

David, a seventeen-year-old (in 1976) son of a hardware store owner, responded:

Well, to me nationalism has been important because it has opened up opportunities for Chicanos. I believe it will give me more opportunities because people who have the power over good jobs will want to give more jobs to those Chicanos they think will be active in the nationalist movement like me, so they can try to stop it [the movement]. I support nationalism partly because I am proud of the culture, but also because I know that it is useful to get things from Anglo society like a chance to get into a good college like Harvard or Yale, which is what I would like to happen.

The people who subscribed to this type of cultural nationalism tended not to identify strongly with the general symbols or goals of Chicano cultural and political nationalism per se but rather to identify with its potential as a political resource to extract direct personal benefits from the dominant Anglo society.[15] It is not surprising to see that all of those who expressed this type of nationalism were from the middle class of Albuquerque and Los Angeles. For in the event that political separation became a reality, the middle class had more to lose than did their lower-class compatriots, and they were apprehensive about that. The comment of Juan, the eighteen-year-old son of a dry-cleaning businessperson in Albuquerque, is a good example of this group's position and concerns:

Well, as a nationalist I am for the maintenance of the culture and for keeping Spanish as the primary language, but some of the things that the radicals [radical nationalists] want, I am not for. Hell, I'd be crazy to be for separation because I would end up being a lot worse off than I am now. I just think that nationalism is good because it can give me, and a whole lot more Chicanos, a better chance to get a good education and good jobs.

SUPPORT FOR POLITICAL NATIONALISM

Now let me turn to those varieties of nationalism that were politically oriented. The first of this type I have called "civil rights" oriented. Those within this category believed that Chicanos had been historically denied their civil rights and that this occurrence had been responsible for prohibiting them as a group from having the same opportunities for mobility that other groups have had. They considered the nationalist ideology an instrument by which Chicanos could be mobilized in order to: (1) press the existing authorities to create opportunities for socioeconomic mobility and protect their civil rights; or (2) elect members of their own group to public office in an effort to create opportunities and uphold the group's civil rights.[16] In this regard traditional culture was thought to be important for purposes of mobilization because it defined the group; and an understanding of the political history affecting the

Chicano's condition was thought to be important for purposes of collective action.[17]

What differentiates these political nationalists from those who will be discussed next is their belief that it is undesirable and unrealistic for Chicanos to think that they would ever be allowed to form a separate country, as the other group wants. In essence, they believe that Chicanos need to be either electorally empowered and/or guaranteed their civil rights (particularly equal protection under the law), and if this is done, the U.S. political system affords Chicanos the best opportunity for a "good life." The comments of Jorge and Denise are representative of this type of nationalism. Jorge is an eighteen-year-old (in 1976) son of an architect in Los Angeles:

> I think of myself as a strong nationalist. I think Chicanos should
> keep traditional culture because it's really what makes us Chicanos
> and it's what keeps the community united. We need to organize
> around what makes us Chicanos, and culture, like language, is the
> one thing that we can do that with. That's why I'm a nationalist. . . .
> Another reason I'm a nationalist is because Anglos have tried to
> keep us down. They discriminate against us so we can't get good jobs,
> so we need to organize around culture and community and elect our
> own people to office and at the same time pressure the government
> to protect us, you know protect our civil rights. Then we will get
> what we deserve.

Denise is a seventeen-year-old (in 1976) daughter of a short-order cook in San Antonio:

> Well, yes, I guess I am a nationalist because I am really for us
> Chicanos keeping our culture . . . I don't support political separation
> from the United States. I know a lot of Chicano nationalists do, but
> I don't because I think we'd be worse off if that were ever to happen.
> Really though, the government wouldn't let us do that anyway. . . . I
> think us Chicanos need to organize because the only way we're going
> to have a chance to get the good things in life is if we get Chicanos
> in government and we get the government to protect our rights and
> stop the Anglos from discriminating against us. . . . The only way
> we'll be able to get the community involved, you know organized,
> is to organize around the culture 'cause that's the most basic thing
> in the community; and you know, if we can do that, we can protect
> ourselves politically.

The fourth type of nationalism is also political in its orientation, and I have labeled it "separatist oriented." Those who identified with this type of nationalism considered traditional culture to be extremely important in the lives of Chicanos. They also thought that the only way in which Chicanos could escape what they considered cultural genocide and socioeconomic inequality was to have their own separate country. Most wanted either all, or at least portions, of the five southwestern states (Texas, New Mexico, southern Colorado, Arizona, and California) that were once part of Mexico to secede from the United States and form a separate Chicano country. This group is quite similar to other separatist groups throughout the world, especially the Québecois in Canada, the Basques in Spain, and some of the Black nationalist groups in the United States.[18] They see traditional culture as the foundation of group identity, and the socioeconomic inequality experienced by the group as the by-product of ethnic/racial discrimination. In their emphasis on the importance of cultural maintenance, this group of nationalists is similar to those with an electoral empowerment/civil rights orientation, although they differ from the electoral empowerment/civil rights group in their belief that the only way Chicanos can hope to maintain their culture and achieve a respectable standard of living is for them to form their own separate country.[19] Of course, they believe separation is a possibility whereas the civil rights–oriented group does not. The comments of Sara and Julian are representative of those from this group. Sara is a seventeen-year-old (in 1976) daughter of a furniture production worker in Los Angeles:

> Separation from the U.S. is necessary if we Chicanos want to keep our culture and have a decent standard of living. You see, the Anglo dominates this system, it's his system, the one he gave us after taking our land and colonizing us. There is no way he is going to let us make a decent standard of living cause he wants us to keep being poor. You see, that way he gets cheap labor. The only way to get out of this mess is to get our own country so we don't have Anglos messing around with us.

Julian is a seventeen-year-old (in 1976) son of a construction worker in Los Angeles:

> Yeah, I am for a separate Chicano country because unless we get one we will always be on the bottom of the society. Plus if we don't get our own country we won't be able to maintain our culture. Everywhere you look you see signs that the Anglos want you to give up your culture like the European groups did and be Anglo American. If we do that we will be nothing—just poor and with no sense of belonging. . . . So if we don't separate we'll just be poor and Anglicized. You know, just poor, brown Anglos!

Having established that there were four different views of nationalism within the group that identified themselves as nationalists, let us now turn to the level of support found for each of these categories of nationalism in the 1986 panel data. As can be discerned from the cell counts in Table 9.3, those who were identified as being cultural nationalists experienced the largest exodus from nationalism. From 1976 to 1986, there had been an 88 percent decline among those who were identified with political nationalism. As discussed above, there are four factors that have directly affected this pattern of attitude change: (1) "air of the times," (2) "life-cycle," (3) "generation," and (4) the local political culture the individual finds himself or herself in. We shall discuss the impact of each of these on the general pattern of decline in nationalist support among the Chicanos in this study.

"AIR OF THE TIMES," "LIFE-CYCLE," AND "GENERATION" EFFECTS

Those respondents who were identified as "self-identity" nationalists consistently said that they had changed because nationalism was no longer an important aspect in either their lives or that of their communities. They consistently said that they had been supporters of nationalism because it had been such an important ideology within the community and among their peers. They also said they thought it was important at the time because Chicanos in general (they included themselves) had had a low sense of self-esteem, due principally to the many years of being told that they and their culture were inferior to that of the Anglo, and nationalism had acted to improve group self-esteem. However, they also believed that as a result of those times when nationalism was a political force within the Chicano community, conditions had changed (some even said improved) such that nationalism was no longer needed as a vehicle for Chicanos to achieve socioeconomic mobility. In essence, their attitude change was the result of the "air of the times" effect. Here are two representative statements from those respondents in this group. Frank is a twenty-seven-year-old (in 1986) electrician in San Antonio:

> Yeah, well, when I was back in high school everybody was into the *movimiento* and so was I. Actually everybody just went along with it. But by saying this I don't want to sound like it was just a fad or something, or that all of us just went along for the hell of it because that's not right. It was something we needed at the time to shake all the prejudices that the Anglos had about us. You know, to start to feel good about being a Chicano and not wishing you'd been an Anglo. So nationalism was important then for everybody—it definitely was

important for me and I supported it. I didn't support separatism and all that radical stuff, but I was for being proud of our culture. Now things are different. We really don't need nationalism cause we are proud of our culture and Chicanos are getting better opportunities; at least that's the way I feel, so I don't support nationalism anymore.

Julia, a twenty-eight-year-old (in 1986) bank teller in Albuquerque, responded:

No, I don't support nationalism anymore, but as you [the author] know, I did when I was back in high school. . . . Well, back then there were a lot of people who were real committed to nationalism and it did make sense then. I mean it was real important in giving us Chicanos pride in our culture, in our parents who were traditional, and in ourselves. I know there were times that I was embarrassed about being a Chicano, I really did believe that I was not as good as Anglos; and Chicano nationalism helped change that for me and a lot of others. I think it helped me. . . . Now I don't support nationalism because I think we've [Chicanos] moved on. We don't need it anymore, we need to be proud of who we are and take advantage of the opportunities that are available now.

For those individuals who had been cultural nationalists from a "self-interest" perspective, the abandonment of nationalism was the result of "life-cycle effects." All but one said that they felt their support for nationalism was just a stage in their lives and that they had simply outgrown their attraction to the ideology. In addition, they all said that their support of nationalism was foolish and a part of being young and naïve. They consistently expressed the view that the opportunities they had seen for themselves in the nationalist ideology had been largely myths derived from adolescent rebellion, immaturity/naïveté, and their own psychological drives of wanting to be socially accepted by their peers. As the quotes will indicate, the prevailing conviction among this group was that nationalism (of one form or another) was prevalent throughout the Chicano community, and while they did not completely believe in it, some went along with it (1) because their parents were against it, (2) to avoid being socially ostracized by their peers, or (3) because it was something new that sounded good. Further, they reported that their decision to support nationalism, even though they did not fully believe in it, was made more palatable through their effort to find ways that nationalism could be useful to them personally, irrespective of whether it was useful to Chicanos as a whole. The comments of Becky and Ron are representative of the views of this group. Becky is a twenty-eight-year-old (in 1986) lawyer in Albuquerque, who said:

Yes, I can remember supporting nationalism when I was in high school. [laughter] That was when I was young and foolish. . . . Well, the answer to why I supported nationalism is really simple, I was young and immature! You see, everybody was into this nationalist thing when we were in school and I was from a middle-class family and felt guilty about that, so I went along with. It was crazy, but I didn't want my high school friends to look down on me. . . . I really did not feel comfortable with all the nationalist stuff—after all, I didn't even speak Spanish—but I saw that some people who were militants got some opportunities by accusing the authorities of being racist, and I thought, maybe I can get something too. I never did, but it kept me talking the line. . . . Then just when I would get to the point of totally thinking it was just crazy, my father would say something against nationalism and I would defend it. . . . I would say my dropping nationalism was just a process of maturation.

Ron is a twenty-eight-year-old (in 1986) dentist in Los Angeles:

When I was in high school I supported Chicano nationalism. I mean I was sort of for strengthening the culture and being proud of it and all that stuff, even though my family was not traditional at all and I did not speak Spanish myself. I never was for separatism, however, even though there were a number of people at my school who were for that too. I really was not that committed to it, but when you're a teenager you care what other people think, and I wanted to be part of the crowd, so I went along with it. I must tell you that I even thought I could use being a nationalist to get into a good college. Is that crazy or what?! I wanted to go to any Ivy League school and I thought that espousing nationalism would put pressure on them to take me. I was a good student, but I thought this could be the deciding factor for me. I was of course incredibly silly, but then that's what you would expect from a teenager. . . . My parents never really did bother me much about my views, they probably knew I would outgrow them, but I thought they cared deep down, so part of me wanted to keep espousing them— Oh the time of youth! . . . What made me change from supporting nationalism was nothing dramatic, I just grew up.

As was mentioned earlier, there was not as dramatic a shift away from pronationalist attitudes among those people whose nationalism was more politically oriented. In fact, among the political nationalists there was a tendency to become even more committed. Of the two types of political nationalists

identified, those who were of the electoral empowerment/civil rights orientation displayed the largest amount of variability between remaining committed to their nationalist beliefs and abandoning them.

Among this group two types of effects were found to influence whether or
not they remained supportive or abandoned their nationalist beliefs. Those
who remained supportive of this type of nationalism were influenced most by
"generation effects." The fact that they were active during the time when Chicanos were striving to ensure that they would be guaranteed the civil rights
entitled to all U.S. citizens and to elect Chicanos to public office had left a
permanent impression on not only their political attitudes but their political
values as well. All of them had vivid memories of what they said and what it
was like when Chicanos were being denied their civil rights of equal protection under the law, the right to vote, the opportunity to pursue good jobs, education, and housing free from racial discrimination. All were extremely proud
of the fact that they had contributed toward improving the lives of Chicanos
through their efforts to pressure the authorities to enforce the civil rights guaranteed them under the U.S. Constitution, and to get Chicanos elected to public office in order to help create more socioeconomic opportunities.

This group also believed that while there had been a good deal of progress
made to ensure that the civil rights of Chicanos were protected, that Chicanos
be elected to office, and to improve the quality of their lives, the work was not
done. It was their contention that there was a definite need to continue to be
vigilant that the civil rights of Chicanos were not being violated and to work
toward ensuring that Chicanos had the same opportunities available to them
that Anglo Americans had. Thus, for those who remained committed to nationalism (a pride in the culture, language, and history and a dedication to improving the group's overall quality of life), their experience of being a part of
the early effort of the *movimiento* to obtain and guarantee the civil rights of
Chicanos and acquire some legitimate political power had left them strongly
committed to nationalism.

The comments of Tomás and María are representative of this group's attitudes. Tomás is a twenty-seven-year-old (in 1986) head of a social service
agency in Los Angeles who said:

> I still consider myself a Chicano nationalist. I am still for the things
> the *movimiento* stood for, things like keeping Chicano culture strong,
> seeing to it that Spanish is no longer looked upon as something bad,
> and making sure Chicanos [are] treated with the dignity and respect
> that other groups [are]. You see, those of us who worked in the
> *movimiento* to improve the community's condition had to struggle to
> get the Anglos to enforce the laws so we could have more opportuni-

ties—I mean we're talking about just obtaining our civil rights and getting a few of us [Chicanos] elected, not anything bold like income redistribution. . . . We worked hard to get the Anglos to give us what every citizen is guaranteed, and it was a real struggle, but we did it by getting the community involved, by emphasizing cultural pride and identity, and using it to strive for better opportunities and protection of our legal rights against discrimination. . . . Yeah, we made some gains, but the experience taught me a lot about the importance of staying committed to the culture and language and the community. So I am as much a nationalist today as I was then [1976].

María is a twenty-eight-year-old nurse practitioner in Albuquerque. She responded:

Yes, I am very much committed to the things I was for when I was in high school. I was a nationalist then and I still think of myself a nationalist today. . . . I believe strongly in maintaining Chicano culture and language, and I am for continuing our struggle to protect our rights from Anglo discrimination. I tell you one thing, if you don't keep an eye out for violations against Chicanos' rights, Anglos will start it all over again. . . . Those like myself who lived through the time when the *movimiento* was trying to get our civil rights and get Chicanos elected know what it was like and know they don't want to go back.

There were people who supported the electoral empowerment/civil rights version of political nationalism in 1976 who had abandoned it by 1986. For these people, their decision to change was influenced most by the effects associated with the "air of the times." All but one of the respondents reported that while they were in high school they thought that Chicano nationalism was necessary because Chicanos were being discriminated against, but since that time things had improved to the point that nationalism was no longer necessary. The comments of Daniel, a twenty-eight-year-old (in 1986) government employee in San Antonio are typical:

I supported Chicano nationalism in high school, but not really anymore. I mean today it's not as necessary as back when I was in high school. Back then we were really discriminated against and we needed to organize so that we could get the government to protect our civil rights. We had to demand that our civil rights be guaranteed. Today we really don't need that kind of stuff, because we have got a lot of our civil rights protected and now we got a Chicano

mayor and Chicanos on the city government. I thought it was important then because the times were different than they are now; we just
don't need to have nationalism now 'cause we got a lot of the civil
rights stuff we were after.

Let us now turn to the group that has remained the most committed to nationalism. They are the people who considered themselves separatists. Of the
total number who supported separatism in 1976, only one had abandoned his
support for separatism in 1986. Those who considered themselves separatists
believed that the Anglo society was intent on destroying the Chicanos' culture and keeping them poor. They also believed that the Anglo American—
dominated political system was being used to systematically facilitate this plan.
So it was their position that the only way for Chicanos to avoid cultural genocide and constant poverty was for them to secede from the United States and
form their own country.

One of the important developments within this group was the fact that
they had become more committed to their nationalist ideology over the ten-
year period. This had occurred as a result of what Latouche and others have
called "generation effects." The people within this group all said that the experience of the *movimiento* had made an indelible impression on them and
that the events surrounding the struggle to liberate themselves from a racist
Anglo society which tried to take away their culture, discriminate against
them, and leave them impoverished had served as a constant source of
influence on their political attitudes.[20] It was their position that things had
not improved for Chicanos in general, and if we look at Table 9.3, we can see
that socioeconomic conditions really had not improved for them. More than
two-thirds (23 of 32) of those who are supportive of this type of nationalism
were of the lower class in 1976 and have remained that way. Thus, their personal socioeconomic histories and their early political experience in *el movimiento* have been mutually reinforcing. Moreover, there is some additional evidence that "generation effects" was the most important factor in this group's
retention of separatist ideology. In Table 9.3 we see that seven of the nine
middle-class respondents who consider themselves separatists were lower class
in 1976, and all reported that they remained committed to separatism as a result of their having lived through the *movimiento* period, which they referred
to as the "Chicano national renaissance." The statements of Rafael, Christina,
and Philipe are representative of the beliefs of this group of nationalists. Rafael and Christina are of the lower class and have remained that way for the
ten-year period, while Philipe was of the lower class in 1976 but since then has
joined the middle class. Rafael is a twenty-seven-year-old (in 1986) worker in
a produce warehouse in Los Angeles:

I am still very committed to a separate Chicano country, and I really
feel it is even more necessary now than ten years ago. . . . You see,
when I first got involved with separatism, conditions for Chicanos
were bad, and those in the separatist movement gave us Chicanos an
alternative for improving our situation, and since then Chicanos are
still being kept in poverty by the Gabacho [a disparaging term for
Anglos]; and if that ain't enough, then they try to take our culture
away from us too! The Anglo will always be racist against Chicanos
and try to keep us at low-paying jobs, that's why we got to get our
own country. . . . I haven't changed concerning separatism because I
know that what was true ten years ago about racism against us and
the need to take back our land from the Anglo is still true today.

Christina is a twenty-seven-year-old (in 1986) worker in a clothing factory in
Albuquerque:

Separatism is the only answer for Chicanos if we want all our people
to share in the good life. There is a growing Chicano middle class,
but the majority of Chicanos are still poor or just low workers. And
the Chicano middle class just acts like Anglos, so you can't really say
that we as a people have improved our status because if you really
look at it, those of us who try to maintain our culture are poor and
those who are well off are not Chicanos anymore, they just be Anglos
with brown skin, if that. . . . I am still strongly for separatism because
my experience during the beginnings for the separatist movement
taught me why it was politically the right thing for Chicanos, and
everything since then has remained the same for Chicanos. . . . I still
think it's possible with constant work to be able to get a Chicano
country, and my readings about other movements like this have told
me that it just takes time. Like Israel, it took time for the Jews to get
an Israel too. . . . Well, if I were Anglo I would just give us the country and say don't bother me anymore. In our group [a political group
she is involved in] we have discussed how the Jews basically said that
to the British and got them to give them Palestine.

Philipe is a twenty-eight-year-old (in 1986) computer programmer for a large
company in Los Angeles:

Well, I know it might sound strange to you, but I am still a separatist
and in many ways even more supportive of it today than I was when
I started some eleven years ago. It's funny because I am middle class
now, so I have made it, but you know things have not really changed
for my parents or the rest of my family. You see a few people like me

make it not just because of hard work, but because we were lucky; and the rest are left behind. What I learned in the beginnings of the *movimiento* is that conditions are not going to get better for Chicanos as a whole unless they get their own country separate from Mexico and the United States. Unless that is done Anglos will always be willing to keep them poor and be racist against them; and of course let a few like myself make it.

THE IMPACT OF THE LOCAL POLITICAL ENVIRONMENT

At this juncture it is important to point out that "air of the times," "life-cycle," and "generation" are not the only factors, or even the most important, in influencing the respondents' attitudes toward Chicano nationalism. The factor which influenced all the respondents regardless of the impact of "air of the times," "life-cycle," or "generation" is the type of city they lived in. If we look at Table 9.3 we see that San Antonio had the smallest number of nationalists in general and only two who were political nationalists. In addition, over the ten-year period all but two respondents in San Antonio had abandoned any nationalist sentiments. Contrast this with Albuquerque or Los Angeles, where there are both greater numbers of people identifying with nationalist sentiments and greater numbers of people distributed among the four types of nationalism described above.

This is not simply a coincidence. Both of these cities have the type of political culture, nurtured by their particular local economies and social demographics, which stimulates and tolerates a wide variety of political beliefs, including a variety of nationalist beliefs. In San Antonio, on the other hand, the political culture, nurtured by its unique local economy and social demographics, has not been tolerant of any ideologies that challenge the status quo.[21] In fact, the administration of sanctions against those who would support deviant views such as Chicano nationalism is readily believed by the vast majority of Chicanos who live there.[22] Thus, in Albuquerque and Los Angeles one observes all three factors ("air of the times," "life-cycle," and "generation") influencing people's views toward nationalism, while in San Antonio one would only observe the "air of the times" and "life-cycle" effects. This is because "generation" effects tend to influence people to maintain their support for nationalism, and in San Antonio the political culture was so conservative in 1976 that there were few supporters of nationalism to begin with; hence the effect that one's "generation" might otherwise have had has been circumvented by the conservative political culture in the city.[23]

The notion that San Antonio was more conservative than Albuquerque and Los Angeles may seem odd given the fact that La Raza Unida Party was

founded in Texas by a number of individuals who went to college in San Antonio. Yet it should not be seen as odd or contradictory for the following reasons. First, the fact that La Raza Unida Party started in San Antonio is simply
a function of the fact that the greatest concentration of Chicano intellectual
elites were living there at the time. Thus, like other places where there are
such elite concentrations, new radical ideas will always be generated. Yet, there
is a large gap between the ideas that emerge out of the academy and those res-
onating from the general society. Likewise, there is usually a rather large gap
between what the general public is willing to support in the way of political
ideologies and what those in the academy are willing to support, and this is
particularly the case when it comes to radical political ideologies. The Raza
Unida Party that began in Crystal City, Texas, was radical in its focus on mobilizing Chicanos to advance their specific interests, but a careful look at the
issues that it began with (e.g., education) demonstrates that the focus was
more oriented toward civil rights and equal opportunity than a profound
change in the structure of the economy or government. In fact, as the Raza
Unida Party spread to other states like New Mexico, Colorado, and California, the focus of the organizations in those states became more radical. In those
states, the Party's ideology became more separatist oriented, taking on a rhetoric similar to that found in Québec, Canada.

This schism in the ideological orientation of the party's elite was brought
to a head in La Raza Unida's 1972 national convention in El Paso. At this convention, the Texas delegation, headed by founder José Angel Gutiérrez, pushed
the party to adopt a platform that was more "third party oriented." That is to
say, it wanted the party to organize around the interests of Chicanos but to
present itself as being a part of the U.S. political system, whereas the delegates
from New Mexico and Colorado, headed by Rodolfo Corky González, were
stressing that the party should adopt a more openly radical position of wanting to politically separate from the United States and form a new country. At
this conference, Gutiérrez won both the leadership and the struggle over the
political orientation of the party, but the battle had been so intense that the
party was not able to create the necessary consensus around a platform, nor
the solidarity it would need to continue to be an effective social movement.

This brief and cursory history of the internal ideological orientations in
the Raza Unida Party is offered simply to highlight that even within a political
organization that was considered radical, the Chicano political elite of Texas
adopted a more conservative position because it understood the restraints and
punitive sanctions of the Anglo political culture in which it and its natural
constituents would have to operate.

Likewise, the establishment of the Southwest Voters Registration Project
by Willie Velásquez, one of the founders of the Raza Unida itself, after that

organization's demise, is another example of an effort to mobilize Chicanos to be active in securing their political interests within a "civil rights orientation." That is to say, within Texas there remains a strong tendency to deemphasize Chicano nationalism (especially political nationalism) and to stress political activities that can be associated within the broader, established orientation of American politics. This strategy among Chicano political elites has been consistent over the years, because in Texas there is a political culture, developed and sustained by the Anglo population, that is intolerant of any beliefs or movements that would threaten the status quo. In Los Angeles and Albuquerque, on the other hand, the political cultures are more diffuse, and as a result more tolerant. Yet, while such "tolerant political cultures" are able to accommodate radical political beliefs and movements more easily, they do not create political environments that are capable of sustaining such beliefs and movements because there are too many competing ideologies.

The fundamental point here is that each of the three factors (generation, life-cycle, and "air of the time") that were found to influence a person's identification with any of the subtypes of nationalism described above are themselves influenced by the political culture of the city in which they are operative.

VIEWS OF NATIONALISM AND PARTY IDENTIFICATION

I now turn our consideration to the question of what, if any, relationship exists between one's decision to abandon or remain supportive of a particular subtype of nationalism and one's identification with a particular political party. As Table 9.4 indicates, among those cultural nationalists who viewed nationalism in "self-identity" terms, the Democratic Party was their overwhelming choice, and this was the case irrespective of whether they had abandoned their support of nationalism or not. Most said that in 1976 they had been supporters of the Raza Unida Party, but since the demise of that party and their abandonment of nationalism, they had identified with the Democratic Party.[24] They said they supported the Democrats because they believed that the Democrats had attempted to: (1) support certain social programs that were sensitive to Latin culture (such as bilingual education); (2) they were instrumental in developing legislation prohibiting racial/ethnic discrimination (the various civil rights bills); and (3) they had developed and supported socioeconomic programs that would aid those minority members who were unemployed. In essence, the Democratic Party was the closest to their present ideological position because it had a record of having supported programs designed to help Chicanos overcome racial or ethnic discrimination.

The comments of Homer are representative of the attitudes of those from

Table 9.4. Views of Nationalism and Party Identification in 1986[a]
(Raw Number Identifying with Each Political Party)

	Democrats	Republicans	Chicano[d] Nationalist Party	Socialist[e]
Cultural				
Self-Identity Nationalists				
Maintained[b]	1			
Abandoned[c]	18			
Self-Interest Nationalist				
Maintained	2	1		
Abandoned		14		
Political				
Civil Rights Nationalists				
Maintained	13	2		
Abandoned	1	6		
Separatist Nationalist				
Maintained			27	5
Abandoned	1			

Notes:

a. Question read: "What political party do you support? Democrat Party; Republican Party; Raza Unida or some other Chicano Nationalist Party; Socialist Workers Party or some other Socialist Party; or no party at all?"

b. Those people who continued to identify with each type of nationalism between '76 and '86 waves. For a discussion of how each nationalism was assigned, see note in Table 9.3.

c. Those people who stopped identifying with each type of nationalism between '76 and '86 waves.

d. The respondents could choose either the Raza Unida Party or any other nationalist party that was organized. They could also choose to identify with a nationalist party that was not yet organized.

e. The respondents could choose either the Socialist Workers Party or any other socialist party. Socialist Workers Party was offered because it was most often mentioned in the two previous panels.

this group. Homer is a twenty-seven-year-old (in 1986) clerk for the local government in San Antonio who responded:

> Well, I never was one of those people who was a nationalist that wanted a separate Chicano country. I was a nationalist because I thought it was important for Chicanos to have a more positive attitude about themselves, and nationalism did do that . . . yes, I supported Raza Unida Party, everybody who was a nationalist did

because the party did give people a lot of pride in being Chicano, and they fought Anglo discrimination against Chicanos. But then it got into financial trouble and just disintegrated, and by that time I wasn't into nationalism anymore because I wasn't for separatism, and I did have pride in Chicano culture, so I stopped identifying with Raza Unida and started to be a Democrat. . . . Well, I was a Democrat because I wasn't a nationalist anymore; Raza Unida was dead and the Democrats supported a lot of programs that Raza Unida also supported, like bilingualism and programs to help the poor and unemployed and antidiscrimination laws. So for me the Democrats just took up where Raza Unida had left off.

On the other hand, those cultural nationalists who viewed nationalism along "self-interest" lines were likely to identify with the Republican Party. Lisa, a twenty-seven-year-old (in 1986) assistant manager of a bank in Los Angeles, said:

When I was in high school I identified with the Raza Unida Party because everybody in my high school was excited about Chicano nationalism then and the Raza Unida Party was a Chicano party . . . but as I got older and realized that nationalism was not going to help anybody, I left both Chicano nationalism and the Raza Unida behind. . . . Now I am a Republican [because] after dropping any attachment I had for Raza Unida, I didn't want to support the Democrats because I didn't think they really help Chicanos, they just get them to be happy with welfare. But the Republicans had policies that help people help themselves. I helped myself, and other Chicanos should do the same. I think the Republicans help you to do that and I support them.

Among the political nationalists who remained supportive of the "electoral empowerment/civil rights" type of nationalism, the Democratic Party was most often identified with. This is because the Democratic Party was viewed as having the best record of supporting the "civil rights" of minorities in the United States. Thus, with the demise of the Raza Unida Party, which all of these nationalists had enthusiastically supported in 1976, they turned to the Democratic Party as their only alternative.

However, for those who had abandoned their support of "electoral empowerment/civil rights" nationalism, the party most often identified with was the Republican Party. The reason for this is that most of the people who abandoned their support of "electoral empowerment/civil rights" oriented nationalism did so because they felt that the whole effort had been successful and there was no more need to work for civil rights or getting Chicanos elected to public office. It was their position that they could now follow their own personal interests (as opposed to the group's), and since most were of the middle class, they viewed their interests as being represented by the Republican Party. Rueben is a twenty-eight-year-old middle-level manager in a business in Albuquerque:

> Back ten years ago I supported nationalism because it was necessary in order for Chicanos to get their rightful opportunities to improve their economic position in life. I felt it was very important to pressure the government to see to it that Chicanos were not discriminated against, that their civil rights were protected, and so I supported the Raza Unida Party because they were the most active in pressing for civil rights for Chicanos. But after a while, we had become successful in guaranteeing that our civil rights would be protected, and so it was time to do something with these rights. After the Raza Unida died, I supported the Republican Party because the Democrats were still stressing civil rights for minorities and we didn't need that anymore, and the Republicans were helping business and I was now involved in that.

When we turn to those individuals who had supported political nationalism along separatist lines, the data indicate that in 1986 nearly all remained supportive of a party like Raza Unida, and some were supportive of the Socialist Workers Party as well. This pattern emerges as a result of the fact that for those who remain committed to separatist ideology, few options exist. Only the defunct Raza Unida Party and the Socialist Workers Party had been at all sympathetic to a separate Chicano country. Thus, among those individuals who remained committed to separatist ideology, 84 percent (27) said they either identified with the old Raza Unida Party or with some new Chicano nationalist party that they hoped would be formed. Daniel is a twenty-seven-year-old (in 1986) janitor for a warehouse company in Los Angeles who said:

> I used to be a strong supporter of Raza Unida, but it stopped being active in elections, so I had really no party that I could support. To this day there isn't any party for those like me who want a Chicano country; all we can do is try to start another separatist party ourselves, like the Québec French did.

The other separatists identified with the Socialist Workers Party because they said that the party had supported Chicano nationalism as part of their effort to assist movements of national/ethnic self-determination. Teresa, a twenty-eight-year-old worker (in 1986) in a garment factory in Los Angeles, responded:

Yes, I now support the SWP [Socialist Workers Party] because Raza Unida folded and there is no other except SWP that has had a long record of supporting the national liberation of oppressed minorities. Plus they have a plan that incorporates the struggle of people like us to get our own country, to assert our right to national self-determination.

In sum, the big change among nationalists had to do with the lessening of identification with the Raza Unida Party and the rise in support for the Democratic and Republican parties. Part of the reason was due to the collapse of the Raza Unida Party, which left nationalists no alternatives, and part was due to the fact that many of those nationalists who were against the U.S. political system in 1976 were now integrating themselves back into it.

POLITICAL PARTICIPATION AND NATIONALIST VIEWS

We end our analysis of the decline of nationalism among Chicanos by addressing the issue of how either the maintenance or abandonment of nationalist ideology has influenced the mode of participation among those who had identified themselves as nationalists in 1976. Table 9.5 indicates the relationship between nationalist identification and the number of times the individual participated in one of these modes of political participation. As one can see, among those people who continued to identify themselves as nationalists, there is a preference for working in a political organization and being involved in direct-action politics. This preference is based on their belief that the only way to effect the type of political change they want is to both get the Chicano community mobilized and have them involved in various forms of pressure politics like strikes, boycotts, and protests. Thus they are active at the local level, focusing in on issues that directly affect the local Chicano residents.

What the nationalists avoid participating in are those types of politics that would work to reify the existing political system, such as contacting political officials or working in the political campaigns of politicians who represent the traditional Democratic or Republican parties. There was some support among the Chicano nationalists in Albuquerque toward voting, but for the most part nationalists refuse to vote, feeling that they do not have a party that represents their interests and that the act of voting is a symbolic act indicating some level of systemic acceptance, which they of course do not accept. The reason that there is some support for voting among the Albuquerque nationalists and not those from Los Angeles is because in Albuquerque there is a larger number of "electoral empowerment/civil rights" oriented nationalists who do not in prin-

Table 9.5. ETA Correlations of Nationalist Identification
and Political Participation

	Voting	Working for Political Organization	Contacting Public Officials	Direct Action
San Antonio				
Nationalism	.07	—	—	—
Albuquerque				
Nationalism	.13*	.32*	.05	.28
Los Angeles				
Nationalism	.04	.35*	.07	.31*

N = 85
*P < .05

ciple reject the American political system, whereas in Los Angeles all the nationalists are "separatist" oriented, and they do reject the U.S. political system.

On the other hand, those people who had been nationalists in 1976 and abandoned their support for that ideology by 1986 had been quite active in those traditional modes of political participation which symbolized the fulfillment of one's civic responsibility.[25] This included, primarily, voting and contacting public officials to articulate their political interests.[26] Basically, they were engaged in those forms of political activity that acted to integrate them into the political system.

Interestingly, while ex-nationalists were found to be active in the political system, those people who had remained committed to nationalism were also active in politics. They had not gone into political isolation as some might have predicted. Rather, they had focused their attention on local Chicano issues and worked to build a base of support among the grassroots of the barrios. The comments of Pedro, a twenty-seven-year old (in 1986) roofer, are indicative of those who remained committed to nationalism in Los Angeles:

Well, I don't work for the Democratic or Republican parties because that's just telling everybody that the system is O.K., but I still do a lot of work in the *barrio*. There is a group of us who help the community get the services they need from the hospitals. We also help people get loans for home improvements, and we got a number of people who will go to people's houses and fix things for them. We're still active in getting people to help themselves and not depend on the government, so we can tell them to go to hell. . . . Yeah, a lot of people think we're all [nationalists] dead because we don't have the demonstrations that we used to have, but they're wrong. We just hanging in there building a community base very slowly. We'll be just like termites: you don't hear from us, but then all of a sudden the house falls in.

CONCLUSION

I began this chapter with the question: where have all the nationalists gone? The present study found that the largest number of those who once supported nationalism had abandoned it and, for the most part, supported the U.S. political system. However, it was also found that there was a smaller, but significant, number of people who had maintained and/or strengthened their support of Chicano nationalism. Having established this, I sought to determine what factors influenced these individuals to either relinquish or maintain their support of Chicano nationalism. In this pursuit I was guided by the work of Daniel Latouche, who found in his study of Québec nationalism that maintenance or withdrawal from nationalism was related to three factors: (1) the effects of "air of the times", (2) the "life-cycle" effects, and (3) the effects of one's "generation." I found that the three factors identified by Latouche for Québec nationalists did in fact have an impact on the decline and maintenance of support for nationalism among Chicanos, but they did so in association with two other factors.

The main argument of this paper is that whether a person decided to abandon nationalism or not was influenced by how he/she conceptually perceived Chicano nationalism in 1976, when nationalism was still an important ideology within the Chicano community. Two relatively broad types of nationalist orientation, with two subtypes within them, were found to be present among those who identified themselves as nationalists in 1976. Those who perceived nationalism within a cultural nationalist framework were inclined to abandon nationalism by 1986, while those who were political nationalists were inclined to maintain and/or strengthen their commitment to it over the ten-year period. Thus, how one originally perceived nationalism had an important impact on whether he or she would maintain it. However, an important factor influencing how a person would conceptualize it had to do with the type of city which the individuals lived in. Those who lived in the politically conservative city of San Antonio generally viewed nationalism in its most benign form (the cultural nationalism of "self-identity" or "self-interest"). Those who lived in the cities of Albuquerque and Los Angeles, with their more liberal and tolerant political cultures, were more inclined to view separatism in its more radical forms (the political nationalism of "electoral empowerment/civil rights" or "separatism"). In essence, the political culture of the city was instrumental in influencing people's perceptions of politics in general and nationalism in particular.

Most importantly, the type of city which influenced the individual's particular view of nationalism also established the environment in which the effects of "air of the times," "life-cycle," and "generation" would have their impact on whether or not an individual maintained his or her nationalist ideology. Those who viewed nationalism in cultural terms were influenced most by the "air of the times" and the "life-cycle" effects, whereas those who identified nationalism in political terms were influenced by both the "air of the times" and "generation" effects.

Let us return to a point I made in the beginning of the chapter concerning recent developments in nationalism in Québec. The 1995 referendum in which the Québec public was asked whether the provincial government should seek to formally separate from Canada indicated that there had been an enormous rise in nationalist support. Given that the referendum was defeated by a mere 1 percent of the vote, cross-generational support for separatism was obvious. How is this explained by the Latouche concepts, and what, if any, are the lessons for the Chicano case discussed here?

First, nationalism, whether it is cultural or political in orientation, is a concept that is deeply tied to an individual's identity, emotions, and socioeconomic condition. As such, unless it is completely extinguished from the individual's worldview, conditions can reappear that reignite nationalist passions. Even those individuals who had seized the ideology as a result of "air of the times" or "life-cycle" effects can be stimulated to support it again, but two situations will need to develop in order for this to occur. Socioeconomic conditions will need to worsen for those who had been nationalists in the past. If this occurs, there will be the tendency on the part of those affected to draw on ethnicity as a political resource to improve and advance their material interests. This was clearly the case in Québec, where even though the socioeconomic situation of the *Québecois* had improved over the years, a significant number of Francophones had been experiencing difficulty in maintaining their desired (subjective) standard of living, creating a sense of status inequality between Francophones and Anglophones. In fact, the Parti Québecois characterized the failure of the Anglophone political leadership to ratify a plan to give Québec special status within the Canadian Constitution at the Meech Lake Summit as evidence of Anglophone resistance to rectify in good faith the structural socioeconomic inequality that was historically instituted by the Anglophone elite and that had so harmed Francophones over the generations. As the close vote on the most recent separatist referendum indicates, this line

of argument resonated with a very large number of the Québec population because it rekindled in the older generation feelings of cultural deprivation and
ignited in the younger generation feelings that they would have a better opportunity to realize their material goals only when the structural impediments
associated with the formal arrangements of Canada could no longer be a factor.

Likewise for Chicanos, situations could arise in which nationalism would
be reignited across generations. For example, if socioeconomic conditions for
significant numbers of the Chicano working and middle class worsen, nationalism among the young and old might be reinvigorated. For the younger generation, the issues will be the disparity between their rising hopes and desires
on the one hand and their increasingly pessimistic expectations that these
hopes and desires can be obtained in the structural arrangements that they
perceive to be biased against people of Mexican origin on the other. For people
who had been nationalists in the past (i.e., the older generation) and found
that the life chances of their children were significantly diminished because
of prejudice against people of Mexican origin, there could (and most likely
would) be a rekindling of support for nationalism. These factors were no doubt
present among the Francophone population in Québec and help to explain
the rise in cross-generation support for the Parti Québecois's 1995 "separatism
referendum."

The second condition necessary for a resurgence of nationalist support
among those who have given up their support of it has to do with the building of an effective social movement. In order for an effective social movement
among Chicanos, or any ethnic group, to arise, there must be political leadership willing to invest time and resources in using nationalist arguments and
symbols in the formal political arena. This condition is best seen in the cases
of Chicano and Québec nationalism. Chicano nationalism was at its strongest
during a time when the Partido La Raza Unida was actively competing in the
formal arena.[27] Although the party was not united in the separatist question,
it was thoroughly nationalist. When it died as a political party, the fire within
Chicano nationalism slowly faded. However, in Québec even when the fire of
separatism had dimmed, the Parti Québecois had remained an active party
within Québec politics. Thus, there remained for the *Québecois* an official or-
gan to represent their nationalist feelings whenever the time seemed appropriate to them.[28]

In conclusion, let me again return to the question I began with: where
have all the nationalists gone? The answer to this question is that while it is
true that many of those who had been nationalists in 1976 have changed and
now support another ideology, it is equally true that nationalism is not dead
in the Chicano community. There still are individuals who remain committed to it, including separatism, its most radical form. They may not believe

that it is possible to realize a separate Chicano nation, but they remain committed to that vision.

This sentiment was captured in an in-depth interview with Jesús, a twenty-eight-year-old (in 1986) truck driver in Los Angeles, when he said, "you know what the Jews used to say before they had Israel, 'next year in Jerusalem'; well, my friends and me think 'next year in a free Aztlán!'" Nationalism's fire has not totally burned out; embers ever so few and ever so low remain waiting for the wind to blow. If socioeconomic mobility becomes stagnant for Chicanos and the inequality gap between them and Anglos widens, or if anti-Mexican immigrant sentiment and actions continue to grow such that they severely impact Chicanos, or if the number of Chicanos incarcerated reaches epidemic proportions, the winds of discontent will increase, and like the mythical phoenix, Chicano nationalism is likely to rise from the depths of Chicano society and reassert itself as a challenging force within American politics.

NOTES

1. See Claybourne Carson, *In Struggle: SNCC and the Black Awakening* (Cambridge, Mass.: Harvard University Press, 1981); and Doug McAdam, *Political Process and the Development of Black Insurgency, 1930–1986* (Austin: University of Texas Press, 1982).

2. Juan Gómez-Quiñones, *Chicano Politics* (Albuquerque: University of New Mexico Press, 1990); Carlos Muñoz, Jr., *Youth, Identity and Power: The Chicano Movement* (London: Verso, 1989); Stan Steiner, *La Raza: The Mexican Americans* (New York: Random House, 1969).

3. Rodolfo Acuña, *Occupied America: A History of Chicanos* (New York: Harper & Row, 1981); David Montejano, *Anglos and Mexicans in the Making of Texas, 1836–1986* (Austin: University of Texas Press, 1987).

4. Harold Isaacs, *Idols of the Tribe: Group Identity and Political Change* (New York: Harper & Row, 1975); Leonard Doob, *Patriotism and Nationalism: Their Psychological Foundation* (New York: Harper & Row, 1964); Karl Deutsch, *Nationalism and Social Communication* (Cambridge: M.I.T. Press, 1966).

5. Daniel Latouche, "Jeunesse et Nationalisme au Québec: Une Ideologie Peut-Ille Mourir," [Youth and Nationalism in Quebec: Can an Ideology Die?] *Revue Francaise de Science Politique* 35 (1985): 240–244.

6. While for Chicanos the period of *el movimiento* was one of critical significance, in the case of Québec it was either the period of "le revolution tranquille" (the quiet revolution) in which the Québecois began to assert their self-identity as Francophones and their interests in politics and economics; or the period of national independence, in which significant segments of Québec society pushed for a separate country. For a general discussion of these periods see Marcel Rioux, *Quebec in Question* (Toronto: James, Lewis, and Samuel, 1971).

7. A more detailed description of the data-gathering procedure used for this survey can be found in Martín Sánchez Jankowski, *City Bound: Urban Life and Political Attitudes Among Chicano Youth* (Albuquerque: University of New Mexico Press, 1986), pp. 237–240.

8. Most studies, like Isaacs's *Idols of the Tribe* and Anthony Smith's *The Ethnic Revival in the Modern World* (Cambridge: Cambridge University Press, 1979) that have dealt with nationalism proceed on an assumption that all those who support this nationalism conceptualize it in the

same way; or they simply do not think it matters that there are a number of conceptions of the ideology within the movement they are analyzing because the process they are studying is the same.

9. See Martín Sánchez Jankowski, "Change and Stability in Political Attitudes among Chicanos: A Panel Study, 1976–1986," paper presented at Western Political Science Association, San Francisco, 1988.

10. All the names used are pseudonyms that have been substituted for the respondents' real names. The other information about the individuals quoted in this paper is accurate.

11. See Martin Kilson, "Blacks and Neo-Ethnicity in American Political Life," in Nathan Glazer and Daniel Patrick Moynihan, eds., *Ethnicity: Theory and Experience* (Cambridge, Mass.: Harvard University Press, 1975).

12. Antonio De Leon, *They Called Them Greasers: Anglo Attitudes Toward Mexicans in Texas, 1821–1900* (Austin: University of Texas Press, 1975).

13. Much of the literature concerning school achievement has found "positive self-image" as the variable with the most impact. In fact, much of the argument in overturning "separate but equal schools" in *Brown v. The Board of Education of Topeka* was based on the precept that separate schools affected a young person's self-image, which in turn affected the student's ability and willingness to learn. See T. Lucas, R. Henze, and R. Donato, "Promoting the Success of Latino Language-Minority Students: An Exploratory Study of Six High Schools," *Harvard Educational Review* 60 (1990): 315–340. The work of Elliot Liebow in *Tally's Corner: A Study of Negro Streetcorner Men* (Boston: Little, Brown, 1967) is an attempt to expose the negative parts of low self-esteem.

14. This view of nationalism made the ideology a tool to be used to extract a desired socioeconomic goal from those with the power or authority to provide it. Those who would use nationalism in this way assumed a posture that Tom Wolfe described as "mau mauing the flak catchers." In brief, nationalism was used as a form of political pressure. See Tom Wolfe, *Radical Chic and Mau Mauing the Flak Catchers* (Toronto: Collins, 1970).

15. See Orlando Patterson, *Ethnic Chauvinism: The Reactionary Impulse* (Cambridge, Mass.: Harvard University Press, 1978).

16. R. Shingles, "Black Consciousness and Political Participation: The Missing Link," *American Political Science Review* 1 (1980): 76–91; Rufus T. Browning, Dale R. Marshall, and David H. Tabb, *Protest Is Not Enough: The Struggle of Blacks and Hispanics for Equality in Urban Politics* (Berkeley: University of California Press, 1984); McAdam, *Political Process*.

17. J. Shockley, *Chicano Revolt in a Texas Town* (South Bend, Ind.: University of Notre Dame Press, 1974).

18. See Anthony Smith, "Toward a Theory of Ethnic Separatism," *Ethnic and Racial Studies* 2, no. 1: 21–38; and his *The Ethnic Revival in the Modern World*.

19. This is similar to the differences one finds between the Black nationalists on the one hand, and those Black politicians and civil rights activists on the other. See R. Hall, *Black Separatism in the United States* (Hanover, N.H.: University Press of New England, 1978).

20. For the definitive studies on "generation" effects, see Glen Elder, *Children of the Great Depression* (Chicago: University of Chicago Press, 1974); John Clausen, *American Lives* (Berkeley: University of California Press, 1993); and Doug McAdam, *Freedom Summer* (New York: Oxford University Press, 1988).

21. See Jankowski, *City Bound*, pp. 77–122.

22. See Jankowski, *City Bound*, pp. 80–122; and "Change and Stability in Political Attitudes among Chicanos."

23. The conservative nature of politics in San Antonio, as well as Chicanos' own conservative response to this particular political culture, is not only supported by the attitudes displayed in *City Bound*, but also, ironically, in the conservative analysis of Mexican American politics presented by Peter Skerry in his *Mexican Americans: The Ambivalent Minority* (New York: Free Press, 1993), pp 23–58.

24. See Armando Navarro, "The Evolution of Chicano Politics," *Aztlán: International Journal of Chicano Studies and Research* 5 (Spring and Fall 1974): 57–84; and Ignacio García, *United We Win: The Rise and Fall of La Raza Unida Party* (Tucson: University of Arizona Press, 1988).

25. See Gabriel Almond and Sidney Verba, *The Civic Culture* (Boston: Little & Brown, 1965).

26. See Nelson Polsby, *Community Power and Political Theory* (New Haven: Yale University Press, 1980).

27. See García, *United We Win*.

28. See Maurice Pinard, "The Dramatic Reemergence of the Quebec Independence Movement," *Journal of International Affairs* 45, no. 2 (Winter 1992): 471–497.

Conclusion

ON THE FUTURE OF ANGLO-MEXICAN RELATIONS IN THE UNITED STATES

DAVID MONTEJANO

I n this essay I speculate on the nature of Anglo-Mexican relations in the twenty-first century, with an emphasis on the southwestern United States. My speculations are based primarily on a consideration of domestic U.S. economics and politics. Although I do not consider events or conditions within Mexico that could affect these relations, it will become clear that the questions of Mexican political stability and economic development, especially as these affect emigration to the United States, figure critically in any future scenario.

The current situation of Mexican Americans can be described in contradictory ways. On the one hand, from a historical perspective, one must recognize a form of political inclusion, in the sense that most structural obstacles, such as the poll tax, at-large elections, and gerrymandered districts, have been removed. One must recognize that Mexican Americans have been granted effective citizenship and that this marks a departure from historical experience. At the state legislative level, Mexican American elected officials today represent significant subregions of the Southwest, an unthinkable proposition in the 1950s and 1960s when the Mexican American electorate was routinely described as "a sleeping giant." In the past twenty-five years, Mexican Americans have become important players in California and Texas politics, and thus in national politics. Their strategic prominence becomes especially visible in any U.S. policy discussion concerning Mexico, as demonstrated in the recent debate over the North American Free Trade Agreement (NAFTA).[1]

On the other hand, it is clear that such political inclusion has not been a paneacea, a general solution, to the economic problems of most Mexican

Americans. In fact, a controversial question in the current public policy literature concerns whether or not a significant "underclass" exists among Mexican Americans.[2] Against the backdrop of political inclusion stands the contrasting evidence of persistent and isolated poverty. In 1990 one of every four Mexican American families lived in poverty. Residential and school segregation of Mexican Americans has actually increased in most cities during the past two decades. Likewise, while the number of Mexican Americans twenty-five years and older completing college has remained "frozen" at the 5 – 6 percent level since 1975, the number failing to complete high school has increased several points, to 56.4 percent.

The evidence suggests that the Mexican American community has been split into a socially incorporated middle class and a socially segregated lower class. The excluded sector is not limited to first- or second-generation immigrants. One source estimates that perhaps 40 percent of third-generation-plus Mexican Americans may comprise something like a Chicano underclass.[3] Political inclusion, in other words, has not signified the "economic assimilation" or any other kind of assimilation of the Mexican American community. What is clear is that inclusion has been quite partial.

Nor does the notion of "inclusion" imply a static condition. Indeed, such a state of affairs is characterized by a constant struggle between exclusion and inclusion. As in previous periods of change and anxiety, in the 1990s there exists a growing literature that speaks about a "Mexican problem," a literature that blames Mexican "immigrants" for every misfortune possible, from the "undoing" of America to crime and traffic jams. These views may sound like hyperbole, but they circulate plainly in both popular and scholarly circles.[4] Bluntly put, the present limited degree of inclusion may be less permanent than it appears. As I have argued elsewhere, the current integrative climate is "not an unchanging condition," for "social forces can move a society in several different directions."[5] I wish to expand on these observations and explore the various possible futures we may face and make.

In the following, I assume that one possible future is that the present-day inclusion, with all its contradictions and unevenness, might continue. As historian Paul Kennedy has aptly put it, we might "muddle through" the twenty-first century.[6] Since I am more concerned with demonstrating the possibility of alternative scenarios—that inclusion might fall apart due to pressing new circumstances—my discussion will center around the factors that might lead to exclusionary policies and practices. This kind of pessimistic speculation will serve to emphasize that even the present state of partial inclusion is based on a continuing struggle to protect gains and increase opportunities.

In short, I aim to provide an "ideal type" sketch of an exclusionary trajectory. The notion of "trajectory" emphasizes the presence of competing forces or pressures that shape or move a society in a certain direction. The methodology for such speculation about the future is provided by the forecasting methods of economics and demography and mediated by the hindsight of history. Forecasting while keeping a sharp memory will suggest the contours of possible futures.[7]

The following discussion focuses on three complexes of contingent factors that may jeopardize the limited and modest advances of Mexican Americans over the last thirty years. The first has to do with the changing global economy, that is, with the projection that, by many accounts, the United States today is in a period of relative economic decline. What impact might such a decline have on ethnic-race relations in the United States, and specifically in the Southwest? The question of U.S.-Mexico economic relations figures critically in this regard.

The second complex of contingent elements that must be discussed are the demographic projections that envision a "browning" or "Latinization" of the United States; more specifically, that within the span of a generation the Mexican-origin population will form a plurality, if not a majority, of the population of the southwestern United States. The most recent awareness of this growing "Latin American" presence has generated much concern and even fear in some quarters of U.S. society, especially over the question of immigration.

The third complex of contingent elements I consider is the intervening process of politics, which basically interpets and articulates responses to changing conditions. While any number of responses or "racial projects" may be entertained in the political arena, the policies envisioned by the traditional political parties are the most critical. Political parties are responsible for generating public support for race relations policies that may be either inclusionary or exclusionary. The electoral arena determines the direction for such policies.

One possible outcome of the interplay of these three complexes of factors is an exclusionary trajectory of social relations (see Figure 10.1). The rise of nativism and scapegoating is a likely political response to the convergence of economic decline and a "browning" demographic pattern. Given sufficient popular support, politicians in a competitive electoral arena will propose measures that restrict or reverse the perceived "unfair advantages" of a distinct population. In the case of Mexicans and Mexican Americans, as we will see shortly, such proposals range from the closing of the U.S.-Mexico border to removing them from the protection of the Voting Rights Act.[8]

Before describing a negative scenario for the future of ethnic/race relations in the Southwest, I will sketch in very brief strokes the recent history of inclusion. This will clarify what I mean by the "politics of inclusion."

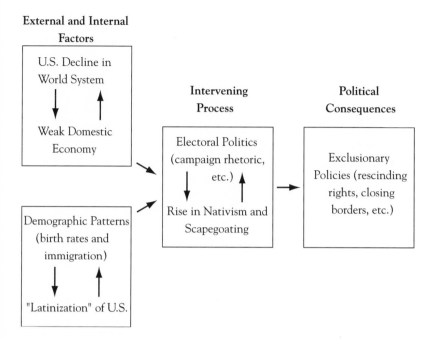

External and Internal Factors

U.S. Decline in World System

↓ ↑

Weak Domestic Economy

Demographic Patterns (birth rates and immigration)

↓ ↑

"Latinization" of U.S.

Intervening Process

Electoral Politics (campaign rhetoric, etc.)

↓ ↑

Rise in Nativism and Scapegoating

Political Consequences

Exclusionary Policies (rescinding rights, closing borders, etc.)

Figure 10.1. A Hypothetical Exclusionary Trajectory

A MATERIAL BASE OF INCLUSION

The current "politics of inclusion" were not just the result of an "awakening" or social protest, although the civil rights movements of the 1950s and 1960s were clearly necessary.[9] As important were the class structural changes that weakened the foundation of Jim Crow segregation. Whether one speaks of African Americans or Mexican Americans, the structures of inequality they confronted were essentially the same, especially in the southern and southwestern sections of the country. At least through World War II, a dominant grower or planter elite maintained low-wage labor through a variety of labor and political controls.[10] Pervasive social segregation of the "races" was the social and cultural manifestation of such elite control. In this setting, any movement "from below" was generally defeated.

The context for successful protest politics was set by the class structural changes accompanying World War II.[11] The move toward integration was catalyzed by the great civil rights protests of the 1950s and 1960s, but its "success" was fundamentally the result of shifting class politics during the post–World War II economic boom. The context for Mexican-Anglo relations was transformed from that of a segregated order that bound Anglo growers and Mexican farmworkers through the mid twentieth century to a present-day inclusion based on an understanding between Anglo urban business elites and middle-class Mexican Americans. The understanding is based on a trade-off: the Anglo business elite desires political support for its development plans, while the Mexican American middle class desires political entry and economic opportunities.

In short, the current integrative situation essentially reflects an inter-ethnic alignment of key organizations from these class groups.[12] This alignment in some places is the result of explicit discussion and agreement; in other places, it merely represents uncoordinated parallel interests. Regardless of which, this represents a pro-development configuration that cuts across partisan and ethnic loyalties.

At one point in the late 1960s, I might note, there was a possibility for a different kind of inclusion based on a broad populist multicultural movement. The failure of the People's March (1972) because of mistrust, lack of knowledge about each community's struggle, identity politics, and perhaps poor leadership, highlighted the difficulties in creating a "rainbow coalition." By the mid 1970s, such efforts had largely dissipated. "Inclusion," in other words, could conceivably have issued from some broadly defined multiethnic middle- and working-class alliance. Instead, the direction beyond Jim Crow was influenced by an interesting alignment between white business elites and the emerging "minority" middle classes.[13]

Perhaps the best example of this present-day alignment between Anglo businessmen and middle-class Mexican Americans was the mayoral tenure of Henry Cisneros, the first San Antonio mayor of Mexican origin since Juan Seguín in the 1840s. The success of Cisneros as mayor in the 1980s did not come about simply because of a mobilized Mexican American electorate, although this was certainly a critical factor. An equally important factor lay in his understanding with the business community. Cisneros promised a "new attitude" toward economic development and expansion, one that would include his active solicitation of new industry. During his eight years as mayor (1981–1989), developers benefited greatly from Cisneros's popularity and the city government's willingness to accommodate their plans. Local voters approved eight bond issues totaling more than half a billion dollars and approved a special sales tax to generate another $180 million for a domed stadium. In turn, the business community supported, however reluctantly, Cisneros's public works programs (involving mainly flood control, sidewalks, and parks) in parts of town where they didn't have an interest. Moreover, citizen pressure groups like Communities Organized for Public Service (COPS), representing many of San Antonio's poor neighborhoods, were included in the city's decision-making process. Cisneros believed that such inclusion represented "the formula needed to build unity."[14] It remains to be seen how much actually "trickled down" from such pro-development policies to the impoverished Mexican American sections of San Antonio. But one clear benefactor has been the city's Mexican American business and professional class.

That in brief is my argument about the current condition and likely future of inclusion: that it is based on a pro-development understanding between an Anglo business elite and a Mexican American middle class. Such politics have long been evident in border cities (Laredo, El Paso, Nogales, for example) and in the state of New Mexico, where an accommodation between Anglo and Hispano elites has historically made for a more relaxed ethnic/race situation. Today these influences are evident in most Southwestern cities but can also be seen at the regional and national level if we analyze the support for the North American Free Trade Agreement (NAFTA), about which I shall say more later.

In the Southwest, then, inclusion is presently contingent on the strength of this political alignment between prominent Anglo and Mexican American class groups.

A GLOBAL FOCUS—THE UNITED STATES IN DECLINE?

Having described the present integrative climate in terms of its internal configuration, I can now ratchet the analysis up another notch and consider its external framing. The "integration" of the post–World War II period was also made possible in part because the United States was a rising world power. Indeed, this ascendancy as a world power, secured with victory in World War II, brought with it unparalleled wealth and political confidence that made Jim Crow social policies seem irrelevant and backward. The ideology of democracy, honed in the fight against Hitler and Aryan supremacy and further developed in the Cold War fight for non-aligned Third World nations, provided the cultural base for challenging race segregation. The national elites proved willing to abandon a Jim Crow system when pressured to do so. Meaningful change was embarrassingly slow, however, and was largely catalyzed by domestic protests and crises. Prosperity alone was an insufficient condition; a social movement was necessary to demonstrate the contradictions of American race policy.

In sum, the weakening of race segregation occurred in the context of the nation's rise as a world power. The converse, that race tensions and conflict increase during periods of decline, also appears to be an axiomatic thesis. This is the prospect I wish to address.

This question of a relative decline of the United States has been discussed so extensively that it has been dubbed the "declinist school." I will focus on one prominent work, the best-selling book *The Rise and Fall of the Great Powers*, by historian Paul Kennedy. Briefly stated, Kennedy argues that the United States today faces the dilemma of all great powers, that of preserving a reasonable balance between the nation's global defense requirements and its technological and economic bases of power. As Kennedy puts it, the United States runs the risk of "imperial overreach," a situation in which a strong military posture throughout the world provides for the emergence of new economic centers that in turn undermine the economic standing of their military protectors.[15] In the present pax americana, it is generally agreed that these emerging competitors are centered in Asia and Western Europe and particularly in the defeated nations of World War II, Japan and Germany.

In his book about the great powers, Kennedy has little to say about Mexico, except to note that if a major international debt crisis is to occur anywhere in the world, it will most likely begin in this region, with very serious consequences to the global credit system, and especially to American banks. Indeed, argues Kennedy, the Polish crisis of the USSR—the crisis that set off a chain of events that ultimately led to the collapse of the Warsaw Pact and of the Soviet Union itself—would "seem small by comparison" with a Mexican crisis: "There is simply no equivalent in the world for the present state of Mexican–United States relations. Mexico is on the verge of economic bankruptcy and default. Its internal economic crisis forces hundreds of thousands to drift illegally to the north each year. Its most profitable trade with the United States is becoming a brutally managed flow of hard drugs, and the border for all this sort of traffic is still extraordinarily permeable."[16]

Unfortunately, this single ominous paragraph contains all that Kennedy has to say about U.S.-Mexico relations, which are obviously critical for understanding the future of the Southwest. Kennedy, in fact, pays very little attention to American domestic politics in this book, but he does warn that high birth rates among American minorities, coupled with the loss of well-paying manufacturing jobs, make it "unwise to assume that the prevailing norms of the American political economy would be maintained if the nation entered a period of sustained economic difficulty."[17] In other words, the forthcoming decline will portend serious difficulties—difficulties of a racial nature—in preserving the U.S. political consensus.

In his sequel, *Preparing for the 21st Century*, Paul Kennedy is more explicit about the matter. Describing the implications of the "browning" of America, the result of differential birth rates and immigration, Kennedy points out, in a characteristically grim assessment, that "the mass migration at the moment is only the tip of an iceberg. We have to educate ourselves and our children to understand why there is going to be trouble."[18]

Critics of the declinist thesis have pointed to the demise of the Soviet Union, the end of the Cold War, and the quick Gulf War victory as powerful contrary evidence. The declinists have countered that the "New World Order" may be an attempt to reestablish the "American Century" on military terms just as American economic dominance is being lost.[19] Whatever the case, the election defeat of President George Bush, who at the time of the Gulf War was seen as infallible, by the economic-oriented campaign of Bill Clinton, demonstrated how short-lived the war-related euphoria was. The initial euphoria following the Persian Gulf War was dissipated by the anxiety of an American public concerned about an uncertain economic future. More relevant to our discussion, such anxiety has also stirred economic protectionist sentiments that threaten to worsen U.S.-Mexico relations over the questions of trade and immigration.

A SOUTHWESTERN FOCUS— A DISSOLVING CONSENSUS?

What, then, does such long-term decline mean for the Southwest and for the United States in general? In the American Southwest there exists an abundance of commentators who have painted very explicit scenarios, especially when the discussion shifts to birth rates and immigration. The public commentaries on Mexican immigration, many of which group Mexican Americans with recent immigrants, illustrates the ambiguous status of Mexican Americans as a "legitimate" citizenry in American society. The practice of the Border Patrol of targeting individuals on the basis of physical appearance underscores this ambiguity dramatically: in San Diego, one-third of the four hundred victims of serious Border Patrol beatings between 1988 and 1992 were U.S. citizens, and in El Paso a federal judge ruled (in 1992) that the Border Patrol was engaging in "excessive force" and "illegal and abusive conduct" against U.S. citizens of Mexican descent "solely because they look Latino."[20] In short, in the context of a "Mexican problem," physical appearance or "race" rather than citizenship easily becomes the salient criterion for public perception and policy.

National security reasons have long been used to support the practice of aggressive border control. In 1975, for example, Immigration Commissioner Leonard Chapman, former commandant of the Marine Corps, warned of "a vast and silent invasion of illegal aliens" numbering some twelve million. In 1978 former Central Intelligence Agency Director William Colby asserted that Mexico was a greater threat than the Soviet Union, with up to twenty million illegals in the country by the year 2000.[21] Likewise in 1983 Governor Bruce Babbitt of Arizona (now U.S. Secretary of the Interior) observed that "the Southwest is being Hispanicized," that "in the War of 1848, we annexed the Southwest and now the Mexicans are taking it back." According to Babbitt, the border has become more and more a juridical figment; it has dissolved in real terms. The Southwest today points to new realities: to problems of population pressure, to massive movements of peoples across uncontrolled borders, to the problems of birth control and cultural levels in education. In fact, warned syndicated columnist Georgie Anne Geyer, if these ominous problems are not dealt with rationally and creatively, we will have "our very own Lebanon right here."[22]

In 1985 another governor, Richard Lamm of Colorado, issued similar warnings in a more strident tone. Speaking of blacks and Hispanics, Governor Lamm argued that these two groups contribute to extraordinary crime, joblessness, and illiteracy rates. In his view, "We are heading for an America in which we will have two angry, under-utilized and under-educated, frustrated, resentful, jealous, and volatile minority groups existing unassimilated and unintegrated within our borders."[23] Given the failure of the American melting pot, Lamm urged that we regain control of our borders and our inner cities.

In the 1990s such political assessments about an American inability to assimilate Latino immigrants are commonplace. The "crowded lifeboat" has become the metaphor of choice for anti-immigrant pundits. In the arch-conservative *National Review*, an assessment of U.S. immigration policy argues that the "melting" dynamics of the past no longer apply: "Just because a danger has been averted in the past does not mean it cannot happen in the future. Many passengers might have climbed aboard the lifeboat safely; one more may still capsize it." Indeed, the assessment warns that "the American ethnic mix *has* been upset. In 1960, the U.S. population was 88.6 per cent white; in 1990, it was only 75.6 per cent white—a drop of 13 percentage points in thirty years."[24] The alarmist assessment concludes, with particular reference to Mexicans, that it may be time to announce that the United States is no longer an immigrant country.[25]

The social science literature describes a no less gloomy scenario. Demographers warn that the combination of "browning" with some "graying" may pose a "troublesome mismatch" for states like California over the next forty years, at which time half of all children are forecast to be Hispanic and whites will compose 60 percent of the elderly. The consequence will be that any fiscal crisis, brought about by the exhaustion of Social Security and health care funds, will have an ethnic/racial cast.[26]

This worst-case scenario may come to pass, according to David Hayes-Bautista, Werner Schink, and Jorge Chapa, *even if we assume no additional immigration*. Hayes-Bautista et al., in warning of the consequences of failing to invest in education, predict that by the year 2030, the U.S.-born Latino population in California, and generally in the Southwest, will nearly equal the Anglo population.[27] This, combined with a long-term failure to reinvest in education and create well-paying employment opportunities, will result in a new social division along generational ethnic lines; specifically, a situation in which a young, undereducated Latino population will find itself supporting a well-educated, retired Anglo generation.

In this future, according to Hayes-Bautista et al., the young Latino population begins to see its predicament as one of exploitation. Huge amounts of their paychecks are eaten up to fund Social Security and health care programs for the elderly. Yet, in spite of high payroll taxes, the young workers see little in the way of benefits returned to them. The school system is failing, and expenditures for roads, water systems, and public programs have dwindled to almost nothing. In time, incendiary literature calls on the younger generation to rebel, to refuse to pay taxes. Strikes break out in assembly plants, security walls are set afire and toppled, and the sale of guns soar in the elderly areas:

> The younger Latinos painted the elderly as parasites, who had enjoyed all the benefits of society when those benefits were free and now continued to tax the workers to maintain their style of living without a thought to the damage it was doing to them. The elderly painted the younger Latinos as parasites, as foreigners who were soaking up benefits that should go to the elderly, as non-Americans who were threatening to dilute American culture as crime-ridden, disease-ridden, and lawless people.[28]

Hayes-Bautista et al. conclude, "Civil revolt was only months away." Thus ends their grim "fin de siecle" vision, essentially a portrayal of a repressive society on the brink of anarchy.

The disturbing aspect of this pessimistic forecast is that many of its features—declining social services, increasing violence, a domestic arms race, frayed ethnic and racial tensions—are already present. In many ways, the Los Angeles riot of April 1992, when more than one-half of those arrested were Latino, appears to have been a preview of the worst scenario portrayed by Hayes-Bautista et al. One immediate consequence of the Los Angeles riot has been the rise of a nativist perception that Latinos, along with African Americans, represent an undesirable element.[29]

The alarmist public discussion of uncontrolled borders and uncontrolled streets clearly reflects the anxiety that surfaces every time the United States enters a period of economic difficulty. The contrast between recession-wrecked California and economically stable Texas is instructive in this regard. In 1990 the arch-conservative Federation for American Immigration Reform (FAIR), which has been lobbying Washington to restrict non-European immigration for nearly two decades, ran commercials on six Houston radio stations linking immigration to such problems as homelessness, drug smuggling, and traffic congestion. The radio commercials, aired as a test for a national campaign, were withdrawn because of public protests. But in depressed California, FAIR found an enthusiastic audience. Three-quarters of Californians, according to a 1992 Roper poll conducted for FAIR, believe that the state has too many immigrants, that they are a financial burden, and that steps should be taken now to limit the population.[30] Leaders from both Republican and Democratic political parties now regularly cite FAIR literature and use FAIR proposals as a basis for their own.

In short, the English-only movement, the anti-immigration campaign, the anti–civil rights sentiment, the reaction to multiculturalism, and so on, all manifest a conservative "lifeboat" reflex to the changing demographics of the United States, and of the Southwest in particular. These views, however strident or exaggerated, should not be discounted, for they suggest a definite political response that gains support in a climate of economic crisis and uncertainty.[31] These groups lack only a legitimizing moment, that time when one of the two major political parties embraces their cause as an element of a campaign platform.

PARTY POLITICS AND RACE

According to the classic work of V. O. Key, Jr., on Southern politics, nativism and racial demagoguery were supposed to fade in importance in the context of an effective two-party system.[32] Key's argument held that the Democratic southern elite was able to maintain political control and to redirect economic class tension among whites through the use of the race issue. This elite generally ruled through a "one-party" Democratic structure, which essentially provided the groundwork for the "politics of disorganization." "One-partyism" thus benefited the Southern ruling class. On the other hand, Key predicted, with industrialization and urbanization and the subsequent emergence of a two-party system, a modified, democratized class conflict would become institutionalized. A two-party system would compete over alternative public programs, mobilize voters, and negotiate the legislative particulars. By so doing, economic issues would come to the fore and the race question would no longer be effective as a diversion.

Or so went the theory. In practice, the results have been mixed. On the one hand, a two-party system has emerged in the South in the 1960s and 1970s, and Jim Crow segregation is legally dead. Yet, on the other hand, appeals to the race issue, or "race-baiting," remain a fundament of American political life. Why has this been the case?

Political sociologist Chandler Davidson argues that this is so because "Race, rather than class, turned out to be the driving force behind party realignment." Beginning with the Goldwater campaign of 1964, a Republican party "bent on capitalizing on the white backlash" endowed the race issue with new life. Nixon's modified use of Goldwater's Southern strategy worked successfully in 1968, and this provided the basis for an explicit statement on the matter by Republican theorist Kevin Phillips.[33]

Phillips identified the key to an "emerging Republican majority" in the United States as a white backlash to minority rights. In fact, Phillips cynically argued that Negro voting rights, so closely associated with Democratic Party policy, should be maintained in order to pressure white conservatives into switching to the Republican Party. A successful Republican strategy for holding their subcoalitions together would play up family and racial issues by implying that street crime, poverty, unemployment, and welfare programs are essentially minority problems. Essentially, Phillips provided a handbook for Republicans on how to encourage racial polarization along party lines without appearing to be racists. The strategy proved successful in the victorious presidential campaigns of Reagan in 1980 and 1984, and the 1988 Bush campaign was infamous for its "Willie Horton" television ad, which played on the fear of African American criminality.[34]

Through the 1980s, much of the "race baiting" was directed at African Americans, with Latinos occupying an ambiguous and contradictory place in Republican strategy. The George Bush–Jim Baker wing of the GOP seemed bent on recruiting Hispanics, who were seen as receptive to a "family values" platform, while other factions of the Republican Party—the English-only, anti–affirmative action, fundamentalist wing—readily identified them as un-American. The Bush-Baker wing, moreover, was characterized by a strong libertarian or "free market" tendency, which supported "open borders" for labor as well as for capital, while the cultural conservatives were basically "neo-isolationists."

This division of opinion between economic and cultural conservatives finally flared into the open in the 1992 and 1996 Republican primaries over the question of immigration and free trade. The presidential candidacy of Pat Buchanan, who explicitly opposed immigration that might "dilute" America's European heritage and who called for tightening the U.S.-Mexico border, brought the conservative unease with "free markets" out into the open. One Buchanan supporter, describing Hispanics as a "strange anti-nation" within the United States, blasted Republican courtship of Hispanics, noting that "Republican success with Hispanics, as with other minorities, is often at the expense of conservative principles."[35]

There is, of course, no need for racist scapegoating to be limited to a particular minority or be contained within one party, especially if this results in electoral success. California, once regarded as the most liberal of states in the country, provides an excellent, contemporary case in point. In California the rise in anti-Mexican sentiment had been evident for some time. In San Diego County the most spectacular example of Mexican-bashing had been the "Light Up the Border" campaign, dating back to November 1989, which attracted more than a thousand who parked at sundown and trained their headlights on the border. As the California economy worsened in the early 1990s and unemployment reached near 10 percent, "citizen groups" began to spring up throughout the state to protest "street hiring" and to urge the INS to conduct raids. Incumbent Governor Pete Wilson, up for reelection in 1994 and with one of the lowest popular ratings in memory, sensed a winning issue. Seizing the immigrant issue to blame for the state's budget difficulties and for problems with the schools, hospitals, and community services, Wilson rallied to easily defeat Democratic challenger Kathy Brown. Proposition 187, the measure championed by Wilson to deny educational and health benefits to "illegal immigrants," also coasted to an easy victory, with nearly 60 percent of the state vote.[36]

On this question of immigration, however, there was little difference between "conservative" Republican and "progressive" Democrat. Republican Governor Wilson called for a constitutional amendment that would deny citizenship to U.S.-born children of illegal immigrants; in response Democratic U.S. Senator Barbara Boxer called for a stationing of National Guard troops along the border. Other Republican and Democratic notables joined in as each side attempted to outdo the other in calling for the closing of the border. The top politicians of both parties, according to policy analyst Andrés Jiménez, engaged in "Willie Horton politics" by making undocumented immigration the central issue in the 1994 elections: "This time, instead of using a single criminal personality to foster a climate of discrimination, political ambitions are causing an entire population — California residents of Mexican ancestry — to be dehumanized and criminalized."[37]

In the span of two short years, 1992–1993, the alarmist anti-immigrant rhetoric was elevated to a commonsense political position. The easy passage in 1994 of the "Save Our State" Proposition 187, which denies health and educational services to undocumented immigrants, and the "Three Strikes — You're Out" Proposition 184, which mandates lengthy sentences for three-time felons, suggested the general unease in California about its "racial minorities." In 1995–1996 this unease gained sharper political clarity. Spurred this time by Governor Wilson's need to galvanize support for a presidential campaign, affirmative action policies were first banned in the University of California system and later statewide through the passage of Proposition 209, the California Civil Rights Initiative. By the mid-1990s the anti-immigrant campaign had become generalized into a sweeping anti-minority one.

The new respectability of the anti-immigrant, anti-minority sentiment can be seen in the pages of the mainstream national media. Imagine, as commentator Jack Miles does for *The Atlantic Monthly*, the specter of school funding collapse in a severely depressed economy—specifically, that the Los Angeles Unified School District, faced with a $400 million cutback in state funding, could conceivably go into receivership: "In such an unthinkable crisis unthinkable remedies might suddenly be thought of."[38] In such a climate, Miles notes, the imposition of a citizenship requirement for elementary and high school education acquires the aura of civility. Indeed, we see, with Governor Wilson's call for denying citizenship to U.S.-born children, that the "unthinkable" has become conceivable.

Thus V. O. Key's prediction (or hope), so common in American social science thought, that economic or class issues would prevail over racial ones was too simply put. These are mutually exclusive only in laboratories or "ideal-type" constructions. In the real world of competitive politics, they compete for attention or salience, and generally they intermix. In California, Governor Wilson was able to redirect the sense of economic malaise to mobilize anti-immigrant and anti-minority sentiment for a successful reelection campaign (a strategy that fell flat in the presidential campaign). In Texas, on the other hand, economic prosperity and significant Texas-Mexico economic ties have moved Republican Governor George W. Bush on various occasions to defend immigrants, Mexico, bilingualism, and so on.

Class and race issues can at times intermix to provide for strange bedfellows. The unexpected arrangements can be seen in the politics of immigration and free trade, where conservative and liberal distinctions quickly break down, as seen already in the apparent consensus between Republican Governor Wilson and Democratic Senator Boxer. Organized labor and right-wingers, for example, found themselves allied in efforts to scuttle the North American Free Trade Agreement (NAFTA), and both continue to call for a tightening of the border. Labor unionists are concerned about competition with Mexico while "groups with thinly veiled racist agendas blame Mexicans for everything from water shortages to the decay of American values to suburban sprawl."[39] Whether the Mexican threat is identified as economic or cultural, the response calls for protection from Mexico and Mexican workers.

On the other side, again in spite of reservations, some Chicano advocacy organizations—the National Council of La Raza, the Mexican American Legal Defense and Education Fund, the Southwest Voter Research Institute, for example—and Anglo business conservatives found themselves allied to promote NAFTA, and both continue to support a flexible "open border" policy. The Chicano advocacy organizations are motivated by a range of concerns—human rights, border development, improved U.S.-Mexico relations—while for business people "open borders" are the logical extension of the open shop. "Too many business interests," as one commentator observed, "have been served by cheap immigrant labor for any Buchananesque, shoot-to-kill sealing of our southern border to gain much Republican support."[40] Indeed, on the bitterly fought issue of NAFTA, it was business rather than labor that staked out an internationalist and historical position, as seen in the statement of Clyde Prestowitz, president of the Economic Strategy Institute: "It is not in our interest to have an impoverished and embittered nation with a rapidly growing population on our southern border. If the Israelis can shake hands with the PLO, surely the United States can take the outstretched hand of Mexico which, after all, has been more sinned against than sinning in the history of our mutual relations."[41] Again the Anglo business–Mexican American middle class nexus, the pro-growth political alignment that has shaped the present form of domestic inclusion, can be seen at work.

In the immediate future, U.S. policy toward Mexico and Mexican immigrants faces a difficult crossroads between providing developmental assistance or increasing the policing of the border, between a "Marshall Plan" or martial law. The debate over NAFTA, in this sense, was basically a debate over a business-sponsored economic development plan. If NAFTA and other initiatives fail to address the problems of Mexican underdevelopment—or worse, if they excaberate these problems—"we might be forced," according to *Atlantic Monthly*'s Jack Miles, "into the martial-law [alternative], and into a particularly severe form of it along our southern border."[42]

SEALING THE BORDER—A FIRST STEP?

U.S. border control polices already point in the direction of martial law. The Immigration Reform and Control Act (IRCA) of 1986, which granted amnesty to long-term illegal residents, has collapsed, and the number of illegal crossings may have increased to pre-IRCA levels. The Immigration and Naturalization Service (INS) estimates that the number of undocumented residents has climbed back to four million, although some scholars disagree, placing the number closer to two million. In the context of such perceived loss of control, the border has become increasingly militarized. The Border Patrol more than doubled in size between 1979 and 1988, with staff increasing from 2,580 to 5,531. The overall INS budget jumped nearly 200 hundred percent, from $304 million to $859 million. Under the Clinton Administration, the INS budget has nearly doubled again, to approximately 1.5 billion dollars. An additional one thousand agents have been placed on active border duty, and additional significant increases are foreseen.

The militarization of the border is most evident in the innovations borrowed from the Vietnam War: in the proposal to create a "DMZ" (ironically meaning "demilitarized zone") or buffer zone and in the deployment of sophisticated, military-related technology. Additionally, the U.S. Congress has altered the legal code to allow U.S. military personnel and equipment to play a greatly expanded role in law enforcement activities along the border. Finally, in the event that the president declares an "immigration emergency," the INS has quietly organized a multiagency govenment group charged with drawing up plans to seal off the border and to control and remove "alien terrorists and undesirables." In essence, this militarization process, concludes sociologist Tim Dunn, amounts to "the implementation of a counter-insurgency doctrine within the United States."[43]

Again the unthinkable has become conceivable. In this sense, U.S. Senator Boxer's proposal to station National Guard troops along the border represents the next logical step to begin the sealing of the border. William Langewiesche, writing in *The Atlantic Monthly*, comments on these proposals in the following way: "This could be done, but only with enormous manpower—for instance, with a large-scale deployment of the U.S. armed forces and the creation of free-fire zones. It would not require much killing: the Soviets sealed their borders for decades without an excessive expenditure of ammunition. The simple fact that there existed a systematic policy of shooting illegal immigrants would deter most Mexicans."[44]

Langewiesche's analogy is not so far-fetched. With the end of the Cold War between East and West, the tensions between the developed North and the underdeveloped South have come into sharp focus. Any new "Iron Curtain" that might be erected in the post–Cold War era would probably be deployed along an increasingly tense U.S.-Mexico border. In the 1990s the stationing of U.S. Marines along the border for the purpose of deterring drug traffickers hints at the outlines of such a militarized barrier. The social costs have become apparent in several controversial shootings—including the 1997 killing of American teenager Ezequiel Hernández of Redford, Texas—that have involved Marines. The problem stems, evidently, from the difficulty armed soldiers have in distinguishing the "drug running" enemy from the peaceful civilians of both countries.

The blockade of the El Paso–Ciudad Juárez border begun in 1993 by the Border Patrol suggests a possible preview of a tense, militarized zone. On September 19, the Border Patrol launched "Operation Blockade" (later renamed "Operation Hold the Line") with a massive show of force. Four hundred agents were stationed around the clock along the Rio Grande from Ysleta to Sunland Park, a distance of twenty miles. Illegal crossings, mostly of Juárez day commuters, immediately dropped from an estimated 10,000 a day to 2,000. In the ensuing days nearly a thousand *Juarenses* protested, chanting "queremos trabajar," blocking international traffic and burning U.S. flags. The National Chamber of Commerce and the Chamber of Industry in Juárez joined the city's politicians and radio disc jockeys in calling for a complete boycott of El Paso. The boycott was named "Operación Dignidad."

On the El Paso side, downtown businesses reported losses in retail sales of 80 percent and protested the blockade. The Catholic Church hierarchy, noting the "serious economic, social and civic consequences in our sister cities," condemned the blockade. Fort Bliss soldiers were ordered not to venture into Juárez because a U.S. military presence might inflame emotions further. But the emotions in El Paso easily matched the resentments in Juárez. The blockade provided an excuse, as the Catholic diocesan newspaper reported, for some "to express their fanaticism, intolerance, racism and even disrespect to church authorities and to whoever disagrees with the operation." In the meantime, Border Patrol officials acknowledged that immigrants appeared to be moving into the U.S. from new points beyond the blockade line, and the best they could hope is that the crackdown had cut down on crime and transients in El Paso itself. One El Paso resident with relatives in Juárez commented: "If it [the blockade] continues, I guess I'll know what people in east and west Germany felt like when families were separated by the Berlin Wall."[45]

Not surprisingly, despite the questionable effectiveness of such a blockade and the worsening of international tensions, California politicians clamored for a similar blockade along their border with Mexico. Operation Gatekeeper in San Diego and Operation Safeguard in Arizona were launched in response.[46]

Adding to the tensions of border control is the "cowboy" image of the Border Patrol itself. As the nation's busiest police force, the Border Patrol makes more than one million arrests per year. Despite this level of activity, the agency has — shockingly — no internal review apparatus for handling complaints or incidents of improper conduct on the part of its officers. Unresolved cases of abuse or brutality number in the hundreds. The *Los Angeles Times*, in a special report, noted that the patrol's record includes "persistent reports of abusive behavior by agents, improper shootings and crimes including drug smuggling, sexual assault and theft." The border in fact already resembles a war-zone in places.[47]

Perhaps more disturbing, from a policy perspective, is the easy manner in which the anti-immigrant sentiment spills over into other areas. One recent line of reasoning in the popular and scholarly literature pits "browns versus blacks," assumes that Mexican Americans are immigrants or "recent" immigrants, and then concludes that they are not as worthy of entitlement programs. Peter Skerry, in his much-publicized *Mexican Americans: The Ambivalent Minority*, for example, holds that the protections of the Voting Rights Act should be withdrawn from Mexican Americans because in his view they are basically immigrants.[48] Invariably negative American views of Mexico and Mexicans are translated into domestic policies that define a subordinate place for Mexican Americans. American citizens, because of appearance and ethnicity, become identified as immigrants so that the sting of the backlash, as one California newspaper put it, is felt also by descendants of Mexicans, Chinese, and Japanese who came to California generations ago.[49]

Historically the pattern is rather evident: in times of economic duress, nativism and racism rise. Such sentiments, while always present in a few groups, are taken up in times of economic difficulties and afforded legitimacy by politicians attempting to capitalize on public discontent. Unthinkable policies become conceivable, and people of color, whether native born or immigrants, become transformed into scapegoats for a variety of social ills.

A CONCLUDING NOTE

In light of this negative assessment, what possible futures await us? We must keep in mind that key elements of this pessimistic scenario may not come to pass. There is considerable disagreement, for example, on the notion of an American decline in the world system. With a successful conclusion to the Cold War, some argue that the United States is now in a process of "renewal."[50] Yet the difficulties of plotting a constructive course are shown in the paradox of California. The end of the Cold War has provided an opportunity to reorient national expenditures away from military ends to regenerative economic projects; but that reorientation, signifying the decline of the defense industry, has resulted in an economic recession that has fueled a vicious anti-immigrant campaign. Such campaigns in turn may determine how the United States deals in the future with increasing international trade competition, whether it withdraws into protectionism or organizes a hemispheric common market.

In a similar vein, the near-term economic dislocations produced by NAFTA may set off serious political difficulties on both sides of the border. The Zapatista rebellion in Chiapas may pale in comparison with other movements if the post-NAFTA Mexican economy continues to deteriorate. One study predicts that NAFTA will add, primarily as a result of the restructuring of Mexican agriculture, an additional 50,000 to 100,000 immigrants per year in the United States. This, of course, would only aggravate an already tense domestic climate in California and elsewhere in the Southwest. To make matters worse, the burden of economic restructuring on the U.S. side will likely fall on its agricultural and textile workforce, which is comprised in large part of Mexican and other minority workers. Indeed, unless employment training and adjustment programs are in place, NAFTA may contribute "to growing class divisions within the Mexican American population."[51]

What of the futuristic domestic nightmare pitting elderly whites against a resentful Latino work force? One scenario for avoiding such a polarizing fiscal crisis calls for investing in education and job development programs that can significantly expand the ranks of the "minority" middle classes. Essentially this strategy envisions a strengthening of the pro-development alignment between the "minority" middle classes and the Anglo business elite, the alignment that has shaped the politics of inclusion in the late twentieth century. Given the significant influence of Mexican American legislators in Texas and New Mexico and their growing influence in California, this pro-development inclusion strategy has powerful support in the Southwest.[52]

Another possible scenario would envision the rise of a broad multiracial working-class and middle-class coalition that could serve as the basis for a populist form of inclusion. This alternative appears somewhat utopian given the increasing tensions between working-class whites, Blacks, and Mexicans, tensions that weaken whatever base may exist for an effective "rainbow" coalition. Latinos and African Americans in Los Angeles, Houston, and Chicago, for example, generally compete for the same jobs, the same rental units, control of the same voting districts, and, according to some conservatives, the same advantages afforded by racial entitlement programs (civil rights, voting rights, affirmative action). On the other hand, the politics of exclusion, evident in the latest anti–affirmative action campaigns in California and throughout the country, may ultimately forge such a coalition. NAFTA and "free trade" with Mexico could likewise compel binational labor organizing.[53]

The worst-case and best-case scenarios, by reminding us of the indeterminate or "open" nature of the future, force us to keep our perspective — to make us realize that despite the advances of the last forty years, the struggle between inclusion and exclusion continues. With the hindsight of history, we know that such sudden shifts in domestic relations are possible, that Mexican American and African American communities as well as white allies are vulnerable to the kind of hysteria and backlashes that erupted during the 1950s. That was a time of reaction to the young civil rights movement, a time of loyalty oaths, job blacklists, book bans and burnings, of raids on ghettos and barrios, of police roundups of "disloyal" and "foreign" elements, even of lynchings and assassinations; in short, of fanatical reaction to desegregation. The same sort of reaction occurred in the 1960s and 1970s during the second civil rights movement. Such a pessimistic scenario is not a fantasy. All these things have already happened, and indeed they are still part of a "living memory."

Society can be pushed along many different trajectories, and the impetus for one or another path comes not just from the larger forces and circumstances I have sketched here, but from our actions and reactions with regard to these forces and circumstances — to decisions made or not made, to policies formulated or not formulated, to organizations formed or dissolved. Politics comprises the critical intervening process for understanding the contrary pull of inclusion and exclusion. Our involvement in that process may decide whether the political inclusion of the late twentieth century was a partial, passing moment or whether it did in fact represent a break from a past history of exclusion.

NOTES

Author's Note: This paper was completed while I was in residence at the Center for Advanced Study in the Behavioral Sciences (Stanford, California) and with support from the Andrew W. Mellon Foundation. I wish to thank Neil Foley, Veronica García-Contreras, Diana Montejano, Ken Bollen, and Norma Chávez for their comments and contributions.

1. The Mexican government reached out directly to Mexican American organizations and politicians to secure support for NAFTA. The responses divided along business-labor lines, with advocacy organizations attempting to forge a "Latino consenus" for a revised NAFTA that included environmental and labor side agreements and a North American Development Bank. See "Mexican Government Lobbying Latinos," *Borderlines*, February 1992; The Tomás Rivera Center, *Debate Series* 2 (Summer 1993); "The Latino Consensus on NAFTA," position paper, Southwest Voter Research Institute, October 1993; "Hispanic Americans Fail to Unite in Support of Free Trade Agreements," *Austin American Statesman*, October 3, 1993.

2. Raquel O. Rivera and Joan Moore, eds., *The Effects of Economic Restructuring on Latino Communities in the United States* (New York: Sage Press, 1993). On the African American underclass, see William J. Wilson, *The Truly Disadvantaged: The Inner City, the Underclass, and Public Policy* (Chicago: University of Chicago Press, 1987).

3. Joan Moore, "An Assessment of Hispanic Poverty: Is There an Hispanic Underclass?," paper presented at the Tomás Rivera Center, Trinity University, San Antonio, April 8, 1988; Jorge Chapa, "The Question of Mexican American Assimilation," LBJ School of Public Affairs Comment, Spring 1989; National Council of La Raza, *State of Hispanic America 1991: An Overview*, February 1992; "Deepening Segregation in American Schools," *Education Daily*, April 8, 1997.

4. During the 1920s, there also was a "Mexican problem" literature that blamed Mexicans for every social ill possible. See David Montejano, *Anglos and Mexicans in the Making of Texas, 1836–1986* (Austin: University of Texas Press, 1987), pp. 179–196; also Carey McWilliams, *North From Mexico: The Spanish-Speaking People of the United States* (Philadelphia: J. B. Lippincott, 1949), pp. 206–226.

5. Montejano, *Anglos and Mexicans*, p. 306. This paper basically extends my argument in Chapter 13, "A Time of Inclusion," pp. 288–307.

6. Paul Kennedy, *Preparing for the 21st Century* (New York: Random House, 1993), p. 324.

7. As Max Weber used the concept, an "ideal type" referred to a pure condition and not an empirical one. Used properly as a tool—when it points to relevant things to study rather than to conclusions to be drawn—it may be valuable. See S. M. Miller, *Max Weber* (New York: Thomas Y. Cowell Co., 1963).

8. Sociologically speaking, exclusionary public policy is what transforms an ethnic situation into a "racial" one. In this sense, Mexican Americans can be considered both an ethnic group and a racial group. See Michael Omi and Howard Winant, *Racial Formation in the United States* (New York: Routledge, 1986).

9. The theme of "awakening" was a popular one in the literature of the late 1960s. A classic

statement is contained in Leo Grebler, Joan Moore, and Ralph Guzman, *The Mexican American People* (New York: Free Press, 1970), pp. 3–11. In this regard, one should note the interesting dissent of Joan Moore from her co-authors in her article "Colonialism: The Case of the Mexican American," *Social Problems* 17, no. 4 (Spring 1970).

10. V. O. Key, Jr., *Southern Politics in State and Nation* (New York: Alfred A. Knopf, 1949).

11. For an excellent elaboration of this argument, see Stanley Greenberg, *Race and State in Capitalist Development: Comparative Perspectives* (New Haven: Yale University Press, 1980).

12. See Montejano, *Anglos and Mexicans*, pp. 259–307.

13. See Manning Marable, *Race, Reform, and Rebellion* (Jackson: University Press of Mississippi, 1991), for a discussion.

14. In the jargon of development studies, this type of alliance between business elites and a middle class is known as the "bourgeois road" to social change. See Barrington Moore, Jr., *Origins of Democracy and Dictatorship* (Boston: Beacon, 1966) for a general treatment. For more details on San Antonio politics, see Rodolfo Rosales, "Personality and Style in San Antonio Politics," in this volume; also "The Prince of the City," *Hispanic Business*, April 1993, pp. 52–61.

15. Paul Kennedy, *The Rise and Fall of the Great Powers: Economic Change and Military Conflict From 1500 to 2000* (New York: Random House, 1987), p. 515. Kennedy explicitly distances himself from Immanuel Wallerstein and others, but his argument is essentially the same. For a similar argument about U.S. decline, see Daniel Chirot, *Social Change in the Modern Era* (San Diego: Harcourt Brace Jovanovich, 1986). For the most recent addition to the declinist thesis, see Donald W. White, *The American Century: The Rise and Decline of the United States as a World Power* (New Haven: Yale University Press, 1996).

16. Kennedy, *Rise and Fall*, p. 517.

17. At another point, Kennedy states that the lack of class politics in the United States has been helped by the fact that the poorest one-third of American society has not been mobilized to become regular voters. In other words, limited democracy has been a good thing. Kennedy, *Rise and Fall*, p. 531.

18. Kennedy, *Preparing for the 21st Century*; also "The Internationalization of Yale," *Yale Alumni Magazine*, February 1992, p. 20, summarizing the faculty presentations at the 39th Assembly of Yale Alumni, October 17–19, 1991.

19. See Jim Mann, "Bush's Gamble to Decide U.S. Future," *Austin American Statesman*, January 17, 1991; Peter Applebome, "After the War: National Mood; War Heals Wounds at Home," *New York Times*, March 4, 1991; William Pfaff, "Gulf War Brought U.S. to Turning Point," *Albuquerque Journal*, April 1, 1991.

20. Patrick McDonnell and Sebastian Rotella, "When Agents Cross over the Borderline," *Los Angeles Times*, April 22, 1993; also William Langewiesche, "The Border," *Atlantic Monthly* (May 1992), p. 73.

21. William Langewiesche, "The Border," *Atlantic Monthly* (May 1992), p.68.

22. Governor Babbitt is quoted by Georgie Anne Geyer. See Geyer, "States Conduct Own Foreign Policy," *Houston Post*, November 10, 1983.

23. Richard D. Lamm, "Two Volatile Groups Threaten to Boil Over Melting Pot," *Albuquerque Journal*, September 23, 1985. The "lifeboat" argument is elaborated in detail in Richard D. Lamm and Gary Imhoff, *The Immigration Time Bomb: The Fragmenting of America* (New York: Truman Talley Books, 1986).

24. Peter Brimelow, "Time to Rethink Immigration?" *National Review*, June 22, 1992, pp. 31, 36.

25. Brimelow, "Time to Rethink Immigration?" p. 46. Kennedy adds, "The root of these ten-

sions lies in foreignness, or, to use another word, race. White Americans have no problem in welcoming to their shores many thousands of well-educated professionals from Scandinavia, Britain, and Germany." Kennedy, *Preparing for the 21st Century*, p. 43. Also see Lawrence E. Harrison, "America and Its Immigrants," *The National Interest*, Summer 1992, p. 45.

26. Kennedy, *Preparing for the 21st Century*, pp. 313, 322–325. In a speculative vein, the Clinton administration forecasts that the average net tax rate for future generations would eventually reach 82 percent of their lifetime earnings unless there is serious reform in health care and Social Security. "How We're Conspiring to Bury Our Children in Taxes," *San Jose Mercury News*, February 20, 1994.

27. David E. Hayes-Bautista, Werner O. Schink, and Jorge Chapa, *The Burden of Support: Young Latinos in an Aging Society* (Stanford, Calif.: Stanford University Press, 1988).

28. Hayes-Bautista, et al., *Burden of Support*, pp. 5, 9.

29. One consequence of the riot was a marked acceleration of the domestic arms race among the citizens of Los Angeles. Legal guns sales alone jumped 64 percent after the riot. The National Rifle Association ran large display ads in the newspapers offering free instruction to new gun owners. See Jack Miles, "Blacks versus Browns: The Struggle for the Bottom Rung," *Atlantic Monthly* October 1992, pp. 41, 48, 50, 52; also see "Return of the Nativist," *The Economist*, June 27, 1992; also "Legacy of Riots in Los Angeles: Fears and Hope," *New York Times*, April 27, 1997, pp. 1, 16.

30. *Austin American Statesman*, January 22, 1990; Miles, "Blacks versus Browns," p. 63; also see "Return of the Nativist."

31. According to Elizabeth Martínez, the right's strategy follows six points: the English-only campaign; undermining Affirmative Action; blocking any new civil rights legislation; creating a buffer of colored elite; teaching whites that any gain by people of color is a white loss; and pitting Blacks against Latinos against Asians against Arab Americans. Elizabeth Martínez, "When No Dogs or Mexicans Are Allowed," *Z Magazine*, January 1991, pp.37–42.

32. V. O. Key, Jr., *Southern Politics in State and Nation* (New York: Knopf, 1949); also see Chandler Davidson, *Race and Class in Texas Politics* (Princeton: Princeton University Press, 1990), pp. 3–10.

33. Davidson, *Race and Class*, pp. 230–231, 239.

34. See Kevin P. Phillips, *The Emerging Republican Majority* (New Rochelle, N.Y.: Arlington House, 1969), pp. 204–206, 467–474; also Davidson, *Race and Class*, pp. 223–239, 256. In 1992 Republicans had intended to go after white working-class votes by tarring the civil rights bill of 1991 as a "quota bill," but the Los Angeles riot of April 1992 apparently made such a strategy too risky and divisive. See Jim Fain, "GOP Knows Racism Works, and It Will Be Back in '92," *Austin American Statesman*, April 24, 1991; also "Return of the Nativist."

35. Patrick Buchanan, "America First Means Chopping Foreign Aid," *San Antonio Express-News*, October 26, 1991; Brimelow, "Time to Rethink Immigration," p. 44; Miles, "Blacks versus Browns," pp.56–58; "Return of the Nativist."

36. "Immigration Number One Election Issue, Local Voters Say," and "State's Diversity Doesn't Reach Voting Booth," *Los Angeles Times*, November 10, 1994.

37. Andrés E. Jiménez, "Six Million Californians Can't Be All Wrong," *Los Angeles Times*, October 27, 1993. Columnist Dan Walters compares the rhetorical "overkill" to the pre–civil rights South when "politicians tried to 'out-seg' each other in opposing integration." See Dan Walters, "Verbal Overkill on Immigrants," *Sacramento Bee*, August 18, 1993.

38. Miles, "Blacks versus Browns," p. 67.

39. Langewiesche, "The Border," p. 69.

40. Miles, "Blacks versus Browns," pp. 56–58. The generally supportive Mexican American

response to NAFTA stemmed from the belief that free trade would boost the economies of the border states, open new opportunities for Mexican American business-people and professionals, and generally improve the standing of Mexicans within the United States. See "Mexican Government Lobbying Latinos," *Borderlines*, February 1992.

41. Clyde Prestowitz, "NAFTA: Why We Hafta," *San Jose Mercury News*, September 26, 1993. For a free-market argument for open borders, see Julian L. Simon, *The Economic Consequences of Immigration* (New York: Basil Blackwell, 1989).

42. Miles, "Blacks versus Browns," p. 68; also see the *San Jose Mercury News*, October 30, 1993.

43. In a historical sense, the U.S.-Mexico border, as the creation of war between these two countries, has always been militarized. Timothy J. Dunn, *The Militarization of the U.S.-Mexico Border, 1978–1990: Low Intensity Conflict Doctrine Comes Home* (Austin: Center for Mexican American Studies, 1996); also see Paul Salopek, "La Migra: The Border Patrol's Wall of Silence," *Texas Observer*, March 12, 1993; Miriam Davidson, "Militarizing the Mexican Border," *The Nation*, April 1, 1991; "Policing the Border—A Military Approach," *Borderlines*, February 1992; "Clinton's New and Improved Immigration Strategy," *Network News*, Newsletter of the National Network for Immigration and Refugee Rights, Jan.–Feb. 1994; McDonnell and Rotella, "When Agents Cross Over."

44. Langewiesche, "The Border," p. 69.

45. *El Paso Times*, September 20, 1993–September 29, 1993; *The Rio Grande Catholic*, El Paso Diocese, November 1993. The El Paso Police Department noted that petty crime and auto thefts have declined about 30 percent, but violent crime, including robbery and assault, has increased. A police spokesperson commented: "We're a city of half a million and we can generate our own crime." See "The New Border Order," *San Jose Mercury News*, November 21, 1993.

46. In response, the governor and other officials of Baja California urged Baja residents to boycott all San Diego businesses. As in Ciudad Juárez, the campaign was called Operation Dignity. Esther Schrader, "State Eager to Copy Border Blockade," *San Jose Mercury News*, October 25, 1993.

47. Along the Arizona-Mexico border, the reckless shootings by agents have been attributed to a "war-zone or drug-zone mentality," in spite of the fact that the overwhelming majority of undocumented immigrants are unarmed and nonthreatening. In the El Paso area, the violence attributed to the Border Patrol between 1988 and 1992 has involved eight shootings (five fatal), a drowning, sporadic beatings, illegal deportations, and even a case of arson. One reporter described El Paso as "a dog-eared variety of Dodge City on the Rio Grande." See McDonnell and Rotella, "When Agents Cross Over"; Salopek, "La Migra."

48. Skerry argues that Mexican Americans consider themselves a racial minority only because of the incentives offered by civil rights legislation. See Peter Skerry, *Mexican Americans: The Ambivalent Minority* (New York: Free Press, 1993); also Miles, "Blacks versus Browns," esp. pp. 52–55.

49. More pernicious have been the armed attacks and sniper shootings of Mexican workers by U.S. civilians and soldiers. One well-known case involved six Marines from Camp Pendleton who were tried, in 1984, for conducting armed "beaner raids" on undocumented farmworkers. In recent years such crimes have become a main agenda item of the Ku Klux Klan, Nazis, violent skinheads, and even a high school paramilitary hate club, "The Iron Militia." Martínez, "When No Dogs or Mexicans," p. 38; "State Leads Anti-Immigrant Wave," *San Francisco Chronicle*, March 29, 1994; "INS Arrests Spur New Rights Group," *San Jose Mercury News*, February 20, 1994.

50. The well-known conservative scholar Samuel P. Huntington has argued that doomsaying seems to be part of a regular political and academic ritual that serves to revitalize an American

resolve to remain competitive. Huntington notes that there have been five such waves of "declinism" in the past thirty years. See Samuel P. Huntington, "The United States: Decline or Renewal?" *Adelphi Papers* 235 (Spring 1989), pp. 63–80.

51. It was this scenario that motivated many Mexican American politicians and organizations to withhold support of NAFTA until commitments to such retraining programs had been secured. "The Impact of the North American Free Trade Agreement on Latino Workers in California and South Texas," Southwest Voter Research Institute Latin American Project Paper 2, September 1992; "How Would Trade Pact Affect State's Hispanics?" *Austin American Statesman*, September 22, 1993; also "Borderline Working Class: Texas Labor Is Feeling Trade Pact's Pinch," *New York Times*, May 8, 1997.

52. Hayes-Bautista et al. have described such a best-case scenario. Drawn together through "enlightened self-interest," the Latino middle class and the aging Anglo Baby Boomers realized that the best guarantee of support for the elderly would be social investment in the younger Latino population. Unfortunately, Hayes-Bautista et al. rest their argument for such an alliance on hope, especially in the "selfless" aging Anglo baby boomers, rather than on any basic material interest. See Hayes-Bautista et al., *Burden of Support*, pp. 145, 147–148.

53. Thus, as a recent issue of *The Economist* put it, "The easy assumption that Latinos and blacks are both minorities and therefore natural allies must be reexamined." See for example, Miles, "Blacks versus Browns"; also "Return of the Nativist." On the other hand, minority bashing can easily mobilize minority communities, as evidenced in the surprising Latino victories in the 1996 California legislature. See "Latino Turnout a Breakthrough Election: Group's Heavy Balloting Could Signal a Historic Pivot Point for Political Relations in L.A.," *Los Angeles Times*, April 10, 1997.

About the Authors

Teresa Córdova is Associate Professor of Community and Regional Planning at the University of New Mexico. She has written extensively about community development, global restructuring, and Chicana studies. She co-edited *Chicana Voices: Intersections of Class, Race and Gender* and is currently studying Chicana grassroots activism in the environmental and economic justice movement.

Margarita Decierdo is a Ph.D. candidate in Sociology at the University of California, Berkeley. She is completing a study of farmworkers titled "Testimonies of Farmworkers in California Agriculture: The Social Construction of Courage and Survival."

Antonio González is Director of the Southwest Voter Research Institute based in Los Angeles. He continues to organize human rights work in the U.S. Southwest, Mexico, and Central America.

Phillip B. Gonzales is Associate Professor of Sociology and Director of the Southwest Hispanic Research Institute at the University of New Mexico. His interests include ethnic identity and political mobilization, urban poverty, and interactional sociology. He is currently working on a history of Hispano ethnic politics in New Mexico.

David Montejano is Associate Professor of History and Sociology and Director of the Center for Mexican American Studies at the University of Texas at Austin. His book, *Anglos and Mexicans in the Making of Texas, 1836–1986*, was awarded the Frederick Jackson Turner prize by the Organization of American Historians.

Mary Pardo is Full Professor of Chicana/o Studies at California State University, Northridge. Her work focuses on women of color and urban politics. Her recent book is titled *Mexican American Women Activists: Identity and Resistance in Two Los Angeles Communities*.

Rodolfo Rosales is Assistant Professor of Political Science at the University of Texas at San Antonio. His interests include comparative urban politics and political theory. His forthcoming book is titled *The Illusion of Inclusion: The Political Story of San Antonio, Texas, 1951–1991*.

Martín Sánchez Jankowski is Professor of Sociology at the University of California, Berkeley. His book *Islands in the Street: Gangs and American Urban Society* won the Robert E. Park award given by the American Sociological Society. He recently co-authored *Inequality by Design: Cracking the Bell Curve*. His next project concerns social change in poor neighborhoods.

Christine Marie Sierra is Associate Professor of Political Science at the University of New Mexico. She has published extensively on U.S. Latino politics, Chicana and Latina women, and Mexican American political activism. Her current book project focuses on Mexican Americans and the politics of immigration.

Roy Eric Xavier received his doctorate in Sociology and Mass Communications from the University of California, Berkeley. He writes about culture and new technologies. Currently he is the chief telecommunications officer for Richmond, California, and the web site manager for KCRT Television in the San Francisco Bay Area.

INDEX